Democracy and Its Others

About the series

Political Theory and Contemporary Philosophy

Political Theory and Contemporary Philosophy encourages a sustained dialogue between the most important intellectual currents in recent European philosophy—including phenomenology, deconstruction, hermeneutics—and key political theories and concepts, both classical and modern. In doing so, it not only sheds new light on today's shifting political realities but also explores the previously neglected consequences of the two disciplines.

Series editor: Michael Marder

Other volumes in the series include:

Medialogies: Inflationary Media and the Crisis of Reality, David R. Castillo and William Egginton

The Sacred and the Political: Explorations on Mimesis, Violence and Religion, edited by Elisabetta Brighi and Antonio Cerella

The Democracy of Knowledge, Daniel Innerarity (translated by Sandra Kingery)

The Voice of Conscience: A Political Genealogy of Western Ethical Experience, Mika Ojakangas

The Politics of Nihilism, edited by Nitzan Lebovic and Roy Ben-Shai

On Hegel's Philosophy of Right, Martin Heidegger (edited by Peter Trawny, Marcia Cavalcante Schuback and Michael Marder, translated by Andrew J. Mitchell)

Deconstructing Zionism, Michael Marder and Santiago Zabala

Heidegger on Hegel's Philosophy of Right, Marcia Sa *Cavalcante Schuback*, Michael Marder and Peter Trawny

The Metaphysics of Terror, Rasmus Ugilt

The Negative Revolution, Artemy Magun

The Voice of Conscience, Mika Ojakangas

Democracy and Its Others

Jeffrey H. Epstein

BLOOMSBURY
NEW DELHI • LONDON • OXFORD • NEW YORK • SYDNEY

BLOOMSBURY INDIA
Bloomsbury Publishing India Pvt. Ltd
Second Floor, LSC Building No. 4, DDA Complex, Pocket C–6&7,
Vasant Kunj, New Delhi 110070

BLOOMSBURY, BLOOMSBURY ACADEMIC INDIA and the Diana logo are
trademarks of Bloomsbury Publishing Plc

First published in India 2024
First published 2016

British Library Cataloguing-in-Publication Data
A catalogue record for this book is available from the British Library

Library of Congress Cataloging-in-Publication Data
A catalog record for this book is available from the Library of Congress

ISBN: 978-93-54356-78-0

Typeset by RefineCatch Limited, Bungay, Suffolk
Printed at Manipal Technologies Limited, Manipal

Contents

Acknowledgments

I am honored to thank all of the friends and colleagues who dedicated countless hours discussing, critiquing, and improving this book. I am especially indebted to Eduardo Mendieta who influenced my thinking and supported this project through every phase. I am grateful to Linda Alcoff, Ed Casey, and Anne O'Byrne whose comments on earlier drafts were frequent and challenging. At the earliest stages, the generous inquiries of Emiliano Diaz, Whitney Howell, Jane Jones, Greg Kirk, and Adam Rosenfeld helped to shape and refine what would come. Finally, a special debt of gratitude is owed to Daniela Winer whose insights were essential to identifying the central features of this work and their relevance to contemporary events.

Introduction

Today, democracy is positioned atop the hierarchy of forms of political rule. This ascendancy of democracy has not coincided with the end of Realpolitik or ushered in an era of global peace, security, and justice (nor have its proponents ever really made that promise). Nevertheless, its historical progression and current global triumph does serve as the basis for the belief that the universalizability of democracy and its fundamental principles and guiding ideals, including freedom, equality, the rule of law, tolerance, and hospitality are the unique and legitimate guarantors of the promise of the possibility for lasting political justice. Despite this belief in the promise of democracy, no democratic state has been able to *fully* actualize these principles constitutive of the very concept of democracy as such and without which democracy remains elusive.

This failure does not mean that democracies do not exist or that existing democracies have not achieved many important ethical and political successes. They have. Rather, it indicates that—throughout history and until today—democratic states are not immune from creating political injustices. Furthermore, in both domestic and global contexts, the exclusionary practices, violence, flaunting of the law, and non-democratic unilateralism of the world's most powerful democracies—almost always performed in the name of and for the sake of democracy—actually threaten to undermine the very principles these democratic powers claim to uphold.[1] Despite the proliferation and promise of democracy, the dominant politic practice today, it seems, is based upon a longstanding, dangerous, and unsatisfactory idea: Justice is the advantage of the stronger. If "might makes right" continues to be the *de facto* definition of democratic justice, then both democracy and justice call out for reconceptualization.

To begin to answer this call, this work examines the political, legal, and moral challenges to democratic legitimacy against the backdrop of the unprecedented levels of human migration into and through sovereign democratic nation-states that has resulted in tens of millions of individuals being denied the most basic democratic and human right, namely membership within a political community.

Democratic legitimacy is premised, at least in part, on the ideal that those who are subject to the laws are also its authors. In this respect, refugees, asylees, guest workers, uninvited (im)migrants, and even native-born individuals denied membership within the sovereign *demos* face systematic and unjust forms of disenfranchisement, political silencing, and denial of civil rights. This raises deep concerns regarding the legitimacy of existing democratic states and the possibility for full legal and moral recognition for those individuals denied political representation and membership.

The exclusion of foreigners from the *demos* is commonly justified by appealing to the sovereign right of the state for self-determination, and this includes establishing and enforcing the rules for political membership and citizenship. In this work, I acknowledge that sovereign self-determination is necessary and may even—in certain instances—pave the way for a just response to the calls for political inclusion and recognition, but I challenge the democratic state's right to self-determination when it is premised upon traditional conceptualizations of sovereign self-identicality—that is, when democratic legitimacy and sovereign self-determination are based upon the ideal of indivisibility, inviolability, wholeness, self-mastery, and unity of a *demos* that has absolute control and supremacy over a bounded geographic territory. The empirical facts of globalization in which humans, capital, information, ideas, and culture cross and re-cross sovereign borders demonstrate the impossibility and undesirability of absolutely closed and impermeable borders and boundaries of the democratic polity. The physical borders that demarcate the territoriality and sovereignty of the democratic nation-state (and whether they should be conceived of as open, closed, or porous) will be a central theme going forward; however, the primary focus in this work will be to examine the construction of the conceptual and symbolic borders of the self-identicality of sovereignty, democracy, and the nation-state.

In particular, I focus on the ways in which foreignness is traditionally conceived of as an absolute threat to the unity of the self-identical sovereign *demos*, which must be repelled, conquered, assimilated, "naturalized," and neutralized. I do not deny that foreignness can be threatening to the sovereign, but against this conceptualization, I argue that there are resources within the history of political philosophy that provide for an alternative understanding of foreignness as that which is an originary, constitutive, and ineliminable structural feature of sovereignty as such that cannot be purged or assimilated. If this is so, then the sovereign nation, state, *demos*, and even democracy as such are necessarily vulnerable to foreignness, and this structural vulnerability is the opening for a democratic ethics and politics that reject the exclusion of foreigners and foreignness in the name of, and for the sake of, the presumed immunity of the self-identical sovereign. Further, I argue that a democracy that fails to extend hospitality and include its foreign others is no democracy at all but rather an ethnic or racial polity. If foreignness is constitutive of democratic sovereignty, then the governing logic of the democratic nation-state in which political membership and citizenship are reserved for members of the nation alone is shattered. Democratic justice, therefore, need not be premised on the advantage of the strong over the weak or the exclusion by the sovereign of the foreign; instead, I show that democratic political identity, political membership and representation, and democratic justice are achieved through—not against—foreignness. The result is a renewed possibility for a just and viable post-nationalist democratic cosmopolitanism.

Chapter 1 begins with an analysis of the ideological politics of modern liberalism and conservative communitarianism and their respective positions regarding the relationships among *ethnos*, *demos*, foreignness, and the unity of a democratic people. I retain the use of the original Greek terms, *ethnos* and *demos*, to highlight a conceptual blurring prominent to the nation-state form of political organization that is integral to the conceptualizations of political justice for both the conservative and progressive sides of the democratic political spectrum. Originally and most broadly, both terms mean "a people." *Demos* is a strictly political term insofar as it conceives of a people along the lines of democratic citizenship and political representation. *Ethnos*, by contrast, originally designated "a people" in a primarily non-political sense.[2] It refers to what today we call ethnicity or "an imagined community of membership and affiliation" (Balibar 2004, 8). In other words, *ethnos* is the set of socio-cultural characteristics (real or imagined) and practices that frequently provide the imaginative basis for a collective identity, belonging, shared fate, and unity distinct from the sphere of political rights and representation proper to the *demos*.

In addition to grouping a people according to certain (again real or imagined) characteristics or lineages, *ethnos*, today, has become a highly charged political concept because it is either understood to be *indistinguishable* from the *demos* or it is deployed in order to highlight those qualities and characteristics that deviate from the dominant (and sometimes hegemonic) characteristics that structure *political* identity, belonging, and unity. Under the organizing principle of the nation-state, sovereign control over a given territory is structured upon not only the historical inhabitance of the territory by a given people but also the ethnic characteristics of that people; hence, the bringing together of two distinct concepts, nation and state. In this way, the apolitical sense of *ethnos* is replaced by the political ideology that certain ethnic characteristics and traditions determine or should determine the physical, linguistic, cultural, and symbolic borders of the *demos* and, by extension, who is or is not foreign to the democratic polity.

This is so even in multicultural, democratic societies such as the United States. For example, the teaching of ethnic studies (primarily Chicano Studies) in public high schools has been eliminated (Arizona's HB2281 in 2010), bilingual education in California's public schools has been made illegal in favor of an English immersion model for non-native speakers (California's Proposition 227 in 1998), and an estimated twelve million (im)migrants who lack official documentation but, nevertheless, live and work within the territorial jurisdiction of the U.S. have been denied voting rights and other basic civil protections. These examples suggest that *ethnos* is expressly political, and that those *ethnoi* that diverge from the imagined American *ethnos* (which, despite the paeans to pluralism, remains white, English-speaking, Judeo-Christian, grounded by certain socio-historical memories, experiences, norms, etc.) are a threat to that which undergirds the political identity and unity of the *demos*. This does not mean that liberal democracies are ethno-nationalist states, far from it. The universal scope of the fundamental principles of freedom and equality mean that, within liberal democracies, some level of diversity must be welcomed and accommodated by both progressive and conservative ideologies. Nevertheless, it remains the case for both the conservative and progressive understandings of the identity of the people within the democratic nation-state that citizenship is reserved for members of the nation alone. Those who are or are deemed to be foreign to the nation's common, unifying bonds of culture, language, shared memories, belief in a common fate, etc., are denied membership within the *demos*. This does not mean that foreigners cannot become citizens, but the very process of "naturalization" is, symbolically, nothing more than the shedding of one's foreignness as one becomes a member of the nation and, by extension, a citizen. In short, today, nationality is a dominant basis for organizing the state while nationalism serves to justify claims to sovereign legitimacy and territorial control through the exclusion of *ethnoi* that are, or are deemed to be, foreign.

After mapping the contemporary terrain between modern liberalism and communitarian conservatism with respect to the relationship between the *ethnos*, *demos*, and foreignness, the second chapter examines Book I of Plato's

Republic where he develops—through both foreigners and foreign themes and settings—a series of critiques against theories of justice that are reducible to religion, tradition, law, and commonly held norms. Plato might appear to be a strange figure to focus on, since he draws upon extant notions of the threat of foreignness to depict one of the central figures of the dialogue, Thrasymachus, as a wild, uncivilized, threatening beast. While Plato articulates the need to eliminate foreigners and foreignness from the just regime, I argue that an alternative reading of this founding text of Western political philosophy reveals an implicit acknowledgment by Plato that a just polity is always already constituted by and must welcome the foreign and the foreigner. In other words, for Plato, the foreigner is indecidable insofar as he is simultaneously a guest to be welcomed and an enemy to be excluded.[3] Despite the indecidability of his status, Thrasymachus is welcomed by Socrates, and I offer that this welcoming is revealing for contemporary political society. Welcoming of the foreigner is a risk, but it is a risk that is required for a radical (re)thinking of foreignness in relation to the politics of exclusion of the democratic nation-state.

Because aspects of the theorizations of sovereignty within the social contract tradition—especially the work of Hobbes, Locke, and Rousseau—remain with us today, they continue to call attention to the relationship between sovereignty and the legitimacy of the democratic nation-state. The examination of the historical origins and conceptualization of sovereignty has been a particularly popular enterprise for contemporary philosophers—particularly in the wake of the September 11 terrorist attacks against the U.S. However, my intention here is to identify what, in my view, is lacking from many of these considerations, namely an explicit treatment of the ways in which foreignness is constructed and theorized as an absolute threat to the sovereign. In other words, I examine sovereignty and sovereign legitimacy, but I do so through the lens of foreignness, a reversal that offers surprising insights into the theoretical construction of sovereignty and the legitimacy of the democratic nation-state.

Despite their differences, Hobbes, Locke, and Rousseau all concur that the legitimate sovereign must protect its members from those who seek to weaken, de-stabilize, or destroy the unity of the people as a whole. Whether it is through violent design or the introduction of traditions, practices, norms, and visions of the good life that ostensibly weaken the original bonds that undergird the people, this model of sovereign legitimacy draws upon the common notion that foreigners are threatening outsiders. Of course, as shown in the analysis of Thrasymachus, the presumed threat of the foreigner precedes the social contract tradition. However, I argue that beyond the foreigner, it is foreignness as such that is implicitly theorized as an absolute threat to the indivisibility, inviolability, inalienability, and self-mastery of the sovereign. In a word, foreignness is the absolute threat to sovereign self-identicality. In order for the sovereign to be and remain sovereign, it must preserve its self-identicality through the elimination of all foreign difference. Accordingly, foreignness becomes a weapon of the sovereign that can be assigned to anyone or anything (insider or outsider, citizen or non-citizen, etc.) that is deemed threatening.

These themes are considered over the next five chapters. Chapter 3 identifies the various ways in which Hobbes, Locke, and Rousseau all posit fear as the origin of political society. These fearful origins of political society will be mirrored in that which threatens political society, namely a foreignness that is equated with the lawlessness, terror, bestial violence, distrust, and tenuousness of life in the state of nature. Chapter Four turns to each thinker's respective considerations of the qualities and characteristics of sovereignty. All three theorists share the belief that sovereign legitimacy is premised upon its ability to mitigate this originary fear of the state of nature by unifying its members into a common body, thereby guaranteeing the protection of each individual only insofar as they are members of a unified whole. All three thinkers share in the idea that sovereignty must be inviolable, inalienable, and empowered to protect the common good. The sovereign that fails to protect its members and the unity of the body politic is vulnerable to that which is foreign, and, as such, is no sovereign at all. It is illegitimate and may, therefore, be disobeyed.

To explicate this relationship between the sovereign and the foreign, the fifth chapter examines the specific ways in which foreignness supposedly poses a threat to the homogeneity and unity of the body politic and sovereign self-identicality. I argue that because political legitimacy and justice is conflated with that which is absolutely eliminative of the de-stabilizing and dis-unifying threat of foreignness, violence is indispensable to sovereignty premised upon self-identicality. In the sixth chapter, however, I detail the contradictory and subversive logic that structures the conceptualization of sovereignty within the social contract tradition. By tracing out this logic, I conclude that sovereignty is not that which is absolutely eliminative of the foreign but rather that which is always already constituted by the foreign. Once this reconceptualization of sovereignty has been established, Chapter 7 argues that when foreignness is conceived of as an originary and constitutive feature of sovereignty, a path opens for developing two im-possible concepts or (non)concepts, namely the foreign-sovereign and the quasi-regime. Both resist traditional conceptualizations of sovereign self-identicality, thereby providing a novel basis for (re)imagining the ways in which foreignness might be included within the sovereign regime.

Beyond a generic account of sovereignty, the remainder of this work considers the dominant form of sovereign political organization today, the democratic nation-state. Contemporary theories of sovereignty have undergone substantive changes since the work of the earliest contractarians. Specifically, within democracies, sovereign legitimacy requires that those who are subject to the laws are also its authors. Thus, the *demos* is, in a sense, always open to reinvention insofar as the imposition of the law upon the individual liberty of the members of the *demos* is perpetually being renegotiated and contested. Be that as it may, the legitimacy of the democratic nation-state continues to rest—at least in part—on a classic formulation, namely that the sovereign is self-identical and that it is obligated to protect each of its members by guaranteeing the unity and stability of the whole. Within democracy, the *demos* is sovereign. Accordingly, "the people" is traditionally conceived of as an always already indivisible, inviolable, and unified whole. In this regard, democratic citizens are only vulnerable when the self-identicality of the sovereign *demos* is threatened. Of course, within the nation-state, inclusion within the sovereign *demos* depends upon first being a member of the nation or *ethnos*. Therefore, the legitimate democratic sovereign's duty to protect is a duty to the nation not simply its individual members. The sovereign that fails to purge or assimilate foreignness is divided and cannot legitimately command obedience from its members. In this way, the governing logic of the nation-state assumes that the unity and self-identicality of the *demos* is achieved through the ideal of a stable, identifiable, and homogeneous *ethnos*, and this means using both the force of law and the law of force to police the physical borders of the state and the symbolic borders of culture, language, history, shared fate, etc. that constitute the *ethnos*.

One might object to this claim by citing the existence of the many pluralistic and multicultural democratic societies. Nevertheless, I maintain that even in pluralistic democratic societies, the self-identicality of the sovereign *demos* is, counter-intuitively, premised on the homogeneity of the *ethnos* or nation. Ethnically diverse and culturally complex societies like the U.S. continue to conceive of the nation as an expansion of the allegiances typical of the biological, genetic, and consanguineous bonds of family or as that which is nourished by the presumed naturalness of geographical proximity and control over a given territory. In other words, access to the *demos* is all-too-frequently (and undemocratically) determined by the extent to which one fits the biological, genetic, or natural conditions for membership within the nation. Our family, neighbors, and those who are familiar to, similar to, and resemble "us" are friends to be welcomed and included. The rest—those whose blood, culture, language, religion, politics, etc. are foreign or do not resemble "us"—threaten to disassemble and divide "us." Therefore, these foreign others must be excluded from both the nation and the state, or if they are welcomed, it is only after they have gone through a transformation—a "naturalization"—whereby they become like "us," a member of the national family, by shedding their foreignness. Accordingly, foreignness is of the utmost importance within the democratic nation-state, since citizenship is reserved for members of the nation alone.

Against this exclusionary logic of the nation-state and democratic legitimacy premised upon the protection of the nation, it might appear that the most efficacious solutions to the unjust exclusion of foreigners and foreignness require exploring the possibilities for a future, more ideal democratic state that will one day be inclusive of more or all *ethnoi*. While praiseworthy, this faith in democratic progress and good conscience elides the violence and injustice experienced daily by those who are or are deemed foreign by the sovereign. To resist the nation-state's politics of exclusion, the quietude of good conscience, and the faith in democratic progress, I draw upon Jacques Derrida's work on autoimmunity as a latticework for analyzing the foreigner and foreignness within the nation-state. Specifically, I argue that the decision of the sovereign *demos* to include or exclude foreigners and foreignness is indecidable in advance insofar it must be rendered within the structural aporia of sovereign self-identicality and the absolute vulnerability to the foreignness constitutive of sovereignty as such. From within this structural aporia, there is no guarantee that the sovereign decision to welcome or exclude the foreigner or foreignness will immunize or destroy the sovereign. Accordingly, the democratic sovereign faces an im-possible decision, namely to violently exclude its others, thereby undermining the universal scope of its fundamental and justificatory principles, or welcoming that which might destroy it in the name of a democratic politics that resists the violent exclusion of foreignness and the quietude of good conscience.

To flesh out these themes, Chapter 8 begins with an analysis of the conceptual mechanisms and operations of power that link sovereign self-identicality to the homogeneity of the nation. In particular, I return to the concepts of *ethnos* and *demos* to examine the ways in which the logic of the democratic nation-state forges a link between nationality and citizenship by conflating these two distinct notions of a people. The result is an excluded class of individuals, norms, traditions, practices, institutions, and beliefs that are or are deemed foreign. A class I refer to as "democracy's others."

I challenge this organizing logic of the nation-state by expanding upon Jacques Derrida's deconstructive figure of autoimmune democracy, which reveals democracy to be simultaneously self-identical and heterogeneous or foreign to it-self. This perpetual differing from and deferral of it-self suggests that democracy will never be fully present as such; its fundamental principles will never be fully instantiated. This does not mean that democracy should be abandoned or that we should not work to create a more inclusive, robust, and just public sphere, but rather that democracy is a "concept that is inadequate to itself" (Derrida [2003] 2005, 72), and, therefore, its meaning and future always already remain to come. To develop Derrida's thinking of the democracy to come, I specifically detail the ways in which foreignness is the source of the structural vulnerability of democracy as such to its others. While this vulnerability is threatening, it is also that which opens democracy to the im-possible, namely a democratic legitimacy that is no longer premised upon sovereign self-identicality and a democratic justice that is no longer reducible to the advantage of the stronger. By linking Derrida's democracy to come to the (non)concepts of the foreign-sovereign and quasi-regime developed in Chapter 7, I conclude that the foreigner and the foreignness of democracy to it-self are constitutive and ineliminable features of democratic sovereignty.

If foreignness and the foreigner represent the only chance and promise for a non-violent justice that refuses the nation-state's politics of exclusion, then the questions of the hospitality owed to foreigners by sovereign states and the possibility for a post-national cosmopolitan democratic citizenship require closer attention. Chapter 9 examines cosmopolitanism in four parts. First there is an analysis of Kant's still-influential *Perpetual Peace*, and his elaboration of the cosmopolitan right to hospitality of each individual and the reciprocal obligations of the sovereign state to welcome foreigners and non-citizens. Of particular interest is Kant's limiting of the cosmopolitan right to hospitality. Kant's skepticism regarding the likely despotism of a single, global regime leads him to insist that a viable cosmopolitanism must be built upon a federation of nations. On this model, the peaceful foreigner does possess the cosmopolitan right to visit and be hospitably welcomed, but permanent residency and political membership remain the gift of the sovereign. While I agree with Kant that a global regime is both undesirable and problematic, his limitation of the right to hospitality raises serious moral and political issues when considered alongside the empirical reality of migration today, in which the political rights of tens of millions of refugees, asylum seekers, and (im)migrants depend upon unenforceable international law or the generosity of the sovereign nation-state, a generosity that is rarely forthcoming.

With the historical and philosophical foundations of hospitality and cosmopolitanism outlined, the second section returns to Derrida and his work on unconditional hospitality, which goes beyond Kant's universal hospitality. For Derrida, conditional hospitality is oxymoronic insofar as hospitality is nothing if not the welcoming of each and all, especially those who have not been invited. Only *the* law of unconditional hospitality, which refuses to demand that the guest identify and give an account of herself, can guarantee and protect the singularity and incommensurability of each and all before she is assigned a status, categorized (refugee, asylum seeker, (im)migrant, friend, enemy, etc.) and turned into a generic subject of the law, a violent transformation that eliminates the singularity and incommensurability of the other insofar as the law must treat each and all as equals. Nevertheless, *the* law of unconditional hospitality is an impossibility that would destroy the sovereign capacity to extend hospitality in the first place, since the guest may very well be an enemy or parasite. As such, the welcoming of the other requires that she be assigned a status and categorized. Paradoxically, it is through this assignation of conditional hospitality that the singularity of the other is recognized and protected (the refugee is not an (im)migrant and the (im)migrant is not a hostile invader, etc.). Without the conditional *laws* of hospitality, *the* unconditional law of hospitality remains an abstraction. In this way, Derrida's analysis of the aporetic structure of hospitality challenges the traditional conception of democratic sovereign right. On the one hand, the hospitable welcoming of the other by the sovereign must be conditional. It depends upon extant laws, legal and political institutions, and local practices and customs. On the other hand, this limited form of hospitality is not, properly speaking, hospitality. Accordingly, while impossible, unconditional hospitality places a hyperbolic demand upon the sovereign to always do more on behalf of democracy's weak, excluded, and foreign others, even when doing so might very well weaken or destroy the sovereign.

The third section moves to the discourse ethics of Seyla Benhabib in order to include an alternative to deconstruction that is also able to navigate the deep tension between the universal cosmopolitan right to hospitality and the sovereign right of the state to self-determination. For Benhabib, a cosmopolitanism worthy of its name must also uphold the democratic principles that underpin universal human rights. The tension, however, is that cosmopolitan citizenship cannot eschew bounded democratic polities precisely because democratic legitimacy requires that those who are subject to the laws are also its authors (alternatively, the laws of one democratic polity have no authority over another polity). However, if cosmopolitanism requires bounded democratic polities, then there is no overarching sovereign power to compel sovereign states to protect cosmopolitan rights. Therefore, Benhabib seeks to resolve this tension by identifying mechanisms internal to democracy that can support cosmopolitanism.

Benhabib rejects the ideas of democratic legitimacy premised upon the unity of the *demos* and its supremacy over inviolable territorial borders. Borders are porous and the *demos* is an always already contested and historically contingent formation; indeed, even the fundamental principles of liberal democratic societies are universal in scope, and it is these universal principles that simultaneously anchor democratic constitutions and transcend the local context and practices of bounded democratic polities. Benhabib insists that democratic polities are justified in determining the conditions for membership within the polity, and this sovereign right to self-determination may often unjustly exclude foreigners; however, it is precisely the universal scope of democracy's founding principles and the democratic requirement for justifying its laws and actions that provide for the perpetual contestation of local norms, practices, traditions, and institutions. She calls this process of perpetual contestation "democratic iterations," and they function to simultaneously posit and challenge precedent and authority in such a way that parochial sources of authority are brought into greater harmony with the universal scope of democracy's founding principles. With a debt to Kant, Benhabib insists that political membership is the purview of the sovereign state, but in a departure, she insists that democratic iterations and the porosity of political borders require that once first admittance has been granted, no obstacles to the universal right to political membership premised on appeals to ethnic or national identity can be legitimately erected by the sovereign state.

The final section brings together and expands upon these respective analyses of cosmopolitanism. Here, I introduce the (non)concept of the foreign-citizen, another deconstructive figure, that recognizes the legal and moral importance of citizenship within bounded democratic polities while simultaneously resisting the exclusionary logic of national citizenship. In particular, I focus on the figure of the itinerant (im)migrant laborer who, like Thrasymachus before her, crosses and re-crosses physical and symbolic borders and boundaries. Rather than simply introducing novel practices, norms, and traditions to be instrumentally appropriated or rejected by the sovereign nation-state, I suggest that it is the itinerant migrant that is at once constitutive of and heterogeneous to democratic sovereignty; she cannot be purged or assimilated. She embodies the deconstruction of democratic citizenship as such insofar as she disrupts the self-identicality of democratic citizenship, thereby revealing the vulnerability of democratic sovereignty to its foreign others. The itinerant migrant is a prominent—though not sovereign—instance of the foreign-citizen who is simultaneously guest and host, friend and enemy, inside and outside, us and them. In these ways, she gives place to a democratic ethics and politics no longer constrained by the ethnic and racial politics distinctive of the political ideologies of the nation-state, and, as such, she merits pride of place within a democracy worthy of its name. Through the disruption of the binary logic of sovereign self-identicality, the foreign-citizen reveals that the legal protections of citizenship are indispensable while displacing the site and structuring logic of nation-state citizenship in the name of a future cosmopolitanism, in the name of democracy's others.

1

Ethnos, *Demos*, and Foreignness

This chapter is an extended discussion of the ideological politics of modern liberalism and conservative communitarianism regarding the relationship between *ethnos* and *demos*, foreignness, and the unity of a people within the democratic nation-state. A few preliminary remarks on terminology are immediately appropriate. The term "modern liberalism" is used throughout to designate the socio-cultural elements of a popular political ideology.[1] Unlike classical liberalism, which primarily emphasized individual freedom, equality, and the right to property rooted in natural law as well as the limitation of the state with respect to the lives of individuals, modern liberalism insists that the state has the unique ability and responsibility to protect individual freedom and equality against the conditions of social decay and corruption. In brief, modern liberalism argues that the state has a fundamental obligation to guarantee the democratic (i.e., human) rights of each individual. This obligation is most frequently met by including previously excluded individuals and groups within the fold of the political community, even if doing so is perceived to be a threat to the identity of the community as a whole or an infringement on the rights of those individuals that comprise this unified whole. This does not mean that modern liberalism rejects the common good of the community, but rather that the common good is dependent upon and even indistinguishable from the state assuming an active role in guaranteeing the individual rights of its members. In this respect, modern liberalism has a communitarian impulse even though it remains anchored by its commitment to protecting individual rights.

By contrast, conservative communitarianism is a more controversial term insofar as political communitarianism itself is neither liberal nor conservative. Nevertheless, communitarianism is critical of liberalism for privileging the individual without properly conceiving of the individual as a member of various forms of community, such as family, neighborhoods, churches, social groups, and finally the nation itself. In this regard, communitarianism, like liberalism, is deeply concerned with the relationship between the individual and the community as well as the protection of individual rights, but it tends to emphasize these local networks of community (i.e., civil society) over and against the state whose powers ought to be limited to protecting a small set of rights without which communities and the individuals who comprise them could not flourish.

By adding the modifier, conservative, to communitarianism, my intention is to bring to the fore a socio-cultural dimension frequently linked to communitarianism. In this case, the rights of the community continue to be central yet its identity and unity is founded upon the conservation of local (up to and including the nation itself) traditions, norms, beliefs, memories, experiences, and practices. Taken together, conservative communitarianism believes in individual rights, but its primary organizing principle is the conservation of the rights and identity of the community as a whole through the limitation of the state intent on expanding individual rights with limited regard for the identity of the political community.[2]

With our terminological house in order, it is worth noting that advocates of modern liberalism and conservative communitarianism are not naïve enough to believe that the full instantiation of all democratic principles is possible in any particular nation-state. Instead, for both ideologies, fundamental democratic principles are viewed as ideals towards which the people and the state strive in order to "form a more perfect union." Accordingly, the approach shared by both ideologies is to eliminate injustice by working towards the (re)unification of the *demos* that has splintered along the lines of unjustifiable exclusions (modern liberalism) or the loss of what are believed to be the common principles, practices, and culture that originally unified the *demos* (conservative communitarianism). While they disagree about how to achieve a unified *demos*, both political ideologies believe that the real and imagined bonds of the common identity of the people are deeply intertwined with the possibility for political unity, a commitment to a shared conception of the common good, and justice. Without this unity produced through the sense of belonging to a people (however it might be imagined or re-imagined), the inevitable result will be a citizenry internally divided, paralyzed, and incapable of passing the laws and instituting the practices that can guarantee "justice for all."

Unsurprisingly, then, the relationship between *ethnos*, membership in the *demos*, and to what extent foreignness can or should be accommodated serves as a primary axis of debate and struggle between modern liberalism and conservative communitarianism. The concern for greater democratic justice is not simply a theoretical exercise where ideas compete for primacy of place to explain the sources of injustice. Real lives, vulnerable lives, are on the line, and the urgency of addressing injustice demands that we acknowledge the failures of existing sovereign democratic nation-states by identifying the mechanisms through which they produce vulnerable others both within and outside of their borders through the dominant and unsatisfying political understanding of the relationship between democracy, sovereignty, and foreignness.[3] With this concern foregrounding what follows, I begin by identifying more fully the political correctives deployed by modern liberalism and conservative communitarianism to ameliorate the failures of existing democratic nation-states to fully instantiate the fundamental and indispensable principles of democracy.

Playing politics: *ethnos* and the (re)unification of the *demos*

Implicitly, modern liberalism holds that democracy's failure to fully instantiate its fundamental principles *results* in the unjust exclusions of certain individuals and groups, exclusions that produce the inequalities that fracture the *demos*.[4] Accordingly, democratic ideals can only be fully instantiated and democratic injustices remedied—if not today, then eventually—through progressive attitudes, laws, and reforms that protect individual rights, thereby fostering ever-widening circles of inclusion, accommodation, and representation within the *demos* for democracy's excluded others.[5] In this case, the possibility for political justice depends upon the belief that democracy's fundamental principles can be fully instantiated only if we conceive of the *demos* as a body that is able to expand beyond its original (and current) composition through the inclusion of diversity and difference that changes the practices and appearance of the *demos* without threatening the common bonds of identity that unify it into an indivisible whole. Accordingly, an expanded notion of the real and imagined features (material, social, historical, linguistic, etc.) that determine the qualities, characteristics, and borders of the *ethnos* is a pre-condition for the possible (eventual) unification of the *demos*.

On the one hand, modern liberalism champions diversity for the sake of diversity, recognizing it not only as innately good and desirable but also practically necessary insofar as it represents the best and only viable possibility for the unity of the *demos* in a globalized world marked by massive flows of persons, goods, practices, and information across increasingly permeable borders. For this reason, while all liberal democracies embrace some level of ethnic diversity, modern liberalism is typically the most vocal defender of multiculturalism and pluralism.[6] On the other hand, this ostensible embrace of diversity for its own sake is frequently touted by modern liberalism to be a mere epiphenomenon of its commitment to the principle of equality as a national value and cornerstone of a unifying democratic identity. In this way, modern liberalism's commitment to diversity—while universal in scope—is also an expression of the "nationalism" of the state that endorses its principles.[7] Against the complex and changing forces shaping the often-conflictual and divided *demos*, the embrace of diversity is believed to strengthen and reproduce the common identity of the *demos in its very plurality* and *a fortiori* diversity both reinforces the primacy of democracy globally because of the universalizability of an equality that respects difference, and, at the same time, it establishes the legitimacy of a nationalism that perpetuates the indivisible (albeit plural) sovereignty of the nation-state. Most simply, for modern liberalism, we are all equal but not the same.

For conservative communitarianism, the inability of democracy to fully instantiate its founding principles does not *result* in a fractured *demos* structured upon systematic exclusions; instead, these principles require a *demos* unified enough to instantiate them. Put another way, the disunity of the *demos* is the *cause* of the democratic nation-state's inability to fully instantiate its founding principles. Rather than exclusion, conservative communitarianism typically identifies the *loss* of original practices, traditions, language, and values as a source of dilution of the common bonds of identity, which then facilitate schisms within the *demos*.[8] The original and indispensable qualities and practices that first gave rise to a unified-yet-contentious *demos* are constitutive of the national character—the *ethnos*—of the state, and it is these same features that should continue to determine the content of and control access to the *demos*. Otherwise, the *demos* risks dissolution through inclusion of populations and practices heterogeneous to the original order.[9] Accordingly, for conservative communitarianism, the principles of democracy can only be fully actualized and political injustice remedied through the unification that results from the re-establishment and stabilization of these same shared common bonds that originally founded and shaped the identity of the *demos*. In a word, political justice can be achieved only through conservatism.[10]

This commitment to conservation or reconstitution of an original *ethnos* does not amount to a rejection of diversity *in toto*. As stated, the very definition of liberal democracy is that it welcomes and promotes at least some level of diversity within the *demos*.[11] In fact, the inclusion of certain differences may be innocuous (e.g., "ethnic food"), or, more importantly, beneficial such as when the inclusion of those previously excluded from the *demos* as well as new arrivals function to reinvigorate, preserve, and reproduce the *demos* through the reaffirmation and choiceworthiness of national values (Honig 2001, 74–76). This primarily occurs through various degrees of *assimilation* (if not total assimilation, then there is at least a minimal requirement to adopt certain national and political characteristics, customs, traditions, respect for the law, language, etc.). Unlike modern liberalism, conservative communitarianism does not typically embrace diversity for the sake of diversity, especially when diversity is contrasted with assimilation and perceived as a threat to the community, as in the case of the imagined hyper-individualism of identity politics in which citizens band together through so-called "divisive" aspects of their identity (race, ethnicity, class, gender, sexuality, etc.) rather than associating as free individuals unified through their common bond of national belonging.[12]

In one respect, conservative communitarianism is similar to modern liberalism because it holds that diversity, when it is present, is a testament to the original democratic principles of freedom and equality that serves as the lodestar for the common bond of the people. However, for conservative communitarianism (and this is a point of divergence from modern liberalism), the progressive expansion of the make-up of the *demos* is not always warranted, since the original and fundamental democratic principles that first gave rise to the *demos* must be preserved against those associations, values, and practices which threaten it and other sources of common identity if democratic ideals are to be fully instantiated. The fundamental principles of freedom and equality suggest that the real and imagined bonds of the *ethnos* that guard the borders of the *demos* ought to be preserved more or less *as is* or *restored* to its original form because—although we are not the same—difference is secondary when measured against the generic and universal freedom and equality of individuals as the primary national (i.e., communal) characteristic.

Against the conflicts and factions internal to democratic self-rule and the exterior strains of globalization on nation-state sovereignty, conservative communitarianism argues for inclusion by means of assimilation (not expansion) in order to strengthen, unify, and reproduce the *demos* through the stabilization of a common identity rooted in founding principles, values, and traditions. Because assimilation limits or eliminates difference, it guarantees the freedom and equality of each individual, thereby establishing the legitimacy of claims for the sovereignty of democratic nation-states whose laws and values demonstrate its commitment to protect its people. While assimilation might not be the basis for a robust cosmopolitanism, neither is it doomed to a rigid ethno-nationalism. Somewhat counter-intuitively, assimilation reinforces the primacy of democracy globally because even though it champions the sovereignty of the nation with its particular organizing *ethnos*, it does so by insisting upon a moral and political obligation to recognize the universalizability of inalienable freedom and equality that respects each and all as an individual.[13]

These brief sketches demonstrate why the opinions of modern liberalism and conservative communitarianism regarding the source of democratic injustices are sometimes incommensurable. A short detour might provide more insight into why this is so as well as point us in a new direction that can shed light on how these disagreements are nevertheless based upon a shared set of assumptions about political identity. In *The Politics* Aristotle argues, "it is the association in these things [perception of good, evil, the just, and the unjust] which makes a family and a city" (Aristotle 1981, 1253a7). While the city may grow for the sake of mere life, it becomes self-sufficient (autarkic) and exists (naturally and teleologically) to secure those common elements necessary for the good life (1981, 1252b27) specific to each form of association or constitution, i.e., democratic, aristocratic, oligarchic, etc. It is not surprising, therefore, when the definition of the good life is at stake that individuals, citizens, partisans, politicians, and so on who might otherwise hold many convictions and beliefs in common will nevertheless disagree about the meaning and scope of the core ideas, values, practices, and beliefs of their association. While Aristotle's claim can help us make sense of why there are often heated disagreements today between modern liberalism and conservative communitarianism, it also shows how these ideologies are merely distinct positions along a unifying spectrum of association, which, in this particular case, holds democracy itself to be indispensable to the good life.[14] This is why both ideological positions, despite their differences, can sincerely claim to be the rightful representatives of democratic values.

In addition to Aristotle's claim regarding the good life and the formation of the city (as well as my innocuous claim that this association also gives rise to often spirited differences of opinion), this detour through Ancient Athens can also help to bring to the fore the theoretical backdrop framing certain exclusionary and isolating practices of the modern nation-state. Aristotle's claim is the (first) culmination of an argument that begins with the famous assertion that "man is by nature a political animal [*politkon zoon*]" (Aristotle 1981, 1253a1). Man is by nature a political animal because the human can only actualize its potential within a political community. However, what makes this actualization of potential and flourishing within political society possible for humans (and not proper to social animals such as bees) is the capacity for language through which a unifying and common view of the good life can be articulated and shared. It is no coincidence that the formation of the *polis*, through the implied assent and unanimity of the association of its members, occurs where it does in Aristotle's text, namely directly after the general claim that the natural capacity for language is proper to humanity as such.[15]

The capacity for language and human flourishing within a political community is especially important to democracy. In a democracy competing ideas must be spoken, heard, debated, and agreed upon ["We *hold* these truths . . ."; my emphasis]. The *polis* can only come into being through a public association structured on a particular set of *articulated* ideas. Nevertheless, Aristotle's argument that the general capacity for language is what allows for the formation (and implied unity) of the *polis* has the potential effect of banning those others (human, animal, or even divine: the *banausoi*) who either cannot speak in the common language or whose speech is deemed irrelevant to political participation. Aristotle certainly differentiates between *ethnos* and *demos*, and although he is at times ambiguous on the issue, he does not hold the position that those features that map out the borders of a particular *ethnos* such as language ought to serve as the sole criterion for citizenship within the *demos*.[16] Nevertheless, by arguing that the capacity for language is a pre-condition for what makes man by nature a political animal, it becomes clear how the potential blurring of the theoretical distinction between *ethnos* and *demos* has ancient roots, since *who* is speaking (or, better still, who is effectively silenced or spoken for, i.e., women, slaves, children, *metics*, foreigners, etc.) and *which* language is being spoken matter greatly to the particular vision of the good life that is and can be articulated, as well as who is permitted to participate in the instantiation of that vision, i.e., become a free and equal member of the *demos*.[17]

While language may be a general capacity—proper to all humans—that makes political association possible and necessary for flourishing, the slippage from the capacity for language in general to "my" or "our" language is particularly dangerous in the era of the nation-state. In the Westphalian model of nation-state sovereignty, legitimacy, and international juridical recognition of the state *as* a nation, the common bond of political identity is frequently expressed in the form of nationality that is inextricably linked to the dominant language of the nation.[18] For example, most contemporary democratic nation-states have basic language requirements for non-natives to become naturalized citizens. However, France, in an attempt to limit citizenship to foreign (primarily Arabic-speaking) immigrants, has recently passed laws which deny citizenship to those applicants unable to successfully pass an exceedingly challenging French language proficiency examination. In both cases—although the Islamophobic tenor of France's case is more troubling—the state only provides access to the *demos* based on the successful acquisition of the language of the dominant *ethnos*. In other words, in the model of the nation-state, there is an ever-present risk that the distinction between *ethnos* and *demos* collapses. Even if outright collapse is guarded against, the easy conceptual and political blurring between *ethnos* and *demos* contributes to (legal, if not just) political exclusions and marginalization structured upon the muddled distinction between the two different notions of a people.[19] As Etienne Balibar convincingly notes: "The democratic composition of people in the form of the nation [leads] inevitably to systems of exclusion" (2004, 8).[20] If this is so, then it is hardly surprising that acrimony, protest, and political violence sometimes accompany attempts by modern liberalism and conservative communitarianism to control the political, legal, and discursive means that shape national identity through the sovereign decisions to include or exclude certain individuals or groups as well as those decisions which demarcate or reinforce the borders meant to mark the interior from the exterior.[21]

While modern liberalism and conservative communitarianism are frequently in disagreement, what this initial examination and the detour through Ancient Athens reveal is that despite their differences, both ideologies share certain (unifying) commonalities and presuppositions regarding the possibilities for political justice. First, beyond the pandering and fear-mongering of politicians, the deeper significance of appeals to the nation or *ethnos* is that they undergird the bonds of common identity and sense of shared purpose. A common bond of identity is necessary for political association, and the fact that the two sides disagree on the composition of this common bond of identity is not surprising. But, their respective ideologies and approaches demonstrate that both sides embrace the belief that the way in which the *ethnos* is imagined, determined, and re-imagined is and ought to be the way in which inclusion or exclusion within the *demos* is rightfully determined.[22]

Second, this shared appeal to *ethnos* as a source of common identity and political unity also reveals that both political ideologies see the possibility for justice and full instantiation of fundamental democratic principles to be related to the question of *scope*, since the possibility for justice through the (re)unification of the *demos* is ultimately dependent upon who is included within and excluded from it as well as the way in which this membership is determined. On the one hand, the scope of the *demos* depends upon the nation-state model of unquestioned, unified, and sovereign control over a given physical territory, whereby the demarcation of an interior and exterior through physical borders visibly marks the difference between included citizen and excluded non-citizen, foreigners, trespassers, enemies, etc. On the other hand, the scope of the *demos* also depends upon a parallel psychic and symbolic "subjective interiorization of the idea of the border" (Balibar 2004, 8) by modern subjects who are inescapably citizens of nation-states. This interiorization of the idea of the border reflects the specific characteristics of the dominant *ethnos* whereby distinctions are made (borders are drawn) between the sovereign self and the counter-sovereignty of the other, citizen and non-citizen, friend and enemy, "us" and "them," etc.[23] The result of this subjective interiorization of the idea of borders along national and ethnic lines is that it tends to obscure the contingencies of any given *ethnos* by conceiving of it as internal, integral, and, as such, natural and indissociable from the modern subject and citizen of the nation-state. In this way, just as humans are, *by nature*, political animals, they also experience *as natural* their distinctness from other individual political animals and other political communities according to a conception of individual self-identicality or a self-identical, homogeneous, unified political body whose sovereignty is determined by borders that are impermeable but also variable according to scope. The point here is not to suggest that *ethnos* does not structure personal and collective identities, but rather to demonstrate the ways in which both modern liberalism and conservative communitarianism structure the *scope* of the *demos* along ethnic or national lines demarcated by physical and symbolic borders.

Finally, both modern liberalism and conservative communitarianism understand their appeals to a nationalism rooted in fundamental democratic principles to work on two levels at once: the particular and the universal. Thus, while their understanding differs as to their meaning and scope of application, the appeals to, for example, "American values" or "French vales" are particular insofar as they aim at reinforcing state sovereignty through nationalism (as well as the two other tenants of civic religion: patriotism and exceptionalism). This nationalistic particularism achieves a certain unity against and through other, foreign nation-states. In contrast to this particularism, there is the notion that fundamental democratic principles are universalizable and, therefore, not to be bound by national borders. In this respect, since at least Rousseau, it is no longer adequate to think of democracy upon the Athenian model of a walled *polis* of limited size and scope.[24] Instead, the influence of Rousseau's emphasis on constitutionalism and juridification make the consideration of the universalizability of democratic principles paramount.

For Rousseau, the very initiation of juridification as humans move out of the state of nature into civil society depends upon "obedience to a law one prescribes for oneself" (Rousseau [1762] 1968, 65) alongside the explicit recognition that all are equal insofar as they, too, autonomously submit to the law. The legitimacy of the social contract rests on an understanding of juridification which transforms each and every individual with her particular, natural freedom and interests into a political being who possesses moral freedom (for Rousseau, natural freedom is transformed into moral freedom in civil society because it is only in civil society that law is introduced and, more importantly, that individuals obey a self-prescribed law). Somewhat counter-intuitively, Rousseau's general will secures universal freedom and equality through the absolute and unconditional alienation of each to all as equals, whereby the private interests of each individual are subtracted out to come up with that which is shared in common, namely the public good or the general will ([1762] 1968, 60–61). On this formulation, a people is best understood as a moral community of free and equal members whose private, subjective interests are secondary to the public good secured through (democratic) juridification. Of course, laws are specific to a given people, but the legitimacy of the law as such cannot be an ethnic law. Instead, the legitimacy of the law depends upon a formal relation of the juridical whole measured against the particular interests of its parts. In this way, juridification among equals is universal because the limits of the law do not end at the physical border of the state. There may be competing general wills in the form of various states, but the condition of possibility for the state as such is that the limit of the law extends universally to those autonomous (*auto-nomos*, literally self-legislating), morally free, and equal individuals who give themselves the law and submit to it. In short, the democratic principles of freedom and equality that were central to the Athenian *polis* walled off from the rest of the world are transformed, through the reconceptualization of the conditions of legitimate juridification, to provide a basis for a *universal* "fraternity" of a democratic moral community.[25]

Even without the notion of the general will so central to Rousseau's political theorizations, juridification still provides the basis for the universalizability of democracy and its fundamental principles (as evidenced by the regimes founded on international law, constitutions, and legal institutions, such as the United

Nations, the Universal Declaration of Human Rights, the International Criminal Court, etc.). Juridification, the rule of law as such, secures the freedom and equality of each individual against the particular, often arbitrary laws of the state, thereby serving as the ground for a "democratic identity" which is itself an *ethnos* or imagined community whose members, despite national borders, are unified by the shared belief in the universalizability and sanctity of democratic values, practices, and rights.[26] The universal scope of democracy and its principles are deeply held tenets of both modern liberalism and conservative communitarianism. In this respect, democratic nationalism both reinforces and threatens nation-state sovereignty, since it is at once a reaffirmation of the limits of a particular *ethnos* bounded by sovereign borders and, at the same time, an expression of a non-statist, universal *ethnos* whose common bond is not a particular language or culture or heritage but rather an unbounded moral community of those who subscribe to fundamental democratic principles.

Here, at the borders between the nation-state and the regime of universal human rights, between the particular and the universal, and between citizenship, *ethnos*, and foreignness, the sovereignty of the nation-state is increasingly put under pressure and challenged by old alliances or new forms of social unity, common cause, and disruption resulting from the forces of economic, cultural, and religious globalization. Despite the differences between modern liberalism and conservative communitarianism, both political ideologies rest on a certain collapsing or blurring between *ethnos* and *demos* through which sovereignty, nationality, and political identity and representation are brought together. Therefore, on the one hand, borders must be opened to allow the free flow of capital and information. On the other hand, this opening is also perceived as a threat to sovereignty and grounds calls to close borders and build walls, if not to capital itself then to those foreigners whose presence, suspected presence, or absence raise deep and complex questions regarding who is and who can become a citizen in a democracy and whether and how foreigners should be included or excluded within the *demos*. These questions and concerns lead us away from policy decisions, ideologies, and attitudes toward an analysis of the conceptual construction of the relationships among *ethnos*, foreignness, sovereignty, and inclusion within or exclusion from the *demos*.

2

Hospitality or War? A Foreigner Approaches

For the vast majority of those born within Athens' walls—slaves, women, and children specifically—democratic citizenship was not an option. Democratic participation was restricted by the walls of the household which divided the public sphere (*polis*) from the private sphere of the household (*oikos*). In the private sphere slaves, women, and children were subservient to and ruled over—albeit in different ways—by their masters, husbands, and fathers (Aristotle 1981, 1259a37–1260b24). Effectively confined to the private sphere, the labor of women and slaves was directed by and toward meeting the basic requirements of survival dictated by the laws of nature (*physis*) such as sustenance and reproduction. By contrast, the *polis* was ranked hierarchically above the *oikos* in importance, wholeness, and self-sufficiency (1981, 1252b27–1253a1) because it was the sphere of convention and lawmaking (*nomos*), where propertied, autonomous, adult males endeavored to articulate and secure the public good through ruling and being ruled by turns as democratic equals.

The fact that that only certain individuals were counted as worthy of democratic freedom and equality was made manifest by the internal walls of the city. However, participation in Athenian democracy was also denied to those born outside of the walls encircling Athens. The physical walls that demarcated the boundaries of Athens—its inside from its outside—also served the political purpose of differentiating the Athenian citizen from the foreigner and (im)migrant. On the one hand, the Athenian model of direct democracy depended upon logistical limitations upon the number of participants. As noted (footnote 24, Chapter 1), Aristotle emphasized that the size of the *polis* ought to be "easily surveyed" (1981, 1326b11–25) while Plato actually posited 5,040 landowners as ideal. On the other hand, the size of Athens was also the result of a particular, though hardly unique, convention in which gaining citizenship was extremely difficult for those who were not born into it.[1] While the power and influence of Athens extended throughout the Peloponnesus, the freedom and equality guaranteed by the Athenian democracy was limited to a select few. Most simply, participation in

Athenian democracy was quite literally, inside and out, circumscribed by its physical walls.

Athens' walls did not simply protect it physically or divide it socially; they also performed a symbolic function just as border fences and walls do today. Symbolically, walls provide a sense of the distinctness, impermeability, purity, and hierarchical ordering between binary pairs of conceptual oppositions that structure political spaces (e.g., public/private, civilized/wild), identity (e.g., self/other, native/foreigner, civilized/barbarian), belonging (e.g., inclusion/exclusion, citizen/non-citizen), common purpose (e.g., friend/enemy, equality/inequality), and law (e.g., nature/convention, necessity/freedom).[2] This sense of distinctness is important, since—in Athens and elsewhere—the physical presence and symbolic function of walls facilitate political decision-making and eliminate indecision by downplaying or denying the existence of any ambiguousness between supposedly pure and distinct concepts.[3]

The intent here is not to map Athenian social and public policy or to point out the obvious fact that walls have and continue to control entry into states, movement within states, and access to the public sphere. Although these are weighty matters, this return to Athens makes it possible to locate and harness conceptual resources from within the Western political and philosophical tradition that can challenge contemporary political decision-making that follows from and further reinforces the notion of the rigidity, purity, and the hierarchical ordering of conceptual binary oppositions. This does not mean that everything is of equal value or that all hierarchical ordering is necessarily problematic; instead, by highlighting the ambiguity constitutive of these inherited conceptual pairings—which are never fully instantiated as such, yet continue to shape the political landscape and discourses as if they were—it becomes possible to identify the sources of and potential points of resistance to homogeneity introduced by categories of political belonging that unjustly exclude some from political membership.

Plato, in particular, is worth revisiting because his works can serve as a rich source for challenging this supposed distinctness and purity of certain concepts. This is not because Plato does not rely upon conceptual clarity and distinctness. He absolutely does, and the history of Platonism reflects an ossification of the purity of conceptual binary oppositions such as forms and appearances, the one and the many, mind and body, *logos* and *mythos*, philosophy and rhetoric, etc. Nevertheless, at times, Plato himself seems to resist the ossification of these binaries through the subtle emphasis upon the ambiguousness of ostensibly opposed and pure concepts. On the one hand, Plato is well aware that Athens' walls represent physical barriers that demarcate the inside of the city from the outside, of democracy from other forms of rule, of citizens from foreigners and barbarians, and so on.[4] On the other hand, Athens' walls also symbolize thresholds, which, when approached or crossed, produce a disorienting effect whereby the previously clear and distinct boundaries between opposing concepts lose their definition.

Some of Plato's richest and most complex insights seem to depend upon those rare occasions when Socrates leaves the city, visits its outskirts, or speaks with foreigners and strangers, suggesting that Plato is well aware of the philosophical, political, and even psychical significance of the symbolic impermeability and power to differentiate that walls have on our sense of place, security, belonging, and identity. While there are many explicit examples of Plato's concern with the walls of the city, I focus primarily on *The Republic* because of its status as the founding text of Western political philosophy.[5] Moreover, as I will argue, Plato's treatment of foreignness in Book I, although not explicit, is itself a sophisticated and complex commentary on the risky indecidability and indispensability of the immigrant and foreigner in the consideration and instantiation of justice.

The Piraeus

The extended discussion of justice that takes place in *The Republic* is set in the port city of Piraeus. Immediately, Plato draws the attention of the reader to the importance of setting with respect to the discussion of political justice in general, and as I will argue, this geographic location is a trope which allows Plato to set the stage for distinguishing and complicating the relationship between foreignness, democracy, and their complex relations to philosophy and sophistry. Physically, the Piraeus is connected to Athens proper by a six-mile-long wall suggesting potential danger even on this brief journey. Moreover, the Piraeus also connected Athens to the outside world and symbolizes Athenian economic prosperity, industry, and trade. Like any port city, the economic activity of the Piraeus is a fertile basis for a dynamic and diverse set of practices and population composed of citizens, legal resident aliens (*metics*), and foreigners (*xenoi*). In addition to economic dominance, the Piraeus is also a symbol of Athenian naval dominance as well as the political and military shame that Plato—writing with the benefit of hindsight—knows will result from Athens' defeat to Sparta in the Peloponnesian War (Tschemplik 2005, 8).

With Socrates' first words reporting that he went down to the Piraeus with Glaucon, Plato emphasizes the conspicuous point that Socrates both leaves the city proper and also remains within the city insofar as he is presumably walking within the walled-road linking Athens to the Piraeus.[6] Both inside and outside of the *polis* at the same time, the content of the ten books that follow is set against a "peculiar ambivalence" (Sallis 1975, 314) of the relationship between the philosopher and the city. Yet, this is not the only ambivalence. The blurring of the distinction between inside and outside that stages the setting also suggests that the barriers meant to separate Athens from the rest of the world, Athenian democracy from Spartan oligarchy, the safety of home from the danger of the outside, friend from enemy, the homogeneity of Athens from the diversity of the Piraeus, and tradition from innovation are not impermeable, and the regions they are meant to secure are not as distinct as they might appear. In short, Socrates' descent points to the risk of indecidability and ambiguity that structures an open discussion on justice that will not be restricted by the immediate watchful eye of the laws and the walled insularity of Athenian democracy. Nevertheless, the discussion, while radical—even revolutionary—will not utterly abandon all things Athenian. Risk is a quality of indecidability and ambiguousness, but arbitrariness need not be.[7]

Socrates tells us that he went down to the Piraeus to offer his sacrifice and witness the inaugural festival taking place there to honor Bendis (Plato 1968: 354a), a new goddess—an imported, foreign goddess—whose festival highlights the innovative spirit of the port city (Bloom 1968, 441). He notes that both the Greek and Thracian processions were of similar quality, i.e., equally good. By doing so, our attention is called to the "lack of distinctions" between "native and foreigner" (Sallis 1975, 318), suggesting that the Piraeus, like other port cities, is a place of equality where the "mixing-up of things which are opposed to one another" is a common result of the leveling effect commercial forms of association have on a population (1975, 318). This mixing up and equality is also political. Indeed, Plato knows that after Athens' loss and Sparta's establishment of the Thirty Tyrants, the Piraeus will become the center for the democratic resistance movement that will eventually overthrow the Thirty (Sallis 1975, 318).

This ceremony and space is political in another sense as well. Bendis is not merely an imported goddess who inspired a cult following. Instead, her importation is the result of an official act. The Athenians adopted her shortly after the start of the war, a decision by Athens that would undoubtedly forge new ties and signal an openness, peace, and common cause with the Thracians that the Spartans did not share. In short, the adoption of Bendis by the Athenians was a "diplomatic concession in order to win the favour and resources of the Thracian king" (Janouchová 2013, 96). War is the unstated reason that Socrates is visiting the Piraeus. More than a place where foreign practices, gods, and mores mix with the authority of Athenian tradition, beliefs, and laws, the Piraeus represents a threshold between the stability and protection of democratic Athens and the uncertainty of that which is outside, exterior, hostile, and threatening.

The threatening undercurrent to this politically charged setting is made explicit as Socrates turns to leave after attending to his sacrifices and witnessing the religious ceremonies. He stops when his cloak is pulled from behind by Polemarchus' servant, dispatched to stop Socrates from returning to Athens. This implication of force becomes an overt threat of violence when Polemarchus—"whose name means 'war-lord'" (Sallis 1975, 321)—arrives and points out his superiority in numbers. He demands that Socrates and Glaucon either prove themselves the stronger or submit and remain in the Piraeus. Socrates replies that a third option remains, namely to use persuasion to convince Polemarchus to grant them leave (Plato 1968, 327c).[8] However, Polemarchus rejects this attempt at diplomacy and peaceful negotiation, insisting that he cannot be persuaded if he refuses to listen.

At this point, it is Glaucon who submits when he states that it would appear as if he and Socrates have no choice but to stay if Polemarchus and his company will not listen to reason (Sallis 1975, 322). Perhaps sensing Socrates' hesitance, Adeimantus, who is with Polemarchus, interjects to participate in a type of negotiation. He tells Socrates of the evening's scheduled activities associated with the festival so that Socrates is enticed (persuaded) to remain. Ultimately, Polemarchus also offers some suggestions of dinner and entertainment. Only then, when the threat of violence is replaced by the practice of persuasion, does Socrates himself agree to stay by wryly announcing in formal, legal language, "if it is so resolved" (Plato 1968, 328b). With this decree, a political community has been formed, a democratic community of sorts insofar as it is one that rests upon "consent" (Bloom 1968, 312), public reason, and the rule of law.

In addition to the uncertainty, the fear of threat, the disorientation resulting from the blurring of distinctions, and the general precariousness of a nascent political community, at least one other element of staging by Plato is extremely important, namely the political status of Socrates' interlocutors. In addition to several silent auditors, there are two Athenian citizens, two *metics*, and a foreigner. Glaucon and Adeimantus are Plato's brothers, high-ranking citizens who are members of the Athenian aristocracy. They will be the primary interlocutors, but their roles are marginal until Book II after the important preliminary discussions of justice in Book I. The extended conversation takes place at the house of Polemarchus' father, Cephalus. Both were *metics* or resident aliens, who ran a lucrative family business manufacturing, among other things, shields and weapons. They were war profiteers, and they formed part of a large, well-established population of immigrant resident aliens that were allowed to live, labor, and prosper under Athenian democracy despite not possessing the full benefits and protections of citizenship. Finally, we meet Thrasymachus, a foreigner, renowned sophist, and a nomadic, migrant laborer whose significance to the debate on justice in *The Republic* and the history of political philosophy as such cannot be overstated.

Before undertaking an examination of the arguments of Book I, a further contextualization is helpful. Each of the foreign interlocutors is indispensable to the consideration of justice, but Thrasymachus holds a special place insofar as he is both a foreigner and a sophist. In *The Apology*, we learn that Socrates will be executed because he is believed to be a corrupting and impious sophist who is dangerous to the city. His defense rests in large part by refuting the claim that he is a sophist (Plato 1961a, 19e–21a), but what cannot be denied is the tension that exists between the philosopher and the city. Socrates may be Athenian, but he is a strange one insofar as he closely resembles a foreigner (not merely because Socrates was famously ugly and quite un-Athenian in this regard) because his speech is taken as threatening to the very foundations of the city in a way that is no different than the foreigner whose different values, norms, and practices can rend the social and political fabric of the city. On this point, Plato's writings often appear to be answering an implicit question: Is there space in the city for the individual who, *in the name of justice*, challenges the deeply held and unexamined norms, beliefs, and practices of the city? Socrates' execution would suggest that there is not, and Plato takes it upon himself to resuscitate Socrates' reputation and the practice of philosophy as such by differentiating between sophistical and philosophical speech within democracy. At stake in Plato's consideration is the very fate of the agora. Will it be a rhetorical space where lovers of speeches gather to further their own interests and become enamored of demagoguery, or will it be a truly public space where lovers of wisdom use speech to seek justice and not personal gain?

All of the sophists in Plato's explicitly political works are foreigners, i.e., they are not Athenians though they may be Greek. There is the foreign, self-proclaimed sophist, Protagoras, who discusses with Socrates the relationship between teaching and justice or whether one needs to be virtuous to teach virtue. Protagoras insists that a good sophist can turn his student into a good citizen who is "able to speak and act most powerfully in the affairs in the state" (Plato 1956, 319e). Socrates, in a rejection of the powers of sophistry, believes that virtue is an "art that cannot be taught or communicated by man to man" (1956, 319b). In defense of his position, Protagoras gives two longwinded speeches replete with rhetorical flourishes (1956, 328d, 334d), which excited those listening to erupt in cheers (1956, 334d). Socrates ironically praises the speeches, but when Socrates requests that Protagoras engage in a dialogical, philosophical form of inquiry, Protagoras is recalcitrant, and the dialogue nearly comes to an abrupt halt. Eventually, Socrates is compelled to remain with the agreement that both will compromise on their styles (1956, 334d–338e). While Socrates' final argument appears to best Protagoras', the conclusion is ironic, since both men change their original position regarding virtue (1956, 361a); nevertheless, what is paramount is that Plato depicts philosophy as superior to sophistry for understanding the important political question of whether virtue can be taught.

Similarly, Plato offers a critique of rhetoric with respect to justice in the *Gorgias* where Socrates argues with the foreign sophist, Gorgias (and a more able interlocutor, Callicles), that rhetoric is a knack (Plato 1987, 462b–463a), a form of self-serving flattery (1987, 463a–463d), which is dangerous and tyrannical because it is deployed to avoid paying for committing an injustice (1987, 474a–481b). By contrast, philosophy alone has the potential to be proper political speech because, unlike the sophistical use of rhetoric, it does not simply tell people what they would like to hear but actually strives "to make them as good as possible" (1987, 521a). In fact, Socrates self-identifies as someone engaged in the "true political craft" (1987, 521e) because "the speeches I [Socrates] make on each occasion do not aim at gratification but at what's best." (1987, 521e).

In *The Sophist*, Socrates silently audits a conversation by an unnamed foreign sophist, the Eleatic stranger, in a notoriously complex examination of sophistry, language, logic, epistemology, and metaphysics. Sophistry is defined by the Eleatic stranger as "the imitative kind of the dissembling part of the art of opinion which is part of the art of contradiction . . ." (Plato 1921, 268d). In this respect, sophistry is suitable to demagogues and is juxtaposed to the speech and wisdom of the philosopher (1921, 268b–c). This particular work is, perhaps, the least explicitly political work of the group, but insofar as speech and its relation to both sophistry and philosophy is central to this text and that sophistry is linked to demagoguery, its broader relation to democracy and public speech cannot be glossed over. Proof of this lies in the fact that the dialogue that follows *The Sophist* is Plato's *Statesman*, where the Eleatic stranger remains to partake in a conversation regarding the art of ruling or statesmanship. Finally, there is the foreign sophist Thrasymachus to whom I will return in short order. However, what the above examples demonstrate is that Plato's differentiation between philosophical and sophistical speech as well as the ways in which both forms of speech are related to foreignness are integral to the philosophical reconceptualization of justice.

Cephalus, the *metic*

The nascent political community moves to the house of the old man Cephalus, a *metic*, who was "induced by Pericles" (Lysias [1979] 2005, 388) to come to Athens, but not even the powerful Pericles was able to help Cephalus gain citizenship. It is worth emphasizing the point that the discussion undertaken in *The Republic* not only occurs in the mixed-up and undetermined space of the Piraeus, but more specifically, Plato stages the discussion in the house of an immigrant.[9] Cephalus begins speaking by welcoming Socrates into his home and demonstrating from the outset that the borders between native and foreigner, inside and outside, and host and guest are going to be problematized. He is led by Socrates through a series of questions regarding old age and Cephalus' commitment to religious sacrifice. Cephalus explains that in his old age, as his erotic desires and pursuit of bodily pleasures have waned, he can finally focus on the promises and rewards of the afterlife. Good sense demands obeying the law and paying his debts to his fellow men and the gods by making sacrifices so that he is cleansed of any "unjust deeds" (Plato 1968, 330e) before death and judgment in Hades.

Cephalus' answers are the source of two important avenues of inquiry going forward in the dialogue. On the one hand, in a subtle play of irony that presupposes the reader's awareness of Socrates' poverty, Cephalus' claims rest on the assumption that to be just requires the wealth necessary to pay one's debts. This is a convenient definition for Cephalus because he is wealthy, thereby effectively distancing himself from those immigrants (or philosophical strangers such as

Socrates) who cannot be just because they are poor. In short order, Socrates will challenge this instrumental and self-serving position in favor of a deontic conception of justice independent of any benefit to the individual. On the other hand, Cephalus' answers also demonstrate his piousness, thereby allowing Plato to first and foremost emphasize the authority of tradition in the form of the gods as guarantors of the city and its laws. Cephalus' mention of "unjust deeds" in the otherwise casual exchange with Socrates on old age provides the opportunity for Socrates to turn the conversation of this new political community toward justice. Cephalus' definition of justice as articulated by Socrates is "speaking the truth and giving back what one takes" (Plato 1968, 331d). Cephalus assents to this definition, but Socrates points out that there are cases when it is not appropriate to pay back what one owes such as returning a borrowed weapon to someone who has gone mad. In this case, one must break the law in order to perform the just act. Cephalus seems to understand this, but this insight does not change his understanding of justice.

The fact that Cephalus does not change his opinion even after Socrates points out the flaws in his understanding makes more sense when viewed in relation to Cephalus' status as a *metic* with limited political rights. Cephalus' relation to Athens is, in one sense, purely economic, and Plato implies this through Cephalus' insistence on paying debts, thereby reinforcing the importance of respecting private property. Cephalus insists that "the possession of money contributes a great deal to not cheating or lying to any man against one's will, and, moreover, for not departing to that other place [Hades] frightened because one owes some sacrifices to a god or money to a human being" (Plato 1968, 331b). In this respect, Cephalus' ability to acquire and retain property, his ability to provide for his family, to pay his debts to gods and men, and his ability to remain and profit in a city that does not recognize his political rights depends entirely upon the sanctity of laws protecting private property. Accordingly, Cephalus could never assent to the fact that, on certain occasions, to be just entails breaking the law. Moreover, for Cephalus, not running afoul of the law is equally important. By paying his taxes, his debts, and all that he owes, he exemplifies a common conception of the "good" immigrant: one who works hard and obeys the law. By doing so, he remains effectively under the radar of the authorities and citizens who may at any time challenge the legitimacy of his acquisition of property or his right to legal residency. In many respects, Cephalus is a "better citizen" than a natural-born citizen insofar as the immigrant's success and safety in his adopted home depends upon knowing and strictly obeying the law.

In a similar vein, Cephalus stands out as one whose allegiance might very easily be called into question, particularly in the instability of wartime politics. His refusal to change his opinion in the face of Socrates' critique compels him to leave the conversation rather than admit that it might be acceptable or even just to break the law because, for Cephalus, "the just is identical to the law of the city, and the law is protected by the gods" (Bloom 1968, 315). Indeed, this understanding of justice still has purchase today, and as Bloom notes, if everyone had to spend their days determining whether or not a law was just and if not what the right course of action would be, the result would be "political anarchy" (1968, 315). Depicted by Plato as neither willing nor able to take on the incredibly risky task of rethinking justice, Cephalus' strict adherence to the law in all cases amounts to an expression of his patriotic allegiance to Athens; however, even this could be called into doubt under the right circumstances precisely because as a *metic*, his allegiance is, in some sense, always uncertain.

Cephalus' definition of justice also reflects various features of the so-called immigrant mentality, including the desire to make a better life for oneself and one's family as well as the proud embrace of the laws and customs of one's new, *chosen* home. As an immigrant (and not merely a generic interlocutor in a dialogue on justice), Cephalus' appeal to the traditional authority of the gods suggests that he is aware that his loyalty to the *polis* requires something more than merely obeying the law; instead, his allegiance, if it is not to be doubted, must be rooted in the divine foundations of the city. Thus, a final guarantee of his loyalty is demonstrated by his commitment to tradition in the form of the authority of the gods. Cephalus' unwavering commitment to the laws, the city, and the gods reveals the great weight that he places not merely on orderliness and tradition but also on a sort of assimilation through the adoption of the values that ground the political and juridical order of his new community. Undoubtedly, on one level, Cephalus' appeal to the traditional authority of the gods as guarantors of the laws of the city serves as a common position that Plato—and philosophy in general—recognizes. Indeed, Plato seems to explicitly acknowledge this point insofar as the conversation on justice cannot even begin until Socrates has first attended to his religious sacrifices.[10] Nevertheless, the appeal to the traditional authority of the gods must be countered if new, non-instrumental conceptions of justice are to be put forward.

Despite Cephalus' piety and strict adherence to the law, Socrates' critique of Cephalus as well as the conception of justice as strictly grounded in either religion or tradition points to a common stereotype faced by immigrants of all epochs, namely that the immigrant's allegiance to the city, its laws, and to the public good is dubitable because his or her actions are motivated by self-interest. Cephalus' practice of making sacrifices only becomes important as he approaches death and contemplates the afterlife. Thus, it is only his concern with his own fate that compels him to "become concerned about his duties to gods and men" (Bloom 1968, 314). On this view, Cephalus is not truly concerned for Athens, its men, its laws, or for that matter justice. For Cephalus, "justice is a matter of self-interest" (1968, 314) because his concern for the law and for justice does not actually extend to the community. He repays his debts and makes his sacrifices without thinking about whether his obedience to the law is actually good for those who the laws are designed to benefit (1968, 315). He desires lawfulness, stability, and tradition, but only insofar as they primarily serve his own economic and spiritual self-interest. In short, for Cephalus, as with the majority: "rewards and punishments in this life and the next are necessary to insure obedience [to the law]" (1968, 315). When Socrates implies, through his counter-example, that his appeal to tradition and obedience to the law is merely an expression of self-interest that may actually hurt this community that he claims to hold dear, Cephalus quickly exits the conversation to continue to attend to sacrifices (i.e., to keep up the appearance of obedience and allegiance) and effectively bequeaths his argument (as his inheritance, his property, his allegiance to the law) to his son, Polemarchus.

Polemarchus, the *metic*

Since a philosophical discourse on justice is only possible after religion and tradition have been properly attended to, the demands and weight upon Polemarchus are that much greater. Polemarchus is also a *metic*, and like his father, he is surely aware that his status places him at risk of having his loyalty questioned. Is he truly loyal or is his loyalty simply at the level of appearances, a ruse that allows him to safely pursue his private interests? However, he is politically savvy in a way his father is not. Unlike Cephalus, whose self-interested conception of justice is thinly veiled by piousness and obedience to the law, Polemarchus' definition of justice is more sophisticated insofar as he is willing to take the risk of acknowledging that justice is not always co-extensive with the law and that tradition and authority can and should be questioned in the name of justice. However, this distinction between justice and law remains risky for

Polemarchus, since it requires that he is able to convincingly demonstrate a sincere loyalty to the common good of the *polis*; otherwise, his disobedience and rejection of the law is criminal and dissident.

While certain stereotypes might facilitate distrust regarding the loyalties of the immigrant by natural-born citizens, natural-born citizens are, of course, also self-interested, and this self-interest frequently clashes with the public good. However, the figure of Polemarchus suggests that Plato is at pains to emphasize the importance of the nexus between political loyalty, self-interest, and foreignness. Polemarchus begins by picking up a similar thread from his father's argument—his inheritance—by emphasizing the authority of tradition. Polemarchus' brief defense of Cephalus' position shows his loyalty to family, *polis*, and ancestral authority. However, unlike Cephalus' commitment to the authority of tradition and the gods, Polemarchus demonstrates his reverence for family and loyalty to the *polis* through a different authority, namely the authority of the poets. By citing the wisdom of Simonides stating that justice is to give to each what is owed (Plato 1968, 331e), Polemarchus demonstrates his familiarity with a cultural reference point and influential style of justification shared by the community.

When a literal interpretation of Simonides is shown by Socrates to be unsatisfactory, Polemarchus is quick to change his position having demonstrated his proper allegiance to his father's position. His conception of justice shifts away from the implication of the self-interested repaying of debts and strict payment of what is owed, especially when it might harm the person or the community. He engages in interpretation (of authority and tradition) by arguing that Simonides' claim really means that one should give friends what is good for them while enemies deserve harm (Plato 1968, 332a–c). Polemarchus shifts the terms of the definition of justice away from traditional authority toward the consideration of two fundamental concerns of politics and philosophy, "friendship, or community, and the good" (Bloom 1968, 317). Put another way, self-interested obedience to the law is rejected for acts that foster the public good insofar as the concern with law and justice is now framed by doing what is good for friends and harmful to enemies. However, if authority and tradition of the gods has been cast aside and now the authority of the poets is in danger, this leaves Polemarchus' commitment to the *polis* in doubt. Perhaps this is why Polemarchus thinks justice is most useful during war when one's loyalty is not about commitment to tradition but one's willingness to join battle with political friends to protect the interests of the community against its enemies.

True to his name, Polemarchus (war-lord) identifies justice as being most useful during times of war when friends can be assisted and enemies harmed. Socrates raises serious doubts regarding inconsistencies in his definition with respect to the usefulness of justice during times of war and peace (Plato 1968, 332b–3334b). Polemarchus, nevertheless, maintains that "justice is helping friends and harming enemies" (1968, 334b), or at least those who we believe to be our friends (1968, 334c). This definition of justice certainly seems sensible to most people, even laudable and patriotic. Nevertheless, the question of who is a friend and how to determine if a friend is really a friend remains, and this concern is one of obvious importance to Polemarchus who must not merely seem to be a friend but must really be a friend if he is not to be deemed insincere, self-interested, or, worse, disloyal during a time of war.

Polemarchus' faith in the good sense that friends are to be benefited and enemies harmed depends upon the seemingly unproblematic, even natural, distinction between insider and outsider that is "identical with love of our own" (Bloom 1968, 318). Just as loyalty to the family as one's own arises almost naturally and is integral to our sense of belonging and identity, inclusion and exclusion, so too does loyalty to the city arise (i.e., "fraternity") as a love of that which is (most nearly) self-identical. The loyalty to family and city is powerful precisely because of the concreteness of the relation and its "exclusiveness" (1968, 318) from the rest, i.e., from outsiders and foreigners. One loves and is loyal to those who share one's sensibilities, ideas, tastes, values, allegiances, etc. Families and cities form exclusive groups that rest upon the sharp and permanent distinction between "insiders and outsiders; and the outsiders are potential enemies" (1968, 318).

Polemarchus identifies as an insider, but he is a *metic* and must convince others that he is, in reality, an insider like them. Thus, his definition of justice is interesting in two senses. On the one hand, it is a hyper-political definition that carves the world up along strict conceptual and geo-political lines between insiders and outsiders, family and others, safety and threat, friend and enemy. On the other hand, as a *metic*, he represents the exact type of person whose position within this strict dichotomy of oppositions is always in need of further justification and tests of loyalty. Paradoxically, his definition of justice is the most common political definition, one that continually reaffirms his loyalty, which simultaneously casts his loyalty into doubt. Insofar as Polemarchus is the very person who might benefit from not defining political belonging along the clear-cut distinction between friend and enemy, Plato appears to use Polemarchus to both reinforce and challenge a strict division between friend and enemy.

Socrates senses the importance of this distinction between seeming to be a friend or enemy and actually being one.[11] He challenges Polemarchus' definition because the seemingly self-evident distinction between the conceptual pair, friend and enemy, is not so easily determined. Socrates insists that we are often in error about who is a friend and who is an enemy (Plato 1968, 334b). This fundamental concept of the political is frequently mistaken, resulting in treating enemies as friends and friends as enemies. When Socrates demonstrates that Polemarchus' definition suggests that it will be just to harm friends and to do good to enemies, Polemarchus immediately changes course because this formulation not only undermines his definition of justice (derived from the authority of Simonides), but it also undermines his implicit claim that, despite being a *metic*, he is a true friend and brother who is not merely self-interested but committed to benefiting his friends and serving the public good. The friend, Polemarchus now claims, is not one who simply appears to be a friend, but rather "the man who seems to be good, and is, good, is a friend" (1968, 335a).

Polemarchus' attempt to save his argument and protect himself from attacks of disloyalty by insisting on the distinction between seeming to be good and being good has an unexpected consequence. It contradicts the implicit justification of his earlier position that rests on the "primitive identification of the good with his own" (Bloom 1968, 323). If those who are closest to us, with whom we share our homes, institutions, public spaces, etc. only seem to be our friends but are really enemies, while outsiders, foreigners, and supposed enemies are actually friends, then for a truly just person "loyalty to family and city is undermined" (1968, 324) because one must benefit those who are good and just, not merely "fellow" citizens who may well be unjust and enemies. Moreover, the implicit claim that Polemarchus is endeavoring to make—that he is a friend and not a stranger or enemy—is put into doubt, since his new position suggests that his loyalties lie with those individuals who are just but not necessarily his (adopted) own. In short, Polemarchus' position reveals something that must be denied if he wishes to retain his property, inheritance, and life, namely that "a man who wishes to be just must be cosmopolitan" (1968, 324).

It is advisable to pause for a moment before moving forward to make sense of this dizzying sequence, which inverts, converts, and calls into question the strict opposition of the conceptual pairing of citizen/foreigner, friend/enemy, and inside/outside. Socrates, the foreigner and the citizen, takes a journey to a new community. There, he discusses justice in the home of an immigrant where the first two definitions are provided by immigrants. Cephalus' definition highlights the importance of the traditional and religious foundation of the law and the city. Next is Polemarchus, a foreign resident, whose definition of justice establishes the criteria for political identity, belonging, and public responsibility. His arguments rely upon the rigid distinction between the conceptual categories of friend and enemy, insider and outsider, and inclusion and exclusion, a curious position given that he does not really fit neatly into either pole of these conceptual oppositions.

The purity of the distinction between friend and enemy seems to arise from the supposed naturalness of the self-same or self-identical rooted in consanguinity. Friends and "brothers" and "fellow-citizens" are unified and committed to promoting their shared interest based on the ties of blood and lineage. However, Socrates shows that consanguinity alone cannot determine who is a friend or enemy. The purity of this conceptual pairing, if it is pure at all, requires a reorientation of insider and outsider, inclusion and exclusion, and citizen and non-citizen. The walls of the city that divide citizen and foreigner and threat from risk may be useful in many respects, but they are arbitrary and even self-defeating if enemies are benefited and fiends harmed.

Things get further complicated later in Book II. Socrates insists that the guardians of the city ought to be like dogs which differentiate between friend and enemy, thereby re-inscribing the importance of a strict delineation between the categories of friend and enemy (Plato 1968, 376a–c). Moreover, in Book III, Socrates insists that the *polis* should be bound together, unified by a shared sense of belonging and place. This is to be accomplished, he argues, with a noble or just lie (1968, 414b) with respect to one's birth. However, as Bonnie Honig points out, this lie that is meant to unify the identity of the *polis* and secure a sense of belonging and shared purpose is itself imported from a foreign source, the Phoenicians (Honig 2001, 3).

Ultimately, Polemarchus' position articulates a widely held political sensibility: loyalty to the group and to perceived friends makes it possible to pursue "collective selfishness" (Bloom 1968, 325) at the expense of outsiders. The irony is that he is both an insider and an outsider who attempts to justify his self-interest by insisting upon the clarity and purity of these distinctions that he himself straddles and complicates. Plato shows that the self-same and self-identical, the consanguinity of family and *polis* is never, it seems, what it is or purports to be. Understood in this way, foreignness is both other than and constitutive of political self-identity and belonging. Plato confronts this conceptual muddling ironically, since he is well aware of Polemarchus' fate at the hands of the Thirty. Accused of conspiring with the democrats, his wealth is confiscated, his family exiled, and he is killed (Lysias [1979] 2005, 387–390). As this exchange ends (in another final ironic twist), Polemarchus agrees to join Socrates in battle (two foreigners united), as a true friend, against any who would insist that it is just to do harm to anyone, including an enemy (Plato 1968, 335e).

Thrasymachus, the indecidable foreigner

At this point the foreign sophist, Thrasymachus, enters the dialogue. At once blustering, aggressive, and terrifying, Plato describes him as a "wild beast" (Plato 1968, 336b) that threatens the tenuous stability of the nascent political community through his rage and blindness to the consent, contract, and the rules of dialogical exchange "which, like laws, govern their association" (Bloom 1968, 326). In fact, Socrates emphasizes that "if I had not seen him before he saw me, I would have been speechless" (Plato 1968, 336d), an allusion to a once-common belief that "if a wolf sees as man first, the man is struck speechless" (Bloom 1968, 444). In other words, this beastly, monstrous, and terrifying foreign sophist leaps in with surprise, cunning, and the threat of a violent silencing put forward to reject the civility and openness necessary for a discourse that is ostensibly democratic, i.e., a discourse that is deliberative, dialogical, and premised on the giving and taking of reasons by equals in the pursuit of establishing consensus regarding the nature of justice.[12] While Plato does not explicitly theorize his foreignness, Thrasymachus is depicted as possessing the negative and threatening qualities stereotypically associated with the foreigner, i.e., uncivilized, wild, irrational, forceful, unable to communicate, unfamiliar with the rules of engagement, ignorant of laws and practices, lacking in good manners, etc.

Socrates' alertness to Thrasymachus suggests that he is on guard and watchful against the risk of deformation that sophistry, embodied by this bestial foreigner, presents to this philosophical and democratic conversation, most especially because this conversation takes place in the build-up to war. Because Socrates has already rejected Cephalus' and Polemarchus' positions on religion and tradition with respect to the law as well as the unifying power of consanguinity and physical proximity, this confrontation between Socrates and Thrasymachus will ultimately decide who leads the new regime (Sallis 1975, 346). Yet—returning to the considerations presented at the beginning of this chapter—this confrontation is also revealing insofar as it highlights the distinction between sophistry and philosophy with respect to democracy and foreignness. Speech is central to democracy, since the skills of debate and legal argumentation are indispensable for achieving power and effecting change in a democracy. Every citizen must both persuade fellow citizens to vote one way or another and convince juries to decide cases in their favor. In Plato's time itinerant, foreign sophists were highly regarded and commanded handsome sums of money because they taught the art of rhetoric, an instrumental use of speech for the sake of victory in debate. Democracy, in short, invites and is dependent upon rhetoric; as such, sophistry is a source of seduction for democratic citizens. Simultaneously, rhetoric is a dangerous threat precisely because it is an instrumental use of speech easily deployed for both personal gain and the unreflective acquiescence of citizens to demagoguery. Most plainly, sophistry and rhetoric are simultaneously necessary and dangerous to democracy.

Plato's depiction of foreign sophists is no doubt based on the historical fact that the most famous sophists were foreigners. The reasons for this fact are varied, but it would appear that, at a minimum, the foreigner is uniquely positioned to profit from sophistry precisely because he can recognize the most important norms, practices, and beliefs of democratic citizens who frequently remain ignorant of their normative presuppositions that influence their understanding of political justice. Sophists are skilled rhetoricians, but they are also manipulative insofar as they draw upon the deeply-held, passionate, and oft-unexamined values of the city to achieve victory in debate without necessarily determining truth. Of course, the philosopher is also skilled in rooting out unexamined values and presuppositions that can blind judgments. Moreover, the methodologies of the sophist and philosopher are frequently assumed to be identical, namely rational debate on a given theme. Thus, it is hardly surprising that the majority makes no distinction between the two practices; indeed, Socrates' execution is proof of this fact.

Nevertheless, Plato goes to great lengths to demonstrate that Socrates' philosophical method is different (*The Apology*, *Crito*, *Meno*, *Protagoras*, *Gorgias*, *The Sophist*, and *The Republic* to name a few) insofar as he engages in questioning and dialogue, not debate. He begins from ignorance and seeks wisdom while the sophist's awareness of his ignorance (if he is aware of it at all) is only relevant if it impedes the likelihood of his victory in debate. Despite these qualitative differences, philosophy is frequently mistaken for a foreign sophistry because philosophy itself and the philosopher are tinged by a foreignness or strangeness.

Philosophy is uncanny and unsettling precisely because it causes the philosopher to become a foreigner to herself and her ideas as well as her community, which is structured upon a dogmatic set of unexamined presuppositions and values. In this regard, philosophy cannot insulate itself from foreignness because its defining feature is that it is a form of self-imposed exile. Given these complexities, Socrates' task in his meeting with Thrasymachus is exceedingly difficult. He must differentiate between the demagogic and instrumental uses of rhetoric and the philosophical use of speech in order to provide a philosophical account of justice which draws upon but is radically foreign to tradition, religion, and the laws of the city.

Fortunately for the nascent community, Socrates is only taken by surprise but not silenced by Thrasymachus. Socrates' initial response is to listen as Thrasymachus spells out his unconditional, non-negotiable, forceful (i.e., *undemocratic*) demands that Socrates abandon his elenctic method (Plato 1968, 336d) and define justice plainly and without further ado. In other words, Thrasymachus attempts to foreclose the very possibility for philosophical inquiry by denying Socrates the opportunity to engage in a questioning dialogue. When Socrates finally does respond, he does so with a "slight tremble" (1968, 336e), insisting that he cannot satisfy Thrasymachus' demands because his options have been so severely limited. Just as Socrates refused to be moved by Polemarchus' threats of force on the road, here, too, Socrates confronts force and violence with an attempt at persuasion and reason.

Thrasymachus spurns Socrates' offer of goodwill, and as the tense negotiating of the terms of engagement seems ready to break down (Plato 1968, 337c), Thrasymachus, perhaps seeking profits, clients, and power in this fecund setting of a new community, offers—as any enterprising sophist would—to provide the definition of justice for a fee. Strictly speaking, Socrates rejects Thrasymachus' demand for ransom in exchange for the continued consideration of justice, and, once again, it is Glaucon who submits to the harsh demands and offers to pay the fee on the condition that Thrasymachus provides a satisfactory definition of justice. To this, Socrates raises no objection. Finally, Thrasymachus hesitates to fulfill his offer, but is eventually persuaded by the entreaties of Glaucon and the rest of the community (1968, 338a). Put differently, the distrust Thrasymachus has for Socrates and his "usual tricks" (1968, 337e) is mitigated by the assurances and entreaties of the rest of the community, a common occurrence even in today's world of international diplomacy when neutral states are called in to insure the good faith of both negotiating parties.

Despite his fear of this aggressive, foreign beast and unwillingness to pay for a cessation to hostilities, Socrates is willing to treat this foreign threat to philosophical and democratic dialogue diplomatically. Thrasymachus' demands favor his rhetorical style of engagement putting Socrates at a serious disadvantage, but Socrates nevertheless encourages him to proceed. When Thrasymachus blurts out his infamous definition of justice—"Justice is nothing other than the advantage of the stronger" (Plato 1968, 338c)—and demands payment, Socrates attempts to draw him further into dialogue by restating his position as he understands it. Thrasymachus bristles accusing Socrates of willful misrepresentation. Eventually, however, Socrates' patient listening and cautious responses manage to achieve precisely what Thrasymachus initially refused to allow, namely a dialogical, philosophical, and democratic conversation regarding justice.

On the heels of Polemarchus' strict delineation of the friend/enemy distinction, Thrasymachus' beastly and aggressive approach might suggest a facile placement of Thrasymachus in the camp of the foreign outsider who is an enemy to be harmed. Indeed, I have just argued that Plato depicts Thrasymachus in this way. Nevertheless, in addition to a lesson about the power of diplomacy in the face of a foreign, possibly violent, threat that might undo the political community, Plato's depiction of Thrasymachus is double-edged insofar as it reinforces and also undermines the relationship between the key concepts of foreignness, outsider, and enemy. To demonstrate this, I examine Thrasymachus' arrival on the scene *qua* foreigner who disrupts the easy distinction between friend and enemy.

Most generally, *xenos* means a foreigner. However, *xenos* also means both host and guest insofar as both host and guest are bound by certain rules of engagement when participating in the rituals of hospitality (*xenia*). Polemarchus' distinction between friends (*philoi*) and enemies (*ekthroi*) is, on the one hand, heightened with the sudden appearance of Thrasymachus; on the other hand, Plato, without changing the specific word, effects a subtle shift in emphasis from the foreigner *qua* personal enemy (*ekthros*) to the enemy of the state (*polemios*) and the foreigner who is the *xenos*.[13] In addition to the political diplomacy offered by Socrates and the group, there is also, in Socrates' accommodating gestures, an expression of the sincere, difficult, and, perhaps, impossible task of offering hospitality to a stranger, a foreigner, who was not invited or expected and whose demeanor makes it exceedingly difficult to know if one is engaging with a *xenos* (foreign guest) or a *polemios*. Moreover, this is an interesting "turning of the tables," since it is Socrates himself who is a visitor to the Piraeus and guest in the home of Cephalus. Socrates, once again, is shown to straddle multiple conceptual categories. In addition to being at home and away from home, an observer and a participant in the ceremony, a citizen and a foreigner, a friend and an enemy of Athens, etc., he is both guest and host (*xenos*).

Why does Socrates decide to welcome Thrasymachus rather than prepare for war, given Thrasymachus' demeanor? One possible answer takes us back to the concern of Book II previously mentioned. Socrates explains to Glaucon that the guardian of the city must be like a dog that barks when strangers and enemies approach but welcomes, as friends, those with whom they are familiar. The guard dog is philosophical because it can make errors regarding who is a friend and who is an enemy. Therefore, the act of determining who is a friend and who is an enemy is a question of knowledge and learning. The determination of the friend is, ultimately, a theoretical and philosophical exercise because it is not simply experience and familiarity that determines the friend, but rather an examination of the good and the true friend to the city beyond consanguinity, the proximate, and the self-same. In this respect, Socrates' hosting of Thrasymachus is a non-violent decision, one that rests on a philosophical openness to the foreigner despite not knowing in advance if the unexpected stranger is a dangerous enemy or deserving of hospitality. Thrasymachus is treated with hospitality (as a *xenos*), and in this respect, Socrates' welcoming of Thrasymachus allows Plato to intentionally complicate the categories of foreigner, stranger, guest, host, friend, and enemy. But why?

The answer seems to hinge on understanding Thrasymachus' definition of justice. Unlike Polemarchus and Cephalus, he has no need to prove his loyalty to Athens. He is a foreign sophist who serves the wealthy and profits handsomely. He has no need to articulate a definition of justice that demonstrates his loyalty to the community or dedication to the common good. Nevertheless, his definition of justice, that it is the advantage of the stronger, does not support an anarchic or even tyrannical ordering of the state. Instead, Thrasymachus argues that the rule of the stronger simply means that whichever group or individual is in power, the laws will reflect that form of constitution and be to its advantage. He states that, "democracy sets down democratic laws; a tyranny, tyrannic laws; and the others do the same. And they declare that what they have set down—their own advantage—is just for the ruled" (Plato 1968, 338d). In this respect, Thrasymachus appears to be a political realist whose definition of justice effectively buttresses the Athenian democracy.[14] Nevertheless, rather than an expression of loyalty to the existing regime, Thrasymachus' position is an open declaration of self-interest. He earns a living from teaching rhetoric, and in a democracy he is guaranteed more clients. Moreover, he gains the satisfaction of siding with the regime that will execute Socrates, a Pyrrhic victory, but a victory nonetheless that would validate his position, which holds sophistry to be superior to philosophy for training future rulers and arranging the best regime. Thus, a position he takes up later in the dialogue, that the ruler knows what is really to his advantage (and not just seems to be to his advantage), rejects a simple legal positivism in favor of an art or skill that can be taught by someone like Thrasymachus (Bloom 1968, 330).

Thrasymachus is hostile toward Socrates, threatening to the new regime, concerned with his private interests, and offers a crude picture of justice and political organization where "might makes right." In this regard, Thrasymachus certainly does not seem deserving of hospitality. Thus, Socrates' willingness to invite this threatening foreigner and possible enemy (to the new regime as well as to philosophy) suggests that Plato is aware that, in some sense, the conceptual distinctions between foreigner, friend, and enemy cannot be made in advance of the arrival of this figure. Socrates' offer of hospitality is, in this sense, not merely diplomatic or a simple political calculation. Instead, his hospitality invites the risk of deformation and annihilation at the hands of the unknown, indecidable *xenos/polemios*, a wild, foreign beast who would silence all or a guest worthy of accommodation. In other words, Socrates' risky hospitality is completely naïve from a political perspective. Nevertheless, his hospitality slowly puts Thrasymachus at ease. He begins to answer questions, offer reasons, negotiate, attempt to persuade, participate in the rules of being a (rough-around-the-edges) hospitable guest and democratic and philosophical interlocutor. Socrates' gamble seems to pay off.

Socrates' welcoming of Thrasymachus suggests a conceptual problem, different from the merely political. Thrasymachus' status is indecidable; moreover, his ultimate status is not really determined through familiarity. Insofar as his status is indecidable, Thrasymachus is both *polemios/xenos* at one and the same time. He is both a threat and a possible guest and friend. It is only after the fact, after an ill-advised and impossible act of hospitality (impossible insofar as Socrates welcomes a potential enemy who would annihilate his very capacity to welcome as a host), that his status is finally determined. Socrates *qua* guardian did not get to know Thrasymachus and then proclaim that he was a guest and possible friend and not an enemy; instead, Socrates' decision is to risk welcoming him as a guest, a decision not made from political naïveté but through the knowledge of his status as one whose status is indecidable. Socrates states as much later when, in Book VI, he proclaims about Thrasymachus: "We've just become friends, though we weren't enemies before" (Plato 1968, 498c).

Through Socrates' hospitality, Plato articulates a defense of both philosophy and a non-violent democracy (a decidedly un-Athenian democracy). Beyond a defense of each, Plato brings these two entities together by suggesting the possibility for a democracy founded upon the dialogical process of philosophical deliberation (and not sophistry) as well as a philosophical openness to the foreign other that the politician cannot risk. In this way, even before the conversation between Socrates and Thrasymachus begins, Socrates' hospitality has already demonstrated a deontic justice that is not grounded in violent force—a justice based on a philosophical openness to the uninvited foreigner in recognition of his indecidability—which shows that justice is not, or need not be, instrumentalized as the advantage of the stronger. As the democratic hospitality and rules of dialogical exchange become re-enforced, Thrasymachus, the wild beast, the foreigner, the great rhetorician, is bested—not in a debate—but according to dialectical, philosophical speech. He famously blushes (Plato 1968, 350d) when it becomes clear that his cynical and realist version of justice (and his future potential earnings as a teacher of justice) has been effectively countered by Socrates' claims regarding a radically different form of justice—a foreign and philosophical justice—which nevertheless draws upon the traditions and practices of democracy, including the importance of speech, equality, hospitality, and the law. While resistant to Socrates' claims regarding justice, Thrasymachus agrees to be hospitable, to remain and listen, as the philosophical city in speech is constructed.

The threat of the foreign enemy was not simply a false alarm; Thrasymachus *is* threatening. However, the inclusion of Thrasymachus into the community not only has political effects such as rendering a potential foreign threat toothless, but it also articulates another vision of political inclusion, one that is built upon an impossible gesture of hospitality that makes a guest out of a foreign enemy.[15] Thrasymachus does not assimilate or integrate into the community, nor does the community expand to include him into an already existing set of norms and values. He remains as an included foreigner with pride of place. A position demonstrated by Glaucon, an Athenian citizen, who takes up Thrasymachus' position insisting that he gave up too easily. Glaucon proceeds to resurrect and deepen Thrasymachus' argument by re-emphasizing the relationship between seeming and being (Plato 1968, 357a) through his recounting of the myth of the Ring of Gyges (1968, 359d) to show that one aspect of Thrasymachus' position—that justice is not performed for its own sake but rather for the benefits that accrue to those who appear to be just—cannot be so easily dismissed. Socrates' response to Glaucon paves the way for the remainder of *The Republic*. In these respects, without Thrasymachus, the founding text of Western political philosophy could not proceed, a tacit acknowledgment, perhaps, by Plato of the ways in which the (nomadic as well as the immigrant) foreigner—the embodiment of the enemy and threat to the distinctness and purity of political identity and belonging—is constitutive of political identity and belonging. Despite the fact that Athenian democracy was literally walled off from the outside, that it was highly exclusionary by design, a people is not formed merely *against* the foreign outsider presumed to be an enemy; rather, it is constituted through and dependent upon foreigners and foreignness as such.[16]

3

The Fearful Origins of Sovereignty in the Social Contract Tradition

Socrates' initial response to Thrasymachus is fear. Plato makes a point to note that Socrates was unable to disguise a "slight tremble" in response to Thrasymachus who bursts into the dialogue on justice. Socrates' fear and trembling is his response to a violent, bestial force. As noted, Thrasymachus is compared to a beast—specifically, a wolf—that is capable of silencing the ostensibly non-violent force of rational persuasion, consent, contract, and the rules of dialogical exchange that will ground this new regime and epitomize its legitimate rulers, the philosopher-kings.[1] Socrates' fear is not simply the fear of the threat that sophistry poses to philosophy but also a fear of the ungovernability of the "wild beast" (Plato 1968, 336b). The beast is lawless, violent, and self-interested, and all of these attributes introduce a chaotic and ultimately destructive element that the well-ordered regime cannot tolerate if it hopes to eliminate divisiveness and defend itself against its enemies whose foreignness renders them beastly threats to the laws distinctive of civilized, political society.[2] Most generally, Plato's brief mention of Socrates' fear implies a concern with the prerequisite that all members of the *polis* obey the established laws, the norms by which they are established, and the legitimate rulers of the regime in exchange for protection against those beastly others who refuse to obey or are deemed to be disobedient.[3] Insofar as the foreigner (in this case Thrasymachus) appears hostile to, unwilling, or incapable of adopting the (philosophical) norms upon which the legitimacy of the law of the new regime is founded, he is depicted as an ungovernable beast, a fearful threat to the regime and its members.

However, I do not wish to dwell on Plato in this chapter. Instead, Socrates' fear marks two important signposts. First, it reminds us of the ancient roots of the theoretical relationship among fear, obedience to the law, the legitimacy of political authority, and the demonization of those others who refuse to obey or appear to do so. Second, it provides an historical foothold for understanding the social contract theorists' modernist narratives regarding the fearful origins of political sovereignty, sovereign legitimacy, and how their fearful conceptualizations of political sovereignty also function as a site of production of the foreigner who embodies the threat to the unification and operations of the state. The theorization of fear and sovereignty within the social contract tradition is most explicit in Hobbes, and I begin with his classic work *Leviathan*. Yet, fear is not unique to Hobbes' theorization. Although Locke and Rousseau depict the state of nature as (initially) peaceful and free from fear, in both theorizations fear is the underlying condition that drives humans out of the state of nature in search of the protection of the sovereign authority of civil society. Accordingly, I will examine each of their important contributions in turn.

The fearful origins of sovereignty in Hobbes

The political instability and ceaseless struggles for political power during Hobbes' life left an indelible mark on his philosophical work.[4] The constant discord of civil war was proof enough for Hobbes that new theorizations of sovereignty were required if the goals of political peace and stability were to be achieved. However, it is not simply the historical events of Hobbes' life that motivated his writings. Hobbes also viewed political instability to be a direct consequence of the failure of both religion and philosophy to provide compelling justifications of the origination and legitimacy of political sovereignty. For example, appeals to God and the divine source of natural law in order to confer legitimacy on the sovereign and the positive laws of the state were inadequate because the interpretation of God's will belonged either privately to each person or in the hands of the politically savvy church itself. Consequently, in the absence of a secular justification (a strictly human, anthropological, and rationally demonstrable justification) for the absolute pre-eminence and authority of the sovereign sheared from traditional appeals to God, "the true sovereign," there would be no end to destabilizing disobedience and sedition within political society.

Similarly, the desire for power and the seeming impossibility of permanently securing it led Hobbes to reject the dominant philosophical framework (itself married to Christianity) of Aristotelian teleology, which viewed man as a social and political animal by nature whose highest and final end is virtuous excellence achievable only within the political sphere.[5] The violence and machinations of man in the struggle for power suggested to Hobbes that Aristotle's conception of man as political by nature—which is to say cooperative and not competitive—was unconvincing because it failed to provide a compelling account of man and his motivations for action, namely securing power for himself or defending himself against the power of every other man, i.e., the competition for self-preservation. Against this doctrine of the teleological potential of cooperative man guided by God and God's natural laws toward virtue, Hobbes' political writings demonstrate his commitment to understanding and theorizing power.[6]

Hobbes' interest in introducing peace, stability, and order into the otherwise messy world of political relations is guided by a complimentary triad of longstanding and fundamental questions: (1) What differentiates man from the beast? (2) How does political society originate, and how are men transformed by it? (3) How can the authority of the sovereign be legitimated without appeals to God or the idea that men are naturally political? Hobbes' answer is deceptively simple: The fear that each individual man experiences when confronted with his physical vulnerability and limited power for self-preservation fosters a violent self-interest that makes survival all but impossible; this "natural right" to violence for the sake of self-preservation requires that we seek agreements to limit exposure to this violence. In a word, the beast within us must be exiled through mankind's own creation of the sovereign—the unchaining of a divine, apocalyptic, and absolutely powerful beast—whose violence or threat of violence functions to protect the life of each individual by domesticating man and commanding the obedience of each and all. The simplicity of this answer is deceptive because Hobbes is not content to simply posit a contrarian, yet plausible, theory of human nature that men are fearsome, fearful, and naturally competitive and violent; instead, to guard against the arbitrary appeals to God, God's natural law, and the teleological unfolding of virtuous man, Hobbes' answer is the product of a highly formalized and systematic science of man, the details of which require further explication.

Hobbes' science rests upon what Jacques Derrida (2009, 42) refers to as a "decisively functional" deployment of the ancient distinction between *physis* (nature) and *nomos* (law or convention) and *physis* and *thesis* (positing). Like the ancients, Hobbes views *physis*/*nomos* and *physis*/*thesis* as conceptual antipodes that demarcate independent and distinct spheres of reality. However, because he rejects appeals to sovereign legitimacy dependent upon dominant conceptions of *physis* (i.e., the sphere of the divine design of natural law and the teleological ends of man as natural animal), Hobbes' account must retain the distinction between these spheres while also subverting the longstanding conceptualizations of the content of these spheres by demonstrating that man's political relations and sovereign legitimacy are an artificial or human creation, something posited (*thesis*) or a convention (*nomos*).

In the introduction to the *Leviathan*, Hobbes sets the stage for his demonstration of the fearful origins of sovereignty and the rationally demonstrable legitimacy of the absolute power of the sovereign by immediately placing political society and the state squarely in the domain of human artifice and convention. He asserts that nature can be understood as God's art that brings forth and "governes the world" (Hobbes [1651] 1985, 81). However, this divine art, this world of nature (*physis*), can be imitated by rational man. For example, man can make artificial machines (engines, watches, and other automata) that are imitative of God's divine ability to create in nature. Just as man is the "Rationall and most excellent worke of Nature" ([1651] 1985, 81), so, too, can man produce an "Artificiall Man" ([1651] 1985, 81), the Leviathan or the sovereign state. Like man, the artificial body of the imitative Leviathan—political society *qua* mechanized automaton—is composed of many parts (e.g., magistrates are the joints, a system of rewards and punishments are the nerves, equity and laws are reason and the will, etc.), but no part is more important than the sovereign or "Artificiall *Soul*" ([1651] 1985, 81 original emphasis) that gives "life and motion" ([1651] 1985, 81) to the body politic. Through mimesis of divine creation, mankind's artificial Leviathan will be a "*mortall god*" ([1651] 1985, 227, original emphasis) who governs mankind's social and political relations. Through this analogy to nature and the divine, Hobbes implies that the artificial Leviathan can become man's most "rational and excellent work" once its origins and operating principles are formalized as an explicit and rigorous science of politics.

In advance of any consideration of the empirical modes of engagement that exist between men, Hobbes' insistence upon the artificiality of the Leviathan demonstrates his commitment to a deductive scientific methodology to explain the origins of political life and the claims to sovereign legitimacy. Put differently, Hobbes' reconceptualization of sovereignty as artificial makes possible a movement away from the arbitrariness of appeals to natural law (along with the discord and instability these appeals make possible) toward a rational, well-ordered, and concrete articulation of the legitimacy of absolute sovereignty which can be deduced from a small set of *a priori* governing principles that order matter, movement, and man in nature. Because Hobbes' claims regarding the artificiality of sovereignty are logically deduced from a simple set of rule-governing principles, his analysis of the fearful origins of sovereignty begins with a formal account of the natural world.

While the details of Hobbes' account of objects and movement in nature would take us far afield, we can usefully pick up with his account of the natural condition of mankind.[7] Hobbes asserts that men are, by nature, equal in ability. While one man may be stronger or smarter than the next, these "inequalities" do not amount to a meaningful difference. Even the weakest has enough strength to kill the strongest (if only through superior intellect or temporary alliances with others); similarly, while one may acknowledge that others are smarter, each is content with his share of intellect suggesting not inequality but rather an "equall distribution" (Hobbes [1651] 1985, 184) of intellect among men. From the natural equality of ability springs an "equality of hope" ([1651] 1985, 184) that each will be able to use his natural power to "obtain some future apparent good" ([1651] 1985, 150), and there is no greater good for man than his self-preservation.

However, the goods necessary for self-preservation are scarce. Even if one man comes to possess something beneficial, he can expect other men to "come prepared with forces united, to dispossesse, and deprive him, not only of the fruits of his labour, but also of his life, or liberty" (Hobbes [1651] 1985, 184). Because of both the scarcity of resources and the drive for self-preservation, men in their natural state—a hypothetical state of nature—are engaged in an unending and violent quarrel.[8] Initially, men violently compete for the goods necessary for self-preservation. Once these goods are secured, a deep distrust or permanent diffidence arises that compels men to violently anticipate other men's attempts to deprive each other of their secured goods. Ultimately, to ward off enemies, violence is used to foster a glorious reputation of invulnerability. Thus, in nature, where there exists no "common Power" ([1651] 1985, 185) to compel men into peaceful relations, man's natural equality and equality of hope fosters a violence that turns each man into the enemy of every other.[9]

The perpetual, violent quarreling in the state of nature grounds Hobbes' claim that man's natural condition is a war "of every man, against every man" ([1651] 1985, 185). In the absence of a "common power" there is no law; instead, man uses his natural power and has a natural right to perform those actions that are necessary for self-preservation. Importantly, Hobbes' claims regarding man in the state of nature explicitly reject traditional conceptualizations of natural law guiding mankind's actions, thereby demonstrating that an account of man is possible without appeals to it. If there is no natural law guiding mankind, then there is also no idea of right or wrong, justice or injustice, and no property, since these are artificial constructs "that relate to men in Society" ([1651] 1985, 188). Moreover, industry, knowledge, culture, and the arts are also impossible in the state of nature. Consequently, for Hobbes, the state of nature is a state of war where there is only "continuall feare, and danger of violent death" ([1651] 1985, 186). Insofar as man is equal by nature and exists in a perpetual state of war, long-term survival is all but impossible. For these reasons, it is man's natural "feare of Death" ([1651] 1985, 188) that compels him, "partly in the Passions, partly in his Reason" ([1651] 1985, 188) to seek and maintain peace by giving up certain natural rights to a "common power."

Hobbes has, in a few short pages, logically deduced from a formal, *a priori* principle regarding man's natural equality (and the dystopic state of war this equality fosters) that fear compels men to seek peace outside the state of nature where—he famously claims—life is "solitary, poore, nasty, brutish, and short" ([1651] 1985, 186). The passion for peace is obvious enough given the brutality, bestial excesses, and difficulties of self-preservation in the state of nature. However, if the basis for peace were simply man's natural desire for survival, then whatever peace could be secured would be indistinguishable from natural cooperation, a premise that Hobbes explicitly rejects. Moreover, all animals share the simple desire for self-preservation; therefore, the passion for peace driven by fear highlights the motivation for leaving the state of nature, but it is insufficient to explain how man departs from the state of nature. While men share passions with beasts, reason is proper to mankind; it is that which raises him above the beast to become the "most excellent work of nature" created by God. As such, Hobbes must also explicate the function of reason with regard to fear in the origination of legitimate sovereignty.

The fear of the state of nature can be quelled by reason which recommends certain "Articles of Peace" (Hobbes [1651] 1985, 188), or, as Hobbes refers to them, "Lawes of Nature" ([1651] 1985, 188). This is Hobbes' first reference to the laws of nature, a notable moment insofar as it comes after the physical description of natural man as well as his natural equality in the state of nature. In other words, Hobbes believes he has successfully rejected traditional conceptions of natural law, thereby avoiding the vagaries of theories that appeal to their divine origin; now, he must confront the task of reconceptualizing the laws of nature and mankind's natural rights according to his science of man. For Hobbes, a law of nature (*Lex Naturalis*) is "a Precept, or generall Rule, found out by reason, by which a man is forbidden to do, that, which is destructive of his life" ([1651]

1985, 189). The laws of nature are suggested to man by reason, which is to say that the very existence of these laws comes into being as a result of rational man comprehending his vulnerable condition in the state of nature. In this way, the secular, scientific, and rational explication of the law of nature points to a subtle shift whereby Hobbes severs laws that govern nature from the divine. The elimination of God from the explication of the laws of nature does not mean that nature (*physis*) and the natural somehow cease to exist or are no longer the art of God, but only that Hobbes' new theorization of "natural law" casts appeals to divine authority out of the garden of man's creation, the Leviathan. In a debt to the simplicity of Euclid's methodology, which posited a small set of basic principles to explain the complexities of geometry, Hobbes posits a short list of nineteen laws of nature (justice, mutual accommodation, mercy, the rejection of pride, etc.), all of which logically follow from the first and fundamental law of nature—derived from man's natural condition—which has two parts: "*Seek peace, and follow it* ... [and] ... *By all means we can, to defend our selves*" ([1651] 1985, 190, original emphasis). In short, Hobbes' laws of nature set the conditions for peace that will guide rational men into political society.

The laws of nature are clearly important for determining the articles of peace; however, because Hobbes' challenge is to explain how it comes to pass that men freely depart from the state of nature, he must also contrast natural law (*Lex Naturalis*) with natural right (*Ius Naturale*). Natural law forbids certain actions by demanding the obedience of rational men to follow the laws that will make peace and self-preservation possible. By contrast, a natural right first requires each to use one's liberty, power, and reason toward the end of self-preservation. Reason dictates that in the violent state of nature where everything can be used by every man in his struggle for survival against his enemies, man has a natural right to everything, including "one another's body" (Hobbes [1651] 1985, 190). In this sense, man's natural right is simply liberty or (according to Hobbes' scientific account) "the absence of externall Impediments" ([1651] 1985, 189), which otherwise might hinder man's power to do what he chooses to secure self-preservation. Because the liberty all men naturally possess grants them the right to everything in the state of nature, there can be "no security to any man" ([1651] 1985, 190). This realization is what suggests to man's reason the laws of nature that can insure his safety. However, the laws of nature suggested to reason can only be followed when men give up a portion of their liberty, i.e., their natural right to everything in the state of nature. Indeed, man's natural right to self-preservation both justifies and requires that he seeks agreements in order to contend with the violence of ourselves and others.

By differentiating between natural law and natural right, Hobbes forges a way out of the state of nature. While natural law must be obeyed, rights can be given up. Sometimes rights are forfeited through inaction, but more important to Hobbes' theorization of sovereignty is the "mutuall transferring of Right ... which men call Contract" ([1651] 1985, 192). In other words, by arguing that men rationally and voluntarily give up their *natural* rights through a covenant or contract, Hobbes demonstrates the artificiality of this new contractual political order. While mankind's right to self-preservation is inalienable, this does not mean that all rights are inalienable. Man can and must give up his right to everything in the state of nature in order to fulfill the obligation of his reason and natural law to secure the peace necessary for self-preservation. Some natural rights, therefore, can be transferred, but because covenants that cannot be enforced are invalid, Hobbes notes that covenants and contracts "without the Sword, are but Words" ([1651] 1985, 223). Without "the terror of some Power" ([1651] 1985, 223) to enforce the covenants between men, a promise from one man to another in the state of nature to uphold the laws of nature (justice, modesty, mercy, etc.), which "are contrary to our naturall Passions" ([1651] 1985, 223) for self-preservation, is rendered meaningless. In short, contracts that are strictly between men in the state of nature have no guarantee of being enforced and are, therefore, void.

For a contract to be valid (where all contracting parties perform their duties), there must be a "common Power set over them both [the contracting parties], with right and force sufficient to compell performance" (Hobbes [1651] 1985, 196). In more stark terms, the social contract is only valid if the contracting parties agree to a third party with the power over life and death, the power of terror. Only a common power terrifying enough to compel obedience from each and all through the threat of or actual punishment of those who violate the terms of the contract to give up their natural right and liberty is sufficient to guarantee the contract. Without this "common Power to keep them all in awe" ([1651] 1985, 225), the instability and continual threats resulting from the egotistical particularity of each man's passion for self-preservation remain, and there can be no exit from the state of nature. In a word, absolutism is the condition of possibility for lawful order, and the state or Leviathan is a divine beast of punishment created by men that domesticates mankind through the threat of beastly violence.

At this point, the role of reason with respect to fear in Hobbes' theorization is more evident. On the side of the laws of nature, reason reveals to men that they must secure their own self-preservation against the fearful threat of violent death in the state of nature. The best way to achieve this end is by obeying the laws of nature, which demand that men seek peace. On the side of natural right, reason dictates, first, that men must give up their natural rights by creating artificial contracts between them. Second, even when men make temporary allegiances or contracts that lack a common power, the possession of natural rights guarantees that men will be directed by "their particular judgments, and particular appetites" (Hobbes [1651] 1985, 224); hence, the violent, egotistical, and discrete particularity of the state of nature will never cease unless all men "conferre all their power and strength upon one man . . . that may reduce all their Wills, by plurality of voices, unto one Will . . . and therein to submit their Wills, every one to his Will, and their Judgments, to his Judgment. This is more than Consent, or Concord; it is a reall Unitie of them all, in one and the same Person, made by Covenant of every man with every man" ([1651] 1985, 227). In short, men must contract to form a commonwealth, a Leviathan or "mortal god," who possesses the power, strength, ability, and right (an artificial or conventional right imitative of the divine and authorized by each signatory to the contract) to inflict terror as "*he shall think expedient*" to provide for men's "*Peace and Common Defence*" ([1651] 1985, 228, original emphasis). He who possesses this power and right to inflict terror is the sovereign, the "artificial soul" of the Leviathan.

Fear is the source of men's passion to leave the state of nature, and in this respect it is the origin of political society. At the same time, reason is the 'divine' power of mankind that discovers the laws of nature and allows them to contract together to create an artificial, absolute sovereign. In this regard, reason, too, has a place in the departure from the state of nature and the subsequent origination of the state.[10] Nevertheless, fear remains at the heart of Hobbes' theorization. No more evidence is needed than the fact that reason does not leave fear behind in the state of nature. Instead, reason ratifies fear as both the origin of political society and the justification for the legitimacy of sovereign powers. The social contract among men requires that a legitimate sovereign is an absolute sovereign powerful and terrifying enough to compel total obedience for the sake of the protection of each and all. In this way, the artificial sovereign is nothing else but the aggregated power of all men's fear of violence and death with an absolute power to inflict punishment. The sovereign *is* terror. Without the absolute power over life and death and right to inflict terror when necessary to protect all signatories to the contract from foreign threats or internal discord and injury, the sovereign is rendered partial and powerless, which is simply to say that the sovereign is not sovereign. Thus, for Hobbes, fear drives men from the state of nature, and terror is what provides the rational and secular justification for the legitimacy of sovereign absolutism.

The fearful origins of sovereignty in Locke

In contrast to Hobbes, Locke's state of nature is a peaceful, cooperative, and normative space. Men are God's property, but they also have property in their own person because freedom is a "fence" (Locke 2003, *Second Treatise* §17, 107) around each man that preserves his life. Thus, freedom is a form of (and protector of) property that each man possesses from God. With freedom acting as a negotiator, the sovereignty of God is transferred, like a piece of property, to each man, thereby providing the basis for the rightful jurisdiction over property in the form of a given territory—in this case one's body, mixing one's labor with the land, and, by extension, material ownership.[11] Moreover, freedom is also the link between individual and political sovereignty insofar as the sole function of political sovereignty is "the preservation of property" (2003, *Second Treatise* §85, 136).[12]

The state of nature within which pre-political man dwells is one of perfect freedom, "yet it is not a state of license" (Locke 2003, *Second Treatise* §6, 102). As such, no man has the right to violate another's freedom (i.e., infringe upon another by trespassing his "fence of freedom") or undermine this God-given freedom and equality by subordinating another. Most generally, each man ought "to preserve the rest of mankind" (2003, *Second Treatise* §6, 102). However, because this space is a normative one where the law of nature can be followed or not (mankind may or may not consult his reason), there will always be that "noxious creature" (2003, *Second Treatise* §10, 104) who violates the equality of the "whole species" (2003, *Second Treatise* §8, 103) of mankind. The existence of transgressors in Locke's otherwise rational, moral state of nature suggests that man frequently acts irrationally and out of self-interest, thereby lowering himself to the level of a "noxious creature" foreign to the rational "species" man (i.e., a beast).[13]

The state of nature is governed by the law of nature. However, as Hobbes had already pointed out, a law that cannot be enforced is no law at all. If the state of nature is to be a moral state, then someone must have the power to secure the peace by enforcing the law of nature. Locke resolves this problem by insisting that because the state of nature is populated with free, rational men who are equals, each has the authority to judge and punish those immoral, irrational, self-interested beasts who transgress the law of nature. While Locke recommends rational restraint that disavows "passionate heats, or boundless extravagancy of his [one's] own will" (2003, *Second Treatise* §8, 103), the victim may, "by right of self-preservation . . . by the right he has to preserve all mankind" (2003, *Second Treatise* §11, 104) kill the irrational and self-interested transgressors just as one would kill a "lion or a tiger, one of those wild savage beasts, with whom men can have no society nor security" (2003, *Second Treatise* §11, 104).

Although each man has the executive authority to punish transgressors, "self-love will make men partial to themselves and their friends" (Locke 2003, *Second Treatise* §13, 105) whereby men may punish disproportionately or punish the innocent. In this respect, self-love and the right to self-preservation lead to irrationality insofar as disproportionality and partiality are expressions of irrational behavior that undermines the stringent (and rational) proportionality of treatment owed universally to each man as a result of his natural equality. Without a common judge for appeal, the "inconveniences" (2003, *Second Treatise* §13, 105) of mankind's self-love and irrationality in the state of nature compel him to seek security and peace within political society.

This initial compulsion is compounded when the lawbreakers go beyond hasty passions by using their reason to make willful designs upon another's life. The result is a "state of war" (Locke 2003, *Second Treatise* §16, 107), a corruption of the state of nature in which the unifying, peace-preserving, common law of reason is subverted. In its place, enmity, mutual destruction, lawlessness, and, in a word, fear is introduced. Exiled by his actions from his moral, peaceful, and cooperative origins, mankind is left no choice but to leave the state of nature entirely to counter the fear that accompanies arbitrariness, bestial irrationality, vigilantism, and the lawlessness and particularism of self-love.

This departure is achieved through reasonable men contracting together in a mutual compact, the terms of which rest upon a trade-off. This emphasis on reason and rationality was present in Hobbes as well, but for Locke, reason functions somewhat differently. The fear of the state of war is assuaged through a rational agreement and consensus that is not the result of a purely selfish calculus of self-preservation. Each man gives up his individual, executive, and God-given sovereign authority to judge and punish those who threaten life and personal property. In return, each man gains the protection of political sovereignty, i.e., the community itself which casts aside divisive self-love for the unity secured by contractual assent to obey a dispassionate, neutral, indifferent, objective, and detached "umpire" (Locke 2003, *Second Treatise* §87, 137). In other words, unlike Hobbes' Leviathan, Locke's umpire does not gain legitimacy through its absolute power and totalizing fear. Indeed, political power and legitimacy for Locke is an explicit rejection of the absolute power of a parent over his or her child, the absolute power of the master over his house (2003, *Second Treatise* §52–76), which leaves mankind fearful of and at the mercy of particularistic, arbitrary, and absolutist decisions. Locke's neutral umpire is purely rational, a "judge on earth" (2003, *Second Treatise* §89, 138) who arbitrates particular disputes and punishes (up to and including death) individual transgressors according to promulgated laws that apply universally to all and are directed toward the protection of "life, liberty, and estate" (2003, *Second Treatise* §87, 137), i.e., property. In this respect, free and reasonable men who recognize their own individual vulnerability (and fear this fact) contract together to transfer a portion of their freedom and their individual sovereignty—itself bequeathed from God through nature—to the community.

More will be said about the attributes and qualities of Locke's rational umpire and his rejection of absolutism as a fear-inducing, illegitimate, and non-political form of rule indistinguishable from paternal power; however, enough has been put forward to grasp that, as in Hobbes, fear is central to Locke's telling of the story of political sovereignty. To eliminate the fears of irrationality and self-love that promote a divisive lawlessness akin to a state of war and the fear of the arbitrariness of absolutism, man contracts to form a political sovereign whose legitimacy rests upon his capacity to eliminate this divisiveness by protecting each member of civil society in exchange for their obedience to the public laws they themselves have instantiated as rational signatories to the social contract.

The fearful origins of sovereignty in Rousseau

In contrast to Hobbes' conceptualization of the scientific and secular reason that guides man out of the state of nature, as well as Locke's theorization of a fear-inducing, bestial irrationality that compels men to leave the state of nature, Rousseau is resistant to a simple identification of reason as the capacity that differentiates man from—and makes him superior to—the irrational, passionate, apolitical beast. For Rousseau, reason is a double-edged capacity that introduces both self-perfectibility and an imbecility that can lower man below the beast. If reason is distinctive of and part of the promise of mankind, so, too, are its deleterious effects. Against the fears of irrationality or the bestial baseness and particularism of desire, Rousseau argues that the idyllic origins of the state of nature are destroyed by the gradual emergence of a vainglorious rationality unrestrained by the passions. Nevertheless, while Rousseau does not possess an abiding faith in reason alone, he does share with Locke the belief that excessive self-interest produces an environment of widespread fear, violence, discord, and disunity that eventually forces man from the state of nature into political society. In this way, fear is also a central feature of Rousseau's state of nature and the legitimacy of sovereign authority.

At its inception, the story Rousseau tells about the state of nature is that it is neither moral nor violent. In fact, Rousseau argues that previous social contract theorists are misguided because "in speaking about savages, they described citizens" (Rousseau [1754] 2004, 2). By contrast, he argues that in the earliest stages of the state of nature, mankind has not yet lost the physicality of the animal. Although man possesses a natural desire for self-preservation (*amour de soi-meme*), his physicality, isolation, nascent and under-developed rationality, and the plenitude of nature, provide him with a peaceful, simple, and innocent existence freed from the fear of death. Most simply, at this stage, man differs little from other animals. Nevertheless, despite these similarities, man *is* different from other animals insofar as he is free to deviate from and reject his natural instincts. Both men and beasts are commanded by nature, but only "beasts obey" (Rousseau [1754] 2004, 9). More importantly, man is aware of this freedom, and this awareness marks the paramount distinction between man and beast.[14] Thus, mankind's awareness of his freedom is the source of "the faculty of improvement" ([1754] 2004, 10) or self-perfection that progressively guides him out of his animal innocence through ever-more sophisticated innovations, advancements, conveniences, and comforts toward the ostensibly unlimited heights of enlightened, civilized virtue.[15]

While the awareness of self-perfectibility implies a rational capacity that men alone possess, Rousseau insists that the relationship between reason and the passions is not hierarchical but dialectical. Reason is not a fully formed capacity at the inception of the state of nature. Instead, like other animals, man's passions and desires are driven by his needs and natural instincts. Accordingly, man initially seeks only simple pleasures, and these pleasures are met with little need for rational reflection (and its corollaries such as language and memory). However, as the needs and passions of the free man change beyond basic natural impulses, these new passions fuel the development of his reason to satisfy the desires, which, over time, foster new passions and needs, new rational capacities, and so on. In short, even at its zenith, reason is neither distinct from nor superior to the passions. Their relationship is dialectical insofar as "it is by the activity of our passions, that our reason improves" (Rousseau [1754] 2004, 11) as man slowly progresses—although not necessarily for the better—toward civilization. In this way, the passions are not synonymous with bestial irrationality, and, therefore, they are not to be feared as a source of debasement of human nature or as that which unleashes the destructive force of violent competition, blinding particularism, and excessive self-interest.

Because the passions are not to be feared as a source of irrationality, Rousseau requires a different explanation for the divisive self-interest that forces men to contract together to create a legitimate political sovereign that unifies all by protecting the interests of each member of political society. Ultimately, reason itself is to blame. While the details are many, a general outline will provide an appropriate basis for understanding Rousseau's critique. He begins by claiming that man in the state of nature is not a moral being. In fact, because there is "no kind of moral relations between men in this state, nor any known duties, they could not be either good or bad" ([1754] 2004, 18). However, man—like other animals who seem to clearly lament death and suffering—does possess pity, which tempers his own natural instinct for self-preservation (*amour de soi-meme*). Mankind—sometimes to his own detriment—pities and empathizes with his own species. Indeed, the capacity for pity is that which makes man more than a savage. Putting the needs of others before one's own needs suggests that pity arises from "the pure motion of nature, anterior to all manner of reflection" ([1754] 2004, 20), since, upon rational reflection, self-preservation and one's own well-being are the highest priority.

Pity in the state of nature brings men together into families and communities. Their cooperation promotes intellectual and rational capacities to develop (e.g., language, collective memory, mutual assistance, technological advancements, etc.), which make life easier for all. However, the progressive taming of nature and the beasts also leads to the first stirrings of pride. As certain skills, forms of beauty, and natural abilities become valorized, vanity emerges, and the "sentiment of preferences" (Rousseau [1754] 2004, 32) toward select natural abilities usher in the first social inequalities among men. The pity that once brought individuals together is replaced by social relations structured upon esteem, deference, and civility. When these mores break down, contempt emerges, resulting in violence and bloodshed. Survival within this new social order becomes more difficult, and the need for mutual assistance arises. Yet, to provide assistance, a surplus of goods is needed. Thus, from mutual need, the creation and legitimization of property and the division of labor emerges. Over time, the naturally strong, skilled, and smart gain the social advantages of wealth, esteem, and status. In this way, natural inequality is "insensibly" ([1754] 2004, 36) and imperceptibly transformed into social inequality, which becomes fixed across generations through inheritance of property (and its corollary, social status). In this way, property, for Rousseau, is the origin of inequality.[16] However, property alone is not what compels men to leave the state of nature for civil society.

Here, in this newly competitive and unequal state of nature, reason is "rendered active" (Rousseau [1754] 2004, 36), and the perfection of the mind is nearly realized, as industry, thought, memory, and language all become more sophisticated and advanced. Reason is praiseworthy as a source of moral excellence and self-perfectibility. At the same time, reason also turns man inward upon himself by separating him from and making him "aloof from everything that can trouble or afflict him" ([1754] 2004, 21). Men use reason to think about others, not pity or empathize with their suffering. In this sense, reason also corrupts the affective dimension that makes mankind noble. For Rousseau, no more evidence of this fact is needed than the observation that it is the rabble and women of the market place who break up fights with no concern for their own well-being while the prudent man—wisely—"sneaks off" ([1754] 2004, 21).[17] In this respect, reason is the source of egocentrism, "self-love, or the desire for self-preservation" ([1754] 2004, 20) that destroys the natural empathy and pity that shapes the state of nature at its inception.[18] Because the value of each person is based not only on the goods one can produce, but also the highly regarded social qualities of wealth, intelligence, beauty, talent, and so on, egocentrism and self-love become indispensable for securing one's interests and survival. Accordingly, one must possess—or appear to possess—these qualities to achieve social recognition and resist the downward force of inequality.

The reason that commands self-preservation now requires cunning and deception, since inequality makes each man dependent on the next. The master requires the slave's labor. The poor need the assistance of the rich. Dependency mandates recognition wherein each attracts or interests the other, which further fosters jealousy, competition, rivalry, and the hidden desire to profit at the other's expense. Theft, crime, deception, and instability come to the fore. In short, the simple, natural instinct for self-preservation (*amour de soi-meme*) that marked mankind at the inception of the state of nature is replaced by a hyper-rational, egocentric mode of self-preservation grounded in vanity, pride, and jealousy (*amour propre*), which brings about a fear-ridden dystopia that once and for all destroys the state of nature.

The reason which could have perfected man leads to the fear, instability, divisiveness, self-interest, and destructiveness of *amour propre* wherein "men reach a point where the obstacles to their preservation in a state of nature prove greater than the strength that each man has to preserve himself in that state" (Rousseau [1762] 1968, 59).[19] Put differently, the destructive force of *amour propre* and the widespread fear it produces ultimately serve as the justification for the legitimacy of political sovereignty produced through a social contract in which free, though socially unequal, individuals willfully adopt a "duty of obedience" ([1762] 1968, 53) to the sovereign in exchange for the unity and protection of each and all. Despite the critiques of his predecessors and his own contributions, Rousseau tells a familiar story: the origin of legitimate political sovereignty is fear. The twist that Rousseau provides is that while fear compels mankind into political society, a deeper fear remains, namely that society and the law, despite its promise of moral excellence, is simply the highest form of mankind's corruption.

4

The Qualities of Sovereignty in the Social Contract Tradition

Although the influence of the social contract tradition had waned within political philosophy until its revitalization by John Rawls' influential *A Theory of Justice* in 1971, the theorizations of political sovereignty by early contractarians such as Hobbes, Locke, and Rousseau continue to have purchase in contemporary nation-states' self-understanding of the sovereign obligation to protect its subjects in exchange for their obedience to local laws and norms. None of these theorizations of sovereignty is reducible to the other, and no more evidence of this point is needed than the fact that each theorist's work has been selectively appropriated by states and governments to legitimate their revolutions, constitutions, laws, and norms of organization.[1] Nevertheless, as argued in the previous chapter, each of these theorists acknowledges—implicitly or explicitly—that the fear that accompanies individual vulnerability (which, broadly construed, also encompasses individual control over private property) is the origin of political sovereignty. Therefore, in what follows, I take the fearful origins of sovereignty as a starting point for considering the attributes and qualities that each of these theorists ascribe to sovereign legitimacy.

Hobbes' absolute sovereign

Hobbes' challenge in theorizing sovereignty is twofold. First, in response to the historical events of his day, he primarily sought to provide a theory that would end the internal discords brought on through seditious acts. Second, to resist the arbitrary claims of the divine right to rule, Hobbes also theorized a rigorously deductive political science to explain the origin and legitimacy of sovereignty. Against the backdrop of the terror that pervades the state of nature, Hobbes' science of politics claims that men, through mutually binding covenants, create an artificial sovereign who protects each and all by eliminating the violent quarrels of the state of nature. In this regard, I argued that Hobbes' legitimate sovereign *is* terror, the amalgamated unity of all men's fears and will to survive that compels fulfillment of men's covenants through obedience to the sovereign. By bringing together the terror of the state of nature and the terrifying Leviathan, Hobbes is well positioned to draw out the consequences of this dual conceptualization of fear with respect to the attributes and qualities of sovereign absolutism.

Leading up to Hobbes' pronouncements regarding the formation of the commonwealth, he explains that no internal stability is possible without a sovereign who is equally well equipped to "defend them [men] from the invasion of Forraigners" (Hobbes [1651] 1985, 227). The force of this claim does not rest upon a theorization of foreignness or foreign threats, but rather in Hobbes' rejection of the temporary alliances of wartime. Individuals might work together, but each party's allegiance to his own particular interests produces a "mutual opposition" ([1651] 1985, 225) that reduces the strength of the alliance. To resist the enervating force of private interest and mutual opposition, Hobbes must show that his soon-to-be sovereign possesses the ability to gather up a multitude and transform it into a "real unity," whereby the destabilizing particularities of self-interested individuals and temporary alliances are eliminated.

The unification of a multitude depends upon a sovereign who possesses the unequivocal *right* to act and judge on behalf of all men. To understand this claim, more must be said about Hobbes' understanding of the terms of men's covenants. Hobbes insists that covenants in the state of nature are void. A covenant is not valid simply because men forswear violent designs on each other's lives; rather, covenants become valid contracts through the enforcement and keeping of these promises. This is only possible through a "visible Power to keep them all [men] in awe, and tye them by feare of punishment to the performance of their Covenants" (Hobbes [1651] 1985, 223). Men rationally and voluntarily agree to give up their individual natural right to everything in the state of nature in order to create a third power—a "common power" or sovereign—whose very existence is the formalization of the "*Right to Present* the Person of them all (that is to say, to be their *Representative*)" ([1651] 1985, 228, original emphasis). In this way, when individual men covenant to give up their natural rights to the sovereign, a single, whole, final, and permanent sovereign will replace the individual wills of men by becoming their representative. Through the sovereign representative, the multitude becomes a unity. Therefore,

Hobbes concludes that, because only the sovereign has the power to unify through representation, this power must be enshrined in a set of rights.

Sovereign right is derived from men's covenants.[2] However, we can imagine a subject under a king insisting that he did not willingly choose this king or even a monarchical ordering of political society. If this objection holds, then individual dissatisfaction and the sedition it fuels would be justified. To guard against claims that sovereign right is illegitimate, Hobbes must counter those who would claim that they did not freely give up their rights to *this* sovereign or *this* form of government. To reject these claims, Hobbes implicitly argues that abstaining from the social contract is to willingly accept death insofar as refusing to enter civil society is to remain in the state of nature where "he [man] might without injustice be destroyed by any man whatsoever" ([1651] 1985, 232). Hobbes is more explicit on a second point. He claims that for those reasonable men who do agree to contract together, they do so willingly. Because the voluntary covenant among men requires a sovereign to make it valid, the final terms of the contract in which the decision is made whether the sovereign shall be a man or an assembly of men comes down to an agreement by the "major part" ([1651] 1985, 228) or a majority vote. The moment a commonwealth is instituted and the multitude of men agree to forge a unity under a sovereign who is the representative of all, "every one, as well he that *Voted for it*, as he that *Voted against it*, shall *Authorise*, all the Actions and Judgements [of the sovereign]" ([1651] 1985, 228–229, original emphasis). In this way, no objections from lack of consent to sovereign right are justifiable, thereby enabling Hobbes to proceed with articulating the sovereign rights necessary to guarantee unity, peace, and security.[3]

The first sovereign right is that the sovereign can justly punish those who seek to disobey or overthrow the sovereign. Accordingly, men are lawfully forbidden—by the sovereign, civil laws they themselves have authored and agreed upon to obey in exchange for protection—from entering into new covenants with each other which would compel obedience to anyone but the sovereign. Those men that do enter into such agreement are justly subject to punishment, including death, at the hands of the sovereign, since he who seeks to overthrow the sovereign through new covenants "is author of his own punishment" (Hobbes [1651] 1985, 229). One might expect that those who claim to disobey the sovereign because they have entered into a covenant with God (i.e., the highest and true sovereign) would be exempt from punishment. However, Hobbes roundly rejects this argument by insisting that "there is no Covenant with God, but by mediation of some body that representeth God's Person" ([1651] 1985,

230), which is to say that man has simply made a covenant with another man—not with God—to disobey the sovereign. Most plainly, the sovereign possesses the right to thwart and punish all disobedience that seeks to justify seditious acts through appeals to new covenants.

The next right of the sovereign, the absolute right to power over his subjects, also follows from the terms of the original contract. Hobbes claims that the covenant that produces the sovereign as the representative of each and all is made between men. There is no covenant with the sovereign.[4] To suggest otherwise is to assume that the sovereign either covenants with the multitude as a whole or with each individual. However, it is impossible to covenant with the multitude as a whole since preceding the contract "they are not one Person" (Hobbes [1651] 1985, 230), and if the sovereign is said to covenant with each individual, then those covenants become void, since any perceived breach of that original covenant by the sovereign is actually authored by each individual and the whole as a unified person.[5] As such, "there can be no breach of Covenant on the part of the Soveraign" ([1651] 1985, 230), which, by extension, means that sovereign right is not granted by "Covenant, that is to say on Condition" ([1651] 1985, 231). Accordingly, men cannot be freed from their "Subjection" ([1651] 1985, 230) to the sovereign by the demand for the forfeiture of his absolute right to power over his subjects. The sovereign right to power is absolute, not conditional

The force of Hobbes' conceptualization of the original contract which insists that all men—even those opposed to the contract—are the authors of sovereign actions and judgments leads him to conclude that it is impossible for the sovereign to perform an injustice upon a subject. The sovereign cannot be unjust, since any injury, real or perceived, upon a subject requires that men blame themselves insofar as they are the authors of sovereign judgment. Moreover, if the sovereign cannot be unjust, then he can never justly be punished, put to death, or overthrown. All casting of blame upon the sovereign or claims of injustice fail to recognize that the sole duty of the sovereign is the protection of his subjects as a whole. Toward this end, the sovereign is justified in using whatever means he deems necessary to secure the "Peace and Defence of them all [his subjects]" (Hobbes [1651] 1985, 232). No subject of the commonwealth may legitimately protest the absolute power of the sovereign except in one case: when the sovereign fails in its obligation to protect the lives of its members as a unified people. In Carl Schmitt's renowned formulation: "*Protego ergo obligo* is the *Cogito ergo sum* of the state" (2007, 52). I protect, therefore, I oblige. Accordingly, it is only if the sovereign does not protect that he can legitimately be disobeyed. Moreover, for Hobbes, man is free in political society because he is always at liberty to perform or not perform an action even if non-performance is ill-advised given the certainty of punishment at the hands of the absolute power of the sovereign. In this way, "Feare and Liberty are consistent" (Hobbes [1651] 1985, 262), and the sovereign right to perform *any* action or pass *any* judgment to secure the peace and safety of all through obedience to the sovereign is absolute.

Hobbes details several other sovereign rights, including the right to determine what is to be taught to the subjects to guarantee peace, the right to take private property, the right to decide all controversies involving the law or even "Fact" ([1651] 1985, 234), and the right to declare war and peace with other sovereign commonwealths, etc. These and the earlier rights examined rest upon a simple principle: The rights of the sovereign are indivisible or "inseparable" ([1651] 1985, 236). The division of sovereign rights into various branches (legislative, judicial, executive, fiduciary, military, etc.) means that the sovereign has lost the "Power to protect his Subjects" ([1651] 1985, 236), since control of only one or a few branches inevitably leads to conflicts as the power of each institutional division to act erodes sovereign power. Therefore, absolute sovereignty entails the indivisibility of sovereign rights.

By detailing the rights of the sovereign representative of the people that arise logically and necessarily from the terms of the contract authored by men, Hobbes begins to fill out his argument in favor of sovereign absolutism. However, Hobbes further develops what attributes must belong to an absolute sovereign capable of perpetually unifying and protecting his subjects by examining the ways in which the weakening or dissolution of the Leviathan occurs. He begins by revisiting a theme from the Introduction, namely that the Leviathan is the artificial representative of all men's interests, a single body, composed of many parts or "institutions" (Hobbes [1651] 1985, 363), which facilitate the function of the artificial body politic. Hobbes agrees that "nothing can be immortall, which mortals make" ([1651] 1985, 363). Nevertheless, despite his recognition of human limitations, these institutions can avoid the "internall diseases" and "*Infirmities*" ([1651] 1985, 363, original emphasis) that weaken or destroy mortal bodies from within as long as each institution is designed according to the dictates of reason. Hobbes' Leviathan is a "mortal god," but insofar as reason allows man to approximate the natural creations of God, the Leviathan is imitative of divine immortality. Accordingly, the Leviathan (and, more specifically, the sovereign) can achieve a certain (human) immortality or perpetuity insofar as it can "live, as long as Man-kind, or as the Lawes of Nature, or as Justice it selfe which gives them [the institutions] life" ([1651] 1985, 363). However, a healthy—even immortal—Leviathan is only possible if the undesirable attributes of diseased and weakened "Imperfect Institutions" ([1651] 1985, 363) produced through the "Defectuous Procreation" ([1651] 1985, 364) of bad reasoning can be eliminated.

Even though absolute power is a sovereign right, the primary internal threat to sovereignty is the lack of absolute power necessary to secure peace. Hobbes analogizes a sovereign commonwealth without absolute power to the offspring of sickly parents.[6] These children, he insists, are subject to "untimely death" or prone to breaking out into "biles and scabbs" (Hobbes [1651] 1985, 364). Accordingly, the lowliness of their "vicious conception" ([1651] 1985, 364) must be purged. Hobbes astutely notes that absolute power is not identical to the simple exercise of power. For Hobbes, absolute power is an originary and constitutional power that is the very condition of possibility for a healthy body politic.[7] When absolute power is not present at the commonwealth's "conception" or when it has been foolishly given up or ignorantly forsworn, any attempt by the sovereign to exercise or reclaim absolute power results in a deep sense of injustice among the subjects of the commonwealth who become all-too-aware of the liberties being stripped from them after the fact of their original covenant. These failures inevitably sow the seeds of rebellion, but they can be cured by eliminating any suggestion that sovereign power is not absolute, i.e., originary and perpetual.

In addition to failing to recognize the absolute power of the sovereign, Hobbes identifies another complex of symptom of the seditious body politic, namely that "every private man is the Judge of good and Evil actions" ([1651] 1985, 365) and that "whatever a man does against his Conscience is sinne" ([1651] 1985, 366). Insofar as the power of the sovereign is absolute, Hobbes concludes that the judgments of the commonwealth are final as well. If men debate the dictates of the commonwealth, then decide "afterwards to obey, or disobey them" ([1651] 1985, 365), Hobbes predicts only weakness and instability. Similarly, even a conscientious objector to the dictates of the commonwealth is a threat to the absolute power of the commonwealth precisely because he "makes himself judge of Good and Evill" ([1651] 1985, 366). The law, Hobbes insists, is the "public Conscience" ([1651] 1985, 366) that every member of the commonwealth is obligated to uphold. As a result, conscientious objectors cannot be tolerated within the commonwealth because they place their private interest over the public good and the law.

These two "diseases" might seem like minor inflictions, but they provide yet another basis for Hobbes' claim that the absolute power of the sovereign is most high and cannot be trumped, even by supposed covenants with God. Hobbes notes that, traditionally, faith and sanctity are thought of as qualities that cannot be taught. One has faith because one is inspired by God. However, if this is the case, then every man's personal revelation becomes the standard bearer for public judgments. If each man appeals to his faith in divine revelation as law, then there can be no compulsion for any man to follow the "Law of his Country" (Hobbes [1651] 1985, 366). While divine inspiration and faith might be unproblematic insofar as it is beneficial for one's private sense of well-being, fulfillment, and private freedom of thought, appeals to God as the highest authority actually weaken the possibility for securing the common good precisely because it is nothing more than the "diseases" of personal judgment of good and evil and conscience. Nevertheless, Hobbes endeavors to retain the important practice of faith and belief in sanctity without reliance upon the supernatural. He insists that faith and sanctity are not miracles; instead, while ultimately guided by God, men are led to faith and sanctity through "education, correction, and other naturall wayes" ([1651] 1985, 366), which is simply to say that faith, sanctity, and reason are complementary. Indeed, Hobbes' conception of the absolute sovereign (the "mortal god") suggests that because reason dictates to men that the power of the sovereign is absolute, the sovereign capacity to "awe" his subjects inspires an abiding faith in the institution of the sovereign, thereby demonstrating the sanctity of man's "most rational and excellent work." Put differently, the sovereign is the unification of the secular and the divine. For this reason, Hobbes' theorization of sovereign absolutism rejects the premise that breaking the public law in the name of personal revelation is ever justified.[8]

The fifth disease of the body politic is the belief that the sovereign is subject to civil laws. Hobbes acknowledges that the sovereign has no right to break the natural laws which direct men toward civil society, since these laws are the very *raison d'être* of the sovereign commonwealth, but to assume that the sovereign is subject to civil laws is to fail to understand that sovereignty is absolute. On the one hand, the commonwealth has no power to perform any action or pass any law except through its legitimate representative, the sovereign. The "Soveraign is the sole Legislator" (Hobbes [1651] 1985, 313) and, therefore, his laws cannot be legitimately disobeyed by any subject nor can he, as the sovereign, be subject to any civil laws, since he may, upon his will, "[repeal] those laws which trouble him" ([1651] 1985, 313). On the other hand, the sovereign cannot be subject to the laws of the commonwealth—or more properly the sovereign himself as the representative of the subjects and the only legitimate legislator—because to be a subject of the commonwealth is to be subject to its laws, which is to be subject to the sovereign. To be subject to oneself is "not subjection, but freedome from the Lawes" ([1651] 1985, 367). If the sovereign is subject to the laws—if he must obey—then there is a judge, an order of authority, above him. Accordingly, he would not be absolute, and, as such, he would not be sovereign.

Similar to his earlier claim that sovereign rights are indivisible, Hobbes also insists "*that the Soveraign Power may not be divided*" ([1651] 1985, 368, original emphasis). Just as the sovereign is not sovereign if there is a judge and lord over him, neither can he be sovereign if his powers are divided because divided powers are competing powers. Like man in the state of nature with the power to secure the goods necessary for self-preservation but who faces certain death at the hands of those other men similarly possessed of this power, the division of sovereign power becomes a competition for absolute power ushering in mutual destruction and the dissolution of the commonwealth. If sovereign power can be divided, the absolute authority of the "Legislative Power" ([1651] 1985, 368) or the power of the sovereign to create civil laws for "*the safety of the people*" ([1651] 1985, 376, original emphasis) is undermined. Accordingly, divided sovereignty is not sovereignty because it is not absolute; therefore, it is another disease that must be excised from the healthy commonwealth.

There are several other diseases of the sovereign commonwealth, but for our purposes one more will suffice. Hobbes is insistent that in the sovereign commonwealth "every man has indeed a Propriety that excludes the Right of Every other Subject" ([1651] 1985, 367). The right of every man to private property is unsurprising given the fact that Hobbes' generic conception of man in the state of nature is not so generic. As C.B. Macpherson notes, Hobbes' natural men are "bourgeois men" (Macpherson [1968] 1985, 11–12); moreover, Hobbes envisages a "bourgeois state" ([1968] 1985, 48) with property rights, taxes, and, of course, a contractual model that brings the commonwealth into being. What is surprising, at first glance, is that Hobbes argues that the sovereign has the right to every man's private property. Yet, upon closer inspection of the logic of absolutism, the sovereign obligation to protect the public interest must include the power to control the goods necessary for protection, including private property. Without such power, the private interest would soon erode the public, an incurable disease that would, in short order, bring about the dissolution of the commonwealth.

In conjunction with sovereign rights, these six diseases of the sovereign commonwealth cement Hobbes' claim that the power of the sovereign is absolute.

In fact, the only legitimate sovereign is an absolute sovereign. Although his absolutism may be fearful, it pales in comparison to the "perpetuall warre of every man against his neighbour" (Hobbes [1651] 1985, 260), which would otherwise consume men in the state of nature. In this respect, Hobbes' depiction of an artificial yet pseudo-divine sovereign—a "mortal god"—brought into existence and authorized through covenants among men is not hyperbole; instead, despite Hobbes' movement away from divine justifications, sovereign legitimacy approximates, through imitation, the absolute and terrifying attributes of God. Whatever succor God provides to men rests in an uneasy tension with the terror of His final judgment. The same holds true for the Leviathan. Accordingly, Hobbes' absolute sovereign is the all-powerful, pre-eminent, perpetual, and sacred protector of all of his subjects; he is the maker of laws, yet he is always above or outside the law; he is whole, complete, total, indivisible, and as such, inviolable. Finally, through the erasure of the destabilizing particularities of the wills of individual men, Hobbes' absolutely terrifying sovereign gathers up the multitudes into a stable, harmonious, obedient, and self-identical unity.

Locke's neutral umpire

Despite the individual risks associated with living under a sovereign with the power over life and death, Hobbes' defense of absolutism rests upon his conviction that the terror of the sovereign is preferable to the terror of the state of nature. In a parallel manner, I have argued that fear is integral to Locke's theorization of the state of nature as well. However, he rejects Hobbes' argument that fear and the liberty of subjects in political society is consistent. Derived from his claim that the state of nature is originally peaceful and moral, Locke's analysis of legitimate sovereignty endeavors to retain liberty while eliminating the fear that forces men into political society. Indeed, for Locke, there is no motivation to compact together to create political society if the power of the commonwealth is unable or arbitrarily unwilling to eliminate the fear of the state of nature by protecting each individual's life, liberty, and estate, i.e., property. Against this backdrop of legitimate sovereignty, two conceptual pairs serve as useful guides through Locke's analysis: fear/security and rationality/irrationality. These two conceptual pairs eventually intersect in Locke's theorization of the attributes and qualities of political sovereignty, which rejects the false security and irrationality of absolutism while, nevertheless, insisting upon the possibility for a unified and secure commonwealth through the elimination of the divisiveness of irrational self-interest.

Legitimate power in political society is created through "compact and agreement, and the mutual consent of those who make up the community" (Locke 2003, *Second Treatise* §171, 177). This compact of mutual consent requires man to give up his "perfect freedom" (2003, *Second Treatise* §87, 136) and natural power for self-preservation to the commonwealth. Even without a terrifying, common power, the compact is guaranteed because naturally peaceful, rational, and moral men formally agree to the establishment of civil law among themselves. The civil law itself compels obedience because it applies universally to all members of the commonwealth insofar as they are, by nature, equal. Moreover, because the law is common law, it can be appealed to directly by every subject of the commonwealth for the resolution of disputes. Locke's emphasis upon the universality of law and the right to direct appeal demonstrates that when a man gives up his natural power to execute the law, he "resign[s] it to the public" (2003, *Second Treatise* §89, 138). In other words, each man transfers his power and right to private execution of the fundamental law of nature over to "the hands of the community" (2003, *Second Treatise* §87, 137) as a public whole and not to a monarch or absolute ruler.

Although Locke's civil society is public, the compact still unites disparate individuals into "one body politic, under one supreme government" (2003, *Second Treatise* §89, 138). However, once again, this unity is not tethered to a terrorizing, absolute sovereign. Instead, the universality of civil or common law eliminates "the private judgment of every particular member" (2003, *Second Treatise* §87, 137) producing a public unified under the law, i.e., a commonwealth empowered only to serve the "public good" (2003, *Second Treatise* §89, 138). Accordingly, Locke's sovereign is capable of unifying disparate individuals, but only because he is an umpire or "judge on earth" whose power is limited to the "indifferent" (2003, *Second Treatise* §87, 137) making, judging, and execution of the universal law established by the compact.

Even at this early stage, Locke's theorizations are critical of absolutism, yet his initial rejection of absolutism is bolstered by his articulation of what powers the commonwealth legitimately possesses. By giving up his natural power to execute the laws of nature, each man has, through consent, "given a right to the commonwealth to employ his force, for the execution of the judgments of the commonwealth" (Locke 2003, *Second Treatise* §88, 137). From the force of man's natural power arises the common-wealth's legislative and executive powers, or the "power of making laws ... [and] ... the power of war and peace" (2003, *Second Treatise* §88, 137) according to the precedent of "standing laws" (2003, *Second Treatise* §88, 137). These public powers to compel obedience to established and universal law, to punish transgressors, to secure unity through the elimination of particular and private execution of the law, to neutrally adjudicate the promulgated law, and to thwart external threats to the commonwealth stand in stark opposition to the absolute monarch who has "both legislative and executive power in himself alone" (2003, *Second Treatise* §91, 138), which is problematic in two ways.

First, the absolute monarch makes and executes the law privately and arbitrarily, including destroying the public good by taking away private property. Through this wanton violation of the laws of nature, men under absolute monarchy are "degraded from the common state of rational creatures" (Locke 2003, *Second Treatise* §91, 139). In other words, because there is no common, neutral, and impartial umpire "with [legitimate] authority to decide" (2003, *Second Treatise* §91, 138) the law or hear appeals to the law, men are effectively treated as beasts. However, more important than Locke's concern regarding the degradation of man's rationality is the fact that the conjoining of legislative and executive power in the hands of the monarch alone—and not the public as a whole—is nothing more than the establishment of private judgment and the divisiveness of irrational and excessive self-interest as legitimate political power. In this respect, Locke views the absolute sovereign as both absolutely terrifying and absolutely irrational. If the private judgment of an absolute ruler is the order of the day, then men remain trapped in the murky, unpredictable, violent depths of the state of nature, as does the "absolute prince, in respect of those who are under his dominion" (2003, *Second Treatise* §90, 138).[9] Accordingly, Locke can faithfully claim that "absolute monarchy ... is indeed inconsistent with civil society, and so can be no form of civil-government at all" (2003, *Second Treatise* §90, 138)

Locke deepens this critique by acknowledging the common notion that the absolute ruler is thought to be above the law. However, if this is the case, then men are rendered defenseless (they have lost their "fence of freedom") "against the violence and oppression of this absolute ruler" (Locke 2003, *Second Treatise* §93, 140). For Locke, political society is the placement of the power to execute the law into public hands; hence, the legitimacy of the commonwealth and the possibility for unity is achieved only through the subjection of each and every man, as an equal, to the public law "which he himself, as part of the legislative [power], had established" (2003, *Second Treatise* §94, 141). On this model, "no man in civil society can be exempted from the laws of it" (2003, *Second Treatise* §91, 141). Because every man who is subject to the arbitrary dictates of an absolute ruler effectively remains in the state of nature, he retains the right and the need to unshackle himself from this ruler—to legitimately rebel and overthrow the ruler—by immediately seeking "safety and security in civil society" (2003, *Second Treatise* §94, 140). At this point, the upshot of Locke's argument is clear: Absolutism is illegitimate (and not a true instance of political society) because it is mired in the private, excessive self-interest of a single man who only compels obedience through force or its threat without performing the reciprocal duty to protect and preserve each man's property.

Through his critique of absolutism, the initial attributes and qualities of Locke's conception of political sovereignty come into focus, and it is worthwhile to provide a brief recap before detailing further qualities. First and foremost, political sovereignty is the public execution of the fundamental law of nature. The power to punish domestic and foreign threats to the public good shows that political sovereignty alone can eliminate the fear of individual vulnerability that comes to define the state of nature. Thus, for Locke, fear and liberty can never legitimately co-exist in political society, since the end of political society is to eliminate fear by protecting men's liberty. Moreover, because civil law applies equally to every man, it is universal, and the universality of common law unifies the commonwealth into an indivisible body through the elimination of self-interested execution of the law. Although each man must obey the public law in exchange for the sovereign power to protect and preserve property, he, nevertheless, retains the right to appeal to the law to adjudicate disputes. This right of direct appeal is only possible because Locke's "sovereign" is an umpire whose function is to impartially, indifferently, and fairly administer—to each and all as equals—the common law of civil society. Finally, because all the powers of political society derive from each man's consent, the people always retain the right to revolution or the "supreme power to remove or alter the legislative [power]" (Locke 2003, *Second Treatise* §149, 166) when this power fails to fulfill its final end to ensure the "peace, safety, and public good of the people" (2003, *Second Treatise* §131, 157).

This is already a substantial list of the attributes and qualities of political sovereignty. While we have skimmed the surface, we have not yet said enough about the implications of Locke's theorization of sovereignty with respect to the guiding conceptual pair of rationality/irrationality and its relation to the fearful origins of political society. Locke's belief that the state of nature is initially peaceful and moral is evident, he assumes, to reasonable men. Reason reveals the laws of nature, namely that all men are free, equal, and have property in their person. Yet, irrational men, or those who refuse to consult their reason, transgress the laws of nature by making designs on other men's property. In this way, they demonstrate themselves to be immoral and self-interested "noxious creatures" and vicious beasts that destroy the peace that rational men naturally foster among themselves. In response, rational men who understand that the law of nature is toothless if it is not executed take it upon themselves to punish irrational men, i.e., self-interested and immoral beasts.

Locke believes these rational men are justified in punishing irrational transgressors as one would a wild beast that threatens the peace, but the execution of the law of nature requires that strict obedience to the proportionality of treatment owed to each man as a result of his measured equality. For Locke, rational execution of the law would never be disproportionate to the crime, would never punish the innocent, and would never entail the subjective interpretation of the law of nature. However, he recognizes that "self-love" makes men partial to themselves and their friends. Though these men are reasonable, the affective elements of self-love compromise their reason leading inevitably to a structural disproportionality wherein otherwise rational men place their own concerns above the law of nature. The result is the irrational execution of the law in which the dangers of excessive punishment, subjective interpretation of the law, and, eventually, lawlessness and vigilantism are the norm. This is the state of war marred by the fear of unmitigated self-interest and private, particular judgments. In other words, for Locke, the state of war is a state of irrationality.

Based on this theorization, it is not surprising that Locke insists that political sovereignty is, on the one hand, a public phenomenon grounded upon a promulgated law that applies universally to each and all. By insisting that political power lies in the "hands of the community" as a whole, Locke guards against the private judgments and "self-love" that destroys unity. On the other hand, Locke's "sovereign" is merely an "umpire" or "judge on earth" whose function is to protect property by administering the consensual, public law dispassionately, indifferently, objectively, and fairly. In this regard, Locke's umpire is purely rational; in fact, he must be in order to guard against the irrationality coextensive with the self-love that tears asunder the unified body politic. While we should not underestimate the importance of the link between unity and the public nature of Locke's commonwealth, its relevance comes into full view only when rationality and irrationality are more completely elaborated.

Irrationality turns men into savage beasts not only because it leads to a violent rejection of the law destructive of the peace, but also because irrationality leaves men stranded in private subjectivity where the partiality and particularism of self-love made law as such impossible. Laws are universally recognizable (to each member of a particular commonwealth) or they are not laws at all; non-universal laws are only decrees or dictates enforced by arbitrary and unpredictable power. Moreover, Locke's frequent comparisons between irrational men and simple beasts suggest that the tragedy of beasts is that they have no law at all. Beasts are merely temporary, partial, weak beings subject to the vicissitudes, violence, and force of nature and the rule of the strongest (Locke 2003, *Second Treatise* §1, 100). By contrast, the light of man's reason makes possible the observation of law that effectively lifts man up out of the dark, violent, and arbitrary recesses of nature to the permanent, universal, and inviolable heights of consensual and, therefore, reasonable political society. Just as the state of nature is ultimately a state of irrationality, legitimate political society is a state of rationality which makes possible a unified whole that protects vulnerable men from the destructive force and violence of irrationality.

On this reading, Locke's theorization of the public power of the commonwealth as a unifying force against particularism and self-love is rooted in his understanding of reason. Reason demonstrates that all men are free and equal. Reason enlightens men from privation. Reason is the source of the law. Reason is the condition of possibility for universality that destroys the partiality and particularism that fractures men by turning them against each other. In these respects, it is easy to understand why the power of the commonwealth is a public power. Unless it is public, there can be no universal law and no common judge of appeal; thus, the threat always remains that an absolute monarch who epitomizes private, self-interested partiality will come to rule. However, reason does not only unify the people through the public, universality of law, it also establishes a homogeneous whole—a people—through the erasure of individual men's private interests.

In this respect, reason with respect to public unity is a double-edged phenomenon. On the one hand, reason rejects private power as partial and divisive, thereby ushering in a public power solely able to guarantee that all men are treated equally according to the dispassionate calculation of the law by an impartial umpire. On the other hand, this universal equality of all is achieved through a potentially dangerous homogeneity. Homogeneity might not be a damaging social norm for a set of individuals who are broadly possessed of the same traits, language, values, and beliefs.[10] However, in today's more complex societies, a homogenizing and totalizing reason that eliminates divisive difference by rejecting the "irrationality" of self-love, disproportionate allegiances, and private judgments through unification into a public and indivisible whole (i.e., a people) can be violent and is often terrorizing.

While the erasure of individual differences might be dismissed as a necessary evil for achieving a public, unified, and homogeneous political society, there is another danger to Locke's theorization. Implicit to Locke's emphasis upon rationality is that political sovereignty is masculine. Although Locke grants that women possess sufficient reason to be in possession of liberty, there is no doubt that at the time of Locke's writing, women were viewed by a male-dominated society—per Mary Wollstonecraft more than a century later—as mired in "perpetual childhood" (Wollstonecraft [1792] 1996, 364), oriented to simple pleasures, prone to love sickness, docile, and utterly dependent on men ([1792] 1996, 365). Women were not beasts, but they were considered the "weaker vessel" ([1792] 1996, 364), who possessed an anemic rationality best suited for the private endeavors of the refinement of tastes and the minding of manners. Even this feeble rationality was believed to be easily and often trumped by women's emotions and penchant for hysteria and irrationality. In this way, women closely resemble Locke's ugly depiction of irrational men trapped in the privacy of state of nature who are unable to climb to the heights of reason, liberty, and the universality of the law.

These depictions go hand in hand with social oppression whereby women are turned into objects, confined to the private space of the home, and meant to be 'seen and not heard'; however, the silencing of women by an oppressive patriarchy extended beyond the social and into the political sphere. Insofar as women were private—not public—beings, they were barred from political society. They could not debate the public good; they could not vote; and, except on the rarest of occasions, they could not own property.[11] These beliefs regarding women's irrationality combined with the historical fact that women rarely owned property are not irrelevant to Locke's theorization of political sovereignty. Like Hobbes, Locke's embrace of contract points not to a generic conception of humans in the state of nature, but to bourgeois males. Men engaged in business, and men made contracts. Women did not. Men also owned property, and so its preservation primarily served men (and women only through familial association with propertied fathers and husbands). More importantly, Locke's emphasis upon a universalizing, law-producing, fear-eradicating rationality suggests not only that irrational women could never be signatories to the creation of the public compact, but also that because political sovereignty itself is, above all else, rational, it is also implicitly conceived of as being masculine.[12]

The explicit and implicit features of Locke's theorization of the attributes and qualities of political sovereignty can now be succinctly laid out. Locke's political sovereign is "the public" which unifies individual men into an indivisible whole whose power is limited to making only those laws that protect and preserve the property of each individual member of the people. To punish domestic or foreign threats to property and unity, the sovereign acts as a rational and neutral umpire empowered to resolve divisive disputes that arise between men through a fair and impartial judging of common law. For a rational umpire to impartially decide the law, the law itself must be universal and apply to all equally, including those who make, execute, and decide the law. Simultaneously, the rationality which guides the making, judging, and execution of the law possible—and under which the people are united—is also a totalizing force that fosters homogeneousness by eliminating the partiality and particularity of individual men and their private judgments. Finally, because rationality has traditionally been conceived of as a masculine capacity, Locke's emphasis upon rationality as the cornerstone of legitimate political society suggests that he conceives of political sovereignty as masculine. In conclusion, Locke's theorization of the attributes and qualities of legitimate political sovereignty serves as a clear and robust rejection of the terror and irrationality of absolutism, which is, nevertheless, able to compel obedience through the consent of reasonable men to a common, public law constrained by its very publicity and the rationality from which it emerges.

Rousseau's general will

Rousseau's theorization of sovereignty as a general will echoes some of the contributions of Hobbes and Locke. To flesh out Rousseau's unique understanding of the sovereign general will, I begin with his premise that men enter into a social contract to eliminate the divisive, fear-producing, vain egocentrism of private wills (*amour propre*). All social contract theorists tell a story about the origins and legitimacy of political sovereignty. Rousseau is no different, and his story functions much like any other national myth that covers over the disorder, violence, and factionalism of political founding and governance by creating the belief that "there has been on at least one occasion unanimity" (Rousseau [1762] 1968, 59). Rousseau's story of the social contract is also similar to a national myth of originary unity and "unanimity" insofar as it endeavors to explain how "people become *a* people" ([1762] 1968, 59, original emphasis) and legitimate sovereignty comes into being.[13] Rousseau's social contract brings together vulnerable individuals who willingly subscribe to and obey the terms of the contract to form a unified, sovereign whole whose strength is the collective force of all and whose common purpose is to protect every member's life, freedom, and (for those who have it) property from each other and non-members, i.e., foreigners.

Rousseau's acute concern with the destructiveness of *amour propre* demonstrates why each man requires the collective force of a sovereign people to protect himself. However, simultaneously, this unification would be counter-productive if men lost or gave up their rights and freedom and received nothing or something of lesser value in return. As we saw in Hobbes and Locke, there is a counter-intuitive demand that man remains free and retains his natural rights while simultaneously giving up his rights and freedom. As examined, Rousseau's depiction of man in the state of nature shows that he rejects the notion of natural rights, but the counter-intuitive features of moving from nature to civil society, nevertheless, remain. Rousseau's solution begins by developing three tenets of the social contract: (1) Each gives himself absolutely to the other ensuring that the conditions are the same for all; hence, no one has any interest in making things "onerous for others" (Rousseau [1762] 1968, 60). (2) Through this absolute alienation, the "union is perfected" ([1762] 1968, 60), since an individual claim to a right amounts to little more than being one's own judge, i.e., the rule of *amour propre* and the continuation of the state of nature. (3) Because every man "gives himself to all, he gives himself to no one" ([1762] 1968, 61), thereby regaining "the equivalent of everything he loses" ([1762] 1968, 61) in the form of a strengthened, unified whole.

Even at this early stage, a clear movement away from Locke and Hobbes is evident. Rousseau does not believe, as Locke does, that men possess freedom and property (in the strict sense of a natural or legal right to property) in the state of nature. Indeed, for Rousseau, man in the state of nature is similar to the beast; hence, natural liberty is simply "the physical power of the individual" ([1762] 1968, 65) and property is mere possession "which is based only on force or 'the right of the first occupant'" ([1762] 1968, 65). What Rousseau's theorization of the state of nature reveals is that man does not give up the same rights that Locke's man in the state of nature gives up. Through the social contract, man does not *transfer* rights; rather his rights are *transformed*.[14] In this way, pre-political man is transformed into "civilized man" because he regains the "equivalent" of what he gave up to the collective force of the whole. For Rousseau, this equivalent is legally protected property, which replaces possession as well as "moral freedom which alone makes man the master of himself; for to be governed by appetite alone is slavery, while obedience to a law one prescribes oneself is freedom" ([1762] 1968, 65). In addition, this emphasis upon moral freedom also demonstrates a departure from Hobbes insofar as Hobbes believed that an absolute sovereign was necessary to compel obedience. However, what Rousseau's notion of moral freedom demonstrates is that men *willingly* obey the law they have given to themselves.

These points will return in short order, but the immediate takeaway is that—through these three tenets of the social contract—"we incorporate every member as an indivisible part of the whole" (Rousseau [1762] 1968, 61). Thus, the first attributes of legitimate sovereign authority are an indivisible wholeness whereby "we" become an "artificial and collective body" ([1762] 1968, 61) and a "simple entity, an individual" ([1762] 1968, 63) that possesses a *general will* whose function is to preserve "the person and goods of each member" ([1762] 1968, 60).[15] To better grasp the indivisible wholeness of the sovereign general will, a brief detour is required. Each individual gives up his person and power to the direction of a general will. However, Rousseau insists that "we incorporate every member." On the one hand, the social contract makes or produces a people, yet Rousseau's use of "we" in this moment suggests that a unified "we" already exists in advance of the contract. This pre-existing unity is the paradox of all theorizations of sovereignty, of the coming-to-be of sovereignty now made explicit by Rousseau.[16] Rousseau does not resolve this paradox so much as he covers it over by positing a mythical and originary unanimity. In this way, he establishes a footing for the transformation of an originary unanimity that is the condition of possibility for a social contract *as such* into a perfectly unified, indivisible sovereign general will.

By theorizing the sovereign general will as "single and identical" ([1762] 1968, 62), Rousseau (in a further rejection of Hobbes) insists that "no one can injure any one of the members without attacking the whole" ([1762] 1968, 63). However, he faces the challenge of navigating the tensions between three wills: the individual will, the collective will of all, and the general will. The social contract that creates the general will does not entail that individuals give up their private interests. Indeed, personal and private allegiances to friends, family, personal gain, etc. frequently trump our allegiance to the will of the community as a whole and the general will. Most plainly, with respect to our actions, the individual will is the strongest. In terms of strength, the collective will of all (the aggregate of individual wills) follows the individual will. To be a member of an association is powerful and frequently compels us to action and belief. The general will is the weakest, and our commitment to it is a passionate one, namely that we are committed to it through our moral will, the will of our heart that we are moral beings.

Despite its relatively weak pull, it is the general will alone that can destroy selfishness and *amour propre*. However, Rousseau insists that no man may "enjoy the rights of a citizen without doing the duties of a subject" ([1762] 1968, 64). Like Hobbes, Rousseau acknowledges that covenants are meaningless without some force to compel compliance to its terms. Yet, unlike Hobbes, Rousseau believes that the man who would disobey the general will in favor of his private interest is "constrained to do so [obey] by the whole, which means nothing other than that he shall be forced to be free" ([1762] 1968, 64). There is a strong force that drives the individual will, but this force is transformed from a physical power and natural drive to the abstract, moral force of freedom. Because political and moral freedom is gained through the social contract, men need not be violently compelled to obey; instead, they must be reminded of and guided toward their newfound freedom (forced to be free), which alone secures men from the fear and danger of the "personal dependence" ([1762] 1968, 64) of *amour propre*. Without the subjection of private wills to the general will, the result would be a "divisive difference" ([1762] 1968, 73) that would be the "ruin of the body politic" ([1762] 1968, 64). As such, all private wills must be subject to a "single and identical" general will which comes into existence only because "it is what is common to those different interests which yields the social bond" ([1762] 1968, 69). In other words, the "single and identical" general will is only conceivable because "separate interests [at one point] coincided" ([1762] 1968, 69).

Because the general will is nothing more than individuals who are indivisible parts of a self-identical whole, it might appear that Rousseau is in concord with Locke that the sovereign must obey the law. However, Rousseau rejects this premise insisting that the general will cannot "set over itself a law which it cannot infringe" ([1762] 1968, 62). To subject the sovereign to the law is to "annihilate" ([1762] 1968, 63) the self-identical wholeness brought into existence through the "original act of association" ([1762] 1968, 63), since this subjection would reveal that the sovereign general will would not be self-identical. If the general will is subject to the law, it would not be sovereign. By rejecting Locke, the conceptual tightrope between Rousseau's self-identical wholeness that makes unity possible and the risk of absolutism is thrown into sharp relief. Yet, Rousseau's position is not equivalent to Hobbes' absolutism precisely because the self-identicality and unity of the general will is founded upon morally free individuals who obey the laws they have created and not a third or common power. Unlike Hobbes' external and totalizing sovereign, Rousseau's sovereign general will can have no "interests contrary to theirs [the individual members' interests]" ([1762] 1968, 63); hence, it need not obey laws nor make "guarantees to the subjects" ([1762] 1968, 63).

To further defend his position that the only legitimate form of political sovereignty is the self-identical general will which is not subject to the law, Rousseau argues that sovereignty must be both inalienable and indivisible. Because sovereignty is inalienable, no part of it can be given away (which is simply to reiterate the claim that sovereignty is self-identical). By giving sovereignty away, Rousseau has in mind a conception of sovereignty that is not general, as is the case when individual or common wills supersede or usurp the general will. It is not impossible for a "private will to coincide with the general will" (Rousseau [1762] 1968, 69), but this coincidence cannot endure because "private will inclines by its very nature to partiality, and the general will towards equality" ([1762] 1968, 69). Even if a private will was in constant concord with the general will, it is not possible that the reverse should be true, namely that the sovereign general will is limited by promises made in advance to the private wills of individuals. For Rousseau, this notion is an absurdity. The sovereign general will is a people and when a people "promises simply and solely to obey, it dissolves itself by that very pledge" ([1762] 1968, 70) because it would thereby alienate its generality to the partiality of private men. Most simply, the sovereign general will is necessarily inalienable precisely because it is what guides the apparatus of the state toward the *common* good.

In addition to inalienability, the general will is also indivisible. The indivisibility of the general will is not to be confused with expressions of power, the division of governments into branches, or applications of laws. Indeed, all of these acts "presuppose the existence of a supreme will they merely serve to put into effect" (Rousseau [1762] 1968, 71). Accordingly, Rousseau's argument for the indivisibility of the sovereign general will depends upon differentiating between power and sovereignty and then splitting the difference between Hobbes and Locke. Contra Hobbes, Rousseau argues that power may indeed be divided into branches of government (executive, judicial, legislative, etc.). Neither government as such nor its officers are sovereign. The sovereign is the general will, and the function of administrators is to use their power to establish laws that reflect the general will of the people. Thus, the division of powers is inconsequential to the theorization of sovereignty.

Contra Locke, Rousseau believes that he collapses the distinction between power and sovereignty. To understand this critique, we must recall that, for Rousseau, individuals do not give up their natural rights to a sovereign, up to and including Locke's expansive notion of sovereignty as "the public" which is then divided into branches to guard against absolutism. A people is a transformation of the individual wills of men into a sovereign body or general will. Rousseau acknowledges that the general will (after its original instantiation) need not be unanimous, but if it is to be indivisible then there can be no "formal exclusion [that] destroys its universality" ([1762] 1968, 70 in footnote). In other words, because the social contract "establishes equality" ([1762] 1968, 76) among all citizens, the general will "derives its generality less from the number of voices than from the common interest which unites them" ([1762] 1968, 76). From here, the crux of his critique against Locke becomes evident: the general will is distinct from the "will of all" ([1762] 1968, 72) because the will of all is nothing more than the aggregation of private wills. Instead, the universality (the generality) of the general will rests only in the "common interests" ([1762] 1968, 72) or what is left over once the individual "pluses and minuses ... [have] ... canceled each other out" ([1762] 1968, 73). If the sovereign will is not a general will (i.e., the will of an indivisible people), then it is merely the will of part of the people, which is to say that it is an expression of a private will or a collection of private wills (even a majority) which may compel obedience through a "mere decree" ([1762] 1968, 70), but it is not sovereign precisely because it is divided internally.[17]

Through his theorization of inalienability and indivisibility, the universality of the general will exceeds and subverts partial private wills by elevating and universalizing what is common among them. Nevertheless, a question remains: what, if any, limits apply to sovereign power? It is here that Rousseau's theorization most closely mirrors Hobbes. For Rousseau, the state is identical to a "legal person" ([1762] 1968, 74), which is composed of the unity of its members. Just like a man, the state must have "a universal and compelling power to move and dispose of each part in whatever manner is beneficial to the whole" ([1762] 1968, 74). In this sense, the power of the body politic is "absolute" ([1762] 1968, 74), and this power is nothing more than the sovereign general will. The general will comes into being by man giving up his natural liberty to the concerns of the unified community, but he does not, as argued above, give up his private will. Rousseau resolves this tension in favor of the general will, insisting that the "sovereign alone is judge" ([1762] 1968, 74) of what concerns the community. Because the general will is always directed toward the common, public good, Rousseau concludes that it can never err. Indeed, Rousseau has no other choice but to conclude in this manner, since to say otherwise would be to do nothing more than place the individual, private will of man above the general will. Hence, the general will is absolute, but, unlike Hobbes, this absolutism does not include the right to "impose on the subjects any burden which is not necessary to the community" (Rousseau [1762] 1968, 75). Although Hobbes' sovereign burdens individuals for the sake of the whole, reason dictates that a general will would not unnecessarily burden itself. In fact, to will such a burden is impossible because the general will is the will of a people, a common, general will produced only when the private similarities and differences have been subtracted away.

The sovereign general will does not unduly burden its members, but Rousseau maintains that it retains the right over life and death over its members. Individuals mutually contract together not only to preserve themselves but also every other member of the newly formed, unified body politic. In this way, "whoever wills the end wills also the means, and certain risks, even certain causalities are inseparable from these means" (Rousseau [1762] 1968, 78). Insofar as one's life might be preserved through the sacrifices of others, so, too, must this individual "give his life for them when it is necessary" ([1762] 1968, 78). If Rousseau had stopped with this, then the extent of sovereign power over life and death would be limited, perhaps, to mandatory military service in order to protect the whole. But, Rousseau immediately takes a bolder step insisting that because no individual man is a proper judge of what the law established by the general will demands of him, then it is entirely within the right of the sovereign to order the death of a member of the body politic, since "it is only on such terms [living in a unified body politic under a general will] that he has lived in security as long as he has and also because his life is no longer the bounty of nature but a gift he has received conditionally from the state" ([1762] 1968, 79).

With the justification for the sovereign power over life and death in place, it is now possible to draw some final conclusions. Rousseau's theorization of sovereignty is enriched if it is understood against the backdrop of a lost, originary unanimity and unity. In this respect, it is quite evident why Rousseau's sovereign is self-identical, inalienable, indivisible, possesses the right of life and death over its members, and is "wholly absolute, wholly sacred, [and] wholly inviolable" (Rousseau [1762] 1968, 77). In these ways, Rousseau's general will—in a manner similar to yet very different from Hobbes' Leviathan—approximates the sacredness and divinity of God by serving as a substitute for individual vulnerability by protecting against the rampant fear fostered by *amour propre*. The "divine" intervention of the general will is also a source of hope for a new conception of universal man. The general will does not come into being through a contract between superiors and inferiors ([1762] 1968, 77); instead, it is a mutually reciprocal contract made between men which establishes the moral autonomy of each man who, in obeying the general will, obeys his own newfound moral freedom, a freedom that is shared equally by all. However, at the same time, we might also usefully extrapolate from these attributes that, beyond the apparent good of unification and moral freedom, Rousseau's desire for a form of sovereignty that serves as a substitute for a lost, originary unanimity and self-identicality also opens a theoretical path toward the more dangerous power of a sovereign duty and right to create a homogeneous body politic purged of any difference that could threaten self-identicality. By excluding domestic forms of difference epitomized by women (see, for example, Book V of Rousseau's *Émile*, which consigns Sophie and women generally to the private sphere) and limiting exposure to external forms of difference by fostering "an instinctive distaste for mingling with the peoples of other countries [foreigners]" (Rousseau 1985, xxxii), the right and duty of the sovereign to insure homogeneity is a danger that should be guarded against, and I take up this issue in Chapters 5 and 6.

A brief summary of sovereignty

I have undertaken this analysis of the historical conceptions of sovereignty because they are not relics of a distant theoretical past. The theorizations of sovereignty by Hobbes, Locke, and Rousseau, as well as the framework of the social contract tradition continue, until today, to influence the ways in which states understand their origins, obligations to citizens, legitimacy, and rights to protect themselves and their citizens insofar as they are sovereign. However influenced a particular state might be by the very distinct theorizations of sovereignty examined here, the qualities of sovereignty most frequently cited by contemporary states tend to be an amalgamation of the dominant themes from these three theorizations, and it is worthwhile to briefly list, one final time, these attributes of sovereignty.[18] Sovereignty continues to be conceived of as inalienable, indivisible, and inviolable. Similarly, despite or because of the ethnic diversity that composes contemporary nation-states, sovereignty continues to be conceived of as self-identical insofar as it is eliminative of the foreign. In democratic societies that pride themselves on the rule of law, legitimate sovereignty can never be above the law, and in this regard it takes on the Lockean tenets of a rational, detached, and neutral umpire to judge the law created publicly by the people and to whom all citizens can equally and commonly appeal. Most importantly—and the end to which all of these individual attributes aim—is that sovereignty is the legitimate possession and use of power to (re)unify and protect its citizens against both domestic and foreign threats through fear (even a Hobbesian terror) which compels obedience and repels foreigners. In brief, sovereignty is the force of a totalizing and equalizing movement of the universalization of right directed against the divisions and instability fostered by threats, disobedience, the partiality of private wills, competition among men, irrationality, and appeals to orders of authority higher than or distinct from the sovereign state itself. With these attributes of sovereignty made explicit, we now have the opportunity to think through the ways in which foreignness is produced at the very site of the conceptualization of sovereignty.

5

Foreignness, Sovereignty, and the Social Contract Tradition

Chapters 3 and 4 highlighted the fearful origins of sovereignty and the various ways in which this fear shapes the qualities attributed to sovereignty by Hobbes, Locke, and Rousseau. Additionally, these chapters showed that legitimate sovereignty compels obedience to the law by the subjects of a state, but this obedience is justified only if the sovereign provides for the protection of its subjects from the fearful threats to self-preservation and property, including nature, man in the state of nature, irrationality, *amour propre*, internal discord, and external wars. Despite their distinct theorizations of legitimate sovereignty, Hobbes' Leviathan, Locke's neutral umpire, and Rousseau's general will are all intended to guard against the threats to the unity of the body politic. This chapter builds upon the fearful origins of sovereignty, but its primary aim is to make explicit the threat of foreignness, which, I argue, is present yet under-theorized in all three analyses of the unified sovereign.

The idea that foreignness is a threat to the unity of a people is not unique to the social contract tradition. In Plato we encountered the already extant view that foreignness poses a danger to political identity and stability. This is precisely why Socrates' welcoming of Thrasymachus is either an act of unprecedented political naïveté or, as I have suggested, an implicit demand by Plato that foreignness be radically reconsidered as constitutive of political identity and philosophical justice. Here, I will argue against the casual, often unreflective, notions of the threat of foreignness put forward by Hobbes, Locke, and Rousseau. All three suggest, implicitly or explicitly, that if legitimate sovereignty is that which protects, then foreignness is that which threatens. Therefore, foreignness must be guarded against, excluded, or purified by and for legitimate sovereignty. By contrast, I argue that all three theorists elide the fact that foreignness is a constructed or artificial concept. This does not mean that foreigners and foreignness do not exist or that foreignness can be threatening. Rather, my claim is that the already extant notions of the negative conceptualization of foreignness are formalized in the social contract tradition insofar as the threat of foreignness is produced simultaneously and in direct opposition to the conceptualization of the qualities of legitimate sovereignty.[1]

The relationship between sovereign protector and foreign threat is developed through an analysis of unity whose organizing logic follows three distinct yet intersecting lines. First, I examine the threat of foreignness against unity understood as inviolable wholeness premised upon the sovereign control of territory. Second, I argue that for Hobbes, Locke, and Rousseau, the possibility for sovereign unity is predicated upon the homogeneity of the contracting subjects. With respect to homogeneous unity, foreignness represents a dangerous difference which legitimate sovereignty must either exclude or purify for the continued unity and protection of the body politic. While this insight is important, I adopt the more contentious position that the homogeneity that underpins unity suggests that foreignness is the originary fear against which the qualities of legitimate sovereign authority are determined.

Territorial exclusions

For Hobbes, Locke, and Rousseau, man leaves the state of nature and joins political society to form a unity, which alone is capable of staving off the fearful threats to his self-preservation and/or property. For this reason, the legitimate sovereign must possess the capacity to unify individuals into a whole. Hobbes notes that the sovereign gathers up the multitude into a "reall Unitie" ([1651] 1985, 227). Locke argues for a commonwealth or public "combined together into one coherent living body" (2003, *Second Treatise* §212, 194). Rousseau insists that the despot who rules over men as a master over a slave is ruler of "an aggregation, perhaps, but certainly not an association, for they would neither have a common good nor be a body politic" ([1762] 1968, 58). Moreover, the very notions of Hobbes' artificial man, Locke's public commonwealth, Rousseau's general will, and the more general terms of "a people," "the body politic," "the common good," "the artificial body," "the coherent, living body," etc., all point to the fact that unity is a primary quality of the legitimate sovereign state. Indeed, sovereign unity is nothing if not a wholeness that is enduring, inviolable, and resistant to internal divisions or external, foreign threats.[2]

The repeated analogies comparing a sovereign people to the human body reinforce the importance of unity. Most simply, human bodies are traditionally conceived of as being bounded, distinct, and single or unified, which is to say that those various parts within the body work in harmony to produce a whole, a viable creature, a man. Similarly, all three contractarians conceive of the political body as possessing these same qualities. Just as the extent and distinctiveness of the human body are determined by its flesh, the political body's extent and distinctiveness are determined by the territory under its control. Put differently, the physical control of territory (achieved through claims of the right of the first inhabitants, the constructions of borders and walls, waging war, etc.) is the pre-condition for individual inhabitants of a territory to be unified according to a common purpose which is "grounded" in local conventions, laws, customs, histories, experiences, memories, etc. Like the dismembered human body or one stripped of its flesh, there can be no unity of the political body without the sovereign capacity to protect, maintain, and control its territory.

The common conceptualization of foreign threats to the integrity of sovereign territory is explicitly operative in Hobbes', Locke's, and Rousseau's accounts of sovereign legitimacy. Hobbes states that the sovereign who cannot protect his subjects from foreign enemies need not be obeyed ([1651] 1985, 272). Locke argues for the necessity of a federative power for declaring war and making peace with foreign powers insofar as distinct peoples with no shared covenant between them remain in the state of nature and are guided by its precepts (2003, *Second Treatise* §146, 165). Rousseau insists upon the sovereign right to compel citizens to fight in wars to defend the state ([1762] 1968, 77–78). Most simply, all three thinkers presuppose that external wars with foreign peoples are inevitable and unavoidable. There is little doubt that history and political reality provide strong evidence for this position. Therefore, the legitimate sovereign commands obedience from his subjects by repelling foreign attacks, or, alternatively, the legitimate sovereign is that which guarantees the inviolability of physical territory necessary for the unity and wholeness of the people.

While the conceptualization of the foreign threat to sovereign territory and the unity of the people is commonplace, for our purposes the goal is to consider how the qualities of foreignness are produced simultaneously and in direct opposition to those of sovereignty. A clue to the theoretical production of foreignness can be found in the etymologies of the terms "sovereign" and "foreign." Through popular orthographic changes, the Old French (*soverain*)—which itself comes from the Latin (*superanus*) meaning chief or principal—is changed to "sovereign" in English to reflect its association with "reign." It is from the sense of "chief" and "principal" that "sovereignty" takes on the meaning of pre-eminence, authority, and rule. By contrast, "foreign," from the Latin (*foranus*) and Old French (*forain*), literally means outside, exterior, or out of doors. Yet, a subtle shift in meaning from the original etymology takes place—made explicit through the spelling of "foreign"—which explicitly links the foreign to the sovereign through the influence of "reign." In this respect, the foreigner is not merely an outsider; instead, she is one who is not ruled over by the sovereign.

This orthographic development is important in two ways. First, the similarity in spelling functions as a linguistic concretization of the absolute conceptual opposition and binaristic logic that differentiates between the sovereign/foreign, inside/outside, included/excluded, us/them, civilized/savage, law/nature, safety/danger, etc. The foreigner can, through the political act of naturalization, become a native, but the foreign can never be sovereign and vice versa. As long as the sovereign is conceived of as being foreign, he can never be legitimate because he is neither author of nor subject to the law. Indeed, he is outside or foreign to the law.[3] In this respect, the foreign is always other than and potentially threatening to the sovereign.

Second, because the foreigner is an outsider, who approaches from "out of doors" and is not ruled by the sovereign, the sovereign is depicted as a gatekeeper or master of the threshold who protects his subjects against the threat of external foreigners who seek to conquer or infiltrate the sovereign territory. The "unruled" foreigner is, at best, worthy of a cautious and temporary hospitality. More frequently, the foreigner is cast simply as a threat because she represents an "unruly" lawlessness, anarchy, and a different order heterogeneous to sovereign rule. The sovereign gatekeeper, therefore, protects the wholeness and unity of the polity and his subjects (and demands their obedience) by repelling, standing guard against, or excluding the threatening foreigner through the physical control of territory. On this account, the unity of the body politic is dependent upon the conceptualization of the legitimate sovereign gatekeeper who protects his subjects against foreigners whose intention is to see that the body politic be (metaphorically and possibly literally) dis-membered.

Because Hobbes, Locke, and Rousseau take for granted that foreigners are threats to the territorial integrity that underpins the unity of a people, territorial exclusion of foreigners is both necessary and just. Because the foreigner is an "unruly" and "unruled" violator, the violable sovereign is no sovereign at all. Accordingly, inviolability is an indispensable quality of legitimate sovereignty.

Yet, as the orthography of "sovereign" and "foreign" suggest, these terms are more deeply linked at the level of conceptuality. Rather than merely drawing upon extant notions of the threat of foreignness or the historical and political reality of fear-inducing foreign enemies, foreignness in the social contract tradition is artificially constructed as the conceptual antipode to sovereignty. Foreigners may or may not attack sovereign territory, but foreignness as such is logically opposed to and threatens the purity and inviolability of the concept of sovereignty itself. Most simply, that which is sovereign absolutely and necessarily excludes that which is foreign.

Homogeneous unity and the sovereign exclusion of foreignness

The arguments above operate on two levels of analysis. On the one hand, the territorial exclusion of foreign threats to the unity of the sovereign body is a practical matter of the state, which includes the operations of armies, police, border agents, immigration checkpoints, construction of walls, etc. On the other hand, a conceptual claim is being made that the meaning of foreignness is produced at the very site of the theorization of the inviolability of legitimate sovereignty. While distinct, these two levels of analysis are mutually reinforcing. Sovereignty is conceptualized as an inviolable unity and wholeness while foreignness is that which violates, breaks apart, and dis-members the body politic. Accordingly, it is the understanding of the meaning of foreignness that justifies the everyday operations of the state to control its territory. In turn, every act of territorial control undertaken by the sovereign gatekeeper (re)produces the strict binaristic logic which absolutely opposes and excludes the foreign from the sovereign.

This section also operates on these same levels of analysis, but its primary intent is to further elaborate the conceptual construction of foreignness as that which is absolutely opposed to and distinct from sovereignty. I begin, therefore, by expanding upon the idea of sovereign inviolability, the control of territory, and the fear of foreigners and foreignness by making explicit the implicit arguments in Hobbes', Locke's, and Rousseau's works that the unity of the body politic presupposes the homogeneity of its subjects, a presupposition predicated upon the self-identicality, self-sameness, or, in Jacques Derrida's useful language to be explored below, the "ipseity" ([2003] 2005, 10) of sovereignty as such.

Through this analysis, foreignness is shown to be both a dangerous difference which legitimate sovereignty must—in its day-to-day operations—exclude in order to unify and protect the body politic and the originary fear of the state of nature against which Hobbes, Locke, and Rousseau respectively determine the qualities of legitimate sovereign authority.

Up to this point, the unified, inviolable body politic has been considered only according to its physical and spatial wholeness. If the foreigner is an outsider who is not ruled by the sovereign, then every foreigner is a potential threat to the sovereign state whose territorial integrity is a precondition for a unified body politic. A parallel etymology of "sovereign" is illustrative of this point. The alternative English spelling *sovran* is also used, suggesting that the word is derived from the Italian *sovrano*, which means not only sovereign but also gold coin. We are all familiar with currency bearing the visages of our sovereigns, yet of interest here is that the sovereign is linked to an economy.[4] Like currency, the rights of the sovereign and subject circulate, are exchanged, are purchased, are banked, etc. The sovereign duty to protect and the reciprocal requirement that subjects obey (and the rights ascribed to both sovereign and subject based on this fundamental requirement) are nevertheless limited insofar as they occur within a given and bounded territory.[5] This is a rather complex way to make the obvious point that there are distinct sovereign economies of power that extend only as far as the sovereign control of physical territory.[6]

This alternative etymology of "sovereign" reveals a different sort of ordering and unity of a people. Not every foreign outsider who arrives at the city walls is intent on conquering the sovereign territory. Indeed, the very notion of the sovereign *qua* gatekeeper suggests that certain foreign outsiders will be welcomed or extended hospitality while others will not. The sovereign (whether a monarchy, an aristocracy, a democratic people, etc.) decides which foreign outsiders are friends to be welcomed into the state and to what extent they will be allowed to participate in the economy of power as well as which foreign outsiders are threats or enemies of the state to be guarded against, excluded, or destroyed. In Carl Schmitt's formulation, the "Sovereign is he who decides on the exception" (1985, 5) by making the distinction between friend and enemy. The sovereign decision to deem certain foreigners to be friends (to transform outsiders into insiders) underscores the fact that foreignness retains its conceptualization as a threat. That the foreigner who is welcomed is transformed into or considered a friend by the sovereign demonstrates that foreignness—not the foreigner—is the conceptual antipode of sovereignty.

Economies of power rest upon an ineliminable conceptual distinction between inside and outside. It is this distinction that the sovereign draws upon and re-enforces in its determination of who is an insider/outsider, friend/enemy, included/excluded, savage/civilized, etc. Insiders are friends who constitute and are protected by the sovereign. Outsiders are foreigners who are potential enemies. However, as Plato understood, just as every outsider is not necessarily an enemy, not every insider is necessarily a friend. Accordingly, the sovereign *qua* gatekeeper also decides which subjects, citizens, natives, insiders, or ostensible friends are actually threatening enemies. Paradoxically, the sovereign also decides which citizens are foreigners. In this way, the conceptual distinction between inside and outside is more than or other than a spatial distinction, even if this conceptual distinction is literally concretized by the walls and borders that represent sovereign control of a territory. Through the unyielding conceptual distinction between inside and outside which structures sovereign economies of power, the unity of a people is achieved not only through the spatial ordering of territory (which excludes certain foreigners *qua* threatening outsiders) but also temporally through the psychosocial unity anchored upon a common identity and shared commitment to the common good (which casts as foreign those insiders who are deemed by the sovereign to be a threat to the unity of the people, thereby justifying their exclusion).

Because the distinction between the inside and outside is not simply a spatial distinction, it is useful and important to examine how the sovereign determines who is an insider and who is an outsider. Traditionally and up until today, there are two dominant legal conceptions of what makes one an insider: *ius soli* and *ius sanguinis*. On its surface, *ius soli* appears to be grounded upon a purely spatial distinction between the inside and outside because citizenship is granted only to those born within a country's physical territory. *Ius soli* serves as a rough and ready guide for inclusion insofar as it grants citizenship to empirical insiders while excluding as non-citizens those born outside of the sovereign, physical territory. Moreover, it has the added benefit of protecting citizens against extra-judicial sovereign violence and even legal decisions to exclude difference in the name of and for the sake of sovereign unity. In the U.S., for example, individuals born on its soil are citizens with all the concomitant rights and protections afforded by the Constitution and its laws. The sovereign may still punish or exclude, but it cannot *legitimately* and *justly* violate the legal rights of its citizens.

Despite this seemingly uncomplicated determination of inclusion based on spatial ordering, others factors related to spatiality and temporality are determinative of who is included and who is excluded from the people. Spatial proximity gives rise to language, values, experiences, histories, and memories that forge a common identity and shared set of allegiances that structure ethnic and national identity. Over time, these qualities associated with the sharing of space are "naturalized" or conceived of as "quasi-genetic." They underpin nationality, an *ethnos* or community of affiliation, which inherits these qualities from its forbearers and passes them on to succeeding generations. In this regard, while *ius soli* might legally entitle an individual to citizenship, this legal recognition does not necessarily guarantee full inclusion as a member of a people.[7] All too frequently, full inclusion is reserved for those who possess the inherited, "quasi-genetic" characteristics of shared proximity.[8] Proximity loses its generic, spatial meaning and becomes a psychosocial form of ordering rooted in the self-proximateness, self-sameness, self-identicality, and homogeneousness of a people. In other words, the psychosocial unity rooted in spatial proximity often serves as a basis for the exclusion of foreignness and difference (or those individuals deemed to be foreign and different by the sovereign) precisely because their inclusion is presumed to dilute the common identity upon which unity is founded and perpetuated.

On this analysis, *ius soli* shares certain features with *ius sanguinis*, which grants the right of citizenship not by birthplace but by the right of blood. Inclusion within the people is granted only if one parent—if not both in more strict polities—is a citizen. Inclusion as a member of a people is entirely genetic, inherited as one might inherit eye color. Language, culture, histories, experiences, memories, etc. are not artificial constructs; they need not be "naturalized" because they are the qualities of a people, an *ethnos*, whose unique characteristics are "in the blood." Nation, common identity, and allegiance to the whole course through the veins of a people. Analogous to a family united by blood, individuals come together as a people—become "brothers"—and are committed to promoting their shared interest based on the supposed naturalness of self-identicality rooted in consanguinity, the ties of blood and lineage.[9] Psychosocial unity is produced through the preservation and perpetuation of biological sameness, and, therefore, *ius sanguinis* is a potent model for inclusion that is not subject to the arbitrariness of the bonds of neighborly proximity. However, this seemingly natural mechanism for determining inclusion within the people has an obvious danger. If the purity of the bloodline is requisite for psychosocial unity, then foreigners are easily cast as parasites whose traits, languages, beliefs, practices, histories, experiences, memories, etc., which differ from those of the dominant ethno-racial group, must not only be excluded but also expunged.

In both models, the intent is to identify and promote that which gives rise to the common identity underpinning the shared commitment to the common good by including only those individuals who are like us, i.e., those who possess the characteristics that determine the common identity of the people. Because inclusion within a people is not simply spatial but also a temporal psychosocial ordering based on genetic or "quasi-genetic" notions of a people, the inviolable sovereign unifies its people not only by excluding outsiders but by excluding that which is different, heterogeneous, not like us, not self-same, not self-identical, etc. Inclusion, therefore, is not granted to all spatial insiders. Instead, one's status as an insider is reserved for those who reinforce and reproduce the psychosocial unity of a homogeneous people. More plainly, the inviolable sovereign excludes foreignness.[10]

While each of these models for including individuals as members of a sovereign people may be susceptible to unfair or unjust sovereign decisions to exclude some individuals or groups, sovereign states frequently resort to the argument that the fact remains that the common identity of a people is rooted in shared commonalities. Therefore, there must be some mechanism for determining which languages, histories, values, etc. are to be included within the state and which individuals will be included as members of the people. The sovereign duty to protect its subjects involves destroying or keeping enemies at bay *and* guarding against the qualities and traits that dilute the common identity of the people upon which its unity is founded. Some states, therefore, implement *ius soli*, and the more diverse and liberal among these states will stand guard against the exclusionary effects of the "naturalization" of the qualities of spatial proximity. Other states will choose *ius sanguinis*, and the more diverse and liberal among these will reject the narratives and practices which call for or promote ethnic and racial purity.

Whether spatial or psychosocial (and, hence, temporal), the basic claim is that sovereign states must retain the right to determine who is a member of a people and who is not in the name of protecting its members. In this respect, foreignness is presumed to be a neutral concept that simply marks that which is different from or other than the common. A foreign language is simply a different language than the one spoken *here*, in this sovereign land. Different peoples have different histories, practices, experiences, etc. that are foreign to *us*. Accordingly, different peoples are foreign peoples, but this does not mean that foreigners and their differences are threatening. In fact, foreigners in the most liberal states are often celebrated for introducing ethnic, racial, social, religious, linguistic, and cultural diversity that strengthens the common bond of the people by expanding its self-understanding of common identity. Therefore, only those individuals who undermine the sovereign inviolability and unity of a people are legitimately excluded.[11]

This sort of rhetoric is inspiring, and the practices of the inclusion of foreigners in some nations produces hope for the elimination of unjust exclusions of foreigners *qua* outsiders. However, the inclusion of foreigners is not the same thing as the exclusion of foreignness. As noted, the foreigner, once included, becomes a friend, which is to say that she loses her foreignness. The distinction between foreignness and foreigner is not arbitrary. Indeed, it is implicit in the very logic of the legitimate, inviolable sovereign gatekeeper who controls the threshold between the spatial and psychosocial inside and outside through its power to decide which differences or actions are or are deemed to be foreign, i.e., threatening to the common identity and shared purpose that unify a people. In more stark terms, the principle sovereign fear is the fear of foreignness. If this is so, then it is easy to understand why the physical outsider and the (im)migrant are so frequently demonized as a threat to sovereign inviolability and unity. Therefore, the challenge is to understand in what sense foreignness or foreign difference is viewed as a threat to the unity of a sovereign people. To examine this point, I return to Hobbes, Locke, and Rousseau in order to demonstrate the ways in which foreignness is the originary fear that gives rise to their respective theorizations of the qualities and characteristics of the legitimate sovereign, how each implicitly constructs foreignness as the fearful antithesis of sovereignty, and how foreignness is a quality assigned by the sovereign to the individual who is or is deemed to be threatening to the sovereign people.

Foreignness in Hobbes' theorization of sovereignty

In any given sovereign state, there will be those insiders, those members of the body politic, who oppose the state or do not share the commitment to the common good. Hobbes' writing, for example, is deeply influenced by the various forms of civil, domestic unrest that marked his life. While differentiating between foreign and domestic threats is reflective of political reality and practically useful, Hobbes' absolutism is not only directed against physical outsiders; instead, his theorization of sovereignty also empowers the sovereign to treat insiders and would-be friends as foreign outsiders and enemies. No further proof is needed than the sovereign right to life and death over his subjects without justification or explanation. The sovereign power over life and death is the power *to deem* anyone a threat to the sovereign on account of his foreign allegiances (to other states, a new ordering of power within the existing state, and even to God). Whether traitors, dissidents, vocal critics of the state, criminals, deviants, or perverts who actively seek or secretly wish to overthrow the sovereign or divide it through deviation from mutually agreed upon public norms of social and political organization, all of these *internal* rogues are *cast* as foreign to the artificial body politic and the agreed upon terms of the social contract. While critics of absolutism might reject the legitimacy of the sovereign power to arbitrarily deem who will live and who will die, few would argue against the sovereign power to protect its subjects from foreign threats. In this respect, insofar as all internal rogues are conceived to have foreign allegiances (i.e., are deemed to be foreign by the sovereign), they are legitimately and rightfully killed, excluded, or sent away from the sovereign body. Most generally, both insiders and outsiders who do not adhere to and follow the terms of the contract are foreign threats to be excluded or eliminated.

Although it is only obliquely present in Hobbes' writing, the shared sense of common purpose and the just destruction and exclusion of foreigners (including domestic threats deemed to be foreign) is underpinned by the presumed self-identicality of individual subjects and the homogeneous, inviolable, self-identical sovereign whole they forge by contracting together to create political society.[12] These sovereign qualities are depicted in the political iconography of the *Leviathan*'s frontispiece. Here—where the image matches the language of the Preface wherein Hobbes explains the artificial and divine nature of the state—the Leviathan is depicted as a single body, an artificial animal, created by mankind whose absolute power and terror is indicated by the symbols of secular and religious power (a mortal god) it holds in each hand. Yet, the Leviathan is not just summoned; rather, the frontispiece reveals that the Leviathan is also forged by man insofar as it is a distinct and whole body, a homogeneous unity composed of self-identical subjects, the composite of mankind and outgrowth of his will to survive.

The political iconography foreshadows Hobbes' telling of the story of the state of nature where, as outlined above, he presents what he believes to be a scientific account of all men. Driven by a natural desire for self-preservation, men in the state of nature are violent, quarrelsome, and competitive. However, this violence and competition makes long-term survival impossible. The only relief from this fearful state is for men to mutually surrender their natural right to everything by contracting together to authorize a common power, a sovereign, to rule over each man for the sole end of guaranteeing his self-preservation. However, this scientific and generic conception of natural man is neither scientific nor generic.

Hobbes' natural man is a stereotypical male who spends his time and energy violently competing with other males. Hobbes pays no heed to the fact that the responsibilities of caretaking—which traditionally (and surely for Hobbes) is solely performed by women—would make this sort of perpetual violent competition impossible and undesirable. Similarly, Hobbes' natural man is also an adult. Hobbes neither considers nor finds it necessary to consider how a child is the kind of being that could protect herself from the violence of the state of nature, understand the terms of the social contract, or perform the duties it commands. The depiction of the violent state of nature devoid of care and occupied by adult males simply reflects the reality of Hobbes' day and culture in which women and children languished under the yoke of patriarchal rule and were confined to the private sphere. In these respects, Hobbes' depiction of natural man is hardly universal; it excludes, as foreign to mankind, all those individuals who are not adult males.

Hobbes' depiction of natural man is not generic in other important ways. His contractual model assumes that natural man must speak and understand the meaning of the contracts and the common language in which they are composed. Moreover, Hobbes believes that property is secured only through the law of the legitimate sovereign. Accordingly, Hobbes organizes natural man according to the legal authority of contracts and the moral obligation to perform one's duties described by the terms of the contract. As noted, his depiction of men in the state of nature is a depiction of "bourgeois men" who rely upon contracts to bring the sovereign commonwealth, a "bourgeois state," into existence. In this way, Hobbes' account makes an illicit move, namely his natural man possesses—as Rousseau astutely notes—the qualities of civilized man.

Rousseau is correct, yet also blinded. The very definition of civilized, of civilization, as that which is structured upon contracts and property fails to meaningfully grasp the myriad ways in which other cultures are civilized, even if they do not value legal contracts or the presupposition of individual property as sacrosanct in the ways championed by social contract theorists. Hobbes' scientific account of natural man does not merely import a conception of civilized man back into the state of nature. Instead, Hobbes (and Rousseau) takes for granted that a culturally determined type of man, the Western, bourgeois man, is an exemplar, a universal, and a permanent, fixed, self-identical archetype representative of mankind as such. To be who he is, natural man is distinct from and sealed off from all differences foreign to the Western, bourgeois man.

A generous reading might forgive Hobbes his sexual chauvinism and parochialism. It is a common error of Western philosophical thinking to envisage the Western subject as both male and to be the universal model of humankind. However, as Hobbes' depiction of man in the state of nature unfolds, it becomes more difficult to extend this principle of charity. Hobbes' highly specific conception of self-identical natural man, exclusive of foreign differences, is unproblematically presupposed to be the basis of a homogeneous "proto-unity" in the state of nature requisite for the creation of the legitimate sovereign. I use the term "proto-unity" here to differentiate from Hobbes' claims regarding the "multitude," or those temporary alliances which are not yet a sovereign whole. For example, Hobbes argues that the multitude that works together to fight a common enemy will ultimately "hinder one another" ([1651] 1985, 225) because their private interest and lack of a common power to unify them secures no lasting bond among them. This multitude conjoined for a time to achieve a particular end is, I suggest, distinct from the "proto-unity" that institutes a sovereign people.

Recall that Hobbes insists that a valid covenant among men is dependent upon a voluntary vote of the majority, which authorizes the legitimate sovereign to rule over all, including those who did not vote for the sovereign. This requirement for a voluntary vote premised on the justness of the will of the majority presupposes that men live together, work together, cooperate, value the same rules and procedures, share cultural convictions regarding voluntary assent, etc. as a unified body and not merely a multitude temporarily and tenuously aligned. Furthermore, the very fact that Hobbes presupposes individuals as consociates capable of instituting a commonwealth suggest that men in the state of nature also share a common language, hopes, desires, experiences, memories, etc. Despite his rejection of Aristotle in which he insists that men are, by nature, naturally competitive and not cooperative, Hobbes' scientific account of mankind and the creation of the sovereign state are dependent upon the presupposition that the bonds of race, class, gender, language, age, common values, shared beliefs, and identical or amenable customs and practices are operative in the otherwise uncooperative and treacherous state of nature. In other words, when Hobbes' non-generic, self-identical natural man joins together with those who are the same as him to vote on the creation of a sovereign, he forms a self-identical and homogenous "proto-unity," exclusive of foreign differences, founded upon the fixed, parochial traits that Hobbes assumes to be universal. Even if, as Hobbes insists, a sovereign is ultimately required to transform this "proto-unity" into a "real unity," the elimination of difference and homogeneity of this "proto-unity" in the state of nature is a condition of possibility for sovereignty as such as well as Hobbes' insistence upon its absolutist qualities.

Previously, I argued that the originary fear of the state of nature that necessitates the social contract and sovereignty is really nothing more than the unrelenting violence that accompanies natural man's right to everything needed to secure his self-preservation. Here, I will complicate this position. Strictly speaking, Hobbes' sovereign does not unify a "proto-unity" into a "real unity" cleansed of this originary fear by eliminating difference. In fact, his conception of the self-identicality of natural man and the homogeneity underlying their association has already eliminated difference. Indeed, without the unexamined presumption of homogeneity in the state of nature, the mutual agreement to give up the right to everything in exchange for the protection of civil society would be impossible, which is simply to say that sovereignty would be impossible. If the elimination of foreign differences is a condition of possibility for sovereignty, then a further step is needed to understand the relationship between foreignness and the originary fear of the state of nature as well as the ways in which foreignness is constructed as the conceptual antipode to sovereignty.

Even though each individual natural man is conceived of as self-identical (with a fixed, permanent, and unyielding set of characteristics believed to represent a universal archetype), natural man as such is, in an important respect, a foreigner insofar as he is foreign to the qualities of civilized man. For Hobbes, natural man is natural to a fault, a victim of his unbounded freedom who is unable to rise beyond his bestial desire for self-preservation generative of diffidence, violence, and war. Furthermore, insofar as he has not created or exists apart from the Leviathan—the artificial, mortal god imitative of the divine—natural man is foreign to the human capacity for mimesis, thereby abandoning him to irrationality, the dictates of nature, all-consuming fear, and the inevitability of an untimely and violent death. In this regard, Rousseau's critique becomes ever more trenchant. Despite Hobbes' claim to the contrary, it is civilized man that is nature's "most excellent work" while natural man is foreign to mankind *qua* his highest (i.e., civilized) self. In this way, natural man is actually shown to *lack* self-identicality which is to say that he is divided, partial, incomplete, foreign to himself, and, therefore, not fully human. Most simply (from the perspective of civilized man), he is a beast.

Insofar as natural man alternates between self-identicality (the self-same Western subject who is distinct from the beast) and difference (in opposition to civilized man), foreignness assumes a central role in Hobbes' analysis of sovereignty. Hobbes' sovereign is absolute not only in the sense that he is the body politic, but also insofar as he is the total and complete artificiality that marks the extent of the conceptual domain of the highest and truest form of man, namely the political domain in which man achieves self-identicality. As such, foreignness, or that which threatens and makes man foreign to himself, is the essence of natural man. In this way, at the very site of the production of Hobbes' notion of sovereignty, foreignness is simultaneously (although implicitly) constructed as the absolutely natural, uncivilized, irrational, lawless, unruly, bestial, amoral, competitive, brutish, and warring desire for self-preservation.[13] In this sense, *foreignness* is the originary fear of the state of nature that is opposed to sovereignty as such.

For Hobbes, internal or external foreigners who threaten the body politic justify the need for an absolute sovereign who commands armies, borders, police, etc. Conceptually, foreignness is that which is opposed to or would destroy the self-identicality of sovereignty. To better grasp the conceptual dimension of sovereign self-identicality, Jacques Derrida's account of ipseity is revealing. *Ipse* is the Latin translation of the Greek term *autos* meaning self. The very essence of the notion of the self, of selfhood, assumes an originary wholeness, completion, and perfection of the self and/or a faith in the teleological unfolding toward wholeness, completion and perfection of the self. Thus, for Derrida, ipseity is the formalized conception of selfhood which presumes "sovereign self-determination, the autonomy of the self, of the *ipse*, namely, of the one-self that gives itself its own law, of autofinality, autotely, self-relation, as being in view of the self, beginning by the self with the end of self in view" ([2003] 2005, 10–11, original emphasis). Put differently, ipseity is the essence of the sovereign self, namely a metaphysical ground of self-sameness and self-identicality that excludes all difference (civilized man, for example, is distinct from and opposed to the beast, God, and himself *qua* natural man). Derrida continues by further claiming that ipseity is "some 'I can', or at the very least the power that *gives itself*, its own law, its force of law, its self-presentation, the sovereign and reappropriating gathering of self in the simultaneity of an assemblage or assembly, being together, or 'living together' as we say" ([2003] 2005, 11, original emphasis). In this regard, even before the state, the monarch, or the rule of the people, etc., "ipseity names a principle of legitimate sovereignty, the accredited or recognized supremacy of a power or force, a *kratos* or *cracy*" ([2003] 2005, 12, original emphasis).

Derrida's conception of ipseity usefully reveals the significance of Hobbes' theoretical emphasis upon the primacy of the natural power each man possesses in the state of nature to secure his *self*-preservation. Hobbes' identification of and emphasis upon the natural power (a force, "*kratos*," "I can," etc.) of man in the state of nature appears to suggest that he conceives of mankind in his origins as a self-identical power. Yet, Hobbes insists that man cannot exist in or maintain this natural, self-identical state. In this regard, his originary self-identicality is put off, delayed, and deferred until he reaches civilized society where the binaristic logic of self-identical and homogeneous sovereignty, exclusive of foreignness, undergirds Hobbes' absolutism. On the one hand, Hobbes' sovereign is the absolute terror who is the amalgamation of all men's fear of vulnerability in the state of nature. On the other hand, with respect to foreignness, the sovereign is the amalgamation of men's existential fear that they are mere beasts who are foreign to themselves *qua* ostensibly self-identical men. The existential fear is that *self-identicality is always already lost*. The absolute sovereign alone, in his approximation of the divine, can thwart the foreign divisiveness of nature, desire, irrationality, and the vicissitudes of individual wills that perpetually haunt civilized man. He is an artificial monster, a Leviathan, summoned and forged by men to guide them toward their teleological destiny of self-identicality and ipseity by protecting them against the monstrous foreignness of ineliminable difference and heterogeneity that deforms mankind as such.

The power and rule of the political body (the *kratos* of the self-identicality or ipseity of the state) is, through the Leviathan, recovered and unified into an inviolable assembly, which bears a semblance to or likeness to itself (Derrida [2003] 2005, 11). In this way, the homogeneity of a sovereign people is both the practico-political/psychosocial concern with "living together" with others who are like "us" and an indispensable conceptual feature of sovereignty as such premised upon the absolute exclusion of all that is foreign, different, and other. On this reading, the unified, indivisible, inviolable whole of the political sovereign is itself conceived of as a homogeneous self-identicality. Hobbes' Leviathan is, in this respect, the lesser of two evils. The only fear greater than the absolute, all-powerful, quasi-divine sovereign terror is the fear of being consumed in the abyss of foreignness, i.e., fear of the loss of the ontological and existential distinctiveness of mankind as such. If the conceptual distinction between the sovereign and the foreign is not absolute and inviolable, then sovereignty as such is inconceivable, since that which is foreign cannot be sovereign and that which is sovereign cannot be foreign.

In that foreignness is the conceptual antipode to sovereignty, it is fairly easy to understand how foreignness is mobilized to establish the social and political stereotypes that define the physical foreigner or the insider who is deemed by the sovereign to be a foreigner. The foreigner is he who opposes and threatens the sovereign. Insofar as he epitomizes a mortal threat to the sovereign, the foreigner is he who remains in or is cast back into the state of nature by the sovereign where he is rightfully hunted and killed like the beast that he is. At the same time, because Hobbes' sovereign is an absolute, all-powerful, self-same, and mortal god, foreignness is pure violation, division, unpredictability, difference, heterogeneity, and unadulterated threat that would disrupt the self-identicality and homogeneity of sovereign ipseity as such. In this respect, foreignness is not merely the conceptual opposite of sovereignty; instead, foreignness is the illogic which illicitly crosses borders, thereby defying the binaristic constructions of nature/convention, man/beast, inside(r)/outside(r), friend/enemy, civilized/savage, us/them, etc. upon which sovereignty is structured and (re)produced in every sovereign decision to include or exclude. On this analysis, the sovereign power over life and death can be understood anew. It is the power to identify and name the foreigner whose very existence is destructive of the self-identicality upon which sovereignty is constructed.

Foreignness in Locke's theorization of sovereignty

The analysis of foreignness in Hobbes' theorization of sovereignty lays the groundwork for a similar critique of Locke's legitimate sovereign authority, i.e., the neutral umpire. Like Hobbes' account, the first trace of foreignness in Locke's political theory emerges in his account of the self-identicality of natural man. God is the only sovereign, and mankind is his property. God has endowed mankind alone with reason through which he discovers the laws of nature that all men are free and equal. Freedom is a fence around each man which protects the property he has in his person, and insofar as each has an equal right to his natural freedom, all are equal. Reason reveals that through freedom and equality, God bequeaths his property to individual men making each sovereign to himself.[14] In this formulation, we discover in Locke, as we did in Hobbes, a supposedly generic and universal account of man. Notwithstanding the liberal tenets of this formulation (that *all* men are naturally free and equal), Locke's ostensibly universal account of natural man is riddled with particularities.

Locke's generic man is (like Hobbes') both male and adult. Reason is the *sine qua non* of natural man, which allows him to discover his own sovereign rights of freedom and equality. Accordingly, children (and those who lack full rationality) are necessarily excluded from his depiction of mankind. Paternal power is nothing more than the right and power of parents to "take care of their off-spring, during the imperfect state of childhood. To inform the mind, and govern the actions of their ignorant nonage, till reason shall take its place, and ease them of that trouble" (Locke 2003, *Second Treatise* §58, 124). Interestingly, Locke explicitly insists that paternal power is a misnomer insofar as paternal power is invested in both men and women (2003, *First Treatise* §6 102). Women, he insists, have an equal role in raising children (2003, *Second Treatise* §52–53, 122). Thus, it appears as if Locke grants to women the same rationality possessed by man. Nevertheless, Locke's depiction of natural man mixing his labor with the land, fencing off the commons, engaging in trade, punishing lawbreakers, forging contracts, owning property, etc. are the activities and rights that belong only to males in Locke's time. Even if we generously allowed that women were to be included in Locke's universal conception of man, it would be difficult to discount the fact that his depiction of the irrational, particular, subjective, private beast of the state of nature is similar to the socially accepted depiction of women prevalent at the time of Locke's writing. Even if Locke's liberalism is in some sense "ahead of his time," there is limited evidence that Locke's universal man is anything but an adult male.

In addition to the theorization of universal man as both male and adult, Locke implicitly posits that mankind as such is fluent in the legal and moral language and authority of contracts. In this regard, Locke's universal man is also a bourgeois, propertied man necessarily exclusive of those others who do not communicate in the spoken language or subscribe to the values, culture, and practices which give rise to the legal and moral authority of contracts. Accordingly, Locke's universal man is also classed and raced. No further proof is needed than his shockingly inconsistent positions with respect to his depiction of men in the state of nature and his views on Native Americans and slaves in the Carolinas.

Because the "natives" in the Americas did not fence the land and practice the same form of agriculture as the Englishman, Locke argues that they had, in effect, not properly mixed their labor with the land (Locke 2003, *Second Treatise* §41, 117–118). Accordingly, the natives of America remained mired in the state of nature where their land remained a commons, which, therefore, was legitimately occupied by the English settler. In this respect, the state of nature is not merely a theoretical construct for Locke; it actually exists, and it is populated by irrational, immoral beasts (i.e., "natives") different from and foreign to the English man of contracts. Similarly, while Locke explicitly condemns slavery in civilized society as unjust, insofar as it is merely a continuation of the state of war, his documented investment in and profiting from the slave trade suggests, at a minimum, that not all men have property in their person. In other words, not all men were free and equal insofar as Locke's depiction of natural man would seem to exclude those who were not white or "propertied."

The exclusion of children, women, those without property, "natives," and slaves reveals that Locke's universal depiction of man depends upon a self-identicality exclusive of difference. All others are foreign to mankind as such. Only when this implicit premise is established does the social contract come into existence. Through the social contract, Locke's self-identical man joins with those who are the same to form a homogeneous unity exclusive of foreign difference. However, in contradistinction to Hobbes, Locke does not theorize a multitude or "proto-unity" that precedes the sovereign political body. Instead, the individual sovereignty of men bequeathed from God is, through the social contract, bequeathed to the public as a whole through rational consent. Thus, in order to understand the homogeneous political unity of self-identical man implicit in Locke's work, the challenge is to articulate the theoretical underpinnings of this transfer of sovereign right through consent in relation to foreignness. By doing so, the ways in which foreignness is produced as that which is absolutely opposed to sovereignty, as well as the way in which sovereignty ties together Locke's analysis of self-identical man and the homogeneous unity of the public commonwealth, will become evident.

Although I have just argued that foreignness is implicitly relied upon in Locke's conception of self-identical natural man, for Locke foreignness and foreigners have no place in the pre-political state of nature. Rather, he conceives of foreignness in its most common formulation, namely a political category that applies only to those individuals who are physical outsiders, i.e., members of other commonwealths. To his credit, Locke recognizes that the foreign outsider can be both threatening and non-threatening to the sovereign commonwealth. For example, he argues that the members of a commonwealth remain distinct individuals relative to other members of the commonwealth. As distinct members of the commonwealth, each is protected by its laws. However, "in reference to the rest of mankind, they make one body, which is, as every member of it before was, still in the state of nature with the rest of mankind" (Locke 2003, *Second Treatise* §145, 165). Accordingly, Locke proposes a federative branch of sovereign government (a sub-division of the executive) that is concerned with responding to "*foreigners,* depending much upon their actions, and the variation of designs and interests" (2003, *Second Treatise* §147, 165, my emphasis). Just as the state of nature can be peaceful or warring, so, too, can foreign relations be non-threatening or threatening. The unified commonwealth, therefore, requires a federative branch that "contains the power of war and peace, leagues and alliances, with all the persons and communities without the commonwealth" (2003, *Second Treatise* §146, 165).[15] In this way, Locke holds the pragmatic position that recognizes foreigners and foreign commonwealths exist and that they ought to be responded to according to their "actions, designs, and interests." Threatening foreign commonwealths call for war, while non-threatening or cooperative foreign commonwealths should be cultivated to forge peaceful alliances.

To contextualize this fairly straightforward understanding of the foreigner, a return to Locke's theorization of the state of nature is necessary. Locke's state of nature is a peaceful and normative space where rational men, who consult their reason, discover the law of nature that all men are free and equal. As mentioned, each man is the property of God the sovereign, and reason dictates that God's sovereignty is bequeathed to each man and made sacrosanct and whole through the freedom which acts as a fence around his property, i.e., his life, liberty, and estate. Men who pursue property according to the dictates of reason that commands respect for all men's freedom and equality live harmoniously. The state of nature, in sum, is an idyllic place where rational and moral men peacefully secure their self-preservation. If this state could continue, there would be no need for political society; however, insofar as the state of nature is a normative state, man is free to not consult his reason and act against the laws of nature.

Recall that the man who does not consult his reason and transgresses another man's fence of freedom is a "noxious creature" who violates the equality of the "whole species" of mankind. In this formulation of the spatial, territorial ordering of self-identical individual sovereignty, an early trace of the foreigner is found. The man who refuses to consult his reason, the "noxious beast" with no regard for the "species," is a transgressor of legitimate territorial borders. In other words, the self-interested, unreasonable, and hence immoral man is, for Locke, explicitly a beast and implicitly a threatening foreigner, an invader, whose irrational "actions, designs, and interests" set the stage for the state of war. For Locke, even in the pre-political state of nature, lawbreakers are conceived of as foreign threats to self-identical mankind and harmonious living that must be guarded against and excluded to preserve and protect both the category of mankind as such as well as each individual sovereign man.

To thwart these beastly, foreign transgressors of God's property (i.e., sovereign man), Locke insists that all men in the state of nature have the authority to execute the law of nature by punishing either for retribution or to deter future transgressions against the law. Because each man in the state of nature is free and equal, those victimized by the foreign, bestial, irrational transgressors of the law may kill transgressors of natural law just as one would kill a savage beast. Here, then, the killing of the savage beast *qua* the foreign invader of sovereign property and territory is both necessary and legitimate. Furthermore, insofar as man is God's property, the foreign invader effectively declares war with God. In this respect, we can identify at least one origin of the stereotype of the political foreign invader who is conceptualized as polluted, unholy, a defiler, a desecrater, an infidel, etc. At the same time, the individual right to execute the law also serves "to preserve all mankind." Thus, the implication is—as we saw in Hobbes—that the physical foreigner or outsider is not the true threat; instead, the threat is foreignness or that which is foreign to self-identical man, i.e., the rationality and morality proper to mankind which makes him what he is.

The power every man possesses to execute the natural law eventually produces unbearable inconveniences as men become partial to themselves and their closest relations. Out of the affective self-love that cripples the objective and neutral rationality requisite for a proportionate and measured execution of the law of nature, man in the state of nature irrationally (i.e., disproportionately) punishes according to his own needs and subjective interpretation of the law of nature. The peaceful and moral state of nature recedes not merely because there are transgressors of property and lawbreakers, but also because otherwise peaceful, moral, and rational men act irrationally out of a self-love. Through their irrational self-love, they, too, become foreign to mankind as such. The originary self-identicality of mankind is always already lost or, put differently, merely posited. The result is a perpetually fearful state of war marred by enmity, lawlessness, vigilantism, bestial behavior, particularism, and partiality which destroys the unifying, peace-preserving, common law of reason operative in the state of nature.

The state of war, then, is a state of irrationality, and in this way, the self-love rooted in irrationality is the originary fear that drives men into civil society through rational consent. Locke's deep concern with the irrational basis of self-love that defines the state of war reveals another trace of foreignness that precedes the political. Mankind in the state of war is like the beast not only because he shares with the beast the natural passion for self-preservation, but also because mankind remains stranded in the shadows of non-universality, private execution of the law, and enmity rooted in his partiality, particularism, lawlessness, and passions representative of irrationality. In short, only reason can replace the divisive and bestial privation of self-love with the public universality of the law, which then legitimately unifies men who have fallen from the original heights of the state of nature to become lowly beasts. Because the man-beast of the state of war is defined by his irrational self-love, he is different from and foreign to self-identical mankind as such. Thus, on this account, the originary fear of the state of nature that compels man into civil society is foreignness as such.

Driven by the originary fear not only of irrational self-love which exposes the physical vulnerability of each and all but also a foreignness to himself (i.e., the loss of self-identicality), the sovereign man gives up his individual sovereignty—his private right to execute the law of nature—by entering into a public commonwealth. Importantly, the transfer of individual sovereignty is only legitimate if it is consensual. Unlike Hobbes' pre-political "proto-unity," which authorizes the sovereign to rule over those who oppose his rule, Locke insists that it is only through consent that one becomes a member of a public commonwealth. The requirement of consent is important for two reasons. First, it serves as a foil against absolutism, which institutes a private sovereign whose authority is akin to paternal power and whose interests often fail to coincide with his subjects' interests, thereby leaving the subjects at the mercy of the absolute sovereign. Second, consent is an expression of a voluntary action rooted in reason. Accordingly, consenting to the social contract is more than giving up one's power to execute the law of nature to any common power; instead, insofar as it is an expression of reason, consent is the voluntary transference of individual sovereignty to the *public* as a whole (in order, interestingly enough, to protect the individual property of each private individual and restore the peace of the state of nature) through the rational action of leaving behind the privation, particularism, and subjectivity of irrational self-love. Consent establishes reason as the legitimate sovereign that rules men, and the sovereign rule of reason takes the form of the public as such, i.e., that entity which is absolutely opposed to the private, subjective, partial, and divisive judgments of individual men. Accordingly, for Locke, the legitimate sovereign is nothing more than the public itself, which acts as a neutral umpire whose sole authority is to dispassionately, objectively, neutrally, and proportionally (i.e., rationally) adjudicate the promulgated laws directed toward the common good and achieved through the preservation of the property of every member of the public commonwealth.

Locke's legitimate sovereign regime of reason explains why he restricts children and foreigners to the private sphere. Children are under the stewardship of their parents until their reason has fully matured. Upon maturity of their reason, they are free, and those who choose to remain in the commonwealth and "enjoy the inheritance [property] of their ancestors" (Locke 2003, *Second Treatise* §73, 131) must follow the laws of the commonwealth, which has jurisdiction over its lands and territory. Yet, "submitting to the laws of any country, living quietly, and enjoying privileges and protection under them, makes not a man a member of that society" (2003, *Second Treatise* §122, 154). Tacit consent is insufficient for full membership in a commonwealth. Upon adulthood, children must expressly declare—as free, rational beings—their consent to the laws and rule of the public commonwealth to be included as a member. Once this express consent is given, a man is "perpetually and indispensably obliged to be, and remain unalterably a subject to it" (2003, *Second Treatise* §121, 153) unless the government he lives under is, by any means, dissolved.

The foreigner is under similar restrictions. He may enjoy privileges and protections, and may "even in conscience" (Locke 2003, *Second Treatise* §122, 154) willingly submit to the laws of the commonwealth, but these acts do not make him a subject. This would require express consent; yet, as a member of a foreign commonwealth, he is only permitted to become a member of the commonwealth in which he resides if the commonwealth to which he has previously consented ceases to exist. In this way, the foreign resident is always restricted to the private sphere for if he is able to consent to the commonwealth, he demonstrates his rationality and commitment to the public as such, and is, therefore, no longer a foreigner; he is a full member or subject of the commonwealth.

With the importance of consent outlined, the function of foreignness in Locke's account is now fully evident. Self-identical, individual men rationally consent to transfer their God-given individual sovereignty (the right to execute the law for the protection of property) to the public as such. Through this rational consent, mankind creates a political sovereign, the public, which reunifies mankind into a self-identical and homogeneous whole through the elimination of foreignness, i.e., the private, particular, subjective, and divisive self-love fostered by irrationality. Most simply, this triumph of reason over self-love via political association enshrines reason as Locke's legitimate sovereign. Sovereign reason—a neutral umpire—creates the law and secures its universality through the dispassionate and proportional adjudication of its tenets. From this account, foreignness is not merely the benign and common insight that the foreign is that which attaches to a member of another commonwealth or is that which is not-yet-known. Rather, foreignness *qua* pure irrationality and pure difference is the absolutely unpredictable, unquantifiable, immeasurable, and fully unknowable threat to self-identicality as such.

If foreignness is the originary fear which drives men into political society (and by extension the subjection to the irrationality and private interests of the absolute sovereign's paternal power), then only legitimate political sovereignty or public reason can make man whole and self-identical again as a unified political body. In this way, foreignness is constructed in absolute opposition to sovereignty itself. More specifically, foreignness is the mortal threat and enemy to the self-identicality of sovereignty as such because it is pure privation, i.e., a perpetual and absolute state of deprivation from God, natural law, universal reason, mankind, consent, the artificial law, the public, unity, and the common good. This is why it must always and necessarily be excluded, cast out, and guarded against in the name of and for the sake of sovereignty.

While Locke's practical attitude toward foreigners and foreign commonwealths is prudent, the conceptualization of sovereignty and the concomitant determination of the meaning of foreignness complicates Locke's position. For proof, we note that Locke insists that in relation to one another, foreign commonwealths remain in and are guided by the precepts of the state of nature. Rational foreign commonwealths will aim toward the preservation of peace and moral relations. Nevertheless, insofar as they are foreign, the "actions, designs, and interests" of foreign commonwealths are ultimately unknowable. This is why foreign alliances must be perpetually and ceremoniously renegotiated with gifts, pledges, oaths, meetings, and renewed consent to constantly make known, at least for the moment, the rationality of the foreign commonwealth. Similarly, the federative power does not merely respond to foreign aggression. Even if a foreign commonwealth proclaims an interest in peace and moral relations, the meaning of their "actions, designs, and interests" can never be fully known. They may be acting duplicitously. Thus, the federative branch, in some respect, remains on a permanent war footing, always prepared to destroy those it *deems* to be a threat.[16]

Most generally, the implicit conceptualization and meaning of foreignness undermines the practical and political position put forward by Locke with respect to foreign commonwealths. Indeed, a surprising result is achieved by fleshing out the implicit conceptualization of foreignness in Locke's account of sovereignty. If legitimate political sovereignty is pure rationality, then the irrational, private sovereign is no sovereign at all; at best, it is a foreign power that cannot legitimately command obedience, i.e., the perpetuation of the state of war. At worst, if foreignness is included into Locke's conceptualization of sovereignty, the result would be none other than Hobbes' illegitimate absolute sovereign, a private, irrational, threatening beast, i.e., a true monster or Leviathan. In this way, Locke's theorization of sovereignty reveals a deep-seated fear of foreignness threatening not only to the commonwealth but also to the conceptualization of mankind as such. Accordingly, it is hardly surprising that his universal conception of man is one that excludes all differences foreign to his parochial understanding of mankind. What does surprise is that Locke's tenets of freedom, equality, rights, toleration, dissent, and revolution are the foundations of liberalism protected by sovereign states that respects the rights of all, including foreigners, but are impossible without the absolute and unyielding elimination of foreignness as such from the qualities and characteristics of sovereignty.[17]

Foreignness in Rousseau's theorization of sovereignty

In contrast to Hobbes and Locke, Rousseau explicitly addresses the question of foreignness in relation to sovereignty even if he is occasionally opaque and indirect. His analysis is, in some respects, nuanced, recognizing that foreigners are both threats to and indispensable components of the sovereign state. Nevertheless, I argue that—similar to his social contract predecessors—Rousseau's conceptualization of the sovereign general will rests upon the implicit presupposition that foreignness as such is a threat which must be absolutely excluded from sovereignty. To defend this claim, I first detail the paradoxical aspects of reason in Rousseau's depiction of mankind: a narcissistic doubling whereby reason both produces and destroys mankind's self-identicality. The loss of self-identicality leads to the originary fear of the state of nature, *amour propre*, being conceived of as a type of foreignness that drives mankind into political society. Political society, at once, renders mankind foreign to himself and offers the only hope for purging this foreignness through inclusion within the self-identical unity of the general will. I then examine Rousseau's explicit mentions of the foreigner in *The Social Contract*, paying special attention to the figure of the foreign lawgiver. By re-examining Rousseau's insistence upon the originary, mythical unanimity of a people, I conclude that his depiction of the foreign lawgiver functions as a scapegoat requisite for establishing the homogeneous unity of a sovereign people, which, in turn, functions as a supplement for the loss of mankind's individual self-identicality.

Despite the critique that his social contract predecessors erred by importing the characteristics of civilized man back into their descriptions of man in the state of nature, Rousseau himself remains vulnerable to the charge that his conceptualization of natural man is premised upon culturally specific characteristics that cannot pass the test of universalizability. Nevertheless, it is important to touch upon Rousseau's initial sketch of the characteristics of man in the state of nature because, unlike the theorizations of Hobbes and Locke, it places mankind's originary self-identicality into question. Rousseau claims that in the earliest stages of the state of nature, man is nearly indistinguishable from the beast. The only important difference is that man is aware that he is free to disobey the dictates of nature, i.e., his passions. While awareness of his freedom is a rational faculty distinctive of man, Rousseau insists that reason *per se* is not what differentiates men from beasts. By doing so, he resists the notion that reason is always and already a fully formed capacity distinctive of a self-identical, fixed, unchanging man who is superior to and exclusive of the beast without reason. Put differently, Rousseau's depiction of natural man suggests that the self-identicality of man *qua* rational being is always already lost. While this position is consistent with what we saw in Hobbes' and Locke's respective accounts, the difference is that Rousseau appears to hold open the possibility that self-identicality is not an originary feature of mankind.

Even if the beast is simply a desiring being and man with his rational awareness of freedom is something different from the simple beast, reason is not superior to desire; instead of a hierarchical relation which places reason above bestial desire, Rousseau claims that they exist in a dialectical relation to one another, whereby desire improves reason and reason creates more and new desires, which, in turn, refine reason and so on as mankind progresses from a beast-like being to a morally free, autonomous being. In other words, contra Hobbes and Locke, Rousseau claims that the passions are not the mark of the beast, partiality, and an unrelenting self-interest foreign to mankind's highest, i.e., rational, enlightened and civilized self. Insofar as mankind can never fully eliminate his bestial, passionate nature that perfects reason, the beast is not foreign to mankind. At the earliest stages of the state of nature, mankind is as much beast as man.

Similarly, while reason is the source of mankind's awareness of his freedom and capacity for self-perfection, Rousseau is careful to note that reason is also the source of mankind's imperfections as evidenced by the so-called civilized man whose vice lowers him below the beasts. The contradictory aspects of reason that Rousseau astutely recognizes suggests that something like the complete, whole, total, perfectible, and self-identical man which earlier theorists presume to be exemplified by civilized man is an impossibility. Taken together, the paradoxical nature of reason and the dialectical relation between reason and desire suggest that Rousseau's conception of mankind does not depend upon a self-identicality which excludes as foreign all that is different from mankind (even if, along the way, Rousseau romanticizes the nobility of the savage). Men are men, but they are also, simultaneously, imperfect and incomplete beasts. This non-self-identicality allows Rousseau to avoid charges (temporarily) that he assigns culturally specific attributes commonly associated with rationality such as gender, age, class, race, belonging to a specific socio-linguistic group, etc. to his generic depiction of man in the state of nature. Indeed, while conceiving of reason as a faculty of perfectibility distinctive of mankind, his depiction of mankind in the earliest stages of the state of nature appears to provide a universal account of man without recourse to an exclusionary self-identicality.

Despite this initial analysis, Rousseau's universal account of man is quickly replaced by the self-identical, non-generic Western subject in which reason proper and all of its culturally ascribed attributes are enshrined as distinctive of mankind as such. Initially, reason is not fully formed in natural man. The result is that pity trumps the self-interest dictated by reason and brings individuals together into caring familial relations and cooperative communities. Socialization fosters rational capacities such as language, collective memories, cooperation, art, technological advances, etc. In a word, culture is born. Mankind at this stage might not be moral or have a fully developed rational capacity, but for Rousseau, this stage in mankind's development is the ideal, even if it cannot last. Most simply, man is an independent being who thrives in small communities with a shared set of cultural preferences and practices. Nevertheless, through his rational capacities, which further refine culture, natural man begins to lose his affinity with the beast. As mankind's reason develops, he starts along the path toward greater self-identicality exclusive of the beast. He is no longer as much beast as he is man; indeed, even if Rousseau laments the fact, the gradual exclusion of mankind's bestial qualities is necessary for him to be who he is at this stage of his development.

The increasing self-identicality of reasonable (though not perfectly rational) mankind enmeshed in culture does not necessarily endanger the universality of his description of natural man. The mere fact that culture exists in the state of nature does not mean that the practices or beliefs of any one culture define mankind as such. Yet, as reason increasingly comes to define natural man, Rousseau's depiction of pre-political culture becomes more and more specific, and his universal conceptualization of mankind becomes lost in cultural specificity. Rousseau claims that the refinement of reason causes pity shared by all social animals to be replaced by hierarchical social relations rooted in esteem, deference, and civility. When these mores break down, violence becomes commonplace. Negative attitudes and sentiments such as pride, vanity, and jealousy emerge. Mutual assistance is needed to survive, and this brings forth the need for surplus, property, and the concomitant requirement for the division of labor. The naturally skilled acquire more property, and this natural inequality—in conjunction with the inheritance of property—slowly and subtly produces an artificial, social inequality. Industry, thought, memory, and language all become more sophisticated, and as reason matures and is finally "rendered active" (Rousseau [1754] 2004, 36), the somatic force of pity felt for seeing others suffer is devalued and replaced by abstract moral reasoning.

Culture may be common to all of humanity, but Rousseau's account of the natural progression of culture in the state of nature demonstrates his own cultural biases. Rousseau's account of the specific cultural group which brings forth civilized, political society and moral freedom (despite its pitfalls) is his own, i.e., the culture of Western enlightenment thinking. Natural man is the European man, and the rational Western subject is now the universal model for mankind. Moreover, as reason increasingly comes to define mankind, natural man becomes more and more self-identical with respect to his specific characteristics. He speaks, writes, or understands the language of contracts, he values the legal and moral authority of contracts, and he subscribes to the belief that contract is the legitimate source for political authority. Furthermore, true to the cultural understanding of Rousseau's day, natural man *qua* rational being is, by default, male, adult, white, European, and respectful of class divisions.[18] In

Rousseau's depiction, reason is "rendered active" through a process unique to Western culture and men; all other humans and all other cultures are necessarily excluded precisely because, it is implied, their reason has not been "rendered active." Natural man lives on in the form of the non-European.[19] Thus, despite Rousseau's cautionary tale of mankind's progressive advancement toward Enlightenment and civilization, the final stage of natural, pre-political man is strikingly similar to Hobbes' and Locke's self-identical bourgeois man exclusive of all differences foreign to this culturally prescribed depiction of man, which nonetheless masquerades as the universal.

Rousseau's awareness of the paradoxical features of reason reveals the centrality of foreignness in his account. While reason is the source of self-identicality that differentiates the bourgeois man from the beast and other non-bourgeois men and women, it is also that which causes man to lose his self-identicality, a loss that leads him into political society. For Rousseau, reason undermines man's sociality. For example, he claims that the wise or prudent man flees a fight while the women of the marketplace and the rabble rush to break it up.[20] Against the simple self-interest and natural desire for self-preservation shared by all animals (*amour de soi me*), reason transforms this innocent simplicity into a vain egocentrism (*amour propre*), a narcissistic doubling wherein mankind's self-interest is achieved through his becoming alienated from himself. Pre-political, rational, and cultured society values specific characteristics (certain forms of beauty, intellect, etc.), is bonded together through particular mores (deference, civility, etc.), and is organized according to division of labor (wealthy property owners require labor and laborers require wealthy property owners). In short, each is absolutely and utterly dependent upon the other, and the demand for recognition becomes paramount, since each must be recognized to secure the assistance of the other.

Self-interest, deception, partiality, and violent disorder dictated by reason become the norm as each must possess, appear to possess, or come to possess through any means necessary those qualities esteemed by all, which will assure that one is recognized. This hyper-rationality of *amour propre*, of narcissistic doubling, unrestrained by the natural passions strips man not only of his animality (pity, innocence, simple desires, etc.), but also the self-identicality which first makes him who he is (a refined beast). His unyielding self-interest spurs partiality, divisiveness, and privation. As such, man becomes utterly divided not only from others but also himself. Paradoxically, reason is the source of mankind's self-identicality and what makes mankind foreign to himself, and in this way, the originary fear of the state of nature which drives man into political society, namely the narcissistic doubling of *amour propre*, is nothing else than the fear of mankind's foreignness to himself, i.e., his loss of self-identicality. Put differently, the state renders mankind foreign to himself, and the price of civilization is the loss of the self.

If the originary fear of the state of nature that drives men into political society is the fear of foreignness, then the legitimate political sovereign that compels obedience from its subjects is only that which absolutely excludes and defends against the threat of foreignness. By differentiating between the individual will, the will of all, and the general will, Rousseau's sovereign general will does not merely eliminate the threat of *amour propre* by identifying and enforcing the common good; rather, the general will protects its subjects by restoring self-identicality through the elimination of the divisive partiality and privation of foreignness and difference as such. Thus, we see why, for Rousseau, the sovereign general will must be indivisible, inviolable, and inalienable. To be otherwise is to open itself up to a foreignness that destroys the self-identicality of the sovereign general will—exclusive of foreign difference—that makes a people unified and whole. Against that which is sovereign, the foreign becomes the beast, difference, irrationality, hyper-rationality, pure self-interest, partiality, division, privation, natural, and uncivilized. For Rousseau, as much as for Hobbes and Locke, the foreign is produced as the conceptual antipode, the absolute threat, to self-identical sovereignty.

Because he conceives of foreignness as a threat to sovereignty, it is unsurprising that Rousseau argues that "all must now fight in case of need for their country" ([1762] 1968, 78), thereby subscribing to the commonplace view that war is a political reality. In this way, Rousseau understands foreigners or foreign countries to be potential threats. Nevertheless, Rousseau offers another depiction of the foreigner, namely the foreign lawgiver. Rousseau's figure of the lawgiver conceives of the foreigner as simultaneously a threat to and indispensable to the founding of a sovereign people. To demonstrate this claim, the ways in which Rousseau's lawgiver is foreign must be detailed.

Rousseau's lawgiver is a curious figure in several ways. On the one hand, the necessity for a lawgiver solves a difficult theoretical question for democracy. The general will (i.e. the will of the people as a unified whole) is distinct from both the private wills of individual men and the collective will of all. The unique quality of the general will is that it guards against the tyranny of any one man as well as the tyranny of the majority. However, if the will of the majority is sometimes a form of tyranny and all men are equal in a democratic society, then the fundamental problem of democracy is that no one possesses the legitimate authority to establish the laws, to forge a constitution, and to "shape the institutions" (Rousseau [1762] 1968, 84).[21] On the other hand, under monarchical or aristocratic constitutions, there seems to be no need for a lawgiver, since this right seemingly belongs to the king or aristocracy. Any lawgiver in these types of regimes would by superfluous or even contradictory to the sovereign. Accordingly, on its surface, Rousseau's positing of the necessity for a lawgiver in all types of regimes appears discordant.

Yet, Rousseau rejects the premise that a lawgiver is superfluous in non-democratic regimes, arguing instead that, "the prince has only to follow a model which the lawgiver provides. The lawgiver is the engineer who invents the machine; the prince is merely the mechanic who sets it up and operates it" (Rousseau [1762] 1968, 84). He justifies this claim by reminding his readers that to establish a people is to "change human nature" ([1762] 1968, 84). Within political society, each man is transformed from a solitary individual into a member of the whole "from which the same individual will then receive, in a sense, his life and his being" ([1762] 1968, 84). Recall that natural man does not transfer his natural rights; instead, his rights are transformed. Upon entering political society, the solitary, independent being whose existence is endowed by nature becomes morally free, i.e., autonomous, self-legislating, and one whose "life and being" are utterly dependent upon and shaped by "communal existence" ([1762] 1968, 85). In political society, man's natural powers are replaced by "external" ([1762] 1968, 85) or artificial powers that can only be exercised with "the help of others" ([1762] 1968, 85). In this respect, it is only when the "acquired power of the whole is equal to, or greater than, the sum of its natural powers of each of its individuals" ([1762] 1968, 85) that a truly unified sovereign whole is achieved. The lawgiver is the one who shapes a constitution that is "best suited" ([1762] 1968, 84) to transform individual men into members of a unified political whole. Legislators (be they kings, aristocrats, or democrats) are simply those who enforce and execute the tenets of the constitution, i.e., the legal, moral, and social ordering which founds a people and its institutions.

Having shown that the lawgiver is necessary in all types of regimes, the question regarding the democratic lawgiver remains to be settled. If the lawgiver is not a legislator in the narrowest sense of that term, then who or what is the lawgiver? Rousseau answers by providing a list of the qualities of the lawgiver: "To discover the rules of society that are best suited to nations, there would need to exist a superior intelligence, who could understand the passions of men without feeling any of them, who had no affinity with our nature but knew it to the full, whose happiness was independent of ours, but who would nevertheless make our happiness his concern, who would be content to wait in the fullness of time for a distant glory and to labour in one age to enjoy the fruits in another" ([1762] 1968, 84).

Based on these qualities, Rousseau's initial answer is that "Gods would be needed to give men laws" ([1762] 1968, 84). Rousseau's lawgiver, however, is not properly divine. Instead, he is a quasi-divine figure capable of determining which constitution is "best suited" to the traits, histories, values, customs, beliefs, etc. of a given group of individuals as well as transforming human nature by establishing these individuals as a unified people. I use the term "quasi-divine" for three reasons. First, because the task of the lawgiver is seemingly "beyond human powers and [rests upon] a non-existent authority for its execution" ([1762] 1968, 86), a common and politically expedient solution to this paradox of the founding of a democratic people has been "to appeal to divine intervention" ([1762] 1968, 87). Nevertheless, while sovereign states frequently appeal to God to justify their constitution and laws, it is human beings who are the "leaders" ([1762] 1968, 84) that found sovereign peoples. Most plainly, lawgivers are humans not gods. Second, there is a historical precedent in the history of philosophy for the quasi-divinity of Rousseau's lawgiver, namely Plato's Socrates and the philosopher-kings. Without going so far as to retrace the emergence of the philosopher-king, suffice it to say that they are humans with "superior intelligence," who "understand the passions of men without feeling any of them," whose "happiness was independent from ours, but who would nevertheless make our happiness his concern," etc. Finally, Rousseau does not argue that God is the lawgiver; instead, he suggests that only "Gods" can give men the law. Here, Rousseau is not advocating a form of polytheism; instead, this strange reference to plural gods is eventually explained by citing legendary political figures. Rousseau explains that the lawgiver is "special not only because of his personal qualities, but also because he is an extraordinary man in the state" ([1762] 1968, 85). Thus, we have our first evidence that the lawgiver is, indeed, a man, but of great interest as well is the second way the lawgiver is extraordinary. He is extraordinary because of his "office" ([1762] 1968, 85). The office of the lawgiver is neither the sovereign nor the government. Instead, "this office which gives the republic its constitution has no place in that constitution" ([1762] 1968, 85). If the giver of the constitution and his office seeks to rule over men, then there can be no general will, for this would simply introduce, once more, the "partial judgments" ([1762] 1968, 85) of the individual will of one man or the majority. Not only must the lawgiver be a quasi-divine outsider of some sort, but his function, role, and office is also temporary and outside of the constitution itself.

Rousseau finally provides an example of this quasi-divine lawgiver when he cites the historico-legendary figure of Lycurgus. Although Lycurgus is referred to by ancient historians, it is the legend of his actions which inform Rousseau's understanding of the extraordinariness of the lawgiver. On the one hand, Lycurgus is believed to have been a wise man. Thus, for Rousseau, his "superior intelligence" enabled him to "discover the rules" that were "best suited" to shape the Spartans. Yet, the legend of his life also tells of him seeking the guidance of the oracle at Delphi who approved and blessed his vision for a Spartan people. In this regard, Lycurgus' legendary status as a wise political thinker is buttressed by divine authority. On the other hand, although Lycurgus is a Spartan, he is said to have founded the Spartan people only by giving up all claims to the office of monarchical rule. Rousseau writes: "When Lycurgus gave laws to his country, he began by abdicating his monarchical functions" ([1762] 1968, 85). The Spartan people was created not through an act of government or decree of the sovereign, but through the separate, distinct, and temporary office of the lawgiver, "which has nothing to do with empire over men" ([1762] 1968, 85). In this respect, the divine, mythical, and legendary basis of Lycurgus' founding of Sparta is revealing as an example of the quasi-divinity of the lawgiver (and the specialized role of the office of the lawgiver) that Rousseau envisages.

Interestingly, however, Rousseau immediately turns to a different example, which suggests that, beyond appeals to the gods or ancient legends, the exemplar of the quasi-divine lawgiver is the foreigner. Rousseau writes: "It was the habit of most Greek cities to confer on foreigners the task of framing their laws. The modern republics of Italy have often copied this custom; the republic of Geneva did so, and found that it worked well" ([1762] 1968, 85). With this claim, Rousseau identifies and draws upon a positive conception of the foreigner that not only extends beyond the simple notion of the foreigner as a dangerous threat to a sovereign people but also runs counter to Rousseau's famed "xenophobia" (Honig 2001, 18) as well as my own claim regarding his implicit positing of foreignness as the originary threat of the state of nature. Like Plato's philosopher-kings, Rousseau's foreign lawgiver is a quasi-divine pedagogue insofar as he understands a people without being swept up by their passions; he has no affinity with the nature of the people he founds, but he knows and understands human nature; he is called upon to found a people, and he performs his function magnanimously. In short, the foreign lawgiver shares a striking similarity with the gods who are foreign to mankind. Indeed, it is the very foreignness of the foreigner lawgiver that provides him with the disengaged, privileged perspective, i.e., the "superior intellect" necessary to lay down the constitution "best suited" to a people.

Insofar as the wise foreign lawgiver is not a member of this group of individuals to be unified into a people, the question of how a democratic people (in which all are equal under the law) legitimately founds itself is eliminated. Nevertheless, while the foreign lawgiver might solve a conceptual problem of democracy, wisdom and pedagogical guidance alone does not disarm the practical problem of the threat of the foreigner. There is a risk that the foreigner will remain to unjustly rule over a people or simply introduce a set of differences that would divide a people against itself. To guard against this threat, Rousseau's insistence that the office of the lawgiver is temporary and distinct from the sovereign begins to make sense. For Rousseau, the foreign lawgiver's purpose is to do what the sovereign lacks the authority to do, namely establish a people. As an outsider, the foreigner has the authority to found a democratic people, but not to rule over them. Once the sovereign people has been founded, the wise, foreign lawgiver departs, dissolves his office, and leaves the ruling of the people to the people as such exclusive of the foreigner. As Bonnie Honig suggests, "If the fortuitous arrival of the foreign-founder seems too good to be true, his timely departure seems almost beyond belief" (2001, 22). In other words, beyond being wise, the foreign lawgiver, like the gods, is also benevolent, and his beneficence is demonstrated by the fact that he has no desire to rule over the people.

These appeals to the divine, myth, or legend notwithstanding, it is Rousseau's reference to the *historical* figure of the foreign lawgiver that solves both conceptual and practical problems of a democracy. Conceptually, the foreign lawgiver alone has the legitimate authority to found a people equal under the law. Practically, his departure also functions to establish and perpetuate the psychosocial unity of a homogeneous people. Because he departs, the foreign lawgiver and his extraordinary office are both distinct from and non-threatening to the sovereign people who now rule. Thus, the emphasis upon the legitimacy and historical reality of the foreign lawgiver allows Rousseau to differentiate between the threatening and non-threatening foreigner. The threatening and illegitimate foreigner is a violent, self-interested, divisive figure (who overstays his or her welcome) against which all sovereign peoples must defend themselves.

By contrast, the foreign lawgiver is a beneficent and wise figure indispensable to a sovereign, democratic people as such.

Rousseau's positing of the foreign lawgiver appears to be a radical rethinking of the foreign with respect to sovereignty and democracy. In Bonnie Honig's formulation, the "foreignness at the heart of Rousseau's ideal democracy invites us to ask whether democracy itself—at its origins and in its daily refoundings—might require not just the (re)construction of the national ... but also the violation of the national" (Honig 2001, 18). I agree with Honig that Rousseau's foreign lawgiver provides conceptual resources within the social contract tradition itself for positing foreignness, difference, and heterogeneity as indispensable to and constitutive of a sovereign, homogeneous, and democratic people. Nevertheless, I maintain that because Rousseau conceives of foreignness as that which destroys individual self-identicality (the narcissistic doubling of *amour propre*) and functions as the originary fear of the state of nature, his conceptualization of legitimate sovereignty remains dependent upon the construction of foreignness as a threat that must be eliminated by the general will. Indeed, the very notion of the beneficent foreigner who willingly departs as well as the temporary and extraordinary nature of his non-sovereign office suggest a distinction between the fact that foreigners will always arrive at the walls of the sovereign state and the requirement that foreignness can and should be eliminated to restore the homogeneity which is presumed to be a prerequisite for the psychosocial unity of a people. If this is so, then Rousseau's foreign lawgiver is a scapegoat whose sacrifice (actual murder, imprisonment, dispatching, or voluntary departure) restores the homogeneous unity and inviolability of a sovereign, democratic people, which, in turn, serves as a legitimate supplement for the loss of individual self-identicality.

Given the authority and legitimacy of divine justifications and legendary figures such as Lycurgus to solve the conceptual problem of democracy's founding, why does Rousseau posit a foreign lawgiver? Rousseau certainly is not an advocate of the view that diversity enriches a people or that tolerance of foreign difference is a great virtue. In fact, early on in *The Social Contract*, he implies the exact opposite. In his attempt to understand "the real foundation of society" ([1762] 1968, 59), Rousseau insists that the challenge is to determine "the act by which people become *a* people" ([1762] 1968, 59, original emphasis). Given the conceptual difficulties outlined above with respect to the founding of democracy, this question is especially poignant. On its surface, Rousseau's answer relies simply on the everyday operations of democracy. If people, a multitude in the classic sense, vote to become *a* people, then the election must be unanimous otherwise there is "no obligation on the minority to accept the decision of the majority" ([1762] 1968, 59). Not only is this unlikely given men's various personal interests, but Rousseau suggests something more fundamental, namely "the law of majority-voting itself rests on a covenant, and implies that there has been on at least one occasion unanimity" ([1762] 1968, 59). Here, there are distorted—democratic—echoes of Hobbes' "proto-unity" in which even those who voted against the sovereign authorize the sovereign because they are (or once were) already unanimous, thereby granting authority to the very process of democratic rule. For Rousseau, the everyday authority and legitimacy of the ideal democratic community rests upon a mythical original unanimity, i.e., a perfect, inviolable unity where dissent, division, partiality, privation, self-interest, and difference do not exist. In a word, foreignness does not exist. Therefore, what gives authority and legitimacy to a democratic people is the mythical belief in the originary self-identicality and homogeneity of the people as such.[22]

The belief in the originary self-identicality or unanimity of a people (even if—or precisely because—it is lost in the everyday operations of a democratic polity) fosters those conservative and progressive longings to uncover, re-establish, and reinvigorate the productive forces, security, inviolability, and harmony of the mythical self-identicality of the founding of the people.[23] So, once again, why does Rousseau introduce the foreign lawgiver here at the very heart of sovereign self-identicality? As noted, the answer is not because of Rousseau's reverence for the foreigner; instead, a more likely answer is to identify a mythical scapegoat whose sacrifice performs both a political and psychological function related to violence and the legitimacy of the sovereign general will.

To develop this point, two analyses are required. I first follow a line of thought developed by Bonnie Honig. For Honig, the foreign lawgiver need not be a foreigner or outsider. He may very well be "one of us." Nevertheless, as a scapegoat, he functions as a foreigner whose sacrifice cleanses the people of the violence of its successful founding and the self-willing of the imposition of the law necessary for social, institutional, and political stability. Second, I turn to my own position. While it is in accord with Honig's claims, I argue that by emphasizing the foreignness of the lawgiver, Rousseau's narrative restores—if only as a myth or ideal—a belief in an originary, homogeneous unity that is exclusive of foreignness as such in order to redress the psychological violence that accompanies the transformation from natural to civilized man, i.e., the violence which accompanies the loss of self-identicality and the narcissistic doubling of *amour propre*. In turn, the belief in this originary, mythical homogeneous unity (and the hope for its (re)instantiation) is or becomes the foundation for the legitimate political sovereignty, exclusive of foreignness, which serves as a supplement for the loss of individual self-identicality.

Honig's analysis begins by working through René Girard's interpretation of Rousseau's foreign lawgiver and the appeal for originary unanimity. For Girard, "the loss of unanimity returns the community to an unending cycle of violence" (Honig 2001, 33). Thus, Girard, like Rousseau, believes that the solution to this divisiveness and faction is an outsider or a scapegoat. Unlike Rousseau, who posits the foreign lawgiver, Girard argues that it is in opposition to the foreigner that unity is achieved. The foreign lawgiver is a scapegoat whose actual or symbolic departure functions to erase the original violence of founding and the perpetuation of violence through factional disputes, thereby restoring the people to itself once again as a harmonious and unified whole. By choosing a foreigner or those from the margins of society as the scapegoat, Girard believes that the psychosocial unity of the people can be restored because violence is "symbolically expunged or absorbed" (Honig 2001, 33) through the sacrifice of the scapegoat.

Honig is quick to note that, despite Girard's insistence that scapegoats must be outsiders, in other writings he is acutely aware that it is not the case that "empirical marginality is what causes their [the outsiders'] scapegoating" (Honig 2001, 34). In other words, scapegoats are not necessarily outsiders or foreigners; rather, in a manner similar to the power of Hobbes' sovereign to deem as an outsider or foreigner those who threaten the community, the scapegoat is simply the one who is cast as an outsider or foreigner without regard for his or her empirical status in relation to the state. In Honig's words, "scapegoating is not caused by the scapegoats—an already existing pool of outsiders. Scapegoating is a social practice that finds or produces the objects it needs" (2001, 34). In this respect, Honig believes Girard's great insight is to identify a "*politics* of foreignness" (2001, 34, original emphasis) in which the sacrifice of the scapegoat serves to restore and (re)unify a people through a "resolution-producing confrontation between 'us' and 'them'" (2001, 34).

For Honig, Rousseau's foreign lawgiver is a sacrificial scapegoat whose expulsion, departure, or death is requisite for social unity, but he need not be an empirical outsider. This fact is important not only for the psychological implication that a people might struggle to take responsibility for the violence of its founding, but also for the political implications associated with the originary violence that accompanies the founding of a people. Honig notes that "democratic life demands a measure of stability and routine that might be impossible to secure for citizens known to be capable of great passion and violence" (2001, 36). In this respect, scapegoats "take it [the originary violence] upon themselves (or suffer its projection onto themselves) and thereby, Christlike, absolve the collectivity of implication in it" (2001, 36).

We recall that Rousseau introduces the lawgiver after a discussion of whether the general will can err. He insists it cannot, but that the will of the majority often passes for the general will, and that the people can be "misled." Rousseau, therefore, suggests that the foreign lawgiver is necessary because what is willed by the general will, namely the imposition of the law, the sovereign right to life and death over the people, the requirement that men are forced to be free, etc. is something which no people would will upon itself. Only the lawgiver can explain the deep imposition of the law upon the individual and the people as a whole; therefore, his status as a scapegoat assumes the mantle of responsibility for the inconveniences of political life. However, Honig pushes this theme further by complicating Rousseau's lawgiver when she asks us to consider the significance of the foreign lawgiver with the assumption that the "project of General Willing . . . has succeeded" (2001, 36).

What if the imposition of the law, the rights of the sovereign, the abdication of self-interest to the general will are, in fact, "generated by the people themselves, imposed upon themselves, and exacted from among their own number" (Honig 2001, 36)? On this reading, the foreign lawgiver is simply a story told to distance ourselves from the violence of our founding for which we, alone, are responsible, a distancing and cleansing requisite for the "daily maintenance of our democratic polity" (2001, 36). Rather than provide a philosophical argument to explain the necessity of political violence, Honig argues that Rousseau opts to tell an origin story which "externalizes the General Will's violence; the willed violence of (re)-founding" (2001, 37) in order to justify the legitimacy of the general will. Rousseau's foreign lawgiver is not an embrace of foreignness at the heart of a people; instead, it is merely the casting as foreign the originary violence of founding, which is expunged through a scapegoat (whether he be a foreigner, a marginal member of society, or even a leader or national hero) for the sake of the political requirements of the everyday operations of the democratic state founded upon the rule and force of law and expunging of the law of force and violence.

Honig's analysis is, in my estimation, highly compelling for two reasons. First, it identifies a politics of foreignness at work in Rousseau's analysis of the ideal democracy, a novel reading at odds with traditional receptions of Rousseau's work. Second, it astutely recognizes that foreignness as such, not the empirical foreigner, is centrally important to Rousseau's account of sovereignty and democracy. Honig's analysis effectively crystallizes the moment of founding—the violence that accompanies the establishment of a people—and the origin stories and myths that we, as a people, tell ourselves. This emphasis upon origins and foundings is essential, yet, in my view, it also has one major drawback, namely it glosses over the substantial efforts that Rousseau puts forth in articulating a vision of the state of nature.[24] Why does he undertake this effort? The most obvious answer is simply to provide a plausible backdrop to explain why political society is both legitimate and preferable to an isolated, natural existence. Yet, another answer is also possible. Rather than demonstrating why a reasonable person would assent to political life, Rousseau's mythical account of the state of nature provides a psychological mooring for the individual against the unsettling fractures and incongruities produced by the violence, fear, and the (at least minimal) accommodation of difference that are inseparable from life in a polity.

While Honig's reading of Girard recognizes the psychological importance of unanimity, unity, and the purging of violence, my intention here is to demonstrate the significance of my earlier claims that foreignness precedes political founding insofar as it is a threat to self-identicality. If this is so, then the purging of foreignness at the moment of founding not only erases our self-willed *political* violence, per Honig, but it is also an attempt by Rousseau to replace an always already lost individual self-identicality with the supplement of political sovereignty rooted in homogeneous unanimity. If the stories of the state of nature point to the need for social and psychological unity, then an explicit analysis of the psychological function performed by the scapegoating of the foreign lawgiver can provide for a more robust understanding of the way in which the legitimacy of the sovereign general will is dependent upon the premise that foreignness is conceived of as absolute violence and unrelenting threat to the self-identicality of both the individual and the general will.

The tales of bloody revolutions, coup d'état, resistance movements, etc. are all familiar, as is the violence that accompanies these political foundings. But what exactly is the violence in Rousseau's state of nature? Certainly, he mentions the thievery, deceit, and general violence that accompany social inequality. These forms of violence are the result of *amour propre*, and it is *amour propre* that is the originary fear of the state of nature that compels men to contract together to forge political society. Yet, my contention is that Rousseau implicitly conceives of *amour propre* as a form of narcissistic doubling, as that which divides man from himself by destroying his presumed self-identicality. In this respect, *amour propre* makes man foreign to himself, which is to say that this narcissistic doubling is itself a kind of foreignness. Foreignness, therefore, is both the originary fear of the state of nature and the source of or origination of violence, which, when taken together, compel men to leave the state of nature.

This account is useful for explaining the violence, thievery, and deceit of the final stages of the state of nature. Nevertheless, it fails to address the psychological violence experienced by men in the state of nature and how the purging of this psychological violence is linked to the legitimacy of the sovereign general will. For Rousseau, the social contract is not the abdication (Hobbes) or transference (Locke) of natural rights in exchange for sovereign protection. Instead, Rousseau claims that through the social contract mankind gives up his independence or natural freedom for "moral freedom which alone makes man the master of himself; for to be governed by appetite alone is slavery, while obedience to a law one prescribes oneself is freedom" ([1762] 1968, 65). In this way, mankind is *transformed* from a natural being into a political, civilized, moral, and autonomous being. However, this transformation comes with a price insofar as it is only possible through the progressive development and refinement of reason which eventuates in a foreignness that strips natural man of his self-identicality. Just as reason is both beneficial and deleterious to mankind, foreignness also is a double-edged phenomenon insofar as it is a *necessary violence* that initiates the transformation of natural man into civilized man through the destruction of self-identicality. As I argue above, the price of civilization is the loss of the self. In this context, this sentiment can be restated in this way: the price of moral freedom is the psychologically unsettling recognition that foreignness is constitutive of individual sovereignty and identity as such.

Rousseau famously claims, "Man was born free, and he is everywhere in chains" ([1762] 1968, 49). He cannot, he says, explain this "transformation" ([1762] 1968, 49), but he can show how to make it legitimate, which is to say that he can convince men that political society is legitimate. Insofar as this transformation (loss of self-identicality) is a violent one, Rousseau's first task in *The Social Contract* is to reject the idea that political society is nothing more than the rule of the strongest or a form of slavery. Once he has assuaged the fear that political society is simply a violent and forced submission, Rousseau moves on to positively construct the legitimacy and authority of the political sovereign. To achieve this goal, Rousseau begins with an attempt to purge the originary psychological violence, which accompanies mankind's foreignness to himself. He explains how individuals become a people through the mythical story of an originary unanimity ([1762] 1968, 58). If there is an originary unanimity, then there was—once upon a time—a perfect unity, an inviolable and homogeneous whole, a self-identical people, which, even after the loss of individual self-identicality, is cleansed of a violent and fearful foreignness. Indeed, for Rousseau, this mythical originary unanimity and cleansing of violent foreignness is the "original covenant" ([1762] 1968, 58), the very condition of possibility for the social contract, the terms of which he lays out only *after* positing the originary unanimity and homogeneous self-identicality of a democratic people exclusive of foreign difference.

With his reunifying origin story and initial purging of the psychological violence of mankind's transformation in place, Rousseau immediately moves on to detail the terms of the social contract. He first argues that the sovereign is the general will before moving on in subsequent chapters to detail its qualities, namely that the general will is inalienable, indivisible, unable to err, has the power over life and death, and that the law acquires its force and legitimacy from the general will itself, i.e., the people as a unified whole. While these qualities of the legitimate sovereign are clear extensions of the necessity to exclude all that is foreign (including individual or private interests if not actual foreigners) from the newly formed people, Rousseau finishes his theorization of these sovereign qualities by voicing either a doubt or, perhaps, an explicit recognition that the story of mythical origination is insufficient to guarantee the legitimacy of the sovereign general will, i.e., that the people might still be threatened by the violence of the loss of self-identicality and their continued vulnerability to foreignness.

He writes, "Individuals see the good and reject it; the public desires the good but does not see it" (Rousseau [1762] 1968, 83). Ostensibly, this is a claim regarding a conceptual problem of democratic founding. On the one hand, individual self-interest undermines the common good. On the other hand, the public regularly fails to identify the common good because it is prone to err insofar as it is unable to differentiate between the will of many or all and the general will. In short, a people—despite its desire for the common good—frequently imposes only a partial will upon its members. Interpreted through the lens of foreignness, the problem that Rousseau identifies is that divisive, private interests (i.e., foreignness) are essentially at odds with a democratic society of equals. Individuals view the general will as a violent and foreign imposition against their self-interest while the public—being nothing more than a collection of individuals—lacks the perspicacity to ensure the general will is, in fact, general; therefore, it is not fully unified and self-identical; it is foreign to itself and its members. In both cases, Rousseau is deeply concerned with an unrelenting partiality, divisiveness, and privation whereby the threat of foreignness remains, resulting in lingering doubts regarding the legitimacy of the sovereign people.

On its own, it seems that the myth of originary unanimity is not sufficient to expunge the psychological violence of transformation that is required to secure the legitimacy of the sovereign general will.[25] Accordingly, to fully purge the psychological violence of the loss of self-identicality and secure the legitimacy of the general will, Rousseau requires a scapegoat, and he finds one in the figure of the foreign lawgiver. He claims that the lawgiver who founds a people is prepared "to change human nature, to transform each individual, who by himself is entirely complete and solitary, into a part of a much greater whole, from which that same individual will then receive, in a sense, his life and being" (Rousseau [1762] 1968, 84). The fact that Rousseau turns to the foreign lawgiver to explain the origination of a people is not arbitrary; instead, it has profound political import, since Rousseau implicitly acknowledges that the foreign violence of transformation and the loss of individual self-identicality is constitutive of a people. Because this originary violence is conceived of as a form of foreignness, Rousseau's exemplar of the lawgiver is a foreigner. Whether he is an insider cast as a foreigner or an empirical outsider is not the primary concern; instead, the lawgiver is the personification of foreignness as such which must be purged if the newly formed sovereign is to acquire legitimacy.

For this reason, Rousseau's foreign lawgiver, essential as he is to a people's founding, must depart or be dispatched. He is or becomes a scapegoat who bears the *psychological* violence of man's loss of his self-identicality and the concomitant transformation into a morally free, political being. Through his departure, the originary foreignness that is constitutive of a people is cast out. This departure of the scapegoated foreign lawgiver restores, at the level of a people, a belief in the homogeneous self-identicality of the general will, which, in turn, functions as a supplement for the loss of individual self-identicality. Through the scapegoating of the foreign lawgiver, Rousseau's myth of originary unanimity is now buttressed by a promise, namely that despite its necessity, the foreignness that destroys individual self-identicality is, once and for all, cast out of the community, leaving behind a self-identical, homogeneous, inviolable, and indivisible general will.

Like his predecessors, Rousseau conceives of and constructs the foreign as that which is absolutely and unalterably opposed to and threatening to the sovereign. For this reason, the sovereign that fails to protect its subjects through the exclusion of foreignness is simply another instance of the imposition of foreign violence upon men. Put differently, the sovereign unable to exclude foreignness is divided, partial, and lacks self-identicality; hence, it is, illegitimate.

6

The Naturalization of Artificial Sovereignty and Foreignness

Because civil society is the result of a social contract among men, for Hobbes, Locke, and Rousseau political sovereignty is conceived of as an artificial construct. Revisiting the distinction between *physis* (nature) and *nomos* (law or convention) or *thesis* (something posited) is useful for understanding why this is the case. To conceive of men being authors of and signatories to the terms of the social contract is simply to claim that they agree to produce and obey certain laws, conventions, and rights, i.e., *nomoi*. In this way, the social contract is not operative in nature (*physis*), but rather something posited (*thesis*) to legitimate sovereign rule over a people.[1] Moreover, as I have claimed, the theorization of the social contract is not only a mechanism for determining sovereign legitimacy but also a tool for positing or artificially constructing the illegitimacy of the foreign in political society. In this chapter, I argue that the attempt to naturalize the artificiality not only of sovereignty but also of foreignness is another tactic common to the social contract tradition which is deployed to establish the legitimacy of the sovereign through appeals to nature or divine creation and to (re)establish the conceptual opposition between the sovereign and foreign as natural, i.e., immutable and inexorable. I begin by examining the naturalization of artificial sovereignty in the works of Hobbes, Locke, and Rousseau before examining the implicit naturalization of artificial foreignness. Finally, I conclude by insisting that despite the attempt to naturalize sovereignty and foreignness, these concepts remain artificial; accordingly, they can be deconstructed and reconceptualized in order to demonstrate the ways in which foreignness is simultaneously opposed to and constitutive of sovereignty.

The artificiality of the social contract does not necessarily mean that it is arbitrary. Indeed, Hobbes, Locke, and Rousseau determine the terms of the social contract based on their respective understanding of the characteristics of men in their "natural state." Be that as it may, if the contract is artificial, then disobedience is always possible because a different set of laws, conventions, and rights can always be proffered to challenge sovereign legitimacy. Most simply, artificial sovereignty is always vulnerable. In this respect, positing the artificiality of sovereignty is a risk that all three theorists are compelled to assume. Hobbes, for example, insists the artificial social contract establishes sovereign legitimacy by explaining how and why individual men leave the violent state of nature in exchange for the sovereign protection of each and all. For his part, Locke found that the natural right to execute the law of nature leads to the untenable inconveniences of the state of war; thus, this right has to be transferred through an artificial contract. Because this transfer of right is consensual, the result is a legitimate sovereign umpire. Finally, Rousseau adopts the social contract as a mechanism for justifying and legitimating the transformation of mankind from a natural to a morally free being.

In order to counter the vulnerability that accompanies sovereign artificiality, the explicit approach undertaken by all three theorists is to detail the qualities and characteristics that confer legitimacy upon the sovereign. While the specific qualities each theorist assigns to sovereignty may sometimes vary (e.g. Hobbes' sovereign has the right to take private property while Locke's sovereign does not), for each theorist the sovereign is legitimate only as long as it can protect the people as a whole. In exchange, individual subjects have a legal and moral duty to obey, thereby severely restricting the right of any individual to (legitimately) disobey the sovereign. In short, the vulnerability constitutive of artificial sovereignty is mitigated by conceiving of sovereignty in such a way so as to guarantee that it never fails in its sole obligation to protect its people.

Simultaneously, to eliminate the vulnerabilities of the artificial sovereign, a subtle—even somewhat deceptive—tactic is undertaken to naturalize the artificial sovereign. By conceiving of sovereignty as an instantiation of the fixed, unyielding permanency of nature and not merely a convention, the question of legitimacy is effectively disappeared. If sovereignty is natural, then so, too, are the rights and powers ascribed to the sovereign. Its indivisibility cannot be challenged; its power over life and death is absolute; its pure rationality is indubitable, etc. Thus, those who would claim that the sovereign is unjust and its powers arbitrary are effectively silenced. Through the naturalization of artificial sovereignty, the sovereign becomes immune to critique, dissent, and sedition.[2] In short, sovereignty is inexorable and irresistible, and in order to demonstrate why this is so, an examination of the ways in which Hobbes, Locke, and Rousseau naturalize artificial sovereignty is required.

Hobbes' naturalization of artificial sovereignty

The claim that Hobbes seeks to naturalize sovereignty appears dubitable upon initial examination. Hobbes is not only explicit about the artificiality of political sovereignty, but his theory of sovereignty depends upon this artificiality. He immediately begins by stating that the Leviathan is an automaton. Like an artificial time-keeping device created by the hands of man with its springs, locks, strings, etc., mankind's imitation of divine creation is the Leviathan composed of laws, magistrates, officers, rewards and punishments, and, most importantly, the sovereign or the artificial soul of the Leviathan. The power of mimesis is the basis for a seemingly straightforward claim, namely that mankind's rational capacity to imitate God's creation of nature results in artifice or the creation of those things which do not exist by nature. Yet, creation in this context is misleading. Jacques Derrida's cautionary note is worth quoting: "The art of this living being, man, imitates the art of God but, being unable to *create*, *fabricates* and, being unable to engender a natural animal, fabricates an artificial animal" (2009, 26, original emphasis). Despite its similarity to man down to the smallest detail, Hobbes' absolute sovereign is not natural; rather, as Derrida explains, "It is the product of a mechanical artificiality" (2009, 27).

Hobbes attempts to establish the legitimacy of the artificial sovereign through the development of a rigorous science of politics that would counter the instability and divisiveness of appeals to God, God's natural law, and Aristotelian teleology as justifications for civil dissent. By excising these natural and supernatural appeals, sovereignty is conceived of as a pure artificiality that is nevertheless legitimate because man authorizes it through his assent to the social contract. Moreover, artificial sovereignty is not arbitrary because the very terms of the contract and the specific qualities of the sovereign are rationally deduced by Hobbes' scientific account of natural man. In these respects, Hobbes demonstrates not only why he believes sovereignty is best conceived of as artificial but also the necessity of sovereign artificiality.[3]

Nevertheless, in the very same moment that Hobbes insists upon the distinction between nature/artifice with regard to the sovereign, he also obscures this distinction. From the very first sentence of a work dedicated to justifying the legitimacy of the sovereign *qua* artificial, the legitimacy of the Leviathan rests upon the claim that it comes into existence through mimesis or imitation of the divine, thereby introducing a deep ambiguity that muddles the distinction between fabrication and creation. On the one hand, human creation (fabrication) is pure artifice; on the other hand, mimesis suggests that man's creation imitates or approximates God's art, which is nothing more than the creation of nature. This ambiguity is reinforced when Hobbes analogizes the artificial Leviathan to the natural, human body. The Leviathan, whose primary function is the preservation and protection of its subjects, must be fabricated to be greater than, stronger than, and more powerful than natural man. Simultaneously, the "larger than life," monstrous, automated machine "must also extend, mime, imitate, even reproduce down to the details the living creature that produces it" (Derrida 2009, 28). In other words, the Leviathan is both greater than and an exact replica of the natural human body whose primary function, like that of the individual man, is also self-preservation. The Leviathan is simultaneously artificial and natural, an outgrowth of each individual's will to survive. Thus, paradoxically, the "political discourse of Hobbes is vitalist, organicist, finalist, *and* mechanicist" (Derrida 2009, 28, original emphasis).

This double-edged theorization of sovereignty is no mere oversight; instead, Hobbes is engaged in a strategic sleight of hand to establish the legitimacy of artificial sovereignty (which cannot be legitimately disobeyed so long as it protects its subjects) by naturalizing this artificiality (whereby disobedience is always illegitimate insofar as sovereignty is a natural and inexorable creation where questions of legitimacy have no place). The result is an unusual contradiction. Hobbes' political science rejects the Aristotelian idea that man is by nature a political animal while simultaneously suggesting that political society—epitomized by the figure of the sovereign, the soul of the Leviathan—is, in some sense, identical to what is natural. If political sovereignty is natural or identical to what is natural, then mankind is, it seems, a political animal because there is no alternative to political society. In this respect, to remain in or be cast back into the state of nature is not, in actuality, an option; instead, it is simply a euphemism for certain death at the hand of the sovereign.

Because Hobbes is explicit in his claim that the sovereign is artificial, perhaps I am simply over-stating my case or, worse, guilty of an interpretive error. After all, Hobbes is simply *analogizing* the state to a physical body while emphasizing the role of imitative capacity of reason distinctive of mankind. This is a legitimate concern, since Hobbes' analogy does, in fact, distance political sovereignty from the natural. Nevertheless, my claim is not that Hobbes argues that political sovereignty *is* natural; instead, I am suggesting that in order to defend against the vulnerability of its artificiality (namely its impermanence, mortality, and the perceived arbitrariness of conventional laws), Hobbes' analogy comparing the sovereign to a physical body performs two contradictory functions: (1) it explicitly distances sovereignty from nature *and* (2) implicitly suggests that the qualities of the sovereign share a similarity, likeness, resemblance, semblance, and effective identicality to God's highest natural creation, i.e., man. In this respect, sovereignty is naturalized or conceived of as natural or identical to nature in order to justify the perpetual "Subjection" (Hobbes [1651] 1985, 230) of individuals by grounding absolute sovereign rule and legitimacy in the inexorability and unyielding permanency of nature itself.

Hobbes provides further evidence for this interpretation in several moments throughout *Leviathan*. First, the rights of the sovereign dictated by the terms of the social contract (the absolute power to punish disobedience, establish the law, take property, decide disputes, determine facts, etc.) are themselves derived from men's natural rights. It is important to note, once again, that Hobbes criticizes earlier theorists for conflating natural law (*Lex Naturalis*) and natural right (*Ius Naturale*). Natural right is simply a scientific term for Hobbes with no political or moral significance. Natural right is identical to the liberty or the power one possesses to secure self-preservation. In this sense, man has a natural right to everything in the state of nature, and this natural right results in a perpetually violent and fearful state that makes self-preservation effectively impossible. By contrast, while rejecting traditional conceptualizations of *natural law*, Hobbes does posit one basic *law of nature*, which demands that men obey the dictates of reason that proclaim that each performs those actions necessary to guarantee self-preservation by seeking peace. Thus, the law of nature dictates to men that they agree to mutually give up, via an artificial contract, their natural right to everything (a portion of their liberty).

By differentiating between natural law and natural right, Hobbes creates a path out of the state of nature through the fabrication of a sovereign empowered to enforce men's contracts. The contract among men that produces the artificial sovereign possessed of certain rights is nothing more than the "mutuall transferring of Right" (Hobbes [1651] 1985, 192). Men in the state of nature do not simply transfer their natural right to the sovereign; instead, they mutually agree among themselves to give up their right to everything. At the same time, men also agree to establish a sovereign empowered to enforce their agreements, since covenants and contracts "without the Sword, are but Words" ([1651] 1985, 223). In this sense, sovereignty is artificial and the rights of the sovereign are artificial rights, since they are simply conventions that men agree upon. Nevertheless, Hobbes' notion of "sovereign right" is a strategic one which distorts the distinction between the natural and the artificial, leaving open the question to what extent the sovereign is empowered to enforce the contract among men.

Hobbes' well-known answer is that the sovereign possesses absolute power to enforce this contract. Put another way, the sovereign possesses the right to everything. In this way, the artificial sovereign right of absolute power is identical to the natural right that individual men in the state of nature have abdicated.[4] Even though individual men do not transfer their natural right directly to the sovereign, the sovereign right of absolute power is grounded in, derived from, determined by, and effectively identical to nature, i.e., each man's natural right. The result is a conceptualization of sovereign right that is both artificial and natural. On the one hand, the artificiality of Hobbes' sovereign allows him to break from the Aristotelian influences of his Scholastic predecessors and contemporaries. On the other hand, Hobbes' notion of sovereign right, which is identical to mankind's natural right, erases or covers over sovereign artificiality at the very moment that it is posited in order to guard against the vulnerability of its artificiality.

The naturalization of artificial sovereignty is implied in yet another way. For Hobbes, the sovereign is the representative of the people, which is to say that the sovereign *represents* individual men as a unified whole or single, inviolable body politic. Yet, to defend against those who would resist the notion that absolute power is a sovereign right necessary for the protection of the body politic, Hobbes, once again, turns to the analogy between the representative sovereign and the human body; however, the analogy changes slightly from its first instantiation. Instead of comparing the artificial sovereign to a human body, Hobbes analogizes a sovereign who lacks absolute power to the offspring of sickly parents. As noted, the sovereign who lacks absolute power is weak, prone to disease and deformity, lacking in permanency, subject to corruption, vulnerable, etc. Thus, Hobbes argues that this "vicious conception" and "defectuous procreation" must be purged if the sovereign is to protect its subjects. Hobbes purges the "vicious conception" of a weak sovereign by conceiving of absolute power as an originary and constitutive feature of legitimate sovereignty.

On its surface, this analogy is simply used to explain the primary internal weakness of the sovereign. For Hobbes, if the sovereign lacks absolute power, it cannot guarantee the protection of its subjects. Nevertheless, I maintain that this version of the analogy goes further by obscuring the artificiality of sovereignty and obfuscating the distinction between fabrication and creation. Above I stated that the artificial sovereign resembles or is a semblance of the human body. I then argued that this resemblance or semblance naturalizes the artificial sovereign insofar as resemblance or semblance suggests that the sovereign is identical to the natural, living human body; however, if we allow that the artificial sovereign simply bears a resemblance to the human body but is not identical to it, then this first analogy to the human body fails to ground the claim that Hobbes seeks to naturalize the sovereign. On its own, this objection might have merit, but it loses its force when this first analogy to the body is read alongside Hobbes' analogy of the birth of sovereignty. By extension of the claim regarding weak sovereignty being an offspring of sickly parents, Hobbes' absolute sovereign is also born but to healthy, not sickly, parents. Whether weak or strong, Hobbes' absolute, legitimate sovereign is born, and through this analogy to biology (to creation and procreation not fabrication), Hobbes' sovereign is as natural as mankind. In this respect, the absolute, legitimate sovereign is *conceived* of as an artificial thing that is posited and simultaneously *conceived*, naturally, as is the child in the womb. If Hobbes' sovereign is mankind's offspring, then it is not a fabrication at all; instead, it is a natural creation. In this way, the legitimacy of Hobbes' absolute sovereign is once again achieved through an analogy that naturalizes sovereign artificiality.

Finally, Hobbes insists that the absolute sovereign approximates the divine. Even in this moment, Hobbes is explicit that the sovereign is something artificial. He insists that "nothing can be immortal, which mortals make" ([1651] 1985, 363) and that any weakness of the sovereign, such as the lack of absolute power, is not the "fault of men, as they are the *Matter*; but as they are the *Maker*, and orderers of them [sovereign institutions]" ([1651] 1985, 363, original emphasis). Nevertheless, the sovereign can achieve human immortality or perpetuity (if it is well-designed/born from healthy parents) because it can "live, as long as Man-kind, or as the Lawes of Nature, or as Justice it selfe which gives them [the sovereign institutions] life" ([1651] 1985, 363). Perpetuity, pre-eminence, omnipotence, inviolability, etc. are all qualities of the sovereign that allow Hobbes to claim that the Leviathan is a "mortal God."

By conceptualizing the sovereign as a "mortal god," Hobbes once again obscures the artificial nature of the sovereign. Insofar as it is divine, the sovereign itself is not natural, but the decrees, actions, rights, and decisions of the "mortal god" are not purely artificial either; instead, they are indistinguishable from divine acts of creation because the artificial sovereign approximates God, the source of nature and natural creation as such. In this way, the dyads of maker/made and artificial/natural are undermined. Mankind makes the artificial sovereign, but the divine/artificial sovereign is that thing which determines, absolutely, the very conditions according to which men must live. Most simply, the legitimate artificial sovereign not only protects man, but insofar as it is divine it also creates men as they are, namely members of political society (even as Hobbes resolutely refuses to conceive of men as political animals). Accordingly, sovereign artificiality is, once again, naturalized, resulting in yet another instance of eliminating sovereign vulnerability by grounding its legitimacy in that which gives men their lives, namely nature or the divine creation of nature.

While I have argued that Hobbes' naturalization of the artificiality of the sovereign functions to eliminate the vulnerabilities of artificiality, it is important to note that Hobbes' sovereign is *simultaneously* artificial, natural, and divine. Despite his best efforts to construct an inviolable, whole, and absolute sovereign, Hobbes' sovereign is never what it *is* as it shifts and oscillates between the artificial, natural, and divine. In a word, Hobbes' sovereign lacks self-identicality. While Hobbes' naturalization of artificial sovereignty is intended to establish the self-identicality of sovereignty eliminative of difference, the opposite result is achieved, namely a perpetual substitution and supplementation of foreignness as such (the simultaneity of the three ostensibly incommensurate realms of the artificial, natural, and divine), which ultimately serves as sovereignty's ground and foundation. The sovereign is foreign to itself, i.e., foreignness is that radical element that perpetually opens and reopens sovereign identity conceived of along the lines of self-containment, hermetic closure, wholeness, and inviolability. If this is so and sovereignty lacks self-identicality, then it is always already vulnerable in the sense that foreignness or difference is not something to be guarded against or excluded, but rather an originary and constitutive element of sovereignty as such. As Derrida notes, "every time one puts an oppositional limit in question [*physis*/*nomos*/*thesis*, natural/divine, etc.] far from concluding there is identity, we must on the contrary multiply attention to differences" (2009, 15–16, original emphasis). I take heed of Derrida's recommendation regarding oppositional limits and the ramifications of the foreignness constitutive of sovereignty, but before developing these themes, it is useful to first detail another instance of the naturalization of artificiality within the social contract tradition by turning to Locke.

Locke's naturalization of artificial sovereignty

Locke recognizes that when political sovereignty is conceived of on the model of an artificial contract, it lacks the immutability, inexorability, and necessity of nature. Thus, it remains vulnerable to alternative orderings of political power and competing *nomoi*—none more dangerous to Locke than absolute monarchy. He insists that absolute monarchy is not a form of civil society because its subjects "are still in the state of nature" (Locke 2003, *Second Treatise* §90, 138) insofar as they are subject to the private judgments and execution of the law by the monarch and, as such, have no right of common appeal. On this formulation, Locke's strict division between nature and civil society becomes evident. While the artificiality of political sovereignty might make it vulnerable to competing *nomoi*, this is the lesser of two evils. The greater evil is the coming to power of an absolute monarch, i.e., the perpetuation of the state of nature. By positing the artificiality of the social contract, Locke is able to justify how political power can be legitimate without appeals to God or nature as well as how it is distinct from the paternal power operative in nature.

Locke's insistence upon the artificiality of legitimate political sovereignty is derived from his rejection of Robert Filmer's arguments for political power. Through the claim that political power is best understood as the natural authority of the father over his children, Filmer defends the divine right of kings and the legitimacy of political authority rooted in patrilineal descent from God's creation of Adam to the time of Filmer's writings. Most generally, Filmer makes no distinction between paternal and political power. The rule of the king over his subjects is identical to the rule of a father over his children. Thus, in order to understand why Locke conceives of sovereignty as an artificiality distinct from nature (which will then clear the way for understanding how Locke also naturalizes the artificiality of sovereignty) requires a brief analysis of his critique of Filmer's once-influential formulation of political power.

The central feature of Filmer's arguments is that the legitimacy of paternal/royal authority comes directly from God and the law of nature. Adam is the one true founding father whose right to rule is derived from his divine creation and his natural or biological role as the original progenitor of all mankind. Just as Adam was completely subjected to God's authority, men are not born free; rather, as childhood proves, they are subjected to the rule of the father, which is simply another way to express "unlimited and unlimitable" (Locke 2003, *First Treatise* §6, 9) royal authority whose origins and powers approach the divine. The king, therefore, legitimately rules his subjects as a father rules his children. Against those who would claim that both parents have authority over their children, Filmer insists it is only Adam who has absolute power over his offspring and posterity, since Eve's actions in the garden make her subservient to him.[5] This lesson teaches us that all wives will be subservient to their husbands for perpetuity. Accordingly, Adam's absolute and unlimited rule extends to his wife, children, and the entire household.[6]

God also grants to Adam, as his highest creation, dominion and the right to rule the earth and all of its creatures. According to Filmer, Adam's dominion over the earth and all of its creatures *includes* his children and posterity (all of mankind). This divine right of governance is, for Filmer, derived from nature and biology as Adam, the father, has a duty imposed by God to reproduce and populate the earth. Adam is, therefore, the *de facto* governor or monarch of the world, and his paternal/royal authority granted as a gift from God is passed on successively to his male heirs. By insisting upon the divine/natural/biological foundation for power, whereby the father is absolute ruler over his children, Filmer extends the absolute and unlimited private, paternal power of the father over his children in nature to the monarch of the public sphere. In Ruth Grant's summation: "all authority is paternal authority. Just as the Lord governs the world as the Heavenly Father of us all, the king governs his subjects, and the earthly father governs his household" (2003, 288).

Despite the brevity of this summation, it is sufficient to highlight the main issues Locke addresses in order to draw a distinction between paternal/natural power and political/artificial power. Locke begins by claiming that the begetting of a child by a father provides no natural right of rule. If it is granted that creation does assign the creator a natural right to rule, then, for Locke, fatherhood provides no natural right to rule over children, since each man's being is given by God, not his father. He writes, "He [God] is king, because he is indeed maker of us all, which no parents can pretend to be of their children" (Locke 2003, *First Treatise* §53, 36). Accordingly, if a father begetting his child provides no right to rule, then Filmer's more ambitious claim that paternal power is the model for political rule already appears dubitable.

By contrast, Locke's foundational claim that all men are born free and equal challenges Filmer's basic premise that the subjection of the child to the father at birth means that men are neither free nor equal. That being the case, Locke does not fail to recognize that "parents have a sort of rule and jurisdiction over them [their children] when they come into the world" (2003, *Second Treatise* §55, 123). However, Locke insists that the rule of a parent is not political rule. Indeed, the subjection of children to parents is temporary and weakens steadily as the child ages and his reason develops. Locke writes, "The power, then, that parents have over their children arises from that duty which is incumbent upon them, to take care of their offspring during the imperfect state of childhood. To inform the mind, and govern the actions of their ignorant nonage, till reason shall take its place" (2003, *Second Treatise* §58, 124). The child eventually matures and gains what is proper to every man: "that equal right that every man hath to his natural freedom, without being subjected to the will or authority of any other man" (2003, *Second Treatise* §54, 123). In brief, Locke's conceptualization of mankind's natural qualities requires that a distinction be made between paternal and political power, a distinction that will ultimately present insurmountable problems for Filmer's position.

Insofar as Filmer does not recognize mankind's natural freedom and equality, he does not and cannot make this distinction between paternal and political power. Yet, for Locke, if paternal power is legitimate political power, the result is nothing more than the continuation of the state of nature or, alternatively, the vicissitudes of irrationality and lawlessness that reduce mankind to the bestial violence co-extensive with nature. Because paternal power is indistinguishable from private, partial, and particular judgments, it grants the sovereign (in this case a monarch) the absolute right and authority to dispose of the life, liberty, and estate (property) of his subjects as he sees fit. Paternal power is the power of the beast and of nature—the force of the stronger—which, paradoxically, de-natures mankind by stripping him of the natural sovereign rule over himself as a free and equal man with property in his person. To counter this apolitical de-naturing of mankind and vision of sovereign right grounded in the bestial irrationality and violent force, Locke differentiates between paternal power and political power by positing the artificiality of political sovereignty.

To establish the artificiality and, hence, legitimacy, of sovereign political power, Locke emphatically rejects Filmer's claim that God gave Adam private dominion over the earth and its creatures, including mankind. Instead, through a close textual reading of the story of Genesis, Locke concludes that God's donation of the earth and its creatures is a "right in common with all mankind" (2003, *First Treatise* §24, 20). If all men are by nature free and equal (this is an indisputable premise for Locke that Filmer does not grant), then each has the right to appropriate the earth in order to survive. Therefore, Locke's notion of a commons performs two functions. First, it effectively undermines the idea that Adam's progeny (and all children of any father) are mere property to be disposed of as the owner/father/king sees fit. God's donation of the earth and its creatures as a common right of all explicitly rules out the right of a father to rule politically over his child. Mankind has dominion in common over the "lesser creatures" and not his fellow men. Second, if the earth is held as a common right of all and each man *qua* free and equal being has the right to appropriate the commons, then the commons and private property are not mutually exclusive. This is critically important for Locke, since the peaceful sharing of the commons is a central feature of the state of nature while the preservation of property is the sole end of legitimate political sovereignty. Paternal and political power, therefore, must be distinct, since dominion over the earth is a right in common with all men and not a divine or natural (patrilineal) right of kings to govern men based on the assumption that God has given private dominion over the earth and all of its creatures to Adam and his heirs.

Enough has been said to show why and how Locke differentiates between paternal and political power. That said, given his sustained critique of Filmer and his insistence upon the distinction between paternal (natural) and political (artificial) power in the *First Treatise*, it is odd that Locke's analysis of property in the *Second Treatise* implicitly endorses the naturalization of artificial sovereignty. As with Hobbes, I am not suggesting that Locke explicitly conceives of political sovereignty as natural; instead, the naturalization of artificial sovereignty is *at once* a subtle rhetorical maneuver to obscure the vulnerability of its artificiality *and* an instance in which Locke's conceptualization of the self-identicality and inviolability of sovereignty is challenged insofar as the legitimacy and authority of artificial sovereignty is secured, paradoxically, through its simultaneous distance from and proximity to nature. Despite his stated claims, Locke's conceptualization of sovereignty is simultaneously artificial and natural. To develop this point, three central features of Locke's conceptualization of property and its link to the legitimacy of civil society must be detailed. First, the artificial commonwealth secures its legitimacy by resembling the state of nature; second, the artificial commonwealth secures its legitimacy by preserving the right for revolution when man's property, established in nature, is not preserved; third, the artificial commonwealth secures its legitimacy by restoring and reassembling (as a unified, inviolable, sovereign public whole) mankind's lost self-identicality and natural sovereignty.

A brief review of Locke's conceptualization of property is required to explain his naturalization of artificial sovereignty. Mankind's God-given, natural reason reveals that each man is equal insofar as he is free, and his freedom is best understood as a fence that protects the property that each man has in his person. Reason also reveals that by mixing the labor of his body (both the body and its labor are the property of each man) with the land (which is held in common by all men), each individual man transforms what was once held in common into private property without the consent of other men. For Locke, no consent is required to appropriate the commons as private property, since, through a man's labor, he "added something to them [the commons] more than nature" (2003, *Second Treatise* §28, 112) which is held in common. Moreover, if consent were needed for every appropriation of the commons, mankind could not survive and the commons would be useless. If consent is not required to appropriate the commons, then private property is best understood as a pre-political right to life, liberty, and estate that reason reveals is a common right shared by all men. As long as men consult their reason, they recognize this natural condition and live peacefully together in the pre-political state of nature.

If mankind followed his reason, there would be no need for civil society, since there is no threat to pre-political property (freedom, body, labor, life, estate). Of course, mankind does not always consult his reason. As such, he must give up his individual sovereign right to execute the law of nature against its transgressors (which results in the divisiveness and partiality of private judgments and irrational, passionate self-love) to an artificial sovereign—established by consent to the social contract—that is empowered to meet the end of the preservation of property. Counter-intuitively, the artificial sovereign and political society only come into being to preserve that which is natural and pre-political, namely mankind's body, his sweat and labor, the earth he has appropriated, etc.

The most stable political society is the one least vulnerable to dissent and revolt, and, ideally, political stability is achieved through the legitimacy of the sovereign. On the one hand, as discussed, Locke's sovereign is explicitly artificial, and its legitimacy depends upon its distance from nature. On the other hand, for Locke, the legitimacy of the artificial sovereign is premised upon preserving the original law of nature, i.e., the law that regulates the private interests and property of pre-political men. Put differently, the legitimacy of the artificial sovereign is achieved only when it effectively resembles the state of nature before its devolution into a state of war. Thus, Locke's conceptualization of property and emphasis upon the body points to the naturalization of artificial sovereignty insofar as sovereign legitimacy is premised upon its artificiality *and* to what extent it is able to resemble and preserve the pre-political state of nature.

Be that as it may, insofar as sovereignty lacks the inexorability and necessity of nature or the divine, Locke's artificial sovereignty remains vulnerable to alternative political orderings. For Locke, the most-fearful and illegitimate alternative political ordering is absolute monarchy, which, as argued, is simply a continuation of the state of nature, the rule of a paternal power that de-natures mankind. Locke's insistence upon the artificiality of sovereignty guards against this concern. Moreover, it also seems to cast doubt on my claim that Locke's conceptualization of property implicitly naturalizes artificial sovereignty, since naturalizing sovereignty would presumably open the door to the legitimacy of absolutism. However, the opposite is, in fact, the case. The naturalization of artificial sovereignty actually functions to buttress Locke's arguments against absolute monarchy (thereby excising nature from sovereignty) by providing a justification for mankind's political right to resist the sovereign that fails to preserve property (thereby including nature *qua* property within his conceptualization of legitimate sovereignty) through revolution.

Obedience to the sovereign is only owed when it protects its subjects. For Locke, the artificial sovereign protects its subjects only by preserving their property. Hence, the legitimacy of the artificial sovereign depends upon protecting and preserving mankind's natural right to property. The failure of the sovereign to preserve property makes the sovereign illegitimate; men are, therefore, permitted to resist the sovereign who fails to preserve property through revolution. Accordingly, the artificiality of sovereignty is only vulnerable to revolution and alternative political orderings when it fails to preserve or infringes upon mankind's property guaranteed to him by nature. The more closely aligned the artificial sovereign commonwealth is—or appears to be (i.e., resembles)—the natural condition and rights of men, the less vulnerable it becomes to legitimate forms of revolution. If this is so, then the naturalization of artificial sovereignty guards against the vulnerability of its artificiality by linking its legitimacy to the preservation of pre-political and natural property.

The naturalization of artificial sovereignty secures the legitimacy of artificial sovereignty through its resemblance to the state of nature before its devolution into the state of war and protecting natural right to property, which, when threatened, serves to reinforce the political right of revolution. At the same time, its legitimacy is also secured in yet another way, namely through the reassembly (as a unified, inviolable, public body) of the individual man who has lost his self-identicality and natural sovereignty in the transition from nature into political society. As noted, mankind's natural capacity for reason structures the normative space of the state of nature. Reason dictates that each man's natural freedom and equality allows all to execute the law of nature to punish its transgressors. These judgments ought to be made according to reason, i.e., in proportion to the crime. However, because mankind is often guided by self-love, he is led astray from the proportionate, objective, and reasonable execution of the law. The state of nature quickly devolves into a state of war wherein reason is replaced by the arbitrary, passionate, private, divisive, and ultimately irrational execution of the law of nature. Locke's state of war is a place of fear—not only of physical insecurity but also the fear of mankind's foreignness to himself, his loss of self-identicality, his irrationality that makes him indistinguishable from the violent and noxious beast.

Alternatively, the loss of self-identicality can be understood as mankind giving up his natural, individual sovereignty. Because each man has property in his person, he is the "master of himself" (Locke 2003, *Second Treatise* §44, 119). In short, he is sovereign, and as sovereign, each man possesses the right to execute the law of nature by punishing its transgressors. However, the inconveniences of the state of war require that each man consent to give up his sovereign right to execute the law of nature to an artificial sovereign. Thus, for Locke, political society only comes into being when all men "resign it [their sovereign to execute the law of nature] to the public" (2003, *Second Treatise* §89, 138). The purpose of the artificial sovereign is to preserve its members' property, and another way to express this same sentiment is that the artificial sovereign—the public umpire—is a substitute for its members' loss of individual sovereignty.

Hobbes expended a great deal of intellectual effort in order to demonstrate that unity, inviolability, self-identicality, power, and sovereignty once assigned to the individual body were replicable in political society. Locke does not go to the same extremes, but he is, nevertheless, concerned with the very same problem. He writes: "That which makes the community, and brings men out of the loose state of nature into *one politic society*, is the agreement which every one has with the rest to *incorporate*, and *act as one body*, and so be *one distinct commonwealth*" (Locke 2003, *Second Treatise* §211, 193, my emphasis). For Locke, as much as for Hobbes, the naturalization of artificial sovereignty achieved by analogy to the human body is an attempt to thwart the greatest threat to civil society, namely its failure to act as a single, unified, inviolable, and self-identical, sovereign whole.

While Locke occasionally relies upon analogies to a unified body, the naturalization of artificial sovereignty is more readily apparent in his conceptualization of legitimate sovereignty. Natural, individual sovereignty is epitomized by the right to execute the law of nature. To execute the law well requires reason, which governs the passions and the will. Locke states: "The freedom then of man, and liberty of acting according to his own will, is grounded on his having reason, which is able to instruct him in that law he is to govern himself by, and make him know how far he is left to the freedom of his own will"

(2003, *Second Treatise*, §63, 126). Whether understood as man is in the state of nature, a child, or anyone else who lacks—or is deemed to lack—a fully developed capacity for reason, irrationality points to an imperfect state or developmental phase in which mankind is foreign to himself, lacking in self-identicality, self-mastery, and, therefore, not sovereign. Reason, in this way, is the natural basis of individual sovereignty insofar as it binds the body, labor, life, and estate into a self-identical, unified individual, a sovereign property protected by a fence of freedom.

Yet, self-love dims mankind's reason; the result is the irrationality, privation, and violence of the state of war that drives mankind into political society. Therefore, the political sovereign (the pure rationality of the neutral umpire and "judge on earth") is an artificial construction which reassembles natural man by repairing the loss of natural reason upon which mankind's self-identicality and individual sovereignty is structured. The legitimate sovereign is a rational umpire whose objectivity and proportional judgment of the law unifies individual men into an inviolable, self-identical, public whole. While sovereignty is absolutely artificial, its naturalization occurs through Locke's recovery of natural reason as the basis upon which its legitimacy depends. In other words, artificial sovereignty appears natural insofar as it is able to reassemble and recreate natural mankind's sovereignty, although this sovereignty is no longer individual or natural; instead, it is a public and artificial body composed of individuals whose consent to a rational sovereign forges a unified, self-identical, and sovereign commonwealth.

While Locke's commonwealth is explicitly conceived of as an artificiality, his conceptualization of property suggests that he, nevertheless, relies upon the naturalization of artificial sovereignty in order to provide a justification for eliminating the irrationality and privation that supposedly threaten the unity, self-identicality, and wholeness of sovereignty. The result is a strange political hybrid in which the sovereign is never what it claims to be (i.e., a self-identical, inviolable whole), but rather a heterogeneous, non-self-identical entity that is foreign to itself insofar as it is simultaneously artificial and natural. Rather than being opposed to one another, nature and artifice operate in a perpetual substitution and supplementation in order to establish both the legitimacy and permanency of sovereign authority. The heterogeneousness of sovereignty, its lack of self-identicality, suggests, as it did in Hobbes, that foreignness is not simply something to be guarded against or excluded; instead, foreignness is constitutive of sovereignty as such even as these perpetual oscillations and supplementations are obscured by Locke in order to evade confronting the conceptual and political danger of an originary and ineliminable vulnerability of the sovereign to the foreign.

Rousseau's naturalization of artificial sovereignty

Like Hobbes, Rousseau explicitly rejects the idea that political sovereignty is natural. There is no general will in Rousseau's state of nature. Rather, civilized, political society is the result of the dialectical unfolding of reason and the passions which eventuates in men producing artificial contracts to institute a sovereign general will that protects men as a whole by eliminating the "obstacles to their preservation" (Hobbes [1762] 1968, 59), i.e., the partiality, self-interest, and egocentrism of *amour propre* which exemplify the final stages of the state of nature. Although Rousseau rejects Hobbes' absolutism, he shares with Hobbes the concern that artificial sovereignty is vulnerable to counter-claims of sovereign legitimacy.[7] For Rousseau, sovereignty conceptualized as a general will defends against those individuals or groups who would charge that the sovereign is illegitimate because it fails to perform its primary function of protecting each of its members. In this way, the sovereign is empowered to act on behalf of the whole even when doing so is at odds with individual wills and the collective will of all.

Following the logic of the sovereign general will, the primary characteristics, qualities, and rights of the sovereign requisite for establishing its inviolability and unity include its inalienability, indivisibility, self-identical homogeneity, inability to err, the right over life and death, etc. As in Hobbes, these sovereign characteristics and rights are made meaningful through comparisons and analogies to the human body. For example, the very idea of a general will suggests that the artificial body politic is best understood as a human body whose will guides it to perform certain actions for the sake of the whole. Rousseau explicitly states as much when he claims: "As soon as the multitude is united thus in a single body, no one can injure any one of its members without attacking the whole, still less injure the whole without each member feeling it" ([1762] 1968, 63). Rousseau's comparisons and analogies between the individual, natural human body and the artificial body politic all function, as they do in Hobbes' work, to buttress his positing of the legitimacy of artificial sovereignty by grounding it in nature or what resembles and mimics the natural.

While these comparisons and analogies to the human body are important, Rousseau also employs a more subtle approach to eliminate the vulnerability of artificial sovereignty. As discussed, Rousseau grounds the legitimacy of the sovereign general will in the presumed originary unanimity of a people. On the one hand, Rousseau's myth of originary unanimity is just another story, something posited and artificial, which compliments his conception of sovereignty as that which is forged through the social contract. On the other hand, this story acquires its force and appeal in another way, namely insofar as it is also presented as if it were a natural history. Rousseau states that people become a people only because "there has been on at least one occasion unanimity" ([1762] 1968, 59). The locution "on at least one occasion" both suggests ("Once upon a time . . .") and moves beyond myth by pointing to an identifiable—though somehow forgotten or lost—past in human history. More emphatically, the claim regarding originary unanimity is an attempt to excavate the natural origins of the sovereign general will.

I have already argued that Rousseau's myth of originary unanimity serves to cleanse individual men of the psychological violence of their transformation from natural to autonomous beings. This cleansing of mankind's deepest trauma is achieved when men become subjects of a legitimate sovereign who guarantees their protection by making them self-identical once again, this time as a whole and indivisible people. As noted, it is only after establishing the legitimacy of the artificial sovereign that Rousseau then proceeds to detail the terms of the social contract and the qualities and rights of the sovereign. However, if this mythical story is also a natural history, then sovereignty is not only legitimate because it symbolically reunifies men into an inviolable, self-identical whole, but also because sovereignty itself is natural.

People do not become a people through the artificial social contract. The social contract simply institutes, through convention, the particular government that will rule over a people (monarchy, aristocracy, democracy, etc.). While the juridical, executive, and legislative features of sovereignty are formalized through the social contract, sovereignty itself appears to precede the social contract, as evidenced by the originary unanimity among men. Sovereignty comes into being when people (with their individual or collective wills) become a people (unified through a general will), and this pre-political—even natural—event is the "real foundation of society" (Rousseau [1762] 1968, 59). Put differently, there can be no "common good nor be a *body politic*" ([1762] 1968, 58, my emphasis) unless individual men were, *before the advent of political society*, unanimous and unified, i.e., sovereign "on at least one occasion." Through the naturalization of sovereign artificiality, the legitimacy of the artificial sovereign is not secured arbitrarily through the qualities, characteristics, and rights that Rousseau ascribes to it, but rather through its foundation in nature itself. If this is the case, then the vulnerability of artificial sovereignty to claims that it is not legitimate are effectively eliminated. In short, Rousseau casts sovereignty as both artificial and natural in order to free himself to posit the rights and characteristics of the sovereign general will while simultaneously covering over its vulnerability as something merely posited by depicting sovereignty as natural and, therefore, a self-identical entity eliminative of all destabilizing ego, vanity, private interests, and destructive differences.

Against this reading, one might simply point to Rousseau's distinction between sovereignty and government. For Rousseau, the sovereign general will is always heterogeneous to the established government. The government can take any number of forms. With respect to the form of government instantiated in any particular state, Rousseau is explicit that the best form of government is that which is best suited to the natural conditions. For example, Rousseau argues that the number of magistrates "should be in inverse ration to the number of citizens" ([1762] 1968, 111). Accordingly, democracy is best suited to small states, aristocracy to medium-sized states, and monarchy to the largest states. Rousseau also notes that certain forms of government are more "voracious" ([1762] 1968, 124) based on the "distance between the people and the government" ([1762] 1968, 125). Therefore, monarchy is best suited to large, wealthy nations, aristocracy to nations of medium wealth and size, and democracy to poor and small nations.[8] Based on this claim, Rousseau insists that climate "necessitates" ([1762] 1968, 125) certain forms of government. For example, barren lands that provide only the barest essentials for survival can have no political society, since there are no resources or surplus to be returned to the state. In this respect, it appears as if Rousseau posits an ineliminable relationship between nature and forms of government.

Just as quickly, however, Rousseau claims that "the object of any political association ... [i.e., legitimate sovereignty, regardless of the form of government in place is a general will directed towards] ... the protection and the prosperity of its members" ([1762] 1968, 130). The legitimate sovereign protects its citizens according to the law established by the general will. If the government "usurps sovereignty" ([1762] 1968, 133) by ruling according to decree and not according to the law established by the general will, "the social pact is broken" (1968, 133). Citizens might be forced to obey, but they are not "morally obliged" ([1762] 1968, 133) to do so; the sovereign general will ceases to exist and revolution is justified.

Accordingly, sovereignty is simply the product of the artificial social contract, not something that precedes it. Alternatively, if sovereignty co-originates with the transformation of natural man to civilized man (an event crystallized by the forging of the social contract), then in what sense can it be argued that sovereignty precedes the social contract and the transformation of man?

The answer hinges on the very possibility for sovereign legitimacy. Because the sovereign is only legitimate if it protects the general will, we are retuned once again to the originary unanimity of a people, which is the condition of possibility for the social contract. As mentioned, those with more fertile lands can spread out and generate more wealth through their labor. Because of the great distances between them, they are less able to assemble and legislate, but they are more able to give over their surpluses to the government. Accordingly, this climate is best suited to a monarchy. While this example might simply appear to explain the connection between natural geography and the form of government that is most appropriate to such a land, Rousseau's claim that barren lands cannot sustain a government points to the relation between nature and sovereignty, not nature and government. It is not merely the case that barren lands cannot support a government because there is a shortage of resources; instead, if there can be no government, then barren lands are incapable of producing a sovereign general will—a people—which, ideally, is reflected in the form of government eventually established by the social contract. Most simply, in barren lands, there are only people, but not a people.

This does not mean that there are no forms of rule among individuals in barren lands, but these forms of rule are not sovereign. They are illegitimate insofar as they compel obedience through force no different from a husband or father over his family or the rule of a master over a slave. If nature (the barren land) determines whether or not people can become a people, then sovereignty itself must, in some sense, originate in nature. It is in this respect that the tale of originary unanimity can be read as a natural history which grounds sovereign legitimacy in something that precedes (nature) and/or exceeds (some form of legendary figure like Lycurgus or quasi-divine figure like the foreign lawgiver) its artificiality.

Originary unanimity naturalizes the legitimacy of sovereignty in other ways as well. The presupposition of originary unanimity explains how people become a people, which then, in turn, institutes a sovereign government through majority voting. Regardless of what type of regime is established through the social contract, Rousseau insists that "the gift itself [a people giving itself to a sovereign] is a civil act; it presupposes public deliberation" ([1762] 1968, 59). Through this claim, Rousseau astutely recognizes that at the founding of political society, there is rarely, if ever, unanimity. There are always those who will seek a different form of political organization, a fact that makes political sovereignty, in all its artificiality, vulnerable to destabilizing private interests and differences. Accordingly, Rousseau argues that *before* the sovereign state is artificially constituted, there is already a public dimension (a people). Without this pre-political, "proto-general will" originating in nature, it would be impossible for a people to willingly assent to being governed.[9] In this way, Rousseau suggests that beyond or in addition to the mythical or supernatural origins of legitimate political society, there is a natural basis for the sovereign general will, and it is by or in nature that "the law of majority-voting itself rests on a covenant, and implies that there has been on at least one occasion unanimity" ([1762] 1968, 59).[10]

Perhaps Rousseau is not positing sovereignty as natural, but rather attempting to capture the unifying spirit that accompanies successful revolutionary events. Undoubtedly, revolution divides an already extant people, but those who will soon come to power and replace the old guard are, in a sense, a unified group with a shared common purpose even if this new regime is not yet properly constituted as a sovereign people. In this way, originary unanimity serves two purposes. First, it diffuses the moral responsibility for the bloodshed and violence that accompany revolutionary acts across a population. Second, it acknowledges the divisiveness of founding and governance while keeping this destabilizing divisiveness at arm's length by emphasizing the originary unanimity that guides the transformation from a revolutionary faction to a sovereign people. In this sense, the story of originary unanimity is either mythical or historical (or both) but not, as I am claiming, a natural history of sovereignty.

This interpretation is compelling, but nevertheless incomplete. Even if one grants that Rousseau does not posit sovereignty as natural, the more general claim holds that he was keenly aware that the violence of founding and the destabilizing divisions ineliminable from political society could be mitigated by obscuring sovereignty's artificiality. Be that as it may, it *is* my contention that Rousseau's story of originary unanimity can also be read as a natural history, and this claim requires further justification. To do so, we must recall that originary unanimity is the foundation for the law of majority voting, which, alone, legitimates all forms of political sovereignty (democracy, monarchy, etc.). Rousseau suggests that central to all forms of artificial, sovereign governance brought into being through the social contract is a pre-political, democratic—even revolutionary—impulse which holds in reserve the possibility for resisting unjust governments whose rule diverges from and distorts the sovereign general will. This democratic impulse squares with the most general goal of *The Social Contract*, namely the positing of the conditions for an ideal democracy. But, in what sense is this democratic impulse underpinning sovereignty natural?

Mankind's transformation into a morally autonomous being rests upon each individual's membership within a "proto-general will" antecedent to artificial sovereignty. Rousseau's emphasis upon the originary unanimity of any sovereign people appears to suggest that mankind possesses or comes to possess through the dialectical unfolding of the passions and reason from nature to civilized, artificial society an innate or natural predisposition for democratic procedures and processes upon which all forms of artificial sovereign legitimacy are grounded. In a word, legitimate sovereignty is both artificially produced through the social contract (as Rousseau explicitly claims) and simultaneously dependent upon a natural democratic impulse that makes possible the formation of a proto-sovereign people capable of instituting the government best suited to reflect the sovereign general will of that people.[11]

While all men living under legitimate sovereign regimes have their natural liberty transformed into the moral freedom to obey a self-prescribed law, Rousseau, nevertheless, claims that "Freedom is not a fruit of every climate, and it is not therefore within the capacity of every people" ([1762] 1968, 124). In this instance, Rousseau's reference to freedom speaks directly to the dispositions and values of a specific people that make it best suited for one form of governance or another. Because freedom is a value and practice belonging to a given people, the originary unanimity requisite for establishing certain forms of government to act according to the agreed upon law is itself determined by natural geography and is different for different peoples. A climate that fosters freedom produces a people that are best suited to democracy while another natural environment produces a people who do not value freedom and are best suited to non-democratic forms of government. While the spark of a democratic impulse is shared by all, some peoples, it would seem, have the capacity for freedom while others do not.

While Rousseau attempts to explain this differentiated capacity for governance through natural geography, this natural description does something more than legitimate different forms of extant political regimes. On the one hand, Rousseau suggests that sovereignty is generic insofar as it is the same for all, namely a general will distinct from individual wills or the collective will of all, which can assume various forms of government. On the other hand, the very fact that a people comes into being according to specific values and capacities determined by geography and nature suggests that the artificial general will of a given people cannot be conceived of in abstraction from natural conditions. No further proof is needed, it seems, than the figure of the foreign lawgiver whose task is "to discover the rules of society that are best suited to nations" (Rousseau [1762] 1968, 84). In this regard, the foreign lawgiver does not arbitrarily establish the law of a people. To do so would render him a despot or sycophant. Rather, his unique, quasi-divine, mythical status is derived in part from his ability to dispassionately identify the shared dispositions, values, beliefs, experiences, and common purpose that anchors the "proto-general will" of a people before engineering the law and establishing the regime which "replace[s] the physical and independent existence we have all received from nature with a moral and communal existence" ([1762] 1968, 85).

The democratic impulse anchoring the originary unanimity of all peoples is never formally extinguished, thereby allowing Rousseau to preserve something like democratic dissent without endorsing anarchy. Nevertheless, it is by nature that the originary unanimity and unity of a homogeneous, self-identical people (with shared capacities and a common purpose, exclusive of all others) comes into being. The fact that a monarchy is not best suited to a democratic people demonstrates that certain forms of government are illegitimate precisely because they fail to adequately represent the general will of the people that precedes the form of government. Moreover, it is by nature that certain others lack the very *capacity* of freedom necessary to forge or become members of a democracy. If the local, natural conditions transform people into particular nations, then nature not only necessitates government as Rousseau explicitly claims, but it also shapes the "proto-general will" of a specific people, which, in turn, artificially constitutes the government best suited to its natural capacities.

Interestingly, however, Rousseau insists that democratic government is not natural. He writes, "In the strict sense of the term, there has never been a democracy, and there never will be. It is contrary to the *natural order* that the greater number should govern and the smaller number be governed" ([1762] 1968, 112, my emphasis). Moreover, the necessary conditions for a legitimate democracy are rarely, if ever, seen in practice (e.g., a small state where members can readily assemble, perfect homogeneity in the form of shared, even identical, manners and morals as a precondition for settling difficult issues without conflict, economic equality, etc.). For this reason, democracy among all forms of government is the most vulnerable to "civil war and internecine strife" ([1762] 1968, 113). Accordingly, Rousseau famously concludes that, "If there were a nation of Gods, it would govern itself democratically. A government so perfect is not suited to men" ([1762] 1968, 114).

While undoubtedly an expression of sincere doubt, Rousseau's claims regarding the unnaturalness and improbability of a legitimate democracy does not necessarily render democracy either a complete artificiality or a wistful prayer. Instead, it is also a revolutionary call for men to become morally autonomous authors and subjects of their own laws and to nourish the democratic impulse so that it becomes an emancipatory source of power eliminative of the divisiveness of *amour propre*. In a word, the originary unanimity of a people is not only a bygone historical moment or a mythical story to ground future hope but also a telling of the natural capacity men have to forge a lasting sovereign general will, and in so doing, to approximate "a nation of Gods."

While Rousseau's democratic-revolutionary spirit extends, on its surface, to all men, his naturalization of sovereignty that binds individual men, according to their natural capacities, into a self-identical, proto-sovereign unity has profound implications for who is to be included and excluded within a body politic. Men who, by nature, are bereft of the capacity for freedom may retain a glimmer of the democratic impulse as an artifact of their being, but as individuals and as a whole, these men have no place in a democratic polity. These men are as ill suited to democratic freedom as those men with the natural capacity for freedom are ill suited to being ruled undemocratically. Neither set of men is properly represented by the sovereign general will, which compels obedience, and each, in his foreignness, would introduce a destabilizing difference into the self-identicality of the people. Accordingly, Rousseau's naturalization of sovereignty functions to eliminate the vulnerability of artificial sovereignty by casting foreign difference as natural, inexorable, and, therefore, always to be excluded. In this sense, Rousseau's famous formulation of the foundations of an ideal democracy and the universal scope of the law extending to all morally free men must be read alongside a persistent xenophobia which calls for the exclusion of those who, by nature, do not possess the capacity for freedom requisite for democratic sovereignty, i.e., a sovereign general will that is not only artificial and natural, but also worthy of the gods.

The naturalization of artificial foreignness

Whether conceived of as a competitive war of all against all, a perpetual state of irrationality, privation, and lawlessness, or the unrelenting divisiveness of the narcissistic doubling of *amour propre*, I have argued that for Hobbes, Locke, and Rousseau foreignness is the originary fear of the state of nature which drives men into political society. Moreover, in the discussion of the implicit construction of foreignness *qua* absolute difference and primary threat to the territorial integrity and psychosocial unity of a sovereign people, foreignness and the foreigner herself have been shown to be conceived of by the contractarians as the embodiment of nature itself. Put differently, foreignness and the foreigner are conceived of as an absolutely untamable, uncivilized, bestial, and violent encroachment that threatens not only a people but the very concept of political sovereignty as such insofar as sovereignty is conceived of as a self-identical, inviolable, artificial unity eliminative of all destabilizing foreign difference.[12] Accordingly, if foreignness is already conceived of as identical to or co-extensive with nature (i.e., the conceptual antipode to artificial political sovereignty), then there appears to be no need to consider the naturalization of foreignness.

However, by examining the naturalization of artificial foreignness, two important insights are revealed. On the one hand, while foreignness and foreigners exist (and may very well be threatening to a sovereign people), their meanings, qualities, and characteristics—like those of sovereignty—are artificial constructs. Just as the naturalization of artificial sovereignty functions to obscure its origins in order to eliminate the vulnerabilities that accompany its artificiality, the naturalization of foreignness obscures its artificial conceptual origins by establishing the threat of foreignness to sovereignty as natural, and, hence, inexorable, unyielding, and absolute. On the other hand, the naturalization of artificial sovereignty is also an attempt to harness this very same inexorability and absoluteness of nature to legitimate political sovereignty. In this respect, when measured against the "naturalness" of sovereignty, foreignness itself *qua* absolute threat is, paradoxically, shown to be naturally unnatural—an absolute and perpetual aberration or deformity of nature—disruptive to the logical ordering and "natural origins" of political sovereignty. Because the naturalization of artificial foreignness simultaneously casts foreignness as both natural and naturally unnatural, the theoretical importance of this paradoxical conceptualization of foreignness against which the self-identicality and homogeneity of sovereignty is established requires further explication.

Insofar as foreignness is artificially conceptualized as co-extensive with or identical to nature, it functions as the binaristic opposite of artificial sovereignty. Nevertheless, as a binaristic pair, the implicit naturalization of artificial sovereignty concomitantly naturalizes the artificiality of foreignness. The result of this naturalization is that foreignness is no longer simply ascribed qualities opposed to sovereignty such as being untamable, irrational, lawless, a source of division, pure difference, etc. Instead, foreignness *is*, by nature, always and necessarily a threat to sovereignty. In this way, the threat of foreignness never wanes, and, therefore, the qualities, characteristics, rights, and powers of the sovereign *qua* protector of a people cannot be legitimately challenged. This is because foreignness, through its naturalization, is instrumentalized to reaffirm sovereign power and legitimacy in such a way that the sovereign *qua* protector is perpetually empowered to protect against the natural—and hence, immutable—destabilizing and destructive differences inherent to foreignness and the foreigner.[13]

Rather than the occasional conflict with this or that foreign enemy, the threat of natural foreignness introduces a permanent state of emergency.[14] Accordingly, the sovereign right and power to protect must also be unlimited, inexorable, irresistible, and absolute, up to and including the right to violate any "natural rights" the sovereign has been constituted to protect. In this way, sovereignty itself is indistinguishable from a natural power, which, in the name of the protection of its people, mirrors foreignness insofar as it acts with unorthodox, unpredictable, illegal, and lawless tactics to wage a constant (even pre-emptive) war against the real or perceived threat of natural foreignness. In this respect, the naturalization of foreignness has the unintended consequence of revealing how, beyond an artificial construction, sovereignty is a hybrid expression of sheer terror, i.e., an artificially sanctioned beast on the hunt or a god raining fire from above whose right to act knows no law or limit. The sovereign is, as much as foreignness, the originary threat to mankind's preservation. In the name of total security, the "natural" sovereign directs its power against both artifice and nature, states and its citizens, foreign outsiders, and those insiders the sovereign deems to be foreign.

This logic of sovereignty is worth restating. The artificiality of the social contract carves out a space for legitimate political authority that is distinct from both nature and the divine no matter how similar the actions of the sovereign might be to the beast or a vengeful god. In the same instant that the artificiality of sovereignty is posited, the naturalization of artificial sovereignty implicit in Hobbes', Locke's, and Rousseau's respective works functions to eliminate the vulnerabilities of artificial sovereignty to various forms of destabilizing and divisive civil dissent foreign to the interests and unity of the body politic. Yet, because sovereignty is conceptualized in binaristic opposition to foreignness, the naturalization of artificial sovereignty concomitantly naturalizes the artificial conceptualization of foreignness. The naturalization of artificial foreignness re-inscribes sovereign invulnerability by revealing the way in which sovereignty itself must be or resemble the natural, i.e., an unyielding, inexorable, irresistible, and absolute power that alone can guard against the perpetual threat of natural foreignness. In this way, the naturalization of artificial foreignness functions to legitimate the unlimited power of the sovereign *qua* protector of a people. Nevertheless, the shared naturalness of foreignness and sovereignty make them effectively indistinguishable from one another. Both are a pure, unlimited, and indiscriminate source of violence and fear.[15]

However, this temporary resting place in the theorization of sovereignty is untenable precisely because sovereignty is conceptualized as that which excludes all foreign difference. If the sovereign is indistinguishable from the foreign, then it is not sovereign. Therefore, just as the artificiality of the social contract constructs the borders between beast, man, and god, a naturalized conceptualization of sovereignty must depict foreignness (and often the foreigner) as a perversion of nature, a monstrous abnormality that threatens to deform the logical ordering of sovereign self-identicality and homogeneity.

In modern parlance, we speak—metaphorically—of the birth of the nation, a locution which both obscures the artificiality and historical happenstance of any given political association and testifies to the shared sense of identity, common values, and psychosocial unity upon which a people is originally constituted. In this respect, legitimate sovereignty is not merely secured through the artificial conventions that empower the sovereign to protect the people, but also through the belief of citizens and subjects that the sovereignty of a people is grounded in and an expression of nature (whether through bloodlines or shared proximity in a geographic location). Although nature is explicitly cast in opposition to sovereignty by Hobbes, Locke, and Rousseau, their contradictory conceptualizations of nature (as both a perpetual threat and the source of sovereign power, right, self-identicality, and unity) is made manifest when we consider how a foreigner becomes a citizen of a sovereign state through the process of naturalization. Most obviously, the threat of nature is mitigated when the foreigner departs from nature by joining a people, i.e., artificial sovereign civilization. Simultaneously, in order to be included as a member of a sovereign people whose sovereignty is "natural," the foreigner—who is the embodiment of natural foreignness as such—must first become *natural or more natural*. In these ways, the foreigner who *naturalizes* both rejects nature and reaffirms the organicity of a self-identical, homogeneous, sovereign people.

Nevertheless, it is not simply nature that is conceptualized in contradictory ways in order to undergird sovereign legitimacy. Indeed, this example shows that legitimate sovereignty requires foreignness itself to be conceptualized as both natural and naturally unnatural.

Foreignness, we recall, does not merely denote an empirical outsider, but rather anything or anyone that differs from the sovereign (dissident insiders, beasts of nature, gods, etc.). In other words, it is against or in opposition to the foreignness of the divine or naturalized foreignness *qua* absolute difference that sovereignty comes into being and is secured. This conceptualization does not mean that an empirical people itself must be self-identical or homogeneous (although this sort of nationalistic ordering is often desired and substituted for the common good or psychosocial unity of a people), but rather that the concept of sovereignty as such ostensibly loses its meaning and power if the binaristic logical ordering underpinning it (i.e., the presumed impermeable conceptual borders between inside/outside, us/them, friend/enemy, nature/artifice, beast/man, civilized/uncivilized, sovereign/foreign, etc.) is not upheld. In this sense, the legitimate sovereign not only protects a people through the empirical control of geographic borders, but also through the vigilant maintenance of the conceptual borders that determine who is to be included within and who is to be excluded from the sovereign people. Accordingly, sovereignty as such (whether it is conceived of as artificial or natural) is understood to be a self-identical, homogeneous, and inviolable whole, which is simply to say that for sovereignty to be *what it is* natural foreignness *qua* absolute difference must necessarily be excluded or expunged. Conceptually, this is achieved through its permanent and fixed positioning as the antipode in binaristic opposition to sovereignty.

However, if sovereignty is conceptualized as natural, then natural foreignness is no longer the conceptual antipode to sovereignty; instead, riven by the absolute difference of natural foreignness, the self-identical homogeneity of sovereignty eliminative of all difference is destroyed. Therefore, if sovereignty is natural(ized), then the logical ordering of sovereignty which necessarily fixes foreignness in binary opposition to itself requires that foreignness be something other than natural. Indeed, we see an example of this in Rousseau's quasi-divine, *supernatural* foreign lawgiver. Yet, an example more in line with the threat that foreignness poses to sovereignty is that foreignness and the foreigner are an aberration, deformity, and perversion of nature, an unadulterated difference whose illicit crossings of physical and conceptual borders compromise the physical territory, psychosocial unity, and binaristic logic of natural sovereignty. More plainly, foreignness is implicitly cast as naturally unnatural, i.e., absolutely, inexorably, and essentially opposed to nature. On this reading, the naturalization process the foreigner undergoes to become a sovereign citizen is revealing. The monstrous and abnormal foreigner who is a pure expression of heterogeneous difference must be stabilized and transformed—*she must become natural and be naturalized*—in order to join the sovereign body. Put differently, the foreigner naturalizes while foreignness remains the naturally unnatural conceptual antipode to sovereignty as such.

Although it is only implicit in Hobbes', Locke's, and Rousseau's analyses, in order for sovereignty to be *what it is*, foreignness must be shown to be that which is *never what it is*. In this sense, foreignness is an unrelenting heterogeneity, a protean deception, pure illusion, and absolutely untrustworthy. It is artificial, natural, unnatural, supernatural, and, simultaneously, none of these. This is why the foreigner can simultaneously be cast as irrational and hyper-rational, lawless and the source of the law, an empirical outsider or insider, a beast, a man, a god, etc. For the contractarians, foreignness is not simply the unknown, but rather that which is never fully knowable. Foreignness either operates in secrecy (the unknowable intentions of a foreign state) or it erases itself as soon as it presents itself (the foreigner who becomes a citizen leaves behind her foreignness). Moreover, insofar as foreignness is never what it is, it is opposed to itself and self-identical homogeneity as such. Accordingly, foreignness is absolute contradiction and, as such, it is the illogic that threatens the logical, natural, and artificial orders. Taken together, foreignness is placed in a negative conceptual double bind that renders it an absolute threat to the sovereign. As natural, foreignness is a lawless, bestial, and violent threat to the universality, moral autonomy, and reason of the state. As a perversion of nature, foreignness defies all rules, categories, conceptualizations, and logic. In both instances, foreignness is brought temporarily into conceptual stasis—deemed to be what it is by and for the sake of the sovereign—in order to re-inscribe, through opposition, the self-identicality, homogeneity, indivisibility, and invulnerability of sovereignty upon which the originary unanimity and real unity of a people is founded.

7

The Foreign-Sovereign

Whether conceived of as absolute, a neutral and public umpire, or a general will, the legitimate sovereign is that power which commands a duty from its subjects to obey insofar as it is the source of and protector of the legal (and often the social) ordering that constitutes a people. Strictly speaking, the obedience owed to the sovereign *qua* protector is not obedience to a legislative body, a president, a monarch, or even to the law itself. While the law—if it is to be legitimate and command obedience—must reflect the terms of the contract which constitute the sovereign will of the people, the sovereign is not reducible to the extant laws of the land. As I have argued above, the threats and inconveniences of the state of nature are conceived of as a foreignness or foreign difference that compels men to depart the state of nature for their self-preservation by establishing a sovereign people. In this regard, sovereignty is best understood as the self-identicality and homogeneity of a unified people that underpins the *force of the law* or the coercive power to decide and execute the law in order to eliminate the various threats and inconveniences of foreignness co-extensive with the state of nature.

The self-identicality and homogeneity of political sovereignty requisite for protecting a people by *enforcing* the law is artificially produced through the social contract. Yet, as noted, the very artificiality of sovereignty renders it vulnerable to the foreign differences of competing *nomoi*, practices, and values. If foreign difference is not absolutely excluded or destroyed, then the sovereign is divided, partial, and violable. Beset by the heterogeneity of foreign differences and enervated by destabilizing dissent, the artificial sovereign loses, in the very moment it is brought into being, its self-identicality, thereby rendering it unable to absolutely guarantee the protection of its people. If this is so, then the sovereign cannot legitimately compel obedience from its subjects because foreignness and dissent are constitutive of artificial sovereignty.

In the name of protecting a people and compelling obedience, maintaining the appearance of self-identicality, and to disguise its vulnerability to foreignness, sovereign power is and must be perpetually performed or put on display. The performance of legitimate sovereign power and right is expressed variously through the policing of the borders and the people, punishments and fines for lawbreakers and dissemblers, mandatory pledges of allegiance, pageantry and ceremony, and declarations of and the fighting of wars. Most simply, the sovereign power to protect a people is always on display through the active *enforcement* of the law. Yet, these displays and representations of sovereign power are mere masks that disguise the true force of the law, namely the silence and unrepresentability of sovereignty.

To understand why this is so, a return to Rousseau is helpful. For Rousseau the sovereign general will never speaks. Brought into existence from an originary unanimity where there is no dissent, no voices, no votes, no decrees—indeed, no politics—the sovereign general will structures a self-identical, homogeneous people which then acts, in a moment of revolutionary constitution, by giving itself *qua* an already established people as a gift to the political order, i.e., the state, government, rulers, legislators, and the law itself.[1] Heterogeneous to the state and its legal and political orderings, the sovereign general will—the force of the law—remains silent as it animates the state and its laws.[2] Rousseau insists, for example, that "the government receives from the sovereign the orders it gives to the people" ([1762] 1968, 103). Moreover, when the government "usurps sovereignty" ([1762] 1968, 133) by ruling according to decree and not according to the law established by the sovereign general will, "the social pact is broken" ([1762] 1968, 133) and the moral requirement to obey is abridged. Similarly, the sovereign sanctuary of silence can never be represented by the state or its laws, for "the moment the people is lawfully assembled as a sovereign body all jurisdiction of the government ceases; the executive power is suspended, and the person of the humblest citizen is as sacred and inviolable as that of the highest magistrate, for in the presence of the represented there is no longer any representation" ([1762] 1968, 139). Representatives may be necessary for the day-to-day operations of the state, but they are just that, representatives of the state and its subjects, but not representatives of citizens insofar as they are sovereign ([1762] 1968, 62).

Silence and unrepresentability are central to Hobbes' theorization of sovereignty as well. Hobbes insists that it is impossible for man to "make covenants with bruit Beasts" ([1651] 1985, 197) because they lack the reason and speech necessary to agree to the terms of the social contract. For the very same reason, man cannot covenant with God because His silence fails to indicate whether the terms of the contract and the transference of rights have been accepted ([1651] 1985, 197). As with the beast and the divine, there is no contract with the sovereign as such. Indeed, Hobbes is explicit that men make covenants amongst themselves, leaving the sovereign unbound by any rules, contracts, or laws.

Sovereign silence is a reserve and credit of power and animating force that stokes the faith of the people in the sovereign. The sovereign, like God, does not and cannot answer (to) its subjects. To do so strips the sovereign of his absolutism, his sovereignty. The sovereign is silent, and while he represents the people, he remains the ethereal, unrepresentable soul that breathes life into the Leviathan. In this respect, Hobbes' absolute sovereign (no less so than Rousseau's general will) is co-extensive with the law but not reducible to it; instead, he is simultaneously above and outside the law, the force that decides, directs, and executes the law. Thus, as Derrida notes, the silence of Hobbes' absolute sovereign, paradoxically, renders him indistinguishable not only from God but also the beast. He writes:

> God himself, like the beast, does not respond, that in any case we cannot be assured of his acceptance, we cannot count on his response. And this is indeed the most profound definition of absolute sovereignty, of the absolute of sovereignty, of the absoluteness that absolves it, unbinds it from all duty of reciprocity. The sovereign does not respond, he is the one who does not have to, who always has the right not to, respond [*répondre*], in particular not to be responsible for [*répondre de*] his acts. He is above the law [*le droit*] and has the right [*le droit*] to suspend the law, he does not have to respond before a representative chamber or before judges . . . like God, the sovereign is above the law and above humanity, above everything, and he looks a bit stupid [*bête*], he looks like a beast, and even like the death he carries within him, like the death that Lévinas says is not nothingness, nonbeing, but nonresponse.
>
> Derrida 2009, 57[3]

The law itself answers and explains. It is open to language, questioning, revision, resistance, and foreign difference; however, the coercive power of the law, the force of the law, revolves around the axes of sovereign silence and unrepresentability, which can never be questioned and has no obligation to respond. Thus, it is along these axes that the sovereign *reinforces* its self-identicality and homogeneity, for the silent, unrepresentable sovereign remains perpetually inviolable and impervious to difference. Yet, simultaneously, the very same self-identicality and homogeneity requisite to enforce the law structured upon silence and unrepresentability provides the justification for the silent and secretive performance of extra-legal and extra-juridical acts. The extra-legal and extra-juridical performance of sovereign power is of a different order from the enforcement of the law not only because it exceeds or stands *outside the law* but also because, in its silence, sovereign power is that which exceeds or stands *outside the artificial order* upon which its legitimacy is founded. In a word, sovereign silence and unrepresentability is not only the *force of law*; they also justify an unrestrained, natural, bestial sovereign violence, i.e., the *law of force*.

Perhaps the most obvious recent example of the silent performance of extra-legal and extra-juridical sovereign violence is the (attempted) clandestine use of torture by the United States. In the name of democratic law, institutions, and values, the sovereign executive of the U.S. regularly violates its own laws, international law, and the very democratic principles it is endeavoring to protect.[4] Even if this silent and secretive performance of illegitimate sovereign power is publicized and criticized (e.g., *leaked*, a term which implies an otherwise hermetically sealed entity; the price for leaking state secrets is high: charges of espionage, treason, and even death at the hands of the state), the effect is the same, namely the extra-legal and extra-juridical coercive power of the sovereign reminds its subjects that destabilizing disobedience and dissent (even in the most robust democracies) that threaten to exploit the vulnerability of artificial sovereignty will be resisted—often violently and most assuredly with the full force of the law—by the sovereign. Paradoxically, the legitimate coercive power of the sovereign to compel obedience and enforce the law is itself undergirded by the extra-juridical, silent, and secretive performances of sovereign violence or the law of force undertaken in secret, without debate, in the name of and for the sake of the people. In a word, the true coercive power of the sovereign is fear. Thus, a question remains: How can the silent law of force, the sovereign use of violence to instill fear and compel obedience, be legitimate?

Because the legitimacy of the artificial sovereign recedes at the very moment it is invoked through appeals to the law, Hobbes, Locke, and Rousseau suggest that the force of law does not arise from an artificial convention among men; instead, the story of sovereign legitimacy is recast so that the sovereign performances of right and power are grounded in and nourished by the absolute and unyielding natural (and sometimes divine) origins of a self-identical sovereign impervious to foreign differences.[5] More succinctly, because the *force of law* is an artificiality riddled with vulnerabilities, it is supplemented by the *law of force* as silent and mysterious as nature and/or the divine.[6] Through the naturalization or re-deification of artificial sovereignty, sovereign power and right exceeds and is unrestrained by the very law it founds, enforces, and protects. The story of sovereignty simultaneously operates on two registers, one audible and the other silent. It is at once an artificiality that protects a people by enforcing the public, promulgated law *and* a natural or divine power, i.e., an unpredictable, violent, non-responsive, and even "stupid" bestial force. When the visible and audible pageantry and performances of sovereignty fail to quell dissent and compel obedience, the state resorts to operating in secret (secret police, spying on citizens, etc.) while simultaneously invoking the stories of its naturalness and/or divinity in order to re-inscribe its self-identical homogeneity, thereby masking the historical artificiality of its founding and legitimizing its use of both legal force and extra-legal violence.[7]

However, because the fictions of self-identical, homogeneous sovereignty are perpetually reinvented, our story of sovereignty also cannot rest here. On the socio-political level, foreigners are always neighboring and inside the sovereign (nation) state. Thus, the sovereign duty to protect its people requires that it identifies those foreigners to be killed, excluded, denied legal status, assimilated, or tolerated in order to preserve the sovereign self-identicality upon which the stability and unity of a people depend. As important as this fact of foreignness is to the day-to-day operations of the (nation) state, it is at the level of sovereignty itself, the conceptualization of sovereignty as such, where the story of sovereignty takes an unexpected turn. Conceptually, foreignness must be excluded because the foreign-sovereign is a contradiction in terms. For the self-identical sovereign eliminative of all foreign differences to be and to remain sovereign, foreignness must always be cast in binaristic opposition to it. Most simply, the foreign-sovereign is no sovereign at all. Nevertheless, as argued above, insofar as sovereignty is conceived of as natural, it is indistinguishable from a foreignness which the stories and logic of traditional sovereignty tell us is mired in and co-extensive with nature. Accordingly, foreignness must not only be natural (when the story and logic of sovereignty appeal to itself as artificial) but also a perversion, deformity, or monstrosity of nature (when the story and logic of sovereignty obscures its artificiality by grounding itself in nature and divine creation). Be that as it may, despite the various efforts of social contract theorists to establish self-identical homogeneity as the basis for sovereign legitimacy, the logical contortions and inconsistent narratives of sovereignty (e.g., the simultaneously artificial, natural, and divine sovereign) suggests that sovereign self-identicality is, paradoxically, structured upon a perpetual substitution, supplementation, and difference. More bluntly, sovereign self-identicality and homogeneity is a fiction. Because sovereign self-identicality and homogeneity is perpetually undermined, the sovereign is never what it is or claims to be. Therefore, it is absolutely vulnerable to competing counter-sovereignties that challenge the legitimacy of both the law and the sovereign itself.

To understand why this is so, we must return to Derrida's requirement that "every time one puts an oppositional limit in question [*physis*/*nomos*/*thesis*, natural/divine, etc.] far from concluding there is identity, we must on the contrary multiply attention to differences" (2009, 15–16, original emphasis). Rather than the self-identicality requisite for legitimacy, the various stories of sovereignty reveal the sovereign for what it is, namely an indeterminate hybrid of beast, man, and god that is always already differing and different from itself. The sovereign is simultaneously artificial, natural, and divine, simultaneously the force of the law and the law of force, simultaneously silent and vociferous, simultaneously legitimate and illegitimate, simultaneously what it is and what it is not. In a word, the sovereign is always already foreign to itself. It *is* a foreign-sovereign. However, one might anticipate an objection: If foreignness is a perversion of nature, don't Hobbes, Locke, and Rousseau provide a conceptual anchor—a binaristic antipode—for the self-identicality of natural sovereignty, since the truth of sovereign legitimacy is the fact that it is self-evident, ahistorical, and the very condition of possibility for the unity requisite to found a people?[8]

A common and convincing rebuttal against this position has been to demonstrate that the naturalization or re-deification of sovereignty is simply one of the seemingly limitless permutations of the stories of legitimate sovereignty repeated so frequently that it is no longer recognized to be what it is, namely a narrative or myth that unifies the people and/or justifies sovereign violence.[9] These critiques are indispensable for demonstrating the ways in which foreign difference has been and continues to be instrumentalized to (re)establish sovereign self-identicality and homogeneity as such (conceptually) as well as the violent nationalisms or well-intentioned pluralisms this conception of sovereignty propagates.[10] Nevertheless, pushing beyond these critiques that reveal the historicity of sovereignty as well as the instrumentalization of foreignness is essential if foreignness is to be re-conceptualized as that which is an originary and constitutive feature of sovereignty generative of novel normative, political, and social orderings.

The quasi-regime

The stories of sovereignty meant to establish its self-identicality are ultimately revealed to be mere symptoms of a sovereignty that is always already a supplementation and heterogeneity insofar as it perpetually oscillates between the artificial, natural, and divine. Despite its fictions and conceptualizations, sovereignty is absolutely vulnerable to a certain foreignness that is neither outside of nor distinct from that which is sovereign. Accordingly, these fictions of sovereignty can be revealed by providing the structural basis for the foreign-sovereign. Once again, it is useful to turn to Derrida's analysis of sovereign ipseity, i.e., the metaphysical presupposition of self-identicality that structures the *autos*/*ipse*/self eliminative of all difference, which, in turn, undergirds the sovereign force to act in order to decide, preserve, and/or violate the law. In this way, ipseity is constitutive of traditional conceptions of sovereignty as such, a metaphysical bedrock that functions as the irreducible locus of the autonomous political actor (both the individual and the state). However, Derrida insists that once sovereignty is shared, divided in space, or spread out over time, it is no longer sovereign because it loses the "indivisible instant" ([2003] 2005, 101) of its ipseity.[11] Therefore, as we have seen, sovereignty must remain silent, for the moment it speaks it is governed by and vulnerable to the "law of giving reasons" ([2003] 2005, 101).

While silence structures the ipseity of the sovereign power to act (thereby providing another way to understand why the secretive and silent performance of sovereignty is the true force of the law), sovereignty must, nevertheless, be verbose, vociferous, diplomatic, or even bellicose precisely because it must constantly justify its silence in order to legitimize *it-self* as sovereign. Because sovereignty—in order to be recognized and received as such—must always speak, judge, rule, and power-share, it is always already partitioned, distributed, and different from *it-self*, thereby revealing its absolute vulnerability to language, questioning, interpretations, alternate values, and competing *nomoi*, i.e., foreign difference. In Michael Naas' useful formulation, sovereignty must always be "introducing within itself counter-sovereignties" (2008, 128). Thus, through its legitimate performances—its enforcing of the law—sovereignty is "always in the process of positing itself by refuting itself" (Derrida [2003] 2005, 101). In this way, the requirement of justification reveals that the *ipse* of sovereignty is not merely self-compromising when it must justify *it-self* in one manner or another; rather, the *ipse*, the *it-self*, and the very power of sovereignty to act is in a "process of autoimmunizing itself" ([2003] 2005, 101) because in the very act of constituting itself, it is constantly "denying and disavowing itself" ([2003] 2005, 101).

The autoimmune structure of sovereignty does not mean that sovereignty does not exist; it most assuredly does. Nevertheless, despite its narratives, performances, silences, laws, and the violence committed for the sake of sovereign self-identicality supposedly requisite for the protection of a people, the autoimmune structure of sovereignty reveals that foreignness and difference are originary to and constitutive of sovereignty and, hence, ineliminable. If this is so, then sovereignty's lack of self-identicality is not simply an accident of the various stories sovereignty tells of *it-self*; rather, the very telling of these stories of sovereign self-identicality—of giving an account of or reasons to justify its legitimacy—exposes sovereignty's fundamental vulnerability, namely that the sovereign is foreign, even as it seeks to legitimize *it-self* as a *self* through the instrumentalization and purging of its originary foreignness. In this way, the attempt to establish total security by identifying, eliminating, assimilating, or tolerating that which is deemed to be foreign to a self-identical, homogeneous sovereign people is not simply misguided but also impossible.

While autoimmunity provides a structural latticework for conceiving of the foreign-sovereign, another step is required to account for the ways in which this structural necessity of foreignness to sovereignty is generative of new normative, political, and social possibilities. Importantly, the conceptual resources for positing the non-instrumental generativity of foreignness can be drawn directly from the history of philosophy and the social contract tradition. The notion of a people whose members are subject to the law implies that each member be counted, represented, accounted for, known or knowable to the sovereign, assigned a status, counted as equals in democratic regimes, etc. Without this counting and accounting, lawlessness pervades the sovereign state. This is why foreignness *qua* the perversion of nature is conceived of as an absolute threat, since it is that which is never what it is. Its very essence is to recede into the shadows, to operate outside of the law, to disappear the moment it appears, to avoid being counted, to remain wholly unknown to the sovereign, to be unrepresented and un-representable (like sovereignty itself, ironically), to openly or clandestinely cross political borders as well as the conceptual boundaries between the binaristic categories of inside/outside, civilized/uncivilized, man/beast, friend/enemy, us/them, same/different, and inclusion/exclusion upon which sovereign legitimacy is premised and perpetuated. In this way, the epithet of perversion assigned to foreignness gains its appeal only insofar as foreignness threatens the sovereign's ability to account for its members. Or, alternatively, it is only by conceiving of foreignness as a perversion of natural, logical, and legal orderings that Hobbes, Locke, and Rousseau provide their full-throated accounts of sovereign self-identicality and homogeneity.

By contrast, when foreignness is conceived of as an ineliminable, originary, and constitutive feature of sovereignty, it can be stripped of the epithet of perversion while, nevertheless, retaining its qualities of pure heterogeneity and difference. Be that as it may, it would be foolish to suggest that these conceptualizations of foreignness and foreign sovereignty eliminate the threat of foreignness. Foreignness is indeed threatening to a sovereign people! However, if the sovereign is always already foreign, then a coherent theory—another telling of the tale—of legitimate sovereignty must recognize foreignness as simultaneously a perpetual threat *and* a structural necessity. Rather than (or in addition to) absolute threat, foreignness is an ineliminable, necessary, and indecidable risk which perpetually opens and re-opens sovereignty to a questioning of its established and shared religious, traditional, and/or legal foundations of political, moral, and social justice.

Within the philosophical tradition, this dual conceptualization of foreignness can be found in Book I of *The Republic*. The analysis of *The Republic* was undertaken at the outset, but only now is its broader significance evident. Plato is at pains to demonstrate that Socrates—who has come to witness the religious festival in honor of the foreign goddess Bendis—is foreign to the Piraeus yet astute enough to both recognize the political importance of the religious festival for Athens and judge the inadequacies of the traditional, religious, and legal foundations of Athenian justice. Yet, unlike Rousseau's foreign lawgiver, the threat of Socrates *qua* a foreigner is not so easily excised. He will neither willingly depart nor be compelled by forced to leave. Instead, he is a foreign founder who remains to become that which is deemed impossible, unjust, and illegitimate, namely a foreign-sovereign, or, in Plato's conceptualization, a philosopher-king. This is not to claim that the foreign-sovereign and philosopher-king are identical concepts. They are not; instead, I am suggesting that Plato establishes a conceptual space—ignored or refused by the tradition—which posits the philosopher-king as simultaneously sovereign and foreign, and this dual conceptualization of sovereign legitimacy has profound implications for contemporary theorizations of the political.

As Socrates' execution makes abundantly clear, philosophy is conceived of as foreign to the political order, a threat to Athens' leaders, institutions, beliefs, and practices. Despite the foreignness of his practices and values, Plato insists in the *Crito* that Socrates is a native, an Athenian, a citizen, whose life is given to him by Athens' laws (1961b, 50a–54e). Plato goes a step further arguing that Socrates' death at the hand of the state (the rule of the political over the philosophical) is legitimate if not entirely just. Nevertheless, *qua* philosopher, Socrates *is* a foreigner—a point made explicitly by Socrates in the *Apology* (1961a, 17d–18a). Indeed, Socrates' death is a rebuke to Athens and a redemption of philosophy precisely because it serves to demonstrate that philosophy is, at once, foreign and autochthonous, i.e., a threat to, product of, and promise of Athenian democracy.

Nevertheless, Plato's explicit acceptance of the governing logic of sovereignty and extant negative conceptualizations of foreignness are worthy of critique. Indeed, it seems incontrovertible that Plato rejects the notion of the foreign-sovereign insofar as he re-inscribes in multiple places throughout *The Republic* the self-identicality and homogeneity of the sovereign philosopher-king's right to act with violence, in secret, and tell lies (noble though they may be) as well as philosophy's sovereign reign over the very possibility for justice. In other words, Plato appears to replace the sovereignty of the political with the sovereignty of philosophy. This may be so, but Plato also provides resources for a not-yet, even impossible, philosophico-political justice—a new source of political tradition and authority—to be inaugurated by the philosopher-king. He implicitly suggests the possibility for a philosophical sovereignty and philosophy's sovereign authority over the history of thought that does not retreat into the silence of the authority of its own self-identical, homogeneous traditions and disciplinarity.[12] The sovereignty of Plato's city in speech (no less so than a certain tradition within philosophy itself) is constituted by heterogeneity, a non-self-identical vulnerability to foreignness. Peter Gratton's notion of a "democratic thinking of philosophy" (2012, 49) while directly addressing the reception of and authority of traditional interpretations of canonical philosophical texts (through his own reading of Michael Naas's reading of Derrida) is worth quoting in full for what it reveals about the rule of the philosopher-king *qua* a foreign-sovereign:

> But what would philosophy be without the *more-than-one* voice within it, without always having something more to say? Like any democracy, philosophy has its traditions and classical views. And we would have to think about who this dēmos of philosophy would be, whether we are capable of thinking a "we" not yet wholly constituted, given the "we" of philosophy that has always signed itself in the singular voice. But philosophy also has an openness—this is essential, for the Socratic questioning and Aristotelian *thaumazein* said to found philosophy are

> meaningless without it—that means leaving itself available for questioning, even under the weight of tradition.
>
> Gratton 2012, 49–50

On this reading, philosophy and, by extension, the reign of the philosopher-king is constituted by a foreignness, structured upon an "openness," that is at once vulnerable to and constituted by multiple voices, dissent, debate, perpetual questioning, and the obligation to respond to the foreign other in ways that go beyond conceiving of him or her as an absolute threat. Accordingly, the sovereignty of philosophy and the philosopher-king rests, at once, upon the authority of tradition and the explicit possibility of re-casting this authority anew. The openness, vulnerability, and loquaciousness of the philosopher-king suggest a reading of Plato's sovereign inauguration of political philosophy in a new light, namely a radical reconceptualization of foreignness in relation to sovereignty and political life. To demonstrate how, we must return to the figure of Thrasymachus.

Book I details Socrates' masterful—even sovereign—demonstration of political naïveté by non-violently welcoming a dangerous and threatening foreigner, Thrasymachus, into the city in speech. Thrasymachus, of course, is a foreigner, a migrant laborer, welcomed by democratic Athens. As Pericles proudly declares in the Funeral Oration: "We throw open our city to the world, and never by alien acts exclude foreigners from any opportunity of learning or observing, although the eyes of an enemy may occasionally profit by our liberality" (Thucydides 1996, 15). While democratic society is epitomized by its openness to outsiders and taking on the risk of welcoming foreigners within its walls, Thrasymachus presents a risk of a different and higher order for the city in speech. Indeed, Thrasymachus is not merely a potential enemy, but rather a "foreign perversion" of the philosophical regime precisely because the violence and bestial nature of sophistry threatens to deform the norms, precedents, and reason-giving upon which the philosophical regime gains its legitimacy. In a word, Thrasymachus, who would silence philosophy, is not just representative of a generic counter-sovereign figure; he is its absolute enemy.

Insofar as Thrasymachus represents the absolute threat of foreignness to the city in speech, Socrates rightfully fears him, fears the silencing of dialectic he pre-figures. Nevertheless, Socrates cautiously welcomes him into the nascent regime and for good cause, since it is Thrasymachus' claim that justice is the advantage of the stronger which ultimately allows the city in speech with its novel conceptualization of philosophico-political justice to be forged. Indeed,

Socrates considers Thrasymachus—who remains unconvinced and recalcitrant throughout the text—a new friend of the regime (Plato 1968, 498c) worthy of pride of place despite the fact that he is explicitly and virulently opposed to its norms, traditions, procedures, and ethos. In short, Thrasymachus is simultaneously an absolute threat and a constitutive necessity of the political order, and Plato never undoes this dual-conceptualization of Thrasymachus. In this respect, Book I of *The Republic* provides a path for thinking through the normative, political, and social possibilities that emerge when foreignness is no longer instrumentalized, but, instead, rightfully—in my view—recognized as an originary and ineliminable feature of sovereignty.

Normatively, Thrasymachus is welcomed, despite the fact that his violent and bestial foreignness threatens to destroy the nascent regime and the very sovereign power to offer hospitality in the first place. The inclusion of Thrasymachus *qua* absolute threat who provides an indispensable definition of justice is no mere case of political naïveté; instead, his inclusion by Socrates suggests a new normative relationship to the foreign grounded in the explicit recognition that foreignness, while dangerous, is a constitutive and originary feature of sovereignty. Rather than falling prey to the naturalistic fallacy by suggesting that the foreignness of sovereignty to itself means that foreign difference and foreigners *ought* to be welcomed, the notion of the foreign-sovereign, a sovereignty premised on heterogeneity and supplementarity, undermines the presupposition of the self-identicality of natural sovereignty and the concomitant ethical harms faced by those targeted for threatening sovereign self-identicality. In other words, the foreign-sovereign is generative of new normative possibilities because it rejects the legitimacy of normative justifications that provide for the instrumental treatment of foreign difference and foreigners in the name of and for the sake of the fictions of sovereign self-identicality and homogeneity. This may or may not result in the welcoming of the foreigner, but the normative backdrop that can inform the decision to welcome or reject the foreigner has been recast, a change in tone and accent from preservation of the self-identical to recognition of the ineliminability of difference.

Does this normative reorientation present a risk to a sovereign people? Yes. Nevertheless, this admittedly risky—even politically naïve—sovereign decision (there is no telling in advance what effects the welcoming of foreignness might have upon a sovereign people, upon its identity) to welcome foreignness unconditionally not only rejects the "noble lies" of sovereignty supposedly requisite to guarantee the unity of a people, but it also provides the possibility for novel traditions, laws, and national identities premised upon foreign difference. In Derrida's words: "Let us say yes *to who or what turns up*, before any determination, before any anticipation, before any *identification*, whether or not it has to do with a foreigner, an immigrant, an invited guest, or an unexpected visitor, whether or not the new arrival is the citizen of another country, a human, animal, or divine creature, a living or dead thing, male or female ([1997] 2000, 77, original emphasis). To "say yes" to Thrasymachus or any foreigner, to welcome who or what might destroy a people, is both the purview and promise of a new normative ordering premised upon the structural vulnerability of the foreign-sovereign.

Politically, the inclusion of Thrasymachus *qua* the absolute threat of foreignness introduces new possibilities for justice. As noted by Rousseau, foreignness seems requisite for founding the laws best suited to a given people. For Plato, Socrates is a foreign lawgiver who will remain; a positioning that suggests that Plato is aware of the centrality and structural necessity of foreignness to the sovereign regime. Nevertheless, while inaugurating philosophy as sovereign, Plato simultaneously recognizes that the justice of the new, philosophical regime cannot be articulated without Thrasymachus. He is welcomed and included, yet he remains apart from and critical of the new regime. In this respect, the rejuvenating and beneficial effects of foreignness are not merely assimilated, thereby expanding the self-identicality of "our" sense of "who we are;" instead, foreignness (whether embodied by Socrates or Thrasymachus) is that which resists the sovereign closure of political justice around the axes of tradition, religion, and the law. Plato's philosophico-political justice, apparently, is that which refuses to exclude the very thing that threatens to destroy it. Indeed, philosophico-political justice is radically cosmopolitan rejecting outright the traditional distinctions between friend/enemy, citizen/foreigner, and inside(r)/outside(r) and the concomitant construction of unity structured upon sovereign self-identicality and homogeneity. The inclusion of Thrasymachus—and foreignness as such—opens and keeps open the possibilities of a new, yet dangerous justice, i.e., the risky opportunity of ineliminable instability, dissent, and counter-sovereignties constitutive of a foreign-sovereign. Ever attentive and resistant to the unjust exclusions and instrumentalization of foreignness, the foreign-sovereign protects a new justice that both *inherits* and *opposes* itself to the authority of religion, tradition, and the laws of the state.

Socially, Socrates' welcoming of Thrasymachus points to both the trepidation and hope of a cosmopolitan openness to foreign difference. Thrasymachus takes pride of place, though he is never assimilated or sworn to allegiance; he observes and monitors, and it is his foreignness that guides the work of the new regime. Thrasymachus both threatens and constitutes the social identity and norms of the city in speech. In this respect, Plato appears to simultaneously embrace and reject the common conception of *ethnos*—the imagined or real qualities of semblance, resemblance, and homogeneity—that functions as the source of unity for a self-identical people. On the one hand, Plato recognizes that a shared social identity and set of norms, beliefs, and practices is required for the formation of a people. Hence, Thrasymachus remains a threatening and dangerous figure, foreign to the social norms and shared identity who cannot be assimilated. On the other hand, there simply is no new regime, no possibility for a radical reconceptualization of justice, without the implicit rejection of the necessity to exclude or instrumentalize foreignness in the name of and for the sake of the protection of the self-identical and homogeneous sovereign people. Because the *ethnos* of this new regime is open to foreignness, never decided in advance, and structured upon a radical alterity, new forms of social inclusion are introduced; hence, the pride of place and overtures of friendship afforded to Thrasymachus by the foreign-sovereign of the city in speech.

Taken together, Book I of *The Republic* suggests that foreignness is generative of novel normative, political, and social possibilities in the exact moment when a people recognizes that it is protected only when the stories of sovereign legitimacy and inviolability are replaced with the simple admission that foreign differences and new *nomoi* are never absolutely eliminated or eliminable. More plainly, a people is protected once it comes to understand itself as a foreign people, a foreign-sovereign, which is legitimately compelled to obey not because of the sovereign promise of perfect unity, inviolability, and self-identicality, but rather because obedience to a foreign-sovereign is premised on the recognition that sovereign political associations are constituted by foreignness as such, and, hence, absolutely vulnerable. The foreign-sovereign protects, but its decisions are made in recognition of the impossibility of sovereign violability. Is the foreign-sovereign a politically naïve idea? Perhaps, yes, but political realism is no less naïve in its belief that violence, secrecy, illegitimate coercion, or even the presumed enlightenment and enlightening of humankind and its sovereign institutions will one day bring "justice for all." Indeed, the foreign-sovereign offers hope that the self-identical sovereign cannot, namely the possibility for a non-instrumental recognition of foreignness that structures a political order that is simultaneously progressive and conservative. On the one hand, by recognizing the structural necessity of foreignness, the foreign-sovereign ends the instrumentalization and scapegoating of foreignness and the foreigner, thereby satisfying the progressive ideology of a heterogeneous *ethnos* through the inclusion of those unjustly excluded according to race, gender, class, sexuality, etc. On the other hand, if the myth and fictions of sovereign self-identicality are cast aside, then the conservation of a given people can shed its blind appeals to language, race, nationalisms, and the longing for an originary purity of the *ethnos* in favor of the conservation of a heterogeneous *ethnos*, i.e., the conservation of a people whose traditions, practices, norms, laws, and unity are founded upon the recognition that a people is always already foreign to *it-self*.

8

Foreign Unto It-Self, the Democratic Nation-State

Democracy's others and the protection of the democratic nation-state

Thrasymachus defines justice as the advantage of the stronger, and this definition is quite similar to the conception of sovereign legitimacy considered up to this point. No matter the form of government, the just regime—the legitimate sovereign—successfully uses its power, force, and laws to protect itself, its resources, its territory, its members, and its interests.[1] Thrasymachus' claim is, of course, an ancient one, but it is worth considering if and to what extent this conception of justice aligns not merely with a generic consideration of the conditions for sovereign legitimacy but also with the widely held, contemporary belief that the most just and legitimate form of political association is the democratic nation-state. Today, the use of force is claimed to be a "last resort," a turn of phrase meant to reflect modernity's political enlightenment epitomized by the secular democratic state that rejects imperialism and empire in favor of a commitment to preserving not only the universal democratic values which hold all human beings to be free and equal but also the human rights which flow from these fundamental human qualities. In Seyla Benhabib's formulation, every human being has a right "to be a *legal person*, entitled to certain inalienable rights, regardless of the status of their political membership" (2004, 3, original emphasis). The just and legitimate democratic nation-state recognizes (and endeavors to uphold) its moral obligations and legal commitments to the human rights of both citizens and non-citizens, and, therefore, no longer subscribes to the antiquated notion that justice is the advantage of the stronger or, more bluntly, that might makes right.[2] That said, the legitimacy of the sovereign democratic nation-state continues to rest upon its duty and ability to protect its citizens, the people, "us," "our" democratic rights, "our" practices, "our" values, "our" way of life, etc.

To make this point is not to argue that the use of force (or the enforcement of the law) by democratic societies is always unjust. There have been and will be just uses of state power to protect against external and internal threats to the people as a whole, the democratic rights of each of its members, and universal human rights and democratic norms. Nevertheless, given the daily instances of violence and legal injustices that continue to be committed by the most powerful democratic nation-states (almost always undemocratically yet, ironically, in the name of democracy or—more properly—the democratic state), it is reasonable to claim that "just and legitimate" democratic nation-states tacitly endorse—at least in part—the common understanding of Thrasymachus' notion of justice. If this is so, and we hope for an alternative conception of justice that refuses to equate might with right, then the question of *who* the sovereign democratic nation-state protects is of paramount importance.

The most obvious answer is that democracies simply protect their own citizens, the members of the *demos*. However, a more nuanced account requires thinking through democratic citizenship within the context of the nation-state in particular and foreignness in general, since minority parties, minorities, "the feminine," and all others deemed by the self-identical sovereign to be foreign (to the nation, to mankind, to reason, etc.) are regularly targeted for political exclusion by the democratic nation-state.[3] Therefore, we must first detail the relationship between sovereign legitimacy premised upon self-identicality and the homogeneity of the people or nation. Only then will we see how this relationship is simultaneously opposed to democracy as such yet essential to the democratic nation-state insofar as it forges the link between nationality and citizenship. Finally, we must examine how the legitimate and just sovereign protection of the democratic nation-state produces an excluded class of individuals (both "insiders" and "outsiders"), norms, traditions, practices, institutions, and beliefs that are or are deemed foreign to the nation and state. I call this excluded class democracy's others.[4] The current analysis focuses on non-citizens who are split into two categories. The first are those whose legal status is recognized in the abstract but whose rights are violated or ignored in the name of the sovereign self-determination and the right of the nation-state. The second are those who are deemed "illegal."

The sovereign is self-identical insofar as it is that which is absolutely distinct from, opposed to, and eliminative of the foreign. Because the sovereign—if it is to be and remain sovereign—must stand guard against the foreign *qua* absolute threat to its self-identicality, it is variously conceived of as possessing the qualities of inviolability, indivisibility, wholeness, unity, self-mastery, mastery over its others, etc. In its vigilance, the abstract conceptual construction of sovereignty touches upon the practical and political operations and duties of the sovereign nation-state to protect itself and "us" from foreign peoples and foreign individuals who come from beyond the walls, borders, and control of "our" sovereign territory. Whether the sovereign destroys, pre-emptively attacks, repels, makes peace with, or tolerates foreigners, all techniques of power can be justified and made legitimate so long as the sovereign protects the safety and unity of the people as a whole. Anything less suggests that the sovereign is not self-identical and vulnerable to the foreign, which is to say that it is not sovereign.[5] As Rousseau notes, a divided or non-sovereign state might compel by force, but it cannot legitimately demand obedience from a people.

This general depiction of sovereign self-identicality makes sense in a palpable way. For example, war between foreign peoples is a political reality, and foreignness and difference are widely regarded as existential threats to the unity of a people. However, when sovereign legitimacy premised upon self-identicality is put into practice within the nation-state model of political organization, a new and dangerous risk emerges. Within the nation-state, the sovereign does not merely protect its individual members or even a generic body politic. Instead, it protects the *ethnos qua* a people or nation (and, all too frequently, the dominant *ethnos* which then becomes co-extensive with the identity of the nation) brought together through geographic proximity, territoriality, and consanguinity, which, by extension, undergirds the common language, traditions, religious beliefs, shared memories and histories, racial and ethnic identification, etc. that provide the imaginative basis for collective belonging, psychosocial unity, and homogeneous national identity. As Hannah Arendt observes, "the very conditions for the rise of nation-states [are] homogeneity of population and rootedness in the soil" (1968, 270). In this way, the nation functions as a litmus test for sovereign self-identicality and legitimacy, since homogeneity, uniformity, and purity provide "empirical verification" that the sovereign is, indeed, inviolable and eliminative of all foreign difference.

Measuring sovereign legitimacy by the homogeneity of the people has been and remains ripe for exploitation in the modern epoch of the nation-state. Today, membership within the nation is frequently a prerequisite not only for citizenship and democratic rights but also political inclusion and representation of any sort. In other words, individuals who have left their countries of birth (by choice or force) are frequently excluded not just from the specific rights that accrue to citizens but also from political membership. Foreigners as well as those "insiders" deemed by the sovereign to be foreign to the nation cannot be citizens, and, as such, they are outside of or exceptions to the law.[6] While each is unique, the most egregious injustices committed by the nation-state—including European colonialism, slavery and Jim Crow in the U.S., the denationalization in Europe beginning after the First World War,[7] the Nazi concentration camps, and the ethnic cleansing at the end of the twentieth and beginning of the twenty-first centuries in Europe and Africa—all share something in common, namely an attempt to destroy, purge, subjugate, dominate, and/or exclude that which is or is deemed foreign to the nation based on the belief that a homogeneous and pure *ethnos* is both the measure and *telos* of sovereign self-identicality.[8]

While these acts are deplorable in every way, the belief underpinning them is not an aberration. What these examples show is that within the nation-state model of political organization, there is a conceptual link between sovereign self-identicality and the homogeneity of the nation that all too frequently results in the predictable treatment of those who are or are deemed to be foreign to it. Admittedly, these are extreme and unfortunate examples that have scarred the psyche of political modernity. Nevertheless, while the most virulent strains of ethno-nationalism and state-sponsored racism have rightly been repudiated as egregious injustices, the relationship between sovereign self-identicality and national homogeneity remains operative today within democratic nation-states. This is troubling for three reasons.

First, in principle, the democratic state is uniquely qualified to guarantee the inalienable political rights of freedom and equality insofar as being a citizen within a democracy is to be an equal member of an autonomous, self-legislating people. The legitimacy of the democratic state is judged, at least in part, according to how successfully it strikes a balance between the rule of law (the particular laws of the state applied equally to all) and individual liberty (universal and inalienable rights for self-determination possessed by all human beings). In other words, the legitimacy of the sovereign democratic state is predicated on it surrendering certain rights and powers to its citizens even as the citizens require the state to protect their rights. Perhaps the most prominent example of the formal divestment of state power and right to the citizens of democracy would be the U.S. Bill of Rights, an enumeration and legal ratification of the individual rights which place restrictions on the scope and use of state power. When the legitimacy of the democratic state is predicated on the extent to which it gives up rights to the individual, the result is somewhat surprising, namely the sovereign "we" of the *demos* is always already disrupted, differentiated, lacks univocity, and is even incoherent in response to individual rights.

This disruption of the "we" of the sovereign *demos* and this tension between democracy and sovereignty runs deeper still. If the balance between the rule of law and individual liberty is determinative of democratic legitimacy, then the sovereign *demos* is also temporally fragmented insofar as there is no predetermined way of knowing what rights future citizens will demand, how the claims to rights will change over time, who can legitimately make claims upon the state, what laws a self-legislating body will pass, and how the general will might change. In this sense, it is not merely that the "we" is disrupted and differentiated; rather, the universal scope of democracy as such resists the sovereignty of the democratic nation-state insofar as democratic legitimacy entails admitting the judgment of the larger community, including those who are not yet citizens (future generations, for example) or who are not citizens at all (foreigners, for example).

This same point might be made in another way. The sovereign democratic state is the exemplar of this relationship between law and liberty; however, as an exemplar, it is always under suspicion. There is always the chance that a different exemplar, another constitution, or a future instantiation of democracy exists or will exist that enacts and enforces this relationship better. In short, *qua* exemplar, democracy is always open and opens itself to critique, which is to say that it admits the judgment of the larger community, including non-citizens, since justice is not reducible to the positive law of any given state, a fact evidenced by the existence of international law, institutions, and the regime of human rights. If this is so, then the non-citizen and the foreigner have a claim to democratic sovereignty that the logic of the sovereign nation-state fails to recognize or cannot accommodate. By denying these claims, the sovereign democratic nation-state risks sacrificing democratic legitimacy at the altar of the nation.[9]

The second concern is that the concept of democracy as such is grounded upon the belief that all human beings, by virtue of their birth, are morally free and equal. This is a fundamental truth of democracy in modernity, and the just recognition of these natural qualities gives rise to a set of inalienable, universal political rights. Put otherwise, each individual is sovereign, and, as such, has the rights to life, liberty, enfranchisement, epistemic authority, freedom of speech and movement, equality, etc. regardless of her political or legal status within the territory in which she resides. Of course, there is an increasingly robust international human rights regime designed to protect the fundamental rights of all, but the sovereign duty and right to protect the nation is regularly invoked by existing states—including and especially the world's most powerful democracies—to justify refusing to recognize or actively violating the most basic democratic and human rights.[10] As Benhabib writes, "There is not only a tension, but often an outright contradiction, between human rights declarations and states' sovereign claims to control their borders as well as monitor the quality and quantity of admittees" (2004, 2). In a similar vein, Hannah Arendt notes that when the laws of a country failed to recognize and protect human rights, countries "were expected to change them, by legislation in democratic countries or through revolutionary action in despotisms" (1968, 293). This holds true today, and the most powerful democracies "speaking and acting on behalf of the international community" apply all forms of political coercion (up to and including the use of force) on countries that violate these international norms. The weakest countries are compelled to acquiesce while the strongest—even when democratic—often do as they see fit.

It is true that the legitimate democratic nation-state must protect its own citizens. However, the sovereign nation-state has obligations to non-citizens as well. International law, treatises, and agreements do have legal force to compel signatory states to recognize the legal rights of non-citizens, even if their enforcement mechanisms are often too weak to guarantee compliance every time. However, the universal scope of democracy as such entails a moral obligation that is heightened and made central by today's historic levels of human migration into and through sovereign territories. Yet, a moral obligation can be met or not. This fact represents the crux of the problem. Despite the universal scope of democratic principles, the nation-state presupposes, in its very concept, the suturing together of two distinct notions of a people: *ethnos* and *demos*. Because membership within the *ethnos*/nation is a pre-condition for citizenship and democratic rights, non-citizens, refugees, asylum seekers, and (im)migrants who arrive at the borders of sovereign nation-states are regularly and systematically excluded from political membership and denied democratic rights. In a word, the logic of the sovereign nation-state justifies ignoring or refusing to recognize the moral rights of non-citizens, of democracy's others, whose claims upon the state are legitimated by our shared humanity.

This thread of what duty existing democratic nation-states owe to foreigners, non-citizens, refugees, and (im)migrants will be taken up in the consideration of cosmopolitanism in the final chapter. At this point, however, the third troubling aspect of the link between the self-identical sovereign *demos* and the homogeneity of the *ethnos* requires immediate attention. To speak generically of the *ethnos* or nation as pertaining to a given population unified according to the particular geo-political territory they control is a misnomer. The *ethnos* or nation is not simply an externally directed entity composed of "us" who live here in this place that is distinct from "them" or the foreign others who live elsewhere. It is also that which undergoes an internal process whereby the "us" of the nation is perpetually re-imagined and reinvented as "we" question who "we" are, what socio-cultural qualities and practices are "ours," what values "we" subscribe to, etc. In this (re)imagining of national identity, it is not simply foreigners or outsiders but also "insiders" who deviate from the imagined *ethnos* of the nation that are cast as foreign based on the presumed threat they pose to national identity.[11]

While the diversity of the *ethnos* within pluralist democracies like the United States has altered the traditional composition of the *demos*, this fact does not justify overlooking or denying its history of sovereign exclusion of insiders who are deemed to be foreign to the ideal and generic exemplar of the democratic citizen, namely the white, Christian, capitalist, English-speaking, adult, heterosexual male (a set of qualities which, not-coincidentally, are nearly identical to the supposedly generic depiction of the man who consents to be governed according to the terms of the social contract). The institution of slavery and subsequent racism, terror, and violence of Jim Crow, the disenfranchisement of women, and the distrust and marginalization of new immigrants, all are instances of the sovereign exclusion of insiders who do not pass the test of American national identity.[12] All are anti-democratic attempts to constitute a self-identical *demos* by controlling access to the *ethnos*. We must not pretend, moreover, that these types of violence no longer exist. The treatment of Muslim-Americans, white supremacy, the exploitation and demonization of undocumented Latin American (im)migrants, and the unequal treatment of homosexuals—to name just four—are unique instances in which the self-identical sovereign *demos* assigns foreignness as a status to certain insiders whose difference threatens the idealized end of a homogeneous nation.[13] By the law of force and the force of law specific to the logic of the nation-state, those deemed foreign to the *dominant ethnos* are justly and legitimately excluded from membership within the *demos*.[14]

These "internal" examples suggest that the governing logic of the nation-state is fundamentally opposed to the democratic value of and belief in every human being's inalienable right to freedom and equality. I have argued that the relationship between sovereign self-identicality and the homogeneity of a people is opposed to *democracy as such*; however, this relationship is essential to the *democratic nation-state*, which—if it is to be just and legitimate—must protect the democratic rights of its national citizens. In this respect, the legitimate and just democratic nation-state is premised upon the exclusion of foreignness from the self-identical sovereign *demos*, an end that can only be forcefully achieved through the perpetual policing of the imaginative and symbolic borders of the *ethnos*, the geo-political borders of the state, and the physical walls meant to keep foreigners out or insiders in. To achieve its end, this perpetual policing is assisted by the sovereign force to deem both "outsiders" and "insiders" to be "illegal" (and therefore justly punished and excluded for breaking the law) or to ignore or violate universal, human rights in the name of the sovereign right of the state and its citizens.

My intention is not to claim that national identity does not or ought not to exist. Moreover, I do not claim that sovereign democratic nation-states have no duty to protect themselves. Instead, by identifying the link between the self-identicality of the sovereign *demos* and the homogeneity of the nation, I am suggesting that democratic justice is enervated through the forceful exclusion of foreignness whereby the *de facto* definition of justice remains indistinguishable from might makes right. One must be counted and recognized as one of "us" to be included within the *demos*, to be provided with the best guarantee that one's human and democratic rights will be recognized and protected. Yet, this very same mechanism (i.e., counting, taking account, surveillance, and monitoring) is designed and deployed to exclude. Legitimate democracy actually resists this exclusionary logic of the nation-state insofar as sovereign right is predicated on the claims of individuals. Yes, the citizen is primary in this respect, but it is precisely the universal scope of these claims that compel the legitimate democratic state to recognize and respond even when it is a non-citizen appealing for political membership. In short, legitimate democratic states are obligated to citizens and non-citizens alike. In this way, the claim of the citizen is mirrored by the claim of the foreigner, and it is the recognition of this fact that is required if we seek an alternative conception of democracy and justice that refuses violence and the force of the stronger directed against the foreign. Accordingly, the next step is to see whether and how democracy in its very concept might break apart the link among nationality, political membership, and citizenship which produces a vulnerable, large, and growing population of democracy's others.

Foreign unto it-self: autoimmune democracy

The logic of the democratic nation-state reserves citizenship for those who are members of the national family. For this reason, bloodlines, birth, and/or the presumed naturalness of geographic proximity and territoriality function as the dominant legal requirements (*ius sanguinis* and *ius soli*) for controlling immigration, determining membership within the nation and citizenship within the state.[15] Yet, as members of a nation who cannot possibly come into contact with or know every other member, our ability to recognize each other *as* members who share common commitments, goals, and allegiances must be extrapolated—at least in part—from our understanding of and experiences of the family. The nation, in this regard, is the imaginary expansion of the presumed biological and natural bonds of affiliation and allegiance typical of familial consanguinity. Most simply, the nation is familiar. Less the soul of the Leviathan, the self-identical, legitimate sovereign of the democratic nation-state is more akin to the immune system of the body politic, at once the skin which repels foreign intruders and the coordinated confluence of systems and processes which detects and eliminates the foreignness that would mutate, dilute, weaken, divide, poison, or even kill the nation-state from within.

Against this conceptualization of sovereign immunity, this chapter begins with an analysis of how Derrida's deconstructive figure of autoimmunity resists this biological and natural model of sovereign self-identicality and legitimacy determinative of who will be included and who will be excluded from the nation and state. I begin by briefly revisiting Derrida's elaboration of ipseity in order to link this essential quality of sovereignty to the freedom and force central to political and, more specifically, democratic rule. Once this connection is detailed, I examine the aporia of freedom as it relates to Derrida's claim that insofar as democracy must immunize itself from real or perceived threats, this process of immunization actually threatens to destroy, in an autoimmune fashion, democracy and the fundamental principles upon which it is grounded. Because autoimmune democracy destroys itself in its attempts to secure itself, it is simultaneously self-identical and heterogeneous or foreign to itself. The goal, however, is not to proclaim that there is nothing more to say about democracy; rather, when democracy's autoimmunity is mapped onto the (non)concepts of the foreign-sovereign and quasi-regime, the biological and natural justifications for excluding the foreign from the *ethnos* and, by turns, the *demos*, lose their force. In short, a democracy that is foreign to itself may be reconceptualized in such a way that its legitimacy is no longer premised upon the forceful exclusion of foreignness in the name of a democratic justice indistinguishable from the old adage that might makes right.

Up to this point, I have largely relied upon the term "self-identicality" to define the essence of sovereignty, since that which is sovereign is absolutely eliminative of the foreign. While self-identicality shares much with Derrida's work on ipseity, I have preferred this term because it makes explicit the complex and varied ways in which foreignness is (implicitly) constructed within the history of political philosophy as an absolute threat to existing sovereign states and the very concept of sovereignty as such. This emphasis must not be lost, since foreignness and the foreigner remain central concerns; however, it is useful to return to Derrida's elaboration of ipseity, since it opens the way forward for considering both foreign difference and the relationship between freedom and force—or, more properly, a certain understanding of freedom *as* force or might—that is central to traditional conceptualizations of democracy (Derrida [2003] 2005, 22).

Ipseity is the quality of sovereignty that undergirds autonomous political action (of both the individual and the state) and responsible moral agency (again of the individual and state). *Ipse* is a common Latin translation of the Greek word *autos*, and the word from which the English term "self" is derived. Ipseity, however, suggests something different from the conscious self. More precisely, following Michael Naas' cue, ipseity is "the system or matrix" (2008, 126) that grounds, frames, and makes operational the collectivity of terms and concepts associated with the *autos* and the self. From autonomy, auto-affection, and autotely to self-sameness, selfhood, and self-determination, ipseity structures the indivisibility and inviolability constitutive of sovereignty as such. It is this originary unity and wholeness of sovereignty as such, which simultaneously directs itself toward its own future completeness—a teleological unfolding and regathering of the self-same to itself through sovereign mastery and self-determining. In short, ipseity suggests sovereign distinction in both senses of the term. First, it is the homogeneity, immunity, and distinctness of the sovereign *autos*/*ipse*/self from the other. Second, ipseity is the sovereign mark of distinction, import, prominence, prerogative, autonomous self-mastery, power, property, authority, strength, legitimacy, etc. (Derrida [2003] 2005, 11).

Given this dual sense of distinction which forges the sovereign self, Derrida insists that "[b]efore any sovereignty of state, of the nation-state, of the monarch, or, in democracy, of the people, ipseity names a principle of legitimate sovereignty, the accredited or recognized supremacy of a power or force, a *kratos* or *cracy*" ([2003] 2005, 12, original emphasis). For Derrida, ipseity alerts us to the force, power, and freedom of the autonomous self to act and decide that (re)produces itself *qua* individual, nation-state, and people, i.e., the legitimacy derived from the sovereign empowered to enforce its will with the result that it maintains and protects its distinction(s). Derrida continues, ipseity is "some 'I can', or at the very least the power that *gives itself*, its own law, its force of law, its self-presentation, the sovereign and reappropriating gathering of self in the simultaneity of an assemblage or assembly, being together, or 'living together' as we say" ([2003] 2005, 11 original emphasis). There is no act or decision without the self-same *autos*/*ipse*/self that acts and decides. Conversely, every use of force or power to freely act or decide (re)inscribes or (re)produces the self-sameness of the *autos*/*ipse*/self *qua* autonomous, responsible, and sovereign actor. Sovereign ipseity anchors freedom and freedom anchors sovereign ipseity.[16] Therefore, democracy (grounded in freedom) must be examined with respect to the conceptual relationship between freedom and sovereign force.

The conceptual link between freedom and democracy is well known, but the longstanding tension that exists between the two concepts is less frequently considered. Derrida draws our attention to an example of this tension in Book VIII of *The Republic* where Plato cites the common belief that democratic freedom simply means that each has the license to do and live as one pleases while its rulers lack the authority, the force, and the resolve to correct this license (Plato 1968, 556a–c).[17] Derrida writes that Plato's "portrait of the democrat associates freedom or liberty (*eleutheria*) with license (*exousia*), which is also whim, freewill, freedom of choice, leisure to follow one's desires, ease, facility, the faculty or power to do as one pleases" ([2003] 2005, 22). One may follow the law or not; one may work or remain idle; one may choose licentiousness over virtue (Plato 1968, 557e). Indeed, one may even have freedom of speech, which can both forge the law or devolve into a cacophonous discord that threatens the univocity upon which the law and sovereign authority depend. This association between freedom and license has persisted into modernity. Recall, for example, Locke's insistence that this association must be broken. He argues that mankind's freedom in the state of nature is not one of license.[18] For Locke as much as for Plato, freedom is simultaneously integral to and that which must be excised from the well-regulated, even free, regime (*exousia* or license must be excised at any rate). Yet, as Derrida notes: "It has always been *hard* to distinguish, with regard to free will, between the good of democratic freedom or liberty and the evil of democratic license. They are hardly different" ([2003] 2005, 21, original emphasis).

This quote already alludes to the aporia of freedom, which will be fully elaborated below, but Derrida's immediate intention is to show that the association between freedom and license as well as the danger this excess of freedom poses to democracy is presupposed even before any meaningful consideration of the central concepts of democracy—the people (*demos*) and power (*kratos*)—is undertaken. This association between liberty and license cannot be overstated, since "it is on the basis of freedom that we will have conceived the concept of democracy [throughout the tradition]" (Derrida [2003] 2005, 22). To understand the meaning of democracy, one must understand freedom, and Derrida, in his reading of the tradition, defines it in this way:

> Freedom is essentially the faculty or power to do as one pleases, to decide, to choose, to determine *one-self*, to have self-determination, to be master, and first of all master of one-self (*autos, ipse*). A simple analysis of the "I can," of the "it is possible for me," of the "I have the force to" (*krateō*), reveals the predicate of freedom, the "I am free to," "I can decide." There is no freedom without ipseity and, vice versa, no ipseity without freedom—and, thus, without a certain sovereignty.
>
> Derrida [2003] 2005, 22–23, original emphasis

Given this conception of freedom, it is evident why Derrida insists that the analysis of the connection between freedom and sovereign force—freedom and ipseity—precedes the nation, state, people, etc. Freedom is the license, power, force, might, and right of the self-same sovereign to impose its will. The sovereign maintains and secures its ipseity—it enacts and enforces its will—by gathering together and assembling those who are similar or by assimilating and integrating those who are different into a unified, homogeneous, and distinct sovereign nation or *demos* premised upon an equality exclusive of all foreign difference.[19] That which is sovereign is the strongest; it is that which is free to impose its will and, in so doing, remains indivisible and invulnerable to foreign difference.

Because this strength and power to enforce its will and protect itself as a self is directed against the weak (or weaker), i.e., the feminine, the minority (party), minorities (ethnic, racial, religious, linguistic, sexual, etc.), the outsider, the other, the foreign, etc., sovereign (democratic) freedom is "hardly different" from the notion that might makes right. That said, Derrida is no "enemy of freedom." Instead, through his deconstructions of freedom and—as we shall see—democracy, Derrida challenges the legitimacy of exclusionary force in the name of the self-sameness and distinction of sovereign ipseity. He solicits sovereignty "in the sense that *sollicitare*, in old Latin, means to shake as a whole, to make tremble in entirety" (Derrida 1982, 21) by conceiving of a freedom no longer aligned with force, a conceptualization of freedom that would cause the very concept of democracy to tremble.[20] In short, Derrida attempts to think freedom and democracy together in a way that rejects those forms of sovereignty and justice that perpetuate the advantage of the stronger.

Because sovereign ipseity is freedom *qua* license, force, power, rule (*cracy* or *kratos*) that originates in and is directed toward preserving the self-same, sovereignty is central to all political constitutions. That which is sovereign gives itself the law and achieves its legitimacy through the (forceful if not always lawful) protection of the people as a unified, inviolable, and indivisible whole. Democracy, in one sense, is no different. The legitimacy of the rule of the people is not only marked by the extent to which it is licensed to enforce its will, but also by the fact that this freedom and autonomy is grounded in the belief in the originary unity of the people (Rousseau's myth of founding, for example) and directed toward its future completeness, univocity, and homogeneity. Whether expressed by a communitarian conservatism that dreams of re-unifying the once unified people or the progressive dream of eventual unification of the *demos* through the inclusion of all democratic friends "yearning to breathe free" (despite their differences), democracy presupposes the ipseity of sovereignty, which forcefully assembles and gathers together the self-same into unified people.

In another sense, however, democracy is different from all other forms of political rule precisely because of its foundation in freedom, and it is here that the aporetic structure of freedom comes into play. Liberty and license are different, yet, as Derrida reminds us, they are "hard" to distinguish; indeed, he insists, "they are hardly different." For example, what are we to make of the philosophical gadfly? Of civil disobedience? Of criminals, dissemblers, rogues, and traitors? Of immigrants who refuse to assimilate or integrate? Of those who reject political allegiances in favor of economic blocs or religious affiliation? Are these acts of liberty or license? Who has the right, power, and authority to decide?[21] Derrida is clear on the tradition: "Democracy is freedom" ([2003] 2005, 23). But, it is precisely this association between liberty and license—freedom as excess that is sovereign power—which suggests the aporia of freedom. Peter Gratton writes, "[F]reedom is always free to be otherwise than freedom, to free itself of itself" (2012, 218). Insofar as "democracy is freedom," democracy is free to be other than it is; it is free to undo itself even as it seeks to preserve, protect, and immunize itself. In a word, democracy is autoimmune.

Autoimmunity might seem an odd choice by Derrida. It is a concept proper to biology, and appeals to biology, nature, procreation, pregnancy, reproduction, etc. have been instrumentally deployed within the history of philosophy to establish the foundation of the Western metaphysics of presence which Derrida tirelessly critiques. For example, in *Symposium*, Plato (1961c) argues that the immortality of the soul is achieved through a pedagogical relationship between two men (the lover educating his beloved). This "procreation" results in a man "pregnant" with rational discourse, and it is against this backdrop that Socrates self-identifies as a midwife of ideas.[22] Similarly, biological (and agricultural) metaphors of the seed are to be found in Aristotle (e.g., woman is the material cause providing only the matter and nutrients for the self-forming, self-replicating agent of change, namely the male seed (1942, II4, 740b19–25)), the Stoics (*logoi spermatikoi*), and Hegel (the germ). Derrida himself points out that Lenin in his interpretation of dialectical materialism endeavored to trace out Hegelian "metaphors" of the "genetic or organic development of the 'germ' or 'seed'" (Derrida and Houdebine 1973, 39). This "logic of the male seed" is longstanding in the tradition of metaphysics given its usefulness as a metaphor for the incorruptible, non-differentiating, iterability of form and identity, the teleological understanding of the individual and history, and an explication of the "origins" of the binary oppositions between self/other, presence/absence, and *physis* and its opposites (*nomos*, *teoria*, *tekhnē*, etc.) to name but a few.

Derrida's critique of Western metaphysics is elaborated in the following section, but more immediately relevant is that biology and nature are also deployed to ground "the birth of the nation" and to establish political legitimacy and inclusion based on the hereditary passage of sovereign power from the king to his son or even the universal fraternity of democracy.[23] To understand why Derrida chooses autoimmunity, we must trace some key moments in its development within his thinking. One of the first uses of autoimmunity appears in *Specters of Marx*. There, Derrida claims that "the living ego is auto-immune . . . To protect its life, to constitute itself as unique living ego, to relate, as the same, to itself, it is necessarily led to welcome the other within . . . it must therefore take the immune defenses apparently meant for the non-ego, the enemy, the opposite, the adversary and direct them at once *for itself and against itself*" ([1993] 1994, 141, original emphasis). Even in this early appearance, it is clear that autoimmunity is being directed against the determination of being as presence, i.e., the perpetual repetition of the self-same that is nothing more than "the possibility for what is called *subjectivity*" (Derrida 1973, 79, original emphasis). Beyond subjectivity, it is life itself that is at stake. While requisite for subjectivity, the machine-like operation and predictability of the perpetual repetition of the self-same reveals that in order for the ego to be fully present as such, it must be or be conceived of as non-living and machine-like. Thus, the enemy, the opposite, the non-ego, the other, the machine, the foreign, artificiality, death, etc. are not simply external threats to the self-same and self-relating living ego; rather, these seemingly opposed and threatening forces disruptive of the perpetual repetition of the self-same are always already internal to and constitutive of the living ego. In this sense, the living ego is autoimmune because the very defenses it requires to immunize itself against the enemy, the non-ego, the other, etc. are simultaneously directed against itself.

Three years later, in "Faith and Knowledge: The Two Sources of 'Religion' at the Limits of Reason Alone" (Derrida [1996] 2002), autoimmunity is explicitly linked to the political. Peggy Kamuf writes that Derrida connects the "pre-modern legal sense [of immunity] (to be immune was to be exempt from taxation and other obligations to the state) to the modern biological or, precisely, immunological sense" (2006, 213–214). Derrida claims that autoimmunity will be developed as "a general logic of deconstruction as a 'contamination' of the proper at the origin" (Kamuf 2006, 214). Kamuf applauds Derrida's early success in establishing a "conceptual graft ... between an organic pathology and legal, institutional, political, religious, and ethical 'normalities'" (2006, 214), a graft that will have important implications for sovereignty in general and the idea of the nation and the *demos* as the unification of the self-same. Derrida's choice of autoimmunity is a risky one because any failure to recast the biological and natural metaphors functions to reinforce the very tradition being deconstructed, but the payoff is high, since autoimmunity can be directed against the determination of being as presence (which will be crucial for Derrida's positing of democracy to come), the exclusion of difference and the foreign from the sovereign, and the biological and/or naturalized requirements for the protection of democratic rights through membership within the nation and, in turn, citizenship.

Rogues is Derrida's sustained consideration of democracy, freedom, and sovereignty within the American context after September 11th, and it is here that autoimmunity is fully developed. Derrida begins by considering rogue states. They are the nation-states involved in the persistent and flagrant flaunting of international laws; they interfere with normal paths of international communication, commerce, and legal or political order; they also go by other names, including pariah states and outlaw states. If there was any doubt as to what a rogue state is, Derrida quotes a former National Security Council staffer under Bill Clinton who unequivocally summed it up: "A rogue state is basically whomever the United States says it is" ([2003] 2005, 96). If we ignore this non-fortuitous, self-proclaimed right of naming and judging, Derrida's aim in *Rogues* is to show that rogue states fail to accurately conceptualize the greatest threat to the security of particular nation-states and the international community.[24] What the terrorist attacks of September 11th make clear is that we must think anew who and what is the enemy of the sovereign state. The enemy is not simply the easily identifiable, bellicose, rogue state which threatens from without; instead, the enemy is the rogue in the broadest sense of the term; it is a non-state or trans-state actor, an affiliation, a network, a cell, a terrorist, a lone wolf, a citizen, an immigrant, a traitor, etc. In this respect, rogues complicate old notions of borders, insiders, outsiders, movement, immigration, national and political identity, military and police, and the very meaning of security and the protection of the people. Given this mixing up of once clear conceptual and geo-political borders, the sovereign state is compelled to act against itself in order to secure itself.

It is against this backdrop of the legitimacy, justness, and power of the sovereign state to immunize itself against threat that Derrida introduces autoimmunity through everyday examples of democratic responses to political crises and the conceptual structure of democracy as such. Derrida begins with the case of Algeria. In 1992, the democratically elected government of Algeria postponed a democratic election because the party that was set to take power planned to end the democracy and replace it with a theocracy. To save democracy in the long run, the election was temporarily suspended—that is, in the name of and for the sake of democracy, democracy was suspended. As Michael Naas points out, because power in a democracy is, by turns, transferred within the *demos*, the "intrinsic possibility" of democracy is that "through the most democratic of elections, a part of the *dēmos* will come to rule that whether wittingly or unwittingly, puts an end to democracy itself" (2008, 136). In this respect, democracy and freedom share the same aporetic features, and this should come as no surprise insofar as "democracy is freedom." Democracy is free to suspend or put an end to itself.[25]

In what sense, though, are the aporias of freedom and democracy autoimmune and not merely bad public policy or the misguided decision of a weak or immature sovereign democracy? Derrida's explication begins with a refined definition of autoimmunity. Autoimmunity, he argues, is "the illogical logic by which a living being can spontaneously destroy, in an autonomous fashion, the very thing within it that is supposed to protect it against the other, to immunize it against the aggressive intrusion of the other" (Derrida [2003] 2005, 123). There is, perhaps, no more vivid example of autoimmunity than the U.S. response to the terrorist attacks of September 11th. One might be tempted to view the U.S. strategy to be a logical attempt to build up its immunity whereby the political body's various modes of defense are released against "terrorists" and the rogue or pariah states believed to harbor these enemies in order to protect both its sovereignty and the fundamental principles of democracy as such. Following Derrida, however, it is helpful to think of this attempt at immunity as an expression of the "illogical logic" of autoimmunity.

In order to protect democracy, democratic values are trampled and suspended. In order to protect freedom, the U.S. curtails the freedoms of its citizens and threatens the freedom of non-citizens (enemies or not). In order to protect the rule of law, the U.S. violates its own and international law. One need look no further than the newspapers replete with verified stories of extraordinary rendition, CIA black sites, indefinite detentions, the torture facilities in Guantanamo, the torture memos, the violent abuses of prisoners in Abu Ghraib, the Patriot Act, unfettered spying on citizens by the NSA, the killing of civilians by unmanned drones, just to name a few. All of these "defenses" of the state, sovereignty, freedom, and democracy (i.e., "Homeland Security") have been undertaken with violent force and the force of law in order to immunize democracy from its others, in this case Islamic terrorist cells. Yet, in each use of sovereign right, freedom, license, and force, the U.S. decimates the very democratic principles it seeks to defend. Derrida writes, "It [democracy] must thus come to resemble these enemies, to corrupt itself and threaten itself in order to protect itself against their threats" ([2003] 2005, 40).

Just as democracy is free to end itself, it is also free to limit its freedom in the name of and for the sake of democracy. Once again, therefore, these acts could be viewed as nothing more than bad policy, the well-intentioned yet excessive proclivities of the sovereign *demos* to protect itself, its ipseity, and the unity of its people against the threat of terror. Freedom and democratic rights may be temporarily curtailed, but new elections and better leaders will result in better policy ... next time. This may or may not be so, but these and similar political examples of the "security apparatus" of the sovereign democratic state attempting to preserve and immunize itself are better understood as unavoidable byproducts of the structural autoimmunity of the very concept of democracy, which is always already in a process of differing from and deferring it-self.

Democracy takes time.[26] It requires discussion, debate, and the recurring and cyclical voting process; it is free to end or limit itself in the name of and for the sake of democracy *or* to criticize, challenge, and question itself, to re-inscribe its very meaning in order to bring about a more just order. Peter Gratton offers a helpful formulation: "democracy is the only system in which one always already has the right, the license, to criticize openly everything, including the concept and history of the idea of democracy; this is both its threat and its chance" (2012, 219). For Derrida, the aporia of democracy founded in freedom—the license that is both its "threat and chance"—is that democracy as such is never fully present; it always takes more time. This does not mean that democratic states do not exist. Of course they do. Rather, Derrida is suggesting that democracy itself is never what it *is* or purports to be because it is always in the process of a "double *renvoi*" ([2003] 2005, 36), i.e., the spatial sending off of the other as well as a referral to the other *and* a temporal putting off or adjournment ([2003] 2005, 36). This double movement of sending off and the putting off of itself is the structural, conceptual basis for the autoimmunity of democracy.

In what sense is democracy always being spatially sent off? Democratic rule is, as Aristotle observed, a rule by turns of equals. "Ruling by turns" implicitly suggests that part of the *demos* is always sent off. This is true even within representative democracies where the ruling of one party entails the temporary sending off of other parties, of another part of the *demos*, to be ruled over (until, at least, the next election). Because part of the *demos* is always being sent off, it is always already differing from—at a remove from—itself. This is why, in Michael Naas' formulation, "a *dēmos* is not exactly 'a people'" (2008, 136), since the part of the *demos* that rules is not, strictly speaking, the people as such.[27] Another more malignant form of sending off occurs when democracy sends off those (both citizens and non-citizens) whose difference threatens or is deemed to be a threat to democracy by excluding them from the *demos*.[28] Even the right of the sovereign *demos* to decide who is or is not to be included as a citizen presupposes the exclusion of certain individuals and groups (non-citizens, undocumented (im)migrants, etc.) from political membership, a limiting of democracy required for the functioning of the democratic state. Internally, these presumed threats are sent back to the private sphere, away from the polls, off to jail, deported, de-humanized, or de-legitimized (Derrida [2003] 2005, 36). Rather than regrettable cases of individual injustices performed by this or that democracy, it is democracy itself that is always already sent off in order to immunize it from the perceived threats to the ipseity and self-identicality of the *demos*. In these ways territory, borders, public spaces for assembly and speech, voting booths, jails, courthouses, detention facilities, etc. are not merely the geographical locations where democracy has taken hold or where it is publicly practiced and instituted within a society; rather, they are also monuments to absence, i.e., to the extent to which the sovereign *demos* has successfully excluded and sent off its others.

Sending off also provides a conceptual explication of why some undemocratic laws are not merely instances of bad governance. For example, until the early twentieth century in the U.S., women were lawfully denied the right to vote to protect the democracy from the threat of "irrational" voters. However, the demand for enfranchisement arises from the very principles of freedom and equality that constitute democracy. In this and so many other cases, freedom is justly and lawfully restricted to ensure freedom. Equality is justly and lawfully disregarded to ensure equality. Voting is justly and lawfully denied to ensure the sanctity of voting. Democracy is justly and lawfully sent off to protect democracy. To reiterate, sending off is the "illogical logic" that structures democracy insofar as its fundamental and indispensable principles are the very same ones that must necessarily be limited if democracy (and the democratic state) is to immunize itself. As Derrida insists, "democracy protects itself and maintains itself precisely by limiting and threatening itself" ([2003] 2005, 36).

Spatial sending off has another dimension. In addition to exclusionary sending off of the perceived threat of foreign difference, there is also a sending off of democracy in the form of a "referral *to* the other" in the form of "respect for the foreigner or for the alterity of the other" (Derrida [2003] 2005, 36, original emphasis). Sovereign ipseity is a central and indispensable feature of democracy, freedom, a people, a nation, etc., but despite the operations of the sovereign state to maintain and preserve its ipseity, the *autos* or self of sovereign democracy "remains incompatible with, even clashes with, another truth of the democratic, namely, the truth of the other, heterogeneity, the heteronomic, and the dissymmetric, disseminal multiplicity, the anonymous 'anyone,' the 'no matter who,' the indeterminate 'each one'" ([2003] 2005, 14–15). Even as democracy excludes the foreign other to protect its freedom and immunize itself, democracy also demands that it welcomes the other, sometimes at great cost to itself. Derrida vividly emphasizes this point, and it is worth quoting at length:

> [It] is perhaps because the United States has a culture and a system of law that are largely democratic that it was able to open itself up and expose its greatest vulnerability to immigrants, to, for example, pilots in training, experienced and suicidal "terrorists" who, before turning against others but also against themselves the aerial bombs that they had become, and before hurling them by hurling themselves into the two World Trade Towers, were trained on the sovereign soil of the United States ... The "terrorists" are sometimes American citizens, and some of those of September 11 might have been. They received help in any case from American citizens; they took American airplanes, took over the controls and took to the air in American planes, and took off from American airports.
>
> Derrida [2003] 2005, 40

This and similar instances of welcoming the "no matter who" is a welcoming not only of the feminine, the foreigner, the minority, and the weak but also the strong, the dangerous, the threatening, and the enemy. The guest may be parasitic, the immigrant may be a sworn enemy, etc., but there is no "calculating technique" (Derrida [2003] 2005, 53) or pre-determined, programmatic law that can tell the democracy *in advance* who will be a threat and who will make democracy more free, more equal, and more just.

In this respect, the "referral to" the other is a limiting of freedom, power, and strength. The power and force of the *demos*—the many, the majority, or even the people as an imaginary unity—is sent off in the address and invitation to the other. Derrida provocatively insists that "one will never actually be able to 'prove' that there is more democracy in granting or in refusing the right to vote to immigrants" ([2003] 2005, 36) because democracy demands the exclusion of the weak for the sake of the majority and the exclusion of the majority for the sake of the weak. One electoral law is, in this respect "always at the same time more and less democratic than another" ([2003] 2005, 36). This does not mean that Derrida opposes robust voting rights or nuanced immigration policy; rather, sending off points to the aporia that structures the concept of democracy itself, namely, it is unable to avoid a certain "indecidability" ([2003] 2005, 35). In referring to the other, it sends off a part of itself; in excluding or sending off the other, it limits and threatens itself. Thus, this moment of free decision—to welcome or exclude the "no matter who"—which constitutes the sovereign ipseity of the *demos* simultaneously and necessarily generates exclusions from itself; it is democracy's foreignness to it-self.[29]

In addition to sending off or the spatial differing from itself, democracy is also always already temporally deferred until another day. In this case there is a *renvoi* or a "*putting off* until later" (Derrida [2003] 2005, 36, original emphasis) of democracy. Referring back to the examples above, the moment of democratic freedom and decision epitomized by the election may be put off indefinitely. Similarly, through the lawful institution and enforcement of undemocratic laws, democracy as such is curtailed and put off. In each case, democracy is deferred until a time when there are no longer foreign or domestic threats. However, because democracy is the one form of political rule that can freely end or curtail itself, there is and never can be absolute security. At the very moment that democracy announces itself by freely declaring the rule of the people, it opens itself to the threat of its own license, its own freedom to undo or limit itself.

Taken together, the "*double renvoi*" of democracy "is an autoimmune necessity inscribed *right onto* [*à même*] democracy, right onto the concept of democracy" (Derrida [2003] 2005, 36, original emphasis). What Derrida is claiming, to emphasize what has already been stated, is that the specific decisions made, for example, by Algeria in 1992 or the U.S. after September 11th are not mere instances of democracy failing to achieve its ideal. Rather, autoimmunity is the autonomous destruction of democracy as such in its logical attempt to immunize itself against that which threatens it. However, this attempt to immunize itself is not the willful suicide of a democracy, but rather the "illogical logic" whereby the attempt to immunize itself is spontaneously turned against itself in an autoimmune fashion. Hence, Derrida claims that autoimmunity "consists not in committing suicide but in compromising the *sui-* or self-referentiality, the *self* or *sui-* of suicide itself" ([2003] 2005, 45). Insofar as autoimmunity is a "necessity" that is "inscribed" onto the very concept of democracy, democracy destroys itself as it constitutes itself. Put differently, democracy is simultaneously self-identical and heterogeneous to it-self; it is simultaneously sovereign and non-sovereign; it is simultaneously sovereign and foreign. Democracy, Derrida claims, is "a concept devoid of sameness and ipseity" ([2003] 2005, 37), which is to say that it is never proper to itself. Democracy always takes more time because "there is no absolute paradigm, whether constitutive or constitutional, no absolutely intelligible idea, no *eidos*, no *idea* of democracy. And thus, in the final analysis, no democratic ideal. For even if there were one, and wherever there would be one, this 'there is' would remain aporetic, under a double or autoimmune constraint" ([2003] 2005, 37, original emphasis).

Derrida's distinguishing between suicide and the autoimmune necessity that destroys "the self or *sui-* of suicide itself" explains why he runs the risk of deploying the biological deconstructive figure of autoimmunity. While the political decisions of Algeria in 1992 and the U.S. after September 11th are symptoms or expressions of the autoimmunity of democracy as such, they are also the decisions made by the sovereign state and on behalf of sovereign right. The principles of legitimate state sovereignty empower the state to protect its sovereignty even when this means undermining or curtailing the very principles upon which it is founded. Even if democracy is always already heterogeneous to it-self and autoimmune, sovereignty, in line with its traditional conceptualization, is that which retains its homogeneity and ipseity. In this way, appeals to sovereign right and the performative expressions of sovereign force undertaken in the name of the state function to (re)establish unity, indivisibility, inviolability, and self-identicality of the one, self-same body politic. In short, sovereignty alone is that which can save autoimmune democracy from itself.

Autoimmunity, however, is more radical still. Before the positing of the "natural" ipseity of the *autos* premised upon the perpetual repetition of the self-same eliminative of all foreign difference, and, thus, before any simple division between *zōē* (the bare life of necessity), *bios* (political life, the possibility for the good life), and "the state of exception" that wields great influence over contemporary debates in "postmodern thinking" on the status and fate of democracy's others (e.g., refugees, the stateless, the (im)migrant, and even its enemies),[30] autoimmunity reveals the heterogeneity constitutive of sovereignty as such. Derrida states that "pure sovereignty is indivisible or it is not at all" ([2003] 2005, 101), and this indivisibility requires the sovereign to remain silent. Derrida continues, "Sovereignty withdraws from language, which always introduces a sharing that universalizes. As soon as I speak to the other, I submit to the law of giving reason(s), I share a virtually universalizable medium, I divide my authority, even in the most performative language, which always requires another language in order to lay claim to some convention . . . To confer sense or meaning on sovereignty, to justify it, to find a reason for it, is already to compromise its deciding exceptionality, to subject it to rules, to a code of law, to some general law, to concepts. It is thus to divide it, to subject it to partitioning, to participation, to being shared" ([2003] 2005, 101). Sovereignty may and must make endless decrees, establish and vociferously promulgate the law, be diplomatic or bellicose in its performances, but if it is to be and remain sovereign (retain its ipseity and be an indivisible, inviolable, and unified whole), then sovereignty must retain or reserve or bank silence.

Recall that sovereign silence is the store of credit, the invisible force, upon which the faith of the people is invested, an inviolable and indivisible remainder to which the people can pledge their allegiance as "one nation under [one] God." This notwithstanding, the sovereign must speak and reveal itself. For this reason, Derrida insists: "Pure sovereignty does not exist. It is always in the process of positing itself by refuting itself, by denying or disavowing itself; it is always in the process of autoimmunizing itself, of betraying itself by betraying the democracy that nonetheless can never do without it" ([2003] 2005, 101). Sovereignty cannot be severed from democracy, but that which is sovereign must break its silence, and in so doing it reveals itself to be constituted by the foreign and open to the counter-sovereignty of its others. Sovereignty, like democracy, is autoimmune.

If so, then sovereignty is always already divided and vulnerable. This is why appeals to state sovereignty are always premised on force and power, and the strongest sovereign states are incorrigible. Derrida writes that "there is no sovereignty without force, without the force of the strongest, whose reason—the reason of the strongest—is to win over [*avoir raison de*] everything" ([2003] 2005, 101). Yet, because sovereignty is autoimmune, there is no telling in advance whether its use of force will be beneficial or detrimental to it. For example, the sovereign democracy must open itself to the foreign, but by doing so it welcomes that which may destroy it and the very democracy able to extend the welcome in the first place. By sending away the foreign, the sovereign democracy limits, curtails, and threatens its fundamental principles and itself. In short, every sovereign decision made by a democracy to freely welcome or exclude is an expression of force simultaneously directed against the other and against itself. For this reason, the use of autoimmunity is worth the risk for Derrida because it brings to the fore the question of the *ipse/autos/sui*/self-referentiality that grounds sovereign force (freedom as force). Put another way, autoimmunity raises the question of life and death.

The life of democracy (the ipseity of the *demos*), of course, is on the line, but also the lives of millions of individuals who are sent off from the democracy (in the name of democracy). They are told to wait until another day, wait until the time is right, wait until the government responds, wait until the people are ready to accept and welcome them.[31] In this way, autoimmunity raises the question of life because it aims directly at the powers that accrue to democracy *qua* an ipsocratic regime of sovereign self-identicality exclusive of the foreign, including the sovereign's right over life and death (of both citizens and non-citizens), the power to decide who is a member of the nation, and, hence, who can be a member of the *demos*.

Autoimmunity also points to the question of life and death in a more general sense. Derrida is clear that democracy requires sovereignty and that the democratic state is a sovereign state even if it is "betrayed" by sovereignty which is always already shared out to counter-sovereignties and foreign others. At the same time, Derrida recognizes that the unity and solidarity of a sovereign people is not only an important and laudable goal but necessary for democratic rule. However, within the nation-state, the solidarity and unity of the *demos*—even in the most progressive democracies—presupposes a natural and biological basis for the self-identicality of the nation.[32] This is why inclusion within the nation-state is traditionally structured upon consanguinity and/or the naturalized conception of geographic proximity and territoriality. Both establish the familiar basis for the self-identicality of the imagined nation. In this way, the nation is restricted according to biology, genetics, and nature (to a greater or lesser extent depending on the particular state), even as these national requirements are strictly at odds with democracy as such, which recognizes the universal freedom and equality of all.[33] The legal and moral claims of non-citizens creates a perpetual opening and vulnerability of the sovereign democratic nation-state that often results in nativistic responses premised upon the belief that the nation—like the state—must be walled off and its borders perpetually policed for fear of the threat of infection, contamination, and mutation, which might threaten social cohesion, political solidarity, and the very life of the nation-state as such.

The sovereign efforts to immunize the nation from foreign difference all too frequently result in the violent targeting, segregation, exclusion, and elimination of the foreigner or casting as foreign the insider who threatens the presumed biological and natural (and, hence, heteronormative) foundations of the nation. However, if, as Derrida claims, the nation *qua* sovereign body is autoimmune, then attempts to immunize the nation from foreignness requires attacking the nation itself (e.g., voter identification laws ostensibly put in place to guarantee the sanctity of the voting booth effectively reduce voter turnout, particularly among minority groups, the poor, and women).[34] The nation premised upon biology, genetics, and nature is an ever-constricting field that requires an ever-expanding set of exclusions directed against both outsiders and insiders. In other words, the policing of the self-identicality of the nation is nothing more than the dominant *ethnos* attempting to enforce its will by exploiting its advantage and might over the weak.

Democracy is autoimmune; it is heterogeneous and foreign to itself. Therefore, within the nation-state model of political organization, the nation becomes the final battlefield and last refuge for guaranteeing the indivisibility, inviolability, ipseity, self-identicality, and unity of the *demos*. Sovereignty endeavors to immunize itself—by rallying biology, genetics, and nature to its side—by freely and forcefully deciding who will be included or excluded from the national family, which is simply to say who will be deemed foreign. Once again, life is on the line; the life of the nation and the lives of those who become victims not only of the most virulent strains of ethno-nationalism but also the equally pernicious—albeit more subtle forms—of national, ethnic, and political exclusion that remain in effect in the most tolerant liberal democracies. Yet, if the nation is autoimmune and always already foreign to itself, the question of life and death is no longer proper to the sovereign; instead, it dangles tenuously by the thread of the possibility for the reconceptualization of foreignness that autoimmunity makes possible.

Unsurprisingly then, autoimmunity returns us to foreignness and the foreigner. Above I argued that the foreigner—she who embodies foreignness no matter if she is an insider or outsider—is conceptualized as lacking an essence. This is why she is simultaneously cast as artificial, natural, and a perversion of nature. She is a shadowy figure whose protean nature and border-crossings are deemed to be absolute threats to sovereign self-identicality and ipseity.[35] As a result, her allegiance and true intentions are always uncertain. Assimilation may be infiltration while remaining apart (ethnic enclaves, for example) indicates a refusal to assimilate. In both cases, the foreigner is conceived of as fundamentally unknowable and untrustworthy.

This does not mean that foreigners are not regularly welcomed and included within democracy. Rather, because the nation is imagined along the lines of familial consanguinity, the foreigner must "naturalize" to be officially recognized as a member of the national family. Only then can she become a citizen whose democratic rights are protected by the law. By naturalizing, she sheds her foreignness, which is to say that she becomes accounted for (known) and accountable to (trustworthy) the national family and the state. Insofar as the link among nationality, citizenship, and democratic right is forged upon the self-identicality supposedly guaranteed by consanguinity, foreignness remains without an essence and, as such, is an absolute threat to sovereign ipseity. It must, therefore, be eliminated.

To counter this negative depiction of foreignness, I argued for the (non) concepts of the foreign-sovereign and the quasi-regime while autoimmunity was used as the structural latticework for theorizing foreignness as constitutive of and ineliminable from sovereignty in general. However, here, we are no longer considering sovereignty in general or democracy in the abstract. Instead, insofar as autoimmunity challenges the very possibility for an indivisible, inviolable, and immune *ipse/autos/*self, it becomes clear that the sovereign, democratic nation-state is always already foreign to it-self. Thus, the effects of every sovereign decision by the democratic nation-state to include or exclude the "no matter who" can never be known in advance, since every attempt at immunity runs the risk of an autoimmune destruction of the self-same. In a word, the decision simultaneously (re)constitutes the nation-state as self-same while opening it to that which is foreign *within itself*.

Autoimmunity, therefore, calls into question the biological and natural foundation of the nation-state. Nature, biology, genetics, and consanguinity may be used to determine membership within the nation-state, but they are revealed for what they are, namely, conceptual mechanisms deployed by the sovereign in its attempt to immunize the nation-state through the forceful exclusion of the perceived threat of foreignness to its self-identicality and ipseity. The sovereign decision to exclude in the hopes of achieving a self-identical nation amounts to a rejection of democracy as such. On the one hand, it forecloses the claims to hospitality and welcoming of democracy's others; on the other hand, it implicitly structures political inclusion and democratic rights on the hierarchical (biological) ordering of *ethnoi* within the nation. Against this conceptualization, the (non)concepts of the foreign-sovereign and the quasi-regime begin to gain traction. They do not simply offer abstract possibilities for the normative, political, and social welcoming of the foreign; instead, when autoimmunity is thought alongside the foreign-sovereign and the quasi-regime, new possibilities emerge for a re-conceptualization of foreignness which recognizes that it is structurally necessary to the *ethnos*, *demos*, democratic political identity, and sovereignty as such, and it is this in-eliminability of the foreign which allows for the possibility of undoing or mitigating sovereign force—of the forceful and free sovereign decision.

As noted, this structural necessity of foreignness does not program or pre-determine the ethical and political response to the foreigner by the sovereign. Rather, insofar as sovereignty is autoimmune, the foreign-sovereign is that which can never know in advance whether welcoming or excluding the foreign will initiate a process of immunization or autoimmunization. The recognition of the structural necessity of foreignness—of sovereign autoimmunity—does not require welcoming any and all that might arrive.[36] The guest may turn out to be a parasite or an enemy; instead, it offers the possibility for an open future—"an exposure to the other, to *what* and to *who* comes" (Derrida [2003] 2005, 152, original emphasis)—in which the decision to welcome or exclude the foreignness of democracy's others is no longer grounded upon the conceptualization of sovereign self-identicality whose legitimacy is measured according to the protection of the nation. If the nation, state, and sovereign are always already foreign to themselves and autoimmune, then ipseity and self-identicality are no longer meaningful qualities of the *ethnos* or *demos*. Foreignness cannot be cast out from the nation-state, which is to say that foreignness perpetually disrupts the sovereign attempts to forge these two distinct notions of a people into one. Foreignness shatters the biological and natural basis of the link among nationality, citizenship, and democratic right, and it is in this way that foreignness can be stripped of its negative conceptualization as an absolute, mortal threat to the life of the nation and state and re-cast as an opening or giving place to a new thinking of democracy no longer tethered to sovereign ipseity.

The question of life and death, therefore, is proper only to the foreign-sovereign ever attentive to the violence and force of sovereign ipseity and ever attuned to the singularity of the what or who that arrives demanding hospitality. It is true that the foreign and autoimmune sovereign cannot know in advance if this welcoming will benefit or harm it, but this absolute risk is what allows the very concept of democracy as such to be re-inscribed and thought anew. If so, then we must attend, in the following chapter, to the ways in which autoimmunity announces the im-possibility of an indecidable democracy, a quasi-regime that remains to-come but nevertheless precedes or exceeds the biological, genetic, and natural divisions and allegiances of the nation, is "ruled" by a foreign-sovereign, and takes responsibility for the political violence which is all too frequently diminished or discounted as we take refuge in faith for the progressive perfection of the democratic nation-state.

Democracy to come and the foreign-sovereign

In the preceding section, I claimed democracy takes time. The balance between the rule of law and protection of individual liberty in democracy requires ongoing negotiation and debate as well as sustained critique of and revisions to democratic laws and institutions. If the "we" of the *demos* is, in good conscience, guided by the possibility for a justice no longer reducible to the advantage and reason of the strong over the weak, a future democracy—one that approaches its ideal—requires time. Most plainly, a common hope and belief is that a more enlightened, future democratic state will finally be able to deliver on the promises of democracy, including liberty, equality, and the protection of basic human rights for each and all regardless of political and legal status.

Democracy in modernity has made great progress in these areas, and I will not pause here to enumerate its myriad political and ethical successes. However, a tension exists between the very concept of democracy and a democracy that takes time to mature toward its ideal. The *double renvoi* of democracy reveals its structural autoimmunity and "suggests the incompletion and essential delay, the self-inadequation of every present and presentable democracy" (Derrida [2003] 2005, 38). Democracy is never proper to itself, and for this reason, Derrida argues that there is no ideal of democracy that will one day in the future be instantiated in a perfect democratic state. Derrida is not suggesting that existing democracies do not, at points, enact their governing principles or just laws, nor is he claiming, as Rousseau did, that a true democracy has never existed.[37] Rather, as long as the "we" of the sovereign *demos* is conceived of according to ipseity and self-identicality, then to wait for and trust in a future, ideal democratic state is to tacitly endorse a stagnating good conscience in response to the daily instances of political exclusion of those deemed by the sovereign to be foreign to itself. To attend to and redress these ills elided by good conscience and faith in democratic progress, Derrida argues that democracy can be reconceptualized in such a way that its future is not reducible to the pre-programmed "decisions points" of a self-identical sovereign *enforcing* its will upon its others in an attempt to bring about the ideal democratic state.[38] He calls this dual reconceptualization of democracy and the future the "democracy *to come*" ([2003] 2005, xv, original emphasis).

To explicate the structural features of the democracy to come, I begin by showing that the very concept of democracy as such does not simply have freedom as one of its fundamental principles; instead, democracy as such is free, which is to say that it is open to radical self-critique and re-invention. I then return to the claim that "democracy takes time" in order to show how this free reconceptualization of democracy both requires and resists sovereignty. Second, by examining Derrida's claim that democracy to come must have the structure of a promise, the "to-come" of democracy is best understood as an "unprecedented event" (Derrida [1994] 1997, 27) distinct from the common conception of a future that will simply arrive tomorrow. Third, this distinction between the "to-come" and the future entails a rethinking of the free, sovereign decision. For Derrida, a decision worthy of its name must resist the violent force inextricably linked to the pre-programmed decisions of the autonomous and self-identical sovereign. To respond non-violently to the unconditional and unprecedented event of the arrival of its others, the sovereign decision must be passive and premised upon a weak force. Finally, while Derrida establishes a deep tension between democracy and sovereignty, I show that he does not endorse an anti-sovereigntist solution to democratic injustices; instead, I argue that the decision of the democracy to come is best understood as one that is "rendered" by a foreign-sovereign, which is simply to say that the democracy to come is at once sovereigntist and anti-sovereigntist. In this regard, before and beyond the exclusions internal to citizenship, birthright, and consanguinity that are, nevertheless, requisite for political inclusion, the foreign-sovereign is that which gives place to its foreign others.

Democracy's others was introduced above to illuminate the logic of the nation-state, which excludes certain individuals from political membership because of their (real or perceived) foreignness to the nation. Democracy's others was also shown to refer to the forms of association—political or otherwise—that are potentially threatening to democratic sovereignty (from theocracy to transnational corporations and NGOs to terror cells with no allegiances to particular states, to rogue states, to lone wolves, etc.). In what follows, democracy's others retains these significations, but it also refers to democracy's autoimmunity or the foreignness and difference internal to or inscribed upon the concept of democracy as such. In this way, democracy's others indicates the structural possibility, unique to democracy as a political concept, for its reconceptualization. Democracy does not simply *have* others; it *is* its own other, and this is democracy's "chance and its fragility" (Derrida [2003] 2005, 87).

Because autoimmune democracy is a concept devoid of sameness and never proper to itself, it is radically open to a reconceptualization that draws upon but is not limited by its traditional theorizations. There is no thinking of the democratic—no matter how novel or foreign—that eschews freedom as a fundamental principle. Freedom, however, is not exhausted by sovereign ipseity understood as a self-identical subject (individual, nation-state, etc.) that possesses the power to enforce its own will over and against its (weaker) others. As shown, Derrida is critical of the bonds between sovereign ipseity and the force indispensable to any autonomous decision, act of self-determination, and establishing (*enforcing*) of the law.[39] In contrast to the force of sovereign freedom, Derrida attempts to think "how another experience of freedom might found in an immediate, continuous, and effective way what would still be called demo*cratic* politics or a demo*cratic* political philosophy" ([2003] 2005, 44, original emphasis). His emphasis on the -*cratic* (the *kratos* or rule) in this quote suggests a difficult challenge, namely to think anew democracy founded in freedom, but a freedom whose meaning is no longer co-extensive with the power and violence of the *autos* or self-identical sovereign that excludes its foreign others in the name of and for the sake of democracy.[40]

Derrida begins at the moment of Plato's hesitation between what is commonly said about the dangers of democracy's excessive license and liberty by taking his own license (the *exousia* at once distinct from and hardly distinguishable from liberty or *eleutheria*) with the interpretation and history of the meaning of the concept of democracy.[41] In addition to social and political freedom, democracy "presupposes, more radically still, more originally, a freedom of play, an opening of indetermination and indecidability *in the very concept* of democracy, in the interpretation of the democratic" (Derrida [2003] 2005, 25, original emphasis). If so, then the claim that democracy takes time sounds a different note. While democracy takes time because it guarantees the right to (re)negotiate and debate its laws and the terms of its legitimacy, it also takes time because it guarantees "the right to self-critique—another form of autoimmunity—as an essential, original, constitutive, and specific possibility of the democratic, indeed as its very historicity, an intrinsic historicity that it shares with no other regime" ([2003] 2005, 72).

To claim that democracy takes time is to oppose it to sovereignty, even as democracy "nonetheless can never do without it" (Derrida [2003] 2005, 101). For the sovereign to be sovereign (i.e., indivisible, inviolable, self-identical, etc.), it must remain silent or hold in reserve the silent moment of decision. To avoid dividing itself and sharing itself out to the counter-sovereignty of the other, "sovereignty withdraws from language, which always introduces a sharing that universalizes. As soon as I speak to the other, I submit to the law(s) of giving reasons" ([2003] 2005, 101).[42] To withdraw from language is also to withdraw from time, from the "time it takes" to give reasons, to explain the sovereign decision, for the sovereign to be held accountable over time for its decisions. On the one hand, sovereign legitimacy is dependent upon a seemingly never-ending string of justifications, narratives, appeals to history, lineage, descent, etc. On the other hand, since sovereignty must withdraw from language and time to immunize itself against its others, it is, paradoxically, ahistorical. In its silent reserve, despite the secularization distinctive of modernity, sovereignty retains its onto-theological foundations insofar as its legitimacy rests upon a purported indivisibility, ipseity, and purity. The silent, ahistorical sovereign remains ensconced within the impermeable walls of the un-deconstructible silence of nature and/or the divine.[43]

By contrast, democracy's normative commitments to negotiation, debate, discourse, and the freedom to publicly criticize the tradition and very concept of democracy as such makes it an historical concept through and through.[44] Democracy requires sovereignty, but its temporality drives a wedge between itself and sovereignty. Because democracy is always already sent off and put off, it is never fully present as such. Democracy is and must remain absolutely open and welcoming to its foreign others and even its future others. In this sense, the temporality of democracy resists the sovereignty of "we, the people" premised on its inviolability, indivisibility, and wholeness. Nevertheless, democracy remains inextricably dependent upon sovereignty (if the *demos* is not sovereign, the regime is not democratic), yet democracy's temporality reveals that a democracy that is not absolutely open to its others is, properly speaking, not a democracy. Within this oscillation between the sovereign and non-sovereign, Derrida situates the democracy to come as a radically open alternative to the resiliency of the onto-theological qualities of sovereignty in modernity that threaten democracy as such in the name of the immunity of the sovereign democratic nation-state. Understood in this way, democracy takes time not because it may one day approach its ideal, but rather because democracy resists the silence of sovereignty. Democracy *qua* an autoimmune (non)concept that is always already foreign-to-itself is radically free to re-inscribe its own meaning and open itself to its others. The autoimmunity of democracy suggests that it always already takes more time. In short, democracy remains to-come.

What, then, is the "to-come" of democracy to come that distinguishes it from a future, more ideal, democratic state? In *The Other Heading*, Derrida writes that the democracy to come is "not something that is certain to happen tomorrow, nor the democracy (national or international, state or trans-state) of the *future*, but a democracy that must have the structure of a promise" ([1991] 1992, 78, original emphasis). This claim operates on two levels. On the one hand, as we have just detailed, democracy's foreignness-to-itself, autoimmunity, and freedom offers the promise for its reconceptualization. On the other hand, these same qualities of democracy guarantee that it will never be fully present, never arrive as such. The structure of a promise is a claim about the meaning and identity of the democratic in which the promise is conceived of as an orientation to a radically open—even impossible—future, which, nevertheless, "*is taking place now* . . . this event [the promise of identity, an alterity ineliminable from identity, the arrival of the foreign other, etc.] takes place as that which comes, as that which seeks or promises itself *today*" (Derrida [1991] 1992, 30, original emphasis). These are complex formulations, and their significance requires a brief detour into Derrida's deconstruction of Western metaphysics.

Derrida's deconstruction begins by identifying the metaphysical moorings of the Western philosophical tradition, namely the pairing of conceptual opposites such as being/non-being, presence/absence, *physis*/*nomos*, self/other, speech/writing, etc. While recognizing that these conceptual pairs are constitutive of thought, Derrida is critical of the hierarchical ordering of these binaristic opposites, which, he claims, are value-laden historical determinations. One of the most sustained efforts throughout all of his works is to challenge this hierarchical ordering by demonstrating the ways in which these conceptual pairs are not inviolable concepts opposed to and absolutely walled off from each other. His effort to disrupt this hierarchical ordering begins with his deconstruction of the "metaphysics of presence" wherein presence is determinative of being and identity. In other words, that which *is* is absolutely eliminative of internal difference, proper to itself, and, hence, fully present as such.

Derrida argues that identity is not the full presence of the self-same; instead, identity is only ever tenuously constituted through a process of *perpetual* repetition into the future. Yet, this repetition is never repetition of the self-same; instead, identity *is* only in its relation and reference to its others and its own iterations both past and future. My emphasis on perpetual, therefore, is intended to show that in order for something to be what it is (or, for that matter, to become something other than what it is), the process of repetition is never complete; repetition is always a repetition in and of difference into a radically open future distinct from the teleological unfolding of the self-same toward its ideal, future completion, or full instantiation. Most plainly, identity always lacks full presence, and if this is so, then deconstruction begins with the questioning of the oppositional logic premised on the self-identicality of the concept (between, for example, nature and convention or law, a distinction that is essential to the legitimacy of the sovereign). Derrida's most well-known term to describe this lack of presence is *différance*, a phrase that captures the alterity of identity by showing the way in which identity is a differing from and deferral of the self-same.[45] Insofar as identity is constituted in and through alterity, difference is originary and *différance* is an originary operation that "is the displacement of this oppositional logic" (Derrida [1994] 2002, 235). Accordingly, repetition is not repetition of the self-same but of the *promise* of the full presence of the self-same that differs from itself and remains deferred into an infinitely perfectible future (when the promise will have been fulfilled) that will never arrive as such. At the same time, the promise also precedes identity, since the promise of full presence is the condition of possibility for identity as such, for the sovereign subject that can remember, make, and fulfill its promises.

This brief detour allows us to grasp why the structure of the promise is an "ontological"—not an empirical—claim. I place ontology in quotes here to emphasize that the promise and the democracy to come are distinct from the ontology of the Western philosophical tradition.[46] On the one hand, the promise is the condition of possibility for the constitution of identity or a sovereign subject that is able to make or potentially fulfill its promises. On the other hand, because the self-identicality of the sovereign subject is merely a promise that will never arrive or be fully present as such, the structure of the promise is, therefore, also the condition of impossibility of identity and—with respect to our current concerns—democracy. Once again, rather than a future democratic state which is simply "an ideal possible that is infinitely deferred" (Derrida [2003] 2005, 84), the democracy that must have the structure of a promise—the democracy to come—is founded in the "*the memory of that which carries the future, the to-come, here and now*" (Derrida [1991] 1992, 78, original emphasis). The structure of the promise is the impossible possibility of the "to-come," thereby situating the democracy to come "under the title of the *im-possible*, of what must remain (in a nonnegative fashion) foreign to the order of my possibilities, to the order of the 'I can,' ipseity, the theoretical, the descriptive, the constantive, and the performative . . . that neutralize the pure eventfulness of the event" (Derrida [2003] 2005, 84 original emphasis).

The democracy to come, the promise of democracy, is not properly sovereign, not proper to itself. For this reason it cannot be brought about, willed, decided upon, or forcefully constituted. Instead, the "to-come" of democracy is an "unprecedented event" because its arrival "would end up contradicting its very origin. It would be an anti-genesis. It would wage war on its own lineage, as the 'metaphysician of all ages' believes; this would be tantamount to a monstrous birth, an 'impossible' origin" (Derrida [1994] 1997, 34). That which is "to-come" cannot be anticipated in advance; it is outside of the horizon of expectation and calculation. The "to-come," therefore, does not simply suggest the inevitable arrival of the foreigner at the border who is perceived as either strengthening or weakening "our" sense of who "we" are. Instead, Derrida insists that "a future that would not be monstrous would not be a future; it would already be a predictable, calculable, and programmable tomorrow" (1992, 387). A future worthy of the name—the "to-come"—is the arrival of foreignness as such, a monstrous future, which simultaneously constitutes and dissolves—here and now—the self-identicality and ipseity of the sovereign, democratic nation-state which must decide whether it will welcome or exclude not only the foreigner but foreignness as such.

Legitimate democracies are, however, sovereign, and this means making decisions intended to protect its members now and in the future. Nevertheless, insofar as democracy has the structure of a promise and foreignness is an originary and constitutive structural feature of it-self, democracy is always beset by an indecidability, an im-possible decision in response to the promise of the arrival of democracy's foreign others in all of its forms, i.e., the immigrant, the refugee, rogue states, terrorists, trans-national global corporations, international law and institutions, *as well as* democracy's historicity, its autoimmunity, its past injustices, its future generations, and its dependence upon and resistance to sovereignty. The impossible decision is "more than an internal contradiction, [it is] an indecidability, that is, an internal-external, nondialectizable antinomy that risks paralyzing and thus calls for the event of the interruptive decision" (Derrida [2003] 2005, 35).

Because democracy is autoimmune, there is no advance knowledge whether the decision to welcome its others will benefit or harm it. However, the decision to welcome or exclude its others is not indecidable. Clearly, sovereign democratic states regularly make decisions in response to their others. Instead, what autoimmunity reveals is that democracy's others are its "opportunity or chance and threat, threat as chance" (Derrida [2003] 2005, 52). Therefore, democracy is indecidable because the very act of sovereign self-constitution is only possible by opening and exposing itself to the counter-sovereignty of its others.[47] The im-possible decision, then, is to assume the risk of welcoming unconditionally the what or who that arrives, thereby interrupting the force and calculating technique of the sovereign decision that forecloses a radically open future in the name of protecting its own ipseity and self-identicality. This is why, for Derrida, the decision worthy of its name is an always already deferred promise—the im-possibility—of the full instantiation of democracy here and now. Peter Gratton's formulation is helpful: "[T]he decision is the event of the 'to-come' of democracy, its future, which is never satisfied with democracy as it stands, here and now" (2012, 225).

To think democracy anew is to reconceptualize democracy premised upon a freedom without autonomy that resists the violence and force of sovereign ipseity. Thus, the democracy to come is a monstrous event because it is the disfiguring promise of and possibility for democracy freed from the force of the autonomous sovereign. Derrida claims the event is "unforeseeable coming of the other, of a heteronomy, of a law come from the other, of a responsibility and decision of the other—of the other in me, an other greater and older than I am. It is thus a question of separating democracy and autonomy, something that is, I concede, more than difficult, indeed im-possible" ([2003] 2005, 84).

The event or promise of the democracy to come faces an im-possible decision with respect to its others, since any sovereign decision is simultaneously an opportunity and chance or threat (threat as chance) to itself, its being, its identity, the people, the nation, etc. Hence, the sovereign endeavors to maintain its purported inviolability, indivisibility, and self-identicality by immunizing itself against threat through the decision to exclude its others. In this sense, we have already caught a glimpse as to why Derrida insists that democracy and autonomy (with all of its ties to sovereign ipseity) must be separated. However, Derrida's attempt to separate democracy and autonomy is developed in another important way. From Plato's hesitation between license and liberty to Aristotle's consideration of equality according to worth or number to the contemporary concerns regarding the balance between liberty and the rule of law within the democratic state and between human rights and the right to sovereign self-determination, the democratic decision is im-possible insofar as it is mired in an inescapable aporia between its fundamental principles of freedom and equality, i.e., unconditional, incalculable, and incommensurable freedom and singularity of each individual and the conditional calculation and counting requisite for the general application of the law, equality under the law, and justice as fairness. The democratic decision is im-possible because it must be made within the indecidable aporia between the unconditional and conditional.

Derrida does not pretend to provide a way out of this indecidability. Whatever decision is made must be made within this aporia. However, he does argue that the aporia between the unconditional and the conditional can be reconceived. "Equality," he insists, "is not simply some necessary evil or stopgap measure; it is also the chance to neutralize all sorts of differences of force, of properties (natural or otherwise) and hegemonies, so as to gain access precisely to the *whoever* or the *no matter who* of singularity in its very immeasurability" (Derrida [2003] 2005, 52, original emphasis). In other words, while equality can serve to limit, for example, the advantage of the stronger, this does not entail destroying the incommensurability and singularity of the other through the blind application of the law indifferent to what claims are being made and who makes them. In fact, it is the opposite, since the neutralization of force which would privilege the claims of certain individuals or groups gives access not just to those with the power and strength to be heard and recognized but to whoever it is that makes a claim or calls for justice. He continues: "Calculable measure also gives access to the incalculable and the incommensurable, an access that remains itself necessarily undecided between the calculable and the incalculable—and that is the aporia of the political and of democracy" ([2003] 2005, 52). In this way, the aporia of democracy (between the unconditional/conditional, immeasurable/measurable, and incalculable/calculable) is not simply the tension that exists between freedom and equality but rather a structural feature of the principle of equality.

Equality is a threat to and may destroy "incommensurable singularity" (Derrida [2003] 2005, 53), but it "is also the chance for the incommensurable; *it is what gives access to it*. A chance given by the political, the juridical, the ethical and their invention, wherever it takes place" ([2003] 2005, 53, original emphasis). Put differently, there can be no response to the call for human or democratic rights—no justice even—without a conditional determination, counting, and measuring of the singular other seeking justice from the sovereign state. In short, there is no possibility for justice without the political, and this means there is no justice without sovereignty and the application of the law, even as the sovereign democratic nation-state threatens to destroy the unconditional calls for justice of the singular other by reserving freedom, equality, and justice solely for the nation and its citizens. Insofar as the conditional is what gives access to the unconditional, Derrida is not wistfully hoping for a politics that welcomes every claim and is cleansed of violence; rather, if the incommensurability and singularity of the other and her unconditional claims for justice are not to be pre-emptively dismissed or put on hold, then what is required is "a *slow and differential* deconstruction of this logic and the dominant, classic concept of nation-state sovereignty . . . without ending with a de-politicization but an other politicization, a re-politicization and therefore *another concept* of the political" (Derrida 2009, 113, original emphasis).

The sovereign democracy surely decides and responds to the unconditional claims for inclusion placed upon it, but Derrida insists that a democracy no longer founded in freedom *qua* autonomy requires a decision that does not foreclose the monstrous event of the "to-come." A decision worthy of its name is im-possible because it divides the sovereign by opening and exposing it to the counter-sovereignty of its others. In short, the im-possible decision is an unavoidable consequence of the structural autoimmunity of democracy. However, Derrida reminds us that "autoimmunity is not an absolute ill or evil. It enables an exposure to the other, to what and who comes—which means that it must remain incalculable. Without autoimmunity, with absolute immunity, nothing would ever happen or arrive; we would no longer wait, await, or expect, no longer expect one another, or expect any event" (Derrida [2003] 2005, 152). Autoimmunity is what exposes democracy to its others, and its im-possible decision is that which offers hope *today* for the future perfection of democracy that will never arrive as such. Per Michael Naas, "Autoimmunity is the very condition of the unconditionality of the event; it is what opens the *autos*, what opens *us*, to time, space, language, and the other" (2008, 139, original emphasis).

A final question lingers: How does the im-possible decision provide a basis for thinking a democracy grounded in freedom but separate from autonomy? Derrida answers: "If an event worthy of its name is to arrive or happen, it must, beyond all mastery, affect a passivity . . . What must be thought here, then, is this inconceivable and unknowable thing, a freedom that would no longer be the power of a subject, a freedom without autonomy, a heteronomy without servitude, in short, something like a passive decision" ([2003] 2005, 152). This passive decision that is the event of the "to-come" of democracy's others is "made" by the sovereign democratic nation-state; yet, it is a decision that is no longer the power or force of the fully self-present and self-identical sovereign. Instead, the im-possible decision—rendered within the inescapable aporia between the unconditional and conditional—is premised upon a "*weak force* . . . [a] . . . force without power" (Derrida [2003] 2005, xv, original emphasis). Therefore, a decision worthy of its name is neither arbitrary nor does it reject precedent, but if it is to attend to the unconditional, then it must, nevertheless, "invent, each time, in a singular situation, its own law and norm, that is, a maxim that welcomes each time the event to come" ([2003] 2005, 151).[48]

Derrida is clear that democracy is imbricated with sovereignty, the state, the nation-state, democratic institutions and laws, conditions for citizenship, etc. Without these structural aspects of the state, there is no access to (no response, responsibility, or decision) the unconditional claims of its other. Thus, my earlier claim that democracy resists sovereignty is explicitly not arguing that Derrida endorses an anti-sovereigntism, i.e., a borderless global political order that is post-statist and post-national that would render citizenship irrelevant to political membership and the protection of human rights. There are countless examples in which the sovereign right of the nation-state functions to include those previously excluded from political membership, and Derrida is well aware of the importance of sovereignty for guaranteeing the rights of citizens as well as the dangers, outlined by Arendt, of denationalization that precedes the loss of citizenship and rights. However, he is also sensitive to the fact that democracy and democratic rights are limited by sovereignty. He writes:

> I would say that according to situations, I am an antisovereigntist *or* a sovereigntist—and I vindicate the right to be antisovereigntist at certain times and sovereigntist at others. No one can make me respond as though it were a matter of pressing a button on some old-fashioned machine. There are cases in which I would support a logic of the state, but I ask to examine each situation before making a statement. It is also necessary to recognize that by requiring someone to be not just unconditionally sovereigntist but rather sovereigntist only under certain conditions, one is already calling into question the principle of sovereignty. Deconstruction begins there. It demands a different dissociation, almost impossible but indispensable, between *unconditionality* (justice without power) and *sovereignty* (right, power, or potency). Deconstruction is on the side of unconditionality, even when it seems impossible, and not sovereignty, even when it seems possible.
>
> Derrida and Roudinesco [2001] 2004, 92, original emphasis

To distinguish between unconditionality and sovereignty is nearly impossible because both "escape absolutely, like the absolute itself, all relativism" (Derrida [2003] 2005, xiv). Indeed, what is the unconditional incommensurability and immeasurability of the singular other if not sovereign identity and subjectivity? Derrida recognizes the challenge of distinguishing these two concepts, but if democracy is to fulfill its promise, to be conceived of in another expression of freedom distinct from the force and power of the self-identical sovereign immune to its others, then its only hope is the unconditional welcoming of its others (the threat that is democracy's chance) regardless of political or legal status. Derrida continues, "I am thinking of a democracy that would no longer be bound in any essential way to citizenship. Here again, I come back to the same apparent contradiction: I am not against citizenship; it is necessary, and one must even fight for certain human beings who have been deprived of it, so that they might finally gain it. But the rights of man must also be extended beyond citizenship" (Derrida and Roudinesco [2001] 2004, 97). He is less ambiguous in *Rogues* when he states: "a *certain* unconditional renunciation of sovereignty is required a priori. Even before the act of decision" (Derrida [2003] 2005, xiv, my emphasis). I emphasize that this is a "certain" renunciation because a democracy that protects the rights of man beyond citizenship by resisting the sovereign closure of the future around the self-same is not anti-sovereigntist, *per se*. Instead, insofar as the democracy to come is autoimmune and foreign-to-itself, we might understand the im-possible decision and alignment with the unconditional (which can, depending on the situation, be a sovereign decision implementing the logic of the nation-state) as one which can only be "rendered" by the foreign-sovereign that always already takes more time even as it attends, here and now, to its others and their unconditional calls for justice beyond or before the laws of the state because "justice, however unpresentable it remains, does not wait. It is that which must not wait" (Derrida [1994] 2002, 255).[49]

The foreign-sovereign "renders" the im-possible decision, but this should not be understood to mean that the foreign-sovereign is akin to a president, a representative, a constitution, a set of laws, or a systematic program for how to respond to the claims made upon the democratic state. Rather, the foreign-sovereign is a political, moral, and legal opening and orientation to counter-sovereignty, to difference, to alterity, to the foreigner without, and the constitutive foreignness within that both enacts and resists the power and hegemony of sovereign self-identicality. In this way, it does not "rule" anything, least of all a territory, a people, a *demos*, a discourse, a decision, etc. Instead, it is that which "makes" the im-possible, passive decision, which is to say that it gives place to its others, although not merely in the sense that it decides to extend hospitality to foreigners. To this point, Edward Casey writes, "giving is an activity, but what is given, room or place, is something *there* into which one enters. It is choric in character; it is a *receptacle* in and through which hospitality happens. It is at once impassive and impersonal, for what gives place is not simply some person freely bestowing admittance to a stranger but the very space itself, its layout" (2011, 45, original emphasis). The foreign-sovereign is not simply another possible conceptualization of sovereignty more attuned to foreignness than traditional conceptualizations. Rather, it is the im-possibility of sovereign self-identicality and ipseity, a promise which precedes and exceeds sovereign identity and the hierarchical binaristic ordering between the conceptual opposites of *zōē* (mere life)/*bios* (good life), *physis/nomos*, sovereign/foreign, self/other, etc., which structure and underlie the order of the political.[50] Put differently, the foreign-sovereign simultaneously and im-possibly gives place to democracy *and* to its others, yet remains immune to these divisions. In this regard, the foreign-sovereign is analogous to what Derrida has in mind when he claims that the "democracy to come would be like the khōra of the political" ([2003] 2005, 82).

Khōra is a concept developed in *Timaeus*, Plato's origin story. After the Demiurge has created the world, Timaeus insists that in order to explain the sensible world of particulars, their interactions with the Forms, and their coming into being, "the new starting point in my account of the universe needs to be more complex than the earlier one" (Plato 2000, 49a). The idea of khōra is introduced at this moment to give an account of metaphysical necessity, epistemology, and justice.[51] Michael Naas writes, "Indeed, khōra comes on the scene in *Timaeus* only after the (effective) withdrawal of the Demiurge" (2008, 248, footnote 21), and, as we shall see, this distinction between religion, the divine, and khōra is a central feature of Derrida's democracy to come. First, however, what is khōra? Khōra is translated as "receptacle," and Plato claims that khōra is "totally devoid of any characteristics" (2000, 50e). Accordingly, it does not, properly speaking, give anything; instead, it receives—it is a receptacle through and in which the sensible world of particulars come into being. Plato continues by describing it as "space, which exists always and cannot be destroyed. It provides a fixed site for all things that come to be" (2000, 52b); it is a wetnurse (49a), invisible (52a), a womb (50e), and that which precedes everything but does not exist at all (52a). Plato admits of its strangeness when he writes: "it is itself apprehended by a kind of bastard reasoning that does not involve sense perception, and it is hardly even an object of conviction [*pistis*]" (2000, 52b).

Insofar as khōra is that which gives place and space for the coming to be of the world, it gives rise, simultaneously, to that which is and its opposites. In Derrida's reading, khōra means "locality in general," which "would make or give *place*" ([2003] 2005, xiv, original emphasis), even as this making or giving of place is that which, properly understood, does not give anything. Khōra gives place "to what is called the coming of the event" ([2003] 2005, xiv), and in this respect, khōra is not sovereign. The giving of place is not part of an economy of power or exchange of obedience for the sovereign gift of life. As Michael Naas notes, unlike all autoimmune sovereign subjects, including the state, the nation, the self, and especially religion, khōra is immune "not because of a sovereign or omnipotent immune system that would protect it from all external aggression—indeed there can be no such thing for *structural* reasons—but immune because it has no identity, no *autos*, to protect" (2008, 132, original emphasis). Permit me to quote Derrida at length on this point. He writes that khōra is:

> without age, without history and more "ancient" than all oppositions (sensible/intelligible) ... [A]s a result, chora remains absolutely impassible and heterogeneous to all processes of historical revelation or of anthropo-theological experience, which at the very least suppose its abstraction. It will never have entered religion and will never permit itself to be sacralized, sanctified, humanized, theologized, cultivated, historicized. Radically heterogeneous to the safe and sound, to the holy and the sacred, it never admits of any *indemnification*. This cannot even be formulated in the present, for chora never presents itself as such ... It is neither Being, nor the Good, nor God, nor Man, nor History. It will always resist them, will always have been ... the very place of an infinite resistance, of an infinitely impassible persistence [*restance*]: an utterly faceless other.
>
> Derrida [1996] 2002, 58–59, original emphasis

For Derrida, the giving of place is not a sovereign act nor something enacted in the name of a future politics, ethics, and law to be "*deduced*" ([2003] 2005, xv, original emphasis) from the qualities of khōra; rather, "the democracy to come would be like the khōra of the political" because it entails a hopeless hope in the promise, "[n]ot hopeless, in despair, but foreign to the teleology, the hopefulness, and the *salut* [health, immunity, indemnification] of salvation" ([2003] 2005, xv).[52] In this sense, the democracy to come perpetually resists the closure of the future by offering and giving place to "another truth of the democratic, namely, the truth of the other, heterogeneity, the heteronomic and the dissymmetric, disseminal multiplicity, the anonymous 'anyone,' the 'no matter who,' the indeterminate 'each one'" ([2003] 2005, 14). With this appeal to another tradition, to democracy's others, the relationship between the foreign-sovereign and the democracy to come becomes evident.

Like the democracy to come, the foreign-sovereign resists sovereignty and its attempts of indemnification of the self-same. Like the democracy to come, the foreign-sovereign is the structure of the promise to come. Like the democracy to come, the foreign-sovereign would be like the khōra of the political because it "precedes" the law, consanguinity, fraternity, nature, religion, the divine, and the oppositional logic upon which sovereign ipseity is premised, which, by turns, forges the logic of the nation-state and its exclusionary violence in the name of democracy and justice. Like the democracy to come, the foreign-sovereign is the im-possibility of freedom without autonomy that solicits democracy. Like the democracy to come, the foreign-sovereign gives place to the conditional law and politics, which, by turns, gives access to the immeasurable singularity of each individual. Like the democracy to come, the foreign-sovereign is immune, not in the sense of sovereign inviolability, but rather because it is absolutely vulnerable to the foreign, there is nothing to protect; it has no self-identicality, ipseity, and autos. Paradoxically, this absolute vulnerability is a source of immunity that makes possible the opening of democracy to its precarious, injurable, and vulnerable others.

While there is no doubt that being a refugee, an asylum seeker, an itinerant or undocumented laborer, a political dissident, etc. make one vulnerable to physical, legal, and moral injury, the precariousness and injurability of democracy's others is not simply the result of their particular, empirical circumstances. Instead, vulnerability, precariousness, and injurability are structural and ontological features of sovereign identity, selfhood, and embodiment. If they were not, there would be no harm, no risk, no danger, no unconditional demand for hospitality, and, by extension, no ethics or politics, especially democratic politics founded upon the ineliminable principle of an absolute openness and hospitable welcoming to all morally free and equal beings, to all of the vulnerable and injurable.[53] For this reason, a democracy that, in the name of an ever-elusive sovereign inviolability, will not open itself to its others is not a democracy. Put differently, a democracy that excludes because it fails to recognize the lack of self-identicality and ipseity of "We, the people"—the foreignness and vulnerability constitutive of any sovereign entity—is not a democracy. Indeed, a democracy that does not open itself to its foreign others demanding hospitality is less a democracy than an ethnic and racial polity, an *ethnos* masquerading as a *demos*. It is in this sense that the onus of the im-possible decision to unconditionally welcome its others falls upon the foreign-sovereign who is the promise that cannot wait for a democracy that gives place to an ethics and politics ever resistant to the mastery, exclusions, and violence of sovereignty.

9

The Foreign-Citizen at the Threshold of Democratic Cosmopolitanism

The conceptual path carved out by the historical development and deconstruction of sovereignty leads to the borders, thresholds, and walls where the foreigner's cosmopolitan right to hospitality meets the right to sovereign self-determination of the democratic nation-state. Given Derrida's own insistence that the democracy to come must not be taken as an ideal from which we might deduce a future politics, ethics, or law, the challenge is to consider what, if any, moral and legal commitments the democracy to come, the foreign-sovereign, and the quasi-regime entail. Because justice cannot and must not wait, the indecidability of democracy cannot result in a paralysis if the calls for justice by democracy's foreign others are to be redressed.

To respond to this concern, this chapter is developed in four parts. First, in order to sketch out the historical basis of the obligations of the sovereign state to the foreigner, I consider Kant's justification of the cosmopolitan right to hospitality. Second, I examine the ways in which Derrida's unconditional hospitality draws upon and goes beyond Kant's formulation of universal hospitality by arguing that any sovereign decision to welcome or exclude the other must be rendered within the inescapable aporia between the unconditional welcoming of each and all and the conditional laws of hospitality of the sovereign state which welcome some and exclude others. Third, I turn to discourse ethics and Seyla Benhabib's notion of democratic iterations to provide another articulation of and possible solution to the tension between the universal cosmopolitan right to hospitality and the democratic nation-state's right to sovereign self-determination. Finally, without positing a post-statist political order, I introduce a final (non)concept, the foreign-citizen, as a deconstructive figure that simultaneously upholds the legal and moral importance and legitimacy of citizenship within bounded democratic communities *and* ceaselessly contests the boundaries of citizenship premised upon the exclusionary logic of the nation-state whereby political membership is reserved for members of the nation alone.

Universal hospitality at the border between the moral and legal

Kant's *Perpetual Peace* remains an influential work regarding the relationship between state sovereignty and the cosmopolitan right to hospitality of each individual *qua* human. He develops three articles requisite for a perpetual peace among nations: "The civil constitution of every nation should be republican;" "The right of nations shall be based on a federation of free states;" "Cosmopolitan right shall be limited to the conditions of universal hospitality" ([1795] 1983, 112–118). Given its emphasis on the duty of hospitality owed to non-citizens who visit a sovereign territory, it is this third article which will primarily concern us here. Kant immediately notes that he is not concerned with "philanthropy, but with right" ([1795] 1983, 118). For Kant, hospitality is not a gift or something offered in the spirit of kindness to be cultivated by generous individuals or the sovereign. Rather, it is a universal right of all human beings because the "common ownership of the earth's surface" ([1795] 1983, 118) and the fact that the earth is a globe means that men "cannot scatter themselves infinitely . . . [therefore, they must] . . . tolerate living in close proximity" ([1795] 1983, 118).

Kant's argument regarding the sphericality of the earth is subtle yet essential. The empirical fact that the earth is a finite sphere means that eventually humans will inevitably come into contact with one another. However, this does not require sovereign states to welcome foreigners upon their arrival. As Benhabib rhetorically notes: "If indeed we were to assume that Kant used the sphericality of the earth as a *justificatory premise* [for the cosmopolitan right to hospitality], wouldn't we then have to conclude that he had committed the naturalistic fallacy?" (2004, 33, original emphasis). Instead, Kant's appeal to the sphericality of the earth suggests that hospitality is a right that is anterior to the distinction between moral or legal rights, and in this way it is outside, above, and precedes the law of the sovereign. Hospitality, in this respect, names and provides a formal requirement to recognize the human right to motility, movement, and emigration across sovereign borders. In this sense, the sphericality of the earth is simply a "limiting condition" (Benhabib 2004, 34) on one's freedom and right to motility. Put another way, the sphericality of the earth is a condition of possibility for perpetual peace (and justice) insofar as it recognizes that while there will be sovereign states, the borders of these states must not be killing zones. All polities draw borders, but the legitimate polity is that which does so in such a way that recognizes not only that foreigners will inevitably arrive but that they possess the cosmopolitan right to demand hospitality, to present themselves to the democratic sovereign. In Kant's language, hospitality is the "right of an alien not to be treated as an enemy upon his arrival in another country. If it can be done without destroying him, he can be turned away; but as long as he behaves peaceably he cannot be treated as an enemy" ([1795] 1983, 118).

For Kant, however, the right to hospitality is only "the *right to visit*" ([1795] 1983, 118, original emphasis). By contrast, permanent residency is a "charitable agreement" ([1795] 1983, 118), a gift of the right to remain indefinitely given from the sovereign to the foreigner. Kant's distinction between the right to hospitality and the gift of permanent residency has both historical and practical motivations. On the one hand, without the universal, cosmopolitan right to visit and enter other nations, commerce is impossible, and it is commerce that fosters peaceful interactions whereby "the human race can gradually be brought closer and closer to a cosmopolitan constitution" ([1795] 1983, 118). On the other hand, because the right to permanent residency is a gift of the sovereign nation, it functions as a bulwark against colonial expansion (itself rooted in commercial and economic interests). Thus, cosmopolitan right is limited only by a universal hospitality, which is to say that all humans (universally) have an incontestable right to visit foreign countries in order to associate with those who live there (for a limited period of time) so long as they are peaceful (or if denying entry does not result in the foreigner's destruction). Nevertheless, the right of universal hospitality is ambiguous in Kant's work insofar as it is not clear whether this right is a moral or legal right.

Universal hospitality and cosmopolitan right do not concern members of a given sovereign state whose interactions are governed by mutually binding laws. Instead, as Benhabib emphasizes: "The right of hospitality is situated at the boundaries of the polity; it delimits civic space by regulating relations among members and strangers. Hence, the right of hospitality occupies that space between human rights and civil rights, between the right of humanity in our person and the rights that accrue to us insofar as we are members of specific republics" (2004, 27). As noted, the right to hospitality is anterior to the sovereign law and its distinction between morality and right. Thus, on the one hand it bridges human rights and civil rights. In Eduardo Mendieta's reading, hospitality is meant to guarantee that, "under no condition is any human to be left without the shelter of law, of the protective canopy of rights" (2011, 184). On the other hand, it points to the liminal space between human, moral, and legal rights, and Benhabib identifies the way in which this ambiguity remains with us today with respect to the rights claims of asylum seekers and refugees when she asks if we are to understand the rights of these individuals and groups "in the sense of being *reciprocal moral obligations* which, in some sense or another, are grounded upon our mutual humanity? Or are these rights claims in the legal sense of being *enforceable norms* of behavior which individuals and groups can hold each other to and, in particular, force sovereign nation-states to comply with?" (2004, 29, original emphasis).[1]

For Kant whose cosmopolitan political order is, per his second article for peace, a federation of nations that do not have a common sovereign governing their interactions, there is no power or force to compel states to recognize the right to hospitality. This is why Benhabib argues that—within Kant's framework—to extend hospitality to foreigners may be obligatory, but it cannot be enforced; thus, it remains the purview of the self-determining sovereign nation-state. In this regard: "The right of hospitality expresses all of the dilemmas of a republic cosmopolitical order in a nutshell: namely how to create quasi-legally binding obligations through voluntary commitments and in the absence of an overwhelming sovereign power with the ultimate right of enforcement" (Benhabib 2004, 29). Recognition of the universal right to hospitality might be a moral obligation of the sovereign state, but as Benhabib concludes, it is an "*imperfect moral duty* to help and offer shelter to those whose life, limb, and well-being are endangered. This duty is 'imperfect"—i.e. *conditional*—in that it can permit exceptions, and can be overridden by legitimate grounds of self-preservation" (2004, 36, original emphasis). I will return to Benhabib's efforts to resolve this ambiguity, but her emphasis on the conditional right to hospitality leads us directly to Derrida's reformulation of Kant's universal hospitality as an aporetic moment of decision between unconditional and conditional hospitality.

Unconditional hospitality and the cosmopolitanism to come

For Derrida, the indecidability of democracy does not result from the fact that there is no advance knowledge whether the decision to welcome or exclude democracy's others will harm or benefit the sovereign state. Decisions of these sorts are institutionalized and made on a daily basis according to the extant laws of the sovereign nation-state. Rather, indecidability is the result of the structural autoimmunity of democracy. Pure sovereignty and absolute sovereign immunity is the withdrawal from history, from time, and from the decision that is necessarily shared out and open to the counter-sovereignty of its others, and this retreat into onto-theological silence is a changeless eternity and death of sorts. The perpetual repetition and iteration of self-identical sovereignty, impermeable to the counter-sovereignty of its others, is impossible. Sovereignty, in this sense, is never fully present as such. Moreover, attempts to achieve this ideal of pure presence, mastery, and sovereignty forecloses the event of the to-come, i.e., a future worthy of its name beyond anticipation and the pre-programmed decision to extend or deny hospitality. Paradoxically, in order for the sovereign to be sovereign, it requires the unconditional welcoming of its others—which may or may not destroy it—without which it could not come into being, time, history, etc. This is its autoimmunity; its threat that is its only chance.

On this account, it appears that Derrida is claiming that the sovereign *demos* must welcome all unconditionally, but this is not the case. To welcome all unconditionally is itself a pre-programmed, calculable decision in accordance with a universal moral law that recognizes each individual's cosmopolitan right to hospitality. Yet, the pre-programmed general application of the law, whether a conditional law of the state or a universal ethical precept, is no decision at all; in fact, this is precisely what results in the loss of the singularity and incommensurability of the who or what that arrives. This is why the democracy to come must not be understood as an idealized, anti-sovereigntist future polity or global *demos* that welcomes all, since this would amount to an untenable de-politicization; instead, as noted, Derrida advocates a "a *slow and differential* deconstruction of this logic and the dominant, classic concept of nation-state sovereignty . . . without ending with a de-politicization but an other politicization, a re-politicization and therefore *another concept* of the political" (2009, 113, original emphasis). This re-politicization, the democracy to come, begins with attention to *who* arrives at the borders of the sovereign nation-state and the decision—which cannot wait—to welcome or exclude this foreign other.

The attention to who arrives is what leads us from the conceptual analysis of foreignness as such to the practical consideration of the foreigner, and Derrida is quick to note that we must differentiate between "the foreigner in general, the immigrant, the exiled, the deported, the stateless or the displaced person (the task being as much to distinguish prudently between these categories as is possible)" ([1997] 2001, 4).[2] Importantly, Derrida suggests that distinguishing between these categories is not always possible. He continues, "Refugee status ought not to be conflated with the status of an immigrant, not even a political immigrant . . . We shall have to maintain a close eye on these sometimes subtle distinctions between types of status, especially since the difference between the economic and the political now appears more problematic then ever" ([1997] 2001, 12).

Historically, countries such as the United States and France have depicted themselves as havens for political refugees and asylum seekers. The U.S., for example, was settled by those fleeing religious persecution, and this right to freedom of religion and expression, enshrined in the First Amendment, is the ethico-juridical cornerstone of democracy in the United States. Internationally, in the wake of two world wars, the Universal Declaration of Human Rights (UDHR) explicitly recognized the right of every human to emigrate without, however, placing obligations upon sovereign states to welcome or grant entry to refugees, asylum seekers, the stateless, (im)migrants, etc. By recognizing the moral considerability of all humans, the UDHR establishes that states do have a moral obligation to uphold and protect the human rights of émigrés, even if these obligations are not enforceable.

Recognizing these shortcomings, the Geneva Convention of 1951 and the Status of Refugees and its Protocols in 1967 are binding international treaties and laws that compel signatory states to welcome refugees and grant asylum in certain cases. Once again, these legally enforceable, international treaties are not always honored, even by its signatories, but they do provide a concrete legal status to refugees, asylum seekers, stateless persons, and displaced persons, which, in principle, obligates states to extend hospitality and welcome these foreigners. Economic migrants and immigrants, by contrast, have a significantly more limited and tenuous legal status.[3] While we must be careful to distinguish between the various types of foreigners and the protections which they require, guest worker programs or even toleration of undocumented (im)migrants effectively create a massive and growing class of foreigners vulnerable to exploitation by the host countries in which they reside. This fact is evidenced time and again by countries such as the U.S. and France whose economic (im)migrants are frequently denied the right to political membership despite their contributions to the economic, social, and cultural flourishing of the host country.

Even if the distinction between the political and economic is arbitrarily invoked by the sovereign state to control immigration when it serves its own social, political, and economic interests, we must, nevertheless, endeavor to distinguish who the foreigner is because, by doing so, the moral and/or legal obligations (or failure to meet these obligations) of the sovereign state are made evident. This is why Derrida's insistence on distinguishing between the categories of foreigner matters. It speaks to the importance of international law, norms of human rights, and determining who is and who is not afforded the protections of legal status. Be that as it may, Derrida will complicate this picture. In response to Kant's arguments for the cosmopolitan right to universal hospitality, Derrida argues that hospitality is aporetic, and to understand this aporia, we must distinguish between the unconditional hospitality (*the* law of hospitality) that preserves the singularity and incommensurability of the foreign other and the conditional hospitality (the *laws* of hospitality) through which the sovereign determines who will be welcomed or excluded.

I have just insisted that Derrida is concerned with determining who the foreigner is. If the singularity of each is to be attended to, then it matters who arrives at the border. For hospitality to take place—for the host to welcome and grant entry to the guest—the guest must be accounted for and must identify herself. This is what determines her status, her right to hospitality, and establishes the contract and agreement of hospitality: namely, you are permitted to visit but not remain permanently so long as you come with peaceful intentions. More succinctly, for the moral obligation of hospitality to be binding and performed, the guest must give an account of herself.[4] In this way, hospitality demands that it must, in principle, be "possible for them [foreigners] to be called by their names, to have names, to be subjects in law, to be questioned and liable, to have crimes imputed to them, to be held responsible, to be equipped with nameable identities, and proper names" (Derrida [1997] 2000, 23). In identifying herself, the foreigner becomes a signatory to the contract or agreement of hospitality.

This questioning of the foreigner has two registers. There is, after all, a difference, if only in accent or "inflections" (Naas 2002, 166) between interrogation ("Who goes there?" "Show me your papers!") and a generous welcoming that implies no contract ("What is your name?" "I would like to know what to call you, who you are, etc."). While identifying (in this sense of interrogation) who arrives is at once essential for determining why the foreigner has come, her status, what her freedoms will be, and what obligations the host has to her, it is also the mechanism by which their singularity and incommensurability are erased. On the one hand, to receive hospitality, every foreigner is obliged to answer, self-identify, give an account of herself, reveal her family name, her nationality, her history, etc., which will make her a subject to the law, thereby either bolstering or diminishing her chances for receiving hospitality. In this respect, the foreigner speaks a common language, the language of right, responsibility, accountability, contract, etc. Yet, by doing so she simultaneously proclaims her singularity and erases this singularity as she becomes a generic subject of the law. On the other hand, the inquiry "What is your name?" ("I would like to know what to call you, who you are, what you call yourself") requires no answer. No accounting is necessary; no responsibility demanded; no subjection to the conditional laws of the sovereign or the master of the house is entailed by this change of accent and inflection in the question. It is here, between accountability and the absence of an account, a name, an identity, a history, a category, and a status that the paradox of hospitality arises.

The foreigner is not, strictly speaking, the absolute other; she has a name, she can be identified, she is knowable, a subject of the law, etc., and it is insofar as she is identifiable and knowable that the host can decide to offer hospitality or not. Hospitality, in this respect, is conditional upon who arrives. However, Derrida writes, "the subtle and sometimes ungraspable differences between the foreigner and the absolute other is that the latter cannot have a name or a family name" ([1997] 2000, 25).[5] With this distinction, unconditional or absolute hospitality "requires that I open up my home and that I give not only to the foreigner (provided with a family name, with a social status of being a foreigner, etc.), but to the absolute, unknown, anonymous other, and that I give *place* to them, that I let them come, that I let them arrive, and take place in the place I offer them, without asking of them either reciprocity (entering into a pact) or even their names. The law of hospitality commands a break with hospitality by right" ([1997] 2000, 25, original emphasis).

I will return below to the emphasis on "place" in the above quote; first, however, more must be said about the inter-dependence of unconditional and conditional hospitality. For Derrida, *the* law of hospitality is an "unconditional, hyperbolic hospitality, as though the categorical imperative of hospitality commanded that we transgress all the laws (in the plural) of hospitality, namely the conditions, the norms, the rights and duties that are imposed on hosts and hostesses, on the men or women who give a welcome as well as the men or women who receive it" ([1997] 2000, 75 and 77). He quickly notes that the usage of the Kantian term "categorical imperative" must be used cautiously and "under erasure" ([1997] 2000, 83), since we are not speaking of a pre-programmed decision, but rather an im-possible, interruptive event of the to-come that cannot be anticipated in advance. Nevertheless, unconditional hospitality is juxtaposed to Kant's universal hospitality—at once a conditioned and imperfect hospitality—as a hyperbolic demand which requires that hospitality be extended to the no matter who or what arrives "before any *identification*" ([1997] 2000, 77, original emphasis). *The* law of unconditional hospitality disallows the questioning (interrogation *and* identification) of the foreigner who arrives, and it requires that the host "give the new arrival all of one's home and oneself, to give him or her one's own, our own, without asking a name, or compensation, or the fulfillment of even the smallest condition" ([1997] 2000, 77). *The* law of unconditional hospitality exceeds or stands outside of the rights, duties, and obligations of the conditional laws and contract of hospitality. Allow me to quote Derrida at length:

> [Unconditional] hospitality must not pay a debt, or be governed by a duty: it is gracious, and "must" not open itself to the guest [invited or visitor], either "conforming to duty" or even, to use the Kantian distinction again, "out of duty." This unconditional law of hospitality, if such a thing is thinkable, would then be a law without imperative, without order and without duty. A law without law, in short. For if I practice hospitality "*out* of duty" [and not only *in conforming with* duty], this hospitality of paying up is no longer an absolute hospitality, it is no longer graciously offered beyond a debt and economy, offered to the other, a hospitality invented for the singularity of the new arrival, of the unexpected visitor.
>
> Derrida [1997] 2000, 83

Unconditional hospitality is, therefore, unusual insofar as the specificity of the foreigner (is she a refugee, stateless, an immigrant, a subject of the law which affords certain protections, etc.?) is, in one sense, lost; she becomes the no matter who or what, the absolute other, the unknowable in advance, etc. However, she also regains her specificity insofar as she is the "singularity of the new arrival." In this way, when she is asked her name and her history, she is identified only by her incommensurability to any other, and, hence, her singularity resists categorization or being assigned a status that enters both guest and host into the economy of the gift, debt, and the circulation of sovereign power and right. In this regard, unconditional hospitality and the absolute other (a certain foreignness as such) disrupts the violence and conditioning of naming and of the law, i.e., the subsumption and loss of specificity under a general or conditional law to be applied according to one's status or ignored based on the sovereign host's right to self-determination.

Yet, in another turn, the unconditional and absolute welcoming of the other carries with it the untenable risk, a paralyzing paradox, since to welcome unconditionally means to welcome even she or those who are not peaceful, the parasite who would take over, conquer, and hold the host "hostage" (Derrida [1997] 2000, 55), and in so doing destroy the very possibility for hospitality as such, i.e., for welcoming and granting entry to the foreigner who arrives at the threshold of "our" home, or on "our" shores, or at "our" borders. In short, *the* law of hospitality requires and cannot come into being without the *laws* of hospitality and vice versa. Permit me, once more, to quote Derrida at length:

> *The* law [of hospitality] is above the laws. It is thus illegal, transgressive, outside the law, like a lawless law, *nomos anomos*, law above the laws and law outside the law ... But even while keeping itself above the laws of hospitality, *the* unconditional law of hospitality needs the laws, it *requires* them. This demand is constitutive. It wouldn't be effectively unconditional, the law, if it didn't *have to become* effective, concrete, determined, if that were not its being as having-to-be. It would risk being abstract, utopian, illusory, and so turning over into its opposite. In order to be what it is, *the* law thus needs the laws, which, however, deny it, or at any rate threaten it, sometimes corrupt or pervert it. And must always be able to do this. For this pervertibility is essential, irreducible, necessary, too. The perfectibility of the law is at this cost. And therefore their historicity. And vice versa, conditional laws would cease to be laws of hospitality if they were not guided, given inspiration, given aspiration, required, even, by the law of unconditional hospitality.
>
> Derrida [1997] 2000, 79

Conditional hospitality is not merely an expression of the power of the sovereign nation-state to offer hospitality in certain instances, but rather that which brings the unconditional law—the welcoming of the no matter who or what within the community of equals—into being and history, even as it necessarily perverts and corrupts the unconditional law that guides its implementation. Hospitality is, in this way, both a chance and threat, the threat as chance, for democracy. The unconditionally welcomed guest might be a parasite; she might never leave, or she might run the host out; however, it is precisely this upending of the host/guest binary which offers the "salutary risk of being reminded that we too are essentially guests in our own home, migrants in our own homeland" (Naas 2002, 166). This paradox of hospitality, however, must not paralyze because extending hospitality to the singularity of the foreigner cannot wait. Thus, Derrida insists that beyond an unresolvable tension between universal cosmopolitan right that obtains insofar as we are human and the particular legal rights that accrue to members of sovereign communities, any decision worthy of its name to include or exclude foreigners must be rendered within an aporia between *the* unconditional law of unconditional hospitality and the conditional *laws* of hospitality without which hospitality as such and the recognition of the singularity of each would be impossible.

Even if unconditional hospitality is im-possible, this does not mean that the political is always already a "fallen" form of a pure politics where justice or hospitality, for example, are possible but infinitely deferred. To conceive of politics in this way is to disregard the aporia that structures the im-possible decision of hospitality in favor of the quietude of good conscience. In other words, to envisage a pure politics is to render justice an abstraction by reducing it to a blind faith in democratic progress whereby the particular laws of the state will—if not today, then in the future—align with the unconditional, universal human rights, etc. This is *not* to claim that justice does not require legal or moral rights or that the particular laws of the state should not be guided by or judged according to standards of right that transcend the particular state, but rather that justice is irreducible to either. If the interruptive event of justice is to come, it requires that the democratic decision be undertaken in the perpetual oscillations between the universal and particular, the unconditional and the conditional, the non-sovereign and the sovereign, and the unconditional (absolute vulnerability) and the sovereign (absolute mastery).[6] Justice—like democracy—remains to come because it is the event that disrupts sovereign ipseity by interrupting the democratic decision and its traditional foundations of authority, namely the supposed inviolability, indivisibility, and immunity of the *demos*. Unconditional hospitality, therefore, is not a recipe for justice or an end toward which sovereign states strive, but rather an im-possible decision that simultaneously demands the exclusion of others (so that "we" might offer hospitality in the first place according to "our" customs, laws, and solutions to the tension between the universal scope of democratic norms and the right to sovereign self-determination) and the "hyperbolic" requirement to welcome the who or what that arrives beyond or outside the economy of the gift, debt, and generosity in the name of and for the sake of the incommensurability and singularity of the other. As Peter Gratton summarizes: "Politics is in the end the only chance for the unconditional, even where it is conditioned, where it is measured, and where justice as an unconditional claim from the other becomes the law of justice as fairness. Ethics and politics is the negotiation, the forever-without-leisure (the non-*otium* of negotiation) of the conditioning of these unconditional demands, the calculation in the face of the incalculable singularity of the other" (2012, 209).

To illustrate this aporia of hospitality and its relation to sovereignty, justice, and cosmopolitanism, I return, once again, to Socrates' welcoming of Thrasymachus in *The Republic*. Before Thrasymachus enters the dialogue, Socrates has rejected the theories of justice posited by the two permanent foreign residents (*metics*), Cephalus and Polemarchus. Specifically, he shows that justice is not reducible to traditional sources of authority like religion, the law, local norms, and consanguinity. By contrast, Socrates suggests a philosophical justice that is cosmopolitan in scope, a conceptualization that will be tested by Thrasymachus. Thrasymachus is a foreigner of a different category and status. He is an itinerant migrant laborer, a sophist whose skill in teaching others how to persuade the *demos* and the courts allows him to profit handsomely from the existing political and legal order of Athenian democracy. Like the *metics*, however, he is excluded from political membership within the *demos*. That itinerant migrants and *metics* are welcome within Athens speaks to the cosmopolitan scope of its democratic norms. Yet, *The Republic* is Plato's most sustained critique of Athenian democracy; therefore, the presence of the various categories of foreigner that populate the founding of the new, philosophical regime in Book I suggests that the cosmopolitan norms of Athens are insufficient to guarantee justice. It is against this backdrop that we might conceive of Thrasymachus as the threat that is the chance for the philosophical regime.

Plato's depiction of Thrasymachus foreshadows his critique of democracy in Book VIII. Specifically, Thrasymachus represents the unrestrained license and the excesses of democracy that not only require—but also are vulnerable to—the power of persuasion. When justificatory reason-giving is replaced by sophistical demagoguery (almost always touting the exceptionalism of the people, the *ethnos*, the nation, etc.), justice, it seems, is easily reduced to the advantage of the stronger. Thus, Plato draws on the extant notions of the foreigner by depicting Thrasymachus as a dangerous, unknown, uncivilized, violent, bestial, and unmannered threat preying on and profiting from the fundamental vulnerability of democracy, namely its liberality. At the same time, Thrasymachus is not simply a foreigner to Athens. *Qua* sophist, he is an absolute threat to philosophy. Thus, Plato's depiction of Thrasymachus must also be understood as one that casts this foreignness as an absolute threat to the nascent philosophical regime.

Thrasymachus is not peaceful. Thus, for Plato, as much for Kant two millennia later, there is no formal duty to welcome him. Indeed, the conditional laws of hospitality require excluding him, since welcoming him vitiates the ability of the host to offer hospitality. Nonetheless, Socrates does welcome him. Rather than a simple case of political naïveté, Socrates' decision to welcome Thrasymachus suggests the exact way in which the philosophical regime will differ from Athens and complicate traditional conceptions of cosmopolitanism, sovereignty, and justice. While the philosophical regime will embrace a certain cosmopolitanism, it is not a cosmopolitanism that is founded upon an imperfect moral duty to foreigners, the beneficence of the sovereign regime, or a limited welcoming in which foreigners are permitted entry to do business but denied political membership; instead, it is founded upon a normative commitment to *the* law of unconditional hospitality, which not only demands welcoming all even before they have given an account of themselves but also extends a place of pride to the foreigner by granting him a political voice and membership in the community without demanding that he assimilate or integrate.

It is true that Socrates knows that Thrasymachus is a foreign sophist, but as I argued above his foreignness is indecidable. He is simultaneously guest (*xenos*) and enemy (*poleimos*), and this is so even after his violent intentions are revealed. This is why it is surprising that Thrasymachus is not only permitted entry, but that it is his definition of justice—taken up by and improved upon by two native citizens—which drives the discourse that ultimately leads to the conception of justice that will anchor the philosophical regime. While Thrasymachus recedes into the background as the text unfolds, he remains physically present throughout the discussion and unbending in his opposition to the founding norms and conceptualizations of justice upon which the new regime is founded. Rather than a "safe" cosmopolitanism that welcomes peaceful visitors, Thrasymachus retains pride of place *qua* indecidable and threatening foreigner, a point Socrates makes much later in the discussion when he states that he and Thrasymachus are not yet friends even though they were never enemies.

Nevertheless, we might still wonder why Socrates ought to embrace the norm of unconditional hospitality (and, as we shall see, Socrates' decision to welcome Thrasymachus is, strictly speaking, not unconditional). The answer, it seems, lies in the relationship among hospitality, sovereignty, and justice. As a sophist, Thrasymachus provides free men with the skill to participate in the dialogical giving and receiving of reasons indispensable to autonomous self-governance. Democracy, it seems, requires not only rhetoric and sophistry but also the sophist *qua* foreign migrant whose distance from and willingness to depart from the regime provides for a non-threatening critical perspective into the operative norms, practices, and sources of authority. The same is true for the philosophical regime. *Without Thrasymachus, the foreign itinerant migrant, there is no reconceptualization of justice and no city in speech.* Insofar as Thrasymachus is an indecidable foreigner, Socrates' decision to welcome him is guided by the norm of universal hospitality.

At the same time, Thrasymachus' name, history, status as a migrant, etc. are known, and he makes known his violent intentions as he leaps into the debate demanding that Socrates abandon the dialogical norms and reason-giving that have structured the regime up to this point. Recall, however, that Socrates resists violence at every turn. When Polemarchus demands that Socrates remain in the Piraeus because he and his friends outnumber him, Socrates refuses to respond. It is Glaucon who acquiesces, and it is not until Polemarchus shifts from violent threat to the offer of observing the festivities taking place that Socrates formally and legalistically decrees his willingness to join them in community. The same commitment to non-violence holds when Thrasymachus violently demands Socrates abandon his dialogical method and provide a clear definition of justice. Socrates refuses. The other interlocutors implore Thrasymachus to give his definition of justice, and he finally agrees to do so for a fee. Socrates himself does not agree to pay this ransom citing his poverty. Instead, it is Glaucon, again, that offers a payment (Plato 1968, 337d). In sum, the welcoming of Thrasymachus by Socrates is not, strictly speaking, unconditional; instead, it is extended only on the condition that he engage non-violently. Those who refuse to engage non-violently, to participate in the norms of the philosophical and dialogical regime, will be excluded. In this sense, non-violence is, ironically, one of the (violent) laws of hospitality in the philosophical regime.

On this reading, unconditional hospitality is an untenable de-politicization, and, as such, it requires a certain violence, namely the conditional laws of hospitality that express the norms of the community which are necessary for determining or (re)imagining the legal and moral obligations owed to foreigners by the host. This claim reinforces Derrida's insistence that there is no pure politics. There are authoritative normative foundations of a given polity (that differ from place to place) that make hospitality possible at all. In this respect, we should not read Derrida—or my own deconstructive reading of *The Republic*—as an appeal to a borderless cosmopolitanism or global *demos*. To welcome all unconditionally is to compromise the ability to extend hospitality in the first place. Unconditional hospitality, in practice, would be aligned with the ideal of a borderless and anti-sovereign future, which suggests a radical de-politicization that provides no possible redemption of the legal and moral rights claims of those who are most vulnerable, even if this vulnerability is the result of the abuses of power by the conditional laws of the sovereign state. In this regard, the norm of unconditional hospitality does not entail welcoming all who come. Instead, it reveals the originary and ineliminable violence of the political and sovereignty within which the sovereign decision must be rendered.

Only now can we see in what sense unconditional hospitality gives *place*. On the one hand, it gives place to the other in advance of the violence that accompanies the loss of incommensurability and singularity as one becomes a subject of and subjected to the law. On the other hand, unconditional hospitality gives place to the host as well insofar as the conditional laws of the sovereign host are grounded in and guided by the unconditional law of hospitality. The sovereign *qua* host is already vulnerable to—even constituted by—the guest because the power and right of conditional hospitality is premised on the absolute welcoming that would undermine this power or right. In other words, the sovereign decision is rendered within the inescapability of the aporia between the unconditional and conditional, and this is the "place" of politics, where justice takes place, for host and guest alike. Perhaps this is why Socrates is depicted as a foreigner to this new regime, at once the guest and the host, the foreign-sovereign, whose decision to welcome Thrasymachus is rendered within the indecidable aporia of unconditional and conditional hospitality.

To revisit Derrida's quote from above: "[I] take place in the place I offer them, without asking of them either reciprocity (entering into a pact) or even their names. The law of hospitality commands a break with hospitality by right" ([1997] 2000, 25). In this sense, hospitality is the guiding norm of the democracy to come because it gives place—unconditionally—to both guest and host outside of or beyond the law and its sovereign enforcement. As such, hospitality is not only a legal or moral right but rather that which opens democracy to the event of the justice to-come, i.e., to that which interrupts the mastery and violence of sovereignty and the sovereign decision that, nevertheless, must—in the name of equality and recognition of the other—demand an account that destroys incommensurability. Thus, unconditional hospitality is not a maxim for perpetual peace. Rather, in the face of the originary violence of the political, it makes possible what Derrida calls a "lesser violence within an *economy of violence*" (1978, 313, footnote 21, original emphasis) that requires, each time, attending to the incommensurability of the foreign other regardless of her name, history, and status. In this way, it is foreignness—not the foreigner—that unsettles sovereignty by demanding a perpetual negotiation and (re)invention of the conditions for inclusion and exclusion. Foreignness is the condition of possibility for a cosmopolitanism that resists the governing logic of the nation-state that attempts the impossible, namely guaranteeing democratic legitimacy, the unity of the *demos*, and justice through the immunization of the sovereign in the name of its presumed self-identicality and ipseity.[7]

Democratic iterations

For Derrida, democracy remains to come, and linking unconditional hospitality to the democracy to come has two important consequences. First, the inheritance of the meaning of democracy is radically free to (re)interpretation and (re) invention even as Derrida himself wants to preserve—however contested it always already will have been—the set of democratic norms concerning the freedom of speech: voting, civil disobedience, public justifications and reason-giving, etc. This is what Gratton calls the "forever-without-leisure of democratic negotiation" (2012), and why Derrida insists that there is "no deconstruction without democracy, no democracy without deconstruction" ([1994] 1997, 105). Derrida's intent is to show that this perpetual contestation and debate over the meaning of democracy and the terms by which membership in the *demos* of a given polity is determined requires a certain unconditional hospitality insofar as it welcomes all viewpoints, including those voices that are hopeful for, critical of, or even hostile to democracy, as well as the voices of those too long silenced, ignored, or strategically excluded from the *demos*.

Second, unconditional hospitality is not a maxim to be blindly followed by the democratic state, but rather the guiding norm of the democracy to come. While Derrida recognizes that unconditional hospitality and absolute openness are impossible and an untenable de-politicization, he nevertheless argues that the hyperbolic demand of unconditional hospitality opens democracy to the im-possibility of a non-sovereign future that would welcome all vulnerable individuals who arrive, uninvited, at the borders and reside inside the walls of the democratic state. To respond to the call for rights from democracy's foreign others—from those with no legal standing or status to demand the right to political voice—challenges the exclusionary logic of the democratic nation-state, which reserves political membership for members of the nation alone. In short, Derrida's unconditional hospitality suggests that democratic justice and legitimacy must be cosmopolitan. He imagines cosmopolitan cities of refuge being the place where "a democracy to come [is] to be put to the test" (Derrida [1997] 2001, 23) even if these cities do not yet exist and this im-possible idea of a non-sovereign yet statist cosmopolitanism remains still to come. However, in order to include a different voice, accent, and set of ideas in support of cosmopolitanism with respect to extant democratic polities and the complexities it poses for democratic legitimacy, I turn now to Seyla Benhabib. Her work on disaggregated citizenship, democratic iterations, and porous borders is indispensable because it provides for a cosmopolitanism that navigates the tensions between the universal cosmopolitan right to hospitality of the individual and the right to self-determination of the sovereign, democratic nation-state.[8]

Throughout this work, I have endeavored to show that the efforts to secure the identity of a democratic people premised upon the belief in an originary homogeneity leads to unjust exclusions of democracy's others. That this conception of identity is a driver for more or less virulent forms of nationalism and questionable immigration policy is well known. I have gone a step further, suggesting that even countries like the U.S. with a pluralistic self-understanding of democratic political identity retain, at least in part, this belief that foreigners and foreignness threaten the homogeneity and self-identicality of the *ethnos* and, therefore, the presumed basis for the unity of the *demos*. For example, "naturalization" suggests that the identity of the nation originates in and is an unchanging fixture of nature. The foreigner must be "naturalized" to be one of "us," a consanguineous member of the political family. Similarly, Benhabib's cosmopolitanism is an attempt to correct misguided ideas of democratic sovereignty and legitimacy premised upon a homogeneous people, a unified *demos*, and efforts to close and secure the border in order to maintain the boundaries of the territory that is ruled by and "nourishes" the sovereign people. Benhabib notes that this belief in the originary homogeneity of the *ethnos* and the unified self-identicality of the *demos* is not just a misguided belief of the nationalistic masses; rather, some of the most important contemporary political thinkers, including Michael Walzer and John Rawls, fail to adequately distinguish between the *ethnos* and the *demos*. She writes, "there is a widespread trend in contemporary political thought to look upon the formation of collective identities and the evolution of cultural solidarities not as having been attained through long, drawn-out, and bitter social and political conflicts, but as if they were stable givens" (Benhabib 2004, 173). In contrast to the static, exclusionary, and exceptionalist conceptualizations of the *demos*, Benhabib attempts to think through the cosmopolitan possibilities of "disaggregated citizenship" (2004, 173).

Proponents of disaggregated citizenship frequently support some form of post-nationalism insofar as they "welcome the uncoupling of political identities from national membership" (Benhabib 2004, 173). From the rise and proliferation of international human rights laws to trans-national economic and religious forms of association to the culturally complex urban centers of the world, new forms of post-national—and post-statist—cosmopolitan allegiances are now proliferating at the subnational, international, and trans-national levels. Benhabib defines cosmopolitanism as "the concern for the world as if it were one's *polis*" (2004, 174), a concern that therefore is not forged on nation, culture, language, race, ethnicity, religion, etc. Disaggregated citizenship provides for forms of political solidarity, belonging, and collective action distinct from the bonds traditionally secured through one's citizenship within the nation-state. In this way, disaggregated citizenship can be a potent tool and practice for challenging homogeneous conceptions of a people that are frequently deployed to champion the exclusionary politics of nationalism that denies even the most basic political rights to foreigners in their midst. However, in its undemocratic instantiations, disaggregated citizenship can also serve to create and sustain dangerous transnational networks of terrorists whose allegiance is to the network or organization and not the political community in which they reside. In this respect, disaggregated citizenship has an "ambivalent potential" (2004, 171), and if we seek to reject the violence of non-statist terror movements yet retain a commitment to cosmopolitanism, then disaggregated citizenship must be consistent with and (re)enforce democratic rights.

The post-statist implications of some versions of disaggregated citizenship appear to clash with a fundamental tenant of democracy, namely that democracy requires borders precisely because it is a form of association in which the laws are authored by the people. Self-governance means that the laws of the *demos* apply only to its members, and, moreover, the bounded *demos* has rules for determining membership even if these rules are contested. While Benhabib is highly critical of the exclusion of foreigners based on appeals to the sovereign authority over a given territory and the cultural identity it is believed to nurture, she acknowledges that "the scope of democratic legitimacy cannot extend beyond the *demos* which has circumscribed itself as a people upon a given territory. Democratic laws require closure precisely because democratic representation must be accountable to a specific people" (Benhabib 2004, 219). To be otherwise is a form of imperialism, which is why Benhabib insists that "empires have frontiers; democracies have boundaries" (2004, 219). If they are to be democratic, cosmopolitan theories of disaggregated citizenship must address the normative questions of boundaries, territory, and borders, since a democratic disaggregated citizenship must "exhibit accountability, transparency, and responsibility toward a given constituency that authorizes them in its own name" (2004, 175). The primary question, therefore, is how individuals can have a cosmopolitan concern for the world, multiple allegiances, and belong to various networks of solidarity distinct from the nation-state while simultaneously recognizing and upholding the normative implications for political inclusion within democracy *qua* a bounded political community whose laws, norms, and institutions might conflict with the universal scope of cosmopolitan right.

While there is a tension between cosmopolitanism and democratic legitimacy, the founding of the *demos* is not the act of a self-identical and homogeneous would-be sovereign citizenry (exclusive of foreignness as such) that wills itself into being *ex nihilo*. The self-identicality of the "we" who is to be protected by the sovereign is not given by nature or the divine; instead, the founding and constitution of a people are the result of historical contingencies that result from the interactions among humans who share the world, including wars, conquests, diplomacy, trade, the proliferation and contestation of ideas concerning the good life, universal moral principles, and the obligations of the state to uphold these principles. If this is so, then appeals by democratic states to nature, the divine, the presumed impermeability of its borders, and the exceptionalism of its people are revealed for what they truly are, namely fictions of sovereign self-identicality deployed to justify the exclusion of its others.

Benhabib frames the problem this way: "This idealized model of democratic legitimacy [a unified *demos* with supreme authority over an autochthonous territory] not only distorts historical facts, but cannot do justice to the normative potential of democratic constitutionalism" (2004, 175). Insofar as "We, the people" hold that *all* men are created equal, "the human rights principles invoked by democratic constitutions have a context-transcending, cosmopolitan character" (2004, 175). Put differently, Benhabib, like Derrida, points to an originary violence. For Derrida, the violence of the political necessarily accompanies the loss of singularity as one becomes a subject of the law. For Benhabib there is an inevitable violence that results from the "territorial delimitation" (2004, 175) of universal human rights. In this way, disaggregated citizenship is an important concept and practice because it reveals the paradox of democratic founding, namely that those who are excluded from the *demos* "will not be among those who decide upon the rules of exclusion and inclusion" (2004, 177). When democratic legitimacy is premised upon the belief in an originary homogeneity that unifies the "we," it ignores the contingencies, contestations, and violence of the political act of founding, which necessarily include some and exclude others. By "normative potential," therefore, Benhabib suggests that the universal scope of democracy's founding principles enshrined in the constitutions of liberal democracies (that anchor the authority of the law) place a demand on democratic polities to (re)imagine the basis of political membership and citizenship with respect to its others that harmonize with the universal moral principles that lend legitimacy to democratic self-constitution.

The attempt of sovereign states to circumscribe the universal scope of democratic rights through appeals to the territory controlled by the nation contradicts the cosmopolitan character of democratic constitutionalism. For this reasons, Benhabib argues that a meaningful and actionable democratic cosmopolitanism initiates a shift from present theories of the homogeneity of a people and the desire for and faith in the impermeability of its territorial boundaries toward "reflexive acts of constitution-making which are cognizant of the fact that political entities act in an environment crowded with other political actors, and that acts of self-constitution are not unilateral gestures" (2004, 175–176). Borders are not natural or even created through the self-willing of a given people isolated and distinct from other peoples or historical and material realities. While Benhabib agrees that democratic legitimacy is not reducible to the polity's ability to seal its borders and justify this closure through parochial appeals to the homogeneity of cultural identity and supreme control over its territory and borders, democratic legitimacy does require that those who are subject to the law are also its authors. Thus, borders are necessary and normatively important, and a democratic cosmopolitanism recognizes this source of legitimacy while simultaneously demanding that bounded polities reflect upon and embrace the tension between the universal scope of democratic principles that serve as the source of authority and legitimation for the sovereignty of the *demos*.

Without borders and boundaries, there is no democratic legitimacy. Despite the universal scope of its norms and principles, exclusion is a constitutive feature of democratic sovereignty. Nevertheless, this does not suggest that a borderless, global *demos* is a viable solution to the exclusion of democracy's others. Instead, because borders and boundaries are ineliminable structural features of democracy, Benhabib endorses Kant's second article for perpetual peace that if there is to be a cosmopolitan political order, then it must be a "federation of world republics" (Benhabib 2004, 176). At the same time, Benhabib is acutely aware of the movements of people, goods, capital, information, and ideas across permeable borders and boundaries. Hence, while she insists that democratic polities must be bounded, this position does not entail equating the *ethnos* with the *demos*. While recognizing the link among "territoriality, representation, and democratic voice" (2004, 219), Benhabib rejects those theorists who fear the dissolution of citizenship from the presence and inclusion of foreigners by arguing for the right to political membership and eventual citizenship that is not delimited or pre-determined in advance by nationality or territoriality, a position buttressed by her idea of democratic iterations.

Democratic iterations are "complex processes of public argument, deliberation, and exchange through which universalist rights claims and principles are contested and contextualized, invoked and revoked, posited and positioned, throughout legal and political institutions, as well as in the associations of civil society" (Benhabib 2004, 179). While the accent is different, this formulation is reminiscent of Derrida's claims regarding the mutual dependence between unconditional and conditional hospitality. For Derrida, the unconditional welcoming of the other requires the authoritative norms and conditional laws of a given polity. By contrast, conditional hospitality requires unconditional hospitality if it is to mitigate the violence inherent to acts of self-constitution and the possibility of a future politics that welcomes those who have traditionally been excluded from the *demos*. For Benhabib, universalist rights claims are worked out and determined within specific contexts, and through this process the historical contingencies that gave rise to a particular polity's laws, institutions, sources of authority, and psychosocial self-understanding are revealed and (re)negotiated in response to the "context-transcending" universal scope of its founding principles.

The similarities between these two formulations is not accidental; indeed, Benhabib takes up the term "iteration" from Derrida's work in the philosophy of language and deconstruction of the Western metaphysics of presence that undergirds sovereign ipseity. Repetition of difference into an infinitely open future grounds Derrida's claim that democracy as such and the self-identicality of a people will never be fully present. They will always already have undergone an iteration and repetition in difference. Benhabib explains her use of the term in this way: "In the process of repeating a term or a concept, we never simply produce a replica of the first original usage and its intended meaning; rather every repetition is a form of variation. Every iteration transforms meaning, adds to it, enriches it in ever-so-subtle ways" (2004, 179).

Benhabib claims that there is no "'originary' source of meaning, or an 'original' to which all subsequent forms must conform" (2004, 179). Nevertheless, she insists (in a way that harmonizes with Derrida's work on *différance*, democracy to come, and hospitality) that while there is no originary source of meaning, this does not mean that there are no forms of precedent and tradition that inform, guide, and authorize the deliberations of a democratic people and its sovereign decision. In other words, one can reject the idea of origins and originary meanings, but nevertheless hold to the position that "every act of iteration might refer to an antecedent which is taken to be authoritative" (Benhabib 2004, 180). The authority and precedents of laws and institutions are simultaneously authoritative and vulnerable to a (re)negotiation in each democratic iteration, each vote, each transfer of power, each new law, each sovereign decision to welcome or exclude, etc. Benhabib summarizes: "*Democratic iterations* are such linguistic, legal, cultural, and political repetitions-in-transformation, invocations which are also revocations. They not only change established understandings but also transform what passes as the valid or established view of an authoritative precedent" (2004, 180, original emphasis).

Cosmopolitan norms are, today, becoming more robust. For example, it is increasingly commonplace that "rights are extended to individuals by virtue of residency rather than cultural identity" (Benhabib 2004, 177). Nevertheless, those individuals whose status is in flux or undetermined, namely undocumented (im)migrants and asylum seekers, are all too often criminalized and deemed illegal by existing democratic nation-states. A cursory glance at the news of the day reveals the ways in which "the right to universal hospitality is sacrificed at the altar of state interest" (2004, 177). While there are instances of legitimate state interest that would result in denying hospitality, Benhabib insists that we must "decriminalize the worldwide movement of peoples, and treat each person, whatever his or her political citizenship status, in accordance with the dignity of moral personhood. This implies acknowledging that crossing borders and seeking entry into different polities is not a criminal act but an expression of human freedom and the search for human betterment in a world which we have to share with our fellow human beings" (2004, 177).

Like Kant, Benhabib endorses the universal right to first admittance precisely because this welcoming and extending of hospitality does not necessarily entail the right to permanent residency, political membership, or even full-fledged citizenship to all who arrive. Insofar as democratic communities are bounded and self-governing, they must make their own laws regarding who will be included or excluded; however, unlike Kant, the decision to grant permanent residency, political membership, or citizenship to those who have been granted first admittance is not merely a gift of the sovereign. For a democracy, this decision must be made in ways that harmonize with the universal scope of fundamental democratic rights.[9] Benhabib concisely summarizes this point and the political and moral obligation of sovereign states to uphold the rights of foreigners when she claims that democratic nation-states "constitute the *demos* as sovereign while proclaiming that the sovereignty of the *demos* derives its legitimacy from its adherence to fundamental human rights principles. 'We, the people,' is an inherently fraught formula, containing in its very articulation the constitutive dilemmas of respect for universal human rights and nationally circumscribed sovereignty claims" (2004, 178). For example, one's status as a guest worker in a host country does not mean that the guest worker has been stripped of her political rights even if the host views granting political voice to this temporary resident as a threat to its own interests. Similarly, undocumented (im)migrants or refugees are not and should not be treated as criminals whose fate is in the hands of the generosity or miserliness of the polity they have entered. It is within the tension between the universal scope of democratic norms and sovereign self-determination that democratic political identity and the legitimacy of the democratic state must be hashed out.[10] Democratic iterations are the perpetual (re)negotiation of this tension that give force to the "normative potential" of democratic constitutionalism to challenge and (re)invent its traditional sources of authority.

Insofar as the right to self-determination of the sovereign state and democratic legitimacy has a long and lingering tradition of protecting the exclusionary logic of the nation-state, democratic iterations provide a corrective capable of attending to the huge numbers of foreigners migrating into and through sovereign states. Democratic iterations outline a fluid understanding of cultural identity and political inclusion that simultaneously respects moral personhood universally without sacrificing the structural necessity of borders and boundaries to democracy. Put differently, the universal, "context-transcending" rights that anchor democratic constitutions always points beyond the local laws and institutions that represent the will of the majority and serve as the sources of authority and legitimacy for the democratic state. At the same time, it is these universal principles that are contested, (re)negotiated, and debated as they are instantiated which provide for their (re)iteration within bounded democratic polities. Democratic iterations uphold the necessity of bounded political communities while exerting a cosmopolitan counter-pressure against the exclusionary logic of the nation-state. In sum, democratic iterations introduce the possibility for establishing a more robust and inclusive *demos* by (re)imagining and (re)inventing the hospitality owed to democracy's others.

Benhabib's elaboration of democratic iterations challenges the idea that democratic legitimacy is premised upon the originary or ultimate unity of the *demos*. Instead, the act of self-constitution that produces a *demos* is the result of a series of historical contingencies and contestations about who is or is not a member. These contestations continue, and with each (re)iteration new laws, rules, and institutions emerge that simultaneously (re)enforce and (re)invent the rules governing membership. Democratic iterations are an expression of the structural potential of democracies to expand the scope of justice and legitimacy beyond their borders.

At the same time, there are no guarantees that a democracy will always make new laws or establish new institutions that fulfill its moral and legal obligations it has to protect the human rights of each and all. For Benhabib, retrograde polices and democratic failures should not be conflated with a democratic iteration. Instead, democratic iterations are only those contestations and (re)inventions of traditional sources of authority within a specific context that come closer to instantiating universal democratic principles. Benhabib rightly points out that even when the highest courts within a democracy make a judgment, which, for example, restrict voting rights for permanent residents based on a conception of citizenship rooted in the imagined cultural identity and the shared fate of the *ethnos*, "finality does not mean irreversibility or infallibility. The complex dialogue between the democratically elected representatives of the people, the judiciary, and other civil and political actors is a never-ending one of complex and contentious iterations. Within such dialogues, the democratic *demos* can reconstitute itself by enfranchising groups without voice or by providing amnesty to undocumented immigrants" (Benhabib 2004, 219–220).

Be that as it may, Benhabib does insist that whatever the promises of disaggregated citizenship and cosmopolitanism to mitigate unjust political exclusion, a viable cosmopolitanism requires bounded democratic polities. She continues, "[I]t is inconceivable that democratic legitimacy can be sustained without some clear demarcations of those in the name of whom the laws have been enacted from those upon whom the laws are not binding" (Benhabib 2004, 220). Therefore, rather than open borders, Benhabib argues for "*porous* borders" (2004, 221, original emphasis). This conceptualization attends to the empirical fact that borders are not impermeable and that they will be crossed by those who seek a better life and with whom the host community shares the world. Porous borders, therefore, provide a viable basis for a democratic cosmopolitanism. On the one hand, they demand that democracies recognize and protect the universal right to first admittance—not only to invited or welcomed guests—but also for those refugees, asylum seekers, and immigrants who, today, are deemed to be and treated as criminals. On the other hand, porous borders are still borders, and in this respect, they uphold the "right of democracies to regulate the transition from first admission to full membership" (2004, 221).

In closing, Benhabib points to various models for citizenship that lend themselves to cosmopolitanism without sacrificing "the principle of territorial membership for undergirding representation" (2004, 217–218). Whether the model is one of dual-citizenship, "flexible citizenship" common in Latin America, which allows those who have left the country to vote in elections and even hold political office, or "citizenship in the city" (cities of refuge, per Derrida) common throughout the European Union (2004, 217), what each of these models of cosmopolitan citizenship share is the necessity of a bounded territory. There can be no democratic representation without "access to, residency upon, and eventual membership within a circumscribed territory" (2004, 218). It is this recognition that gives Benhabib's cosmopolitanism and defense of the rights of others its force. Democratic disaggregated citizenship, democratic iterations, and porous borders provide a conceptual framework that recognizes the necessity and normative importance of borders while resisting unjust immigration policies designed to preserve outdated notions of territoriality premised on the idealized conception of impermeable borders immune to the empirical realities of globalization in which culture, identity, environment, disease, information, and individuals cannot be contained by the walls of the nation-state.

The foreign-citizen

The central claim of this work is that foreignness is an originary and constitutive structural feature of sovereignty. Drawing on this formulation, I introduce a final (non)concept, the foreign-citizen. The foreign-citizen provides a model for cosmopolitan citizenship that respects the requirements laid out by Benhabib that bounded democratic polities determine their own rules for membership, that the conditions for membership are transparent, and that these justifications "respect the communicative freedom of human beings qua human beings" (Benhabib 2004, 139). Moreover, the foreign-citizen provides further support for Derrida's claims regarding unconditional hospitality that political membership for the foreigner is not, contra Kant, a gift of the sovereign.[11] I begin by returning to the distinction between the foreigner and foreignness as such in order to demonstrate the vulnerability and tenuousness of the status of citizenship. This vulnerability of the citizen to the foreign can be abused by the illegitimate sovereign to exclude those it deems to be a threat to its sovereignty; however, this vulnerability of citizenship is also productive insofar as it serves to deconstruct the logic of national citizenship without, however, calling for open borders. By attending to the itinerant (im)migrant who crosses and re-crosses porous borders, I argue that this figure is illustrative of the cosmopolitan foreign-citizen who gives place to the foreigner and the citizen alike to engage in a democratic politics. I conclude by suggesting that the foreign-citizen offers a model for the perpetual (re)imagining of democratic citizenship, a cosmopolitan democratic citizenship to come that embraces the im-possible risk of an ineliminable foreignness.

When considering the theorization of sovereignty in the social contract tradition, I argued that foreignness is distinct from the foreigner. Whether an empirical insider or outsider to a given polity, foreignness is that which is or is deemed to be a threat to the self-identicality of the sovereign. Anyone, including citizens, can be cast as foreign to the sovereign. By the same token, the foreigner need not be threatening. Indeed, the transition from foreigner to citizen through the process of "naturalization" is the shedding of the threat of foreignness as the foreigner becomes known, accountable, and unthreatening to the sovereign. Most simply, foreignness, as much as citizenship, is a *status* assigned by the sovereign.

Insofar as citizenship is a status granted by the sovereign, it is precarious and subject to revocation. While it is more common for naturalized citizens to be denaturalized, native-born citizens can also be stripped of their citizenship for a variety of reasons. However, my interest here is not to identify historical cases of individuals losing their citizenship. Beyond and in addition to revocation, I am suggesting that even if one retains her citizenship, she may, nevertheless, be deemed foreign when her citizenship is effectively held in abeyance. For example, we might point to U.S. citizens who until 2015 were denied the opportunity and right to marry same-sex partners. More extreme cases are those American citizens who are treated as enemy combatants for their real or supposed support for Islamic terrorism.[12] In both cases, one's citizenship does not purge one's foreignness. Because one's status ultimately depends on the justified or unjustified decision of the sovereign, every citizen is, in a sense, a foreign-citizen. This vulnerability to the foreign can be and often is exploited and abused by the sovereign, which is to make the obvious claim that civil and political rights are tenuous even when they are ostensibly protected by one's status as a citizen.

The vulnerability to the foreign is undesirable if it results in the loss of civil and political rights. However, the foreign-citizen also echoes the efforts throughout to show that sovereignty is always already foreign to it-self, and this structural feature of sovereignty offers the possibility for the (re)imagining of democratic citizenship, legitimacy, and justice. In this case, we must not focus on the sovereign *demos* or even the sovereign self but rather the individual *qua* sovereign democratic citizen. Citizenship is a status assigned to the individual, a set of legal rights and protections that accrue to her because she is a member of a given democratic polity. To be a citizen presumes certain things, namely that she be knowable, known, and accountable to the *demos*. It is in this way that the citizen becomes sovereign; she is identified and identifiable as an equal member of the *demos*: each citizen is sovereign insofar as the individual gains herself—her singularity and incommensurability to any other—through her equal membership in democratic political society.

At the same time, in becoming a citizen, the individual also loses something of herself. She becomes foreign to herself, not psychologically, but rather in the sense of a certain alienation that accompanies all juridical subjects who lose their singularity and incommensurability as they become equal—yet generic—subjects under the law. The individual is necessarily transformed from an incommensurable singularity into a measurable identity, and this, to reiterate the point, is the originary violence of the political for Derrida. Nevertheless, without this transformation from the unconditional to the conditional, the singularity of each and all would remain an abstract ideal. Paradoxically, one both gains and loses one's singularity by becoming a citizen. The individual is, at once, an incommensurable singularity and a measurable and calculable citizen, and each requires the other, even as these "identities" might conflict. This, then, is another, positive, way to conceive of the sovereign democratic citizen as always already a foreign-citizen.

This formulation is positive because the foreignness of the citizen to herself is not merely a source of precariousness but rather an opening for the contestation and (re)imagining of citizenship that is indispensable to democracy and democratic legitimacy. I would like to push this point by suggesting, as Derrida does, that the general logic of autoimmunity is operative in any sovereign entity, and this includes the democratic citizen. For the general logic of autoimmunity to hold, citizenship would need to be refuted by its indispensable principles and the very acts that constitute it. Put differently, the fundamental expressions and performances of democratic citizenship that would constitute the individual as a citizen and immunize her from any threat to this status must also threaten to destroy democratic citizenship *from within*. There is, perhaps, no better example of the autoimmunity of democratic citizenship than the act of voting.

The citizen who votes her conscience (i.e. who uses her sovereign freedom and force in good faith to pass a law or elect a representative) performs and enforces democratic citizenship. This does not mean that those citizens who do not vote are not citizens or that abstention is not, in specific contexts, a political act and free voicing of one's sovereign opinion; however, even though voting is simply one among many civil and political rights of democratic citizenship, it is fundamental and paradigmatic precisely because democratic legitimacy rests upon the authoring of the laws by those who are subject to them. Beyond the right to vote, it is the performance of this right that is indispensable to democratic citizenship because it is in this way that the individual becomes known and accountable to the *demos*. Moreover, by voting, the citizen declares her own sovereignty as a democratic citizen *and* (re)affirms the sovereignty and legitimacy of the democratic *demos* as a whole as well as the citizenship of each and all *qua* sovereign and equal political actors.

As fundamental as voting is to citizenship, it is also that which exposes the sovereign citizen to the counter-sovereignty of the other, a sharing out of her sovereign right as a citizen, since the very act of voting—one's declaration of independence—is also that which, in an autoimmune fashion, threatens democratic citizenship as such. Whatever the consequences, the democratic citizen is free to vote to limit her democratic rights, the democratic rights of some individuals or groups, or—as we saw in Derrida's example of Algeria—the democratic rights of all members of the polity. This is a structural feature and intrinsic possibility of democratic citizenship. Taking liberty with an earlier example provided by Derrida is illustrative of this point.[13] The citizen, in good conscience, might vote to deny undocumented (im)migrants the right to vote in elections based on the view that one's status as a citizen is strengthened by denying this right to non-citizens. What, after all, is citizenship worth if non-citizens can vote? If this vote carries the day, it not only sends off foreign residents who, nevertheless, are indispensable to the viability of the polity, but it also effectively sends off part of the *demos*, the minority. Meanwhile, the minority in this example holds the conviction that extending voting rights to undocumented immigrants strengthens the status of citizenship by establishing a more legitimate democracy, which guarantees that those who are subject to the law are also its authors. On this minority view, the rights of democratic citizenship are, somewhat counter-intuitively, weakened by denying undocumented immigrants the right to vote, thereby putting off—until another day—the full instantiation and inalienability of democratic citizenship.

There is no telling in advance if the sovereign act of voting performed in good faith by the citizen will strengthen or weaken citizenship. Accordingly, voting both constitutes and sends off and puts off citizenship. As with democracy, there is a *double renvoi* of democratic citizenship, an "autoimmune necessity inscribed" onto its very concept. Voting, therefore, is the performance of autoimmune citizenship, since it is that which would constitute and immunize oneself *qua* citizen and that which threatens to pervert, weaken, or destroy democratic citizenship.[14] The autoimmune democratic citizen is accountable, known, calculable, native-born or "naturalized," yet it contains within itself an aspect of the unknown, the nameless, the unaccountable, the incalculable, the heterogeneous, and the foreign. Most plainly, the autoimmune citizen is a foreign-citizen, and it is this foreignness to it-self that reveals that democratic citizenship will never be fully present as such. This lack is the threat and opportunity, threat as opportunity (per Derrida), for democratic citizenship, since it is in the spacing between the unconditional and conditional, the human and the juridical subject, the moral and the legal, the self-same and the foreign where the scope, meaning, and requirements of citizenship are not only determined but perpetually (re)negotiated and contested. Just as democracy is a project, so too is democratic citizenship. We have not yet learned how to be proper citizens, and, as such, there is always already more to be done in this project. Indeed, vibrant and legitimate democracies are precisely those in which its citizens work to become proper citizens through the tireless efforts to understand and engage in democratic politics. The democratic citizen remains to come, and this has important consequences for the democratic nation-state.

Citizenship within the nation-state is reserved for members of the nation alone, and we have elaborated throughout the threat of disenfranchisement, political marginalization, and civic death faced by empirical insiders and outsiders that result from linking political inclusion and citizenship to membership within the nation. Within the nation-state, the foreign-citizen is impossible precisely because one who is a citizen is by definition not foreign. She is a national or "naturalized" member of the people but never foreign. On this model, the unity of the *demos* is premised, at least in part, on the belief in the homogeneity of the nation and the self-identicality of the citizen. Like the foreign-sovereign and the quasi-regime, the foreign-citizen is im-possible, yet it is precisely this im-possibility that reveals it as a (non)concept perpetually resistant to sovereign appeals to the impermeability, inviolability, indivisibility, and self-mastery of the *ethnos* and *demos* as well as the logic linking these two distinct notions of a people in the figure of the citizen. As such, the foreign-citizen disrupts traditional justifications for the exclusion of democracy's others from political membership based upon their real or perceived foreignness, including race, ethnicity, gender, religion, linguistic group, sexuality, etc. In this way, the foreign-citizen provides for a post-nationalist cosmopolitanism which rejects the exclusion of foreignness and foreigners based on appeals to sovereign self-identicality by demanding that the sovereign decision to admit, include, and eventually grant citizenship to its others attends to the ineliminable and structural necessity of foreignness to citizenship and democratic legitimacy as such.

While the foreign-citizen holds the meaning (and make-up) of democratic citizenship perpetually open to its foreign others and cosmopolitan (re)iterations, this does not mean that citizenship within bounded democratic polities is either impossible or undesirable. Indeed, on this point, I side with both Benhabib (democracy must be bounded since its laws cannot apply to those who did not author them) and Derrida (the rejection of sovereignty as such or a borderless/stateless world is an untenable de-politicization and abstraction) that democratic cosmopolitanism requires bounded polities of some kind (e.g., cities of refuge) to establish the institutions and laws necessary to guarantee the human rights and unconditional singularity of the foreign others who arrive at or reside within the borders of a given polity. As Benhabib argues, this does not mean that there are not non-territorial sub- and super-national forms of political solidarity and political community whose existence is in dialogue with state-based forms of representation and solidarity (2004, 218–219); however, citizenship within a particular democratic polity resists the hegemony of the most powerful democracies precisely because it allows for local variation and determination of the rules for membership, laws, and institutions informed by and responsive to specific historical, material, and cultural contexts and traditions.

This position is not an implicit endorsement of relativism; instead, because the citizen is always a foreign-citizen, the justifications for exclusion of the foreigner from political membership must always be both transparent and acceptable to the citizen insofar as she is also a foreigner and the foreigner insofar as she is also a citizen. In other words, per discourse ethics, "reasons that barred you from membership because of the kind of being you were, your ascriptive and non-elective attributes such as your race, gender, religion, ethnicity, language community, or sexuality, would not be permissible, because I would then be reducing your capacity to exercise communicative freedom to those characteristics given to you by chance or accident and which you did not choose" (Benhabib 2004, 138–139).[15] Per deconstruction, the decision to include or exclude foreigners from political membership and citizenship is rendered by the sovereign but always in view of the unconditional singularity of the other and the foreignness constitutive of sovereignty as such. To exclude the foreigner because of her differences (race, ethnicity, gender, sexuality, etc.) is to foreclose the possibility for a justice distinct from the pre-programmed application, mastery, and violence of the law.

Despite its advantages for challenging the unjust exclusion of foreigners, the foreign-citizen has not yet answered the question of whether the civil right of political membership is also a universal human right. In other words, does the figure of the foreign-citizen simply provide, per Kant, the right to sojourn and visit? Or, should political inclusion and eventual citizenship for those foreigners who have been admitted be an inalienable and non-fungible right of each and not a charitable gift of the sovereign? What about those who have not been invited by the host? Do refugees or (im)migrants temporarily or permanently residing in a given polity have a right to political membership? To answer these questions, I turn to the contemporary figure of the uninvited itinerant migrant who reveals the impossibility of sovereign inviolability and the possibility for a robust hospitality in which the foreigners residing within a democratic polity are guaranteed admittance to the *demos*.

The itinerant migrant leaves her country of birth in order to better her life and the lives of her family. In this regard, we should demand, as Benhabib does, that the emigration and movement of individuals across sovereign borders be decriminalized. The argument above that the right to hospitality precedes and names the right to motility reveals a deep agreement between my own view and Benhabib's on this point, but I would push further by suggesting that the itinerant migrant is the cosmopolitan foreign-citizen. The itinerant migrant crosses and re-crosses the sovereign borders intended to demarcate and distinguish between inside/outside, sovereign/foreign, us/them, citizen/non-citizen, friend/enemy, host/guest, etc. In this respect, the movements of the itinerant migrant reveal the artificiality, historicity, and, hence, the deconstructibility of the conceptual borders and boundaries of sovereignty. Moreover, while the native-born citizen may or may not belong to cosmopolitan networks and associations, the itinerant migrant, by definition, participates in and has allegiances to multiple polities, cultures, histories, languages, religions, familial networks, etc. These allegiances are not delimited by the borders of the state. In fact, these borders are hindrances to these allegiances, and it is precisely insofar as she is itinerant that she does not and cannot give up one set of allegiances simply because she crosses a political border.

The itinerant migrant challenges the hierarchical and binaristic logic and ordering of sovereignty. Her life is proof of the impossibility of sovereign inviolability. She embodies the deconstructive potential and cosmopolitan scope of the foreign-citizen whose foreignness is constitutive of sovereignty as such and the sovereign citizen that can never be purged. In other words, the model for cosmopolitan democratic citizenship is best expressed by the itinerant migrant who simultaneously requires the legal protections of citizenship and who—through the generative potential of foreignness, difference, and multiple allegiances to the law and the state—resists the exclusion of foreigners from political membership in the name of and for the sake of sovereign self-identicality. Indeed, it is those who have no right to demand rights, no legal status to demand the rights reserved for full citizens (or those citizens that are marginalized or disenfranchised once they are deemed to possess the qualities of foreignness) that serve as the impetus for the contestation of the terms, conditions, and laws for determining citizenship. If, however, the itinerant migrant embodies the deconstructive possibilities of the foreign-citizen toward a cosmopolitan democratic citizenship, then she must also give place to the possibility of the political for both the citizen and the foreigner alike. To understand this claim, I return, one final time, to the figure of Thrasymachus. Despite the different historical contexts and their respective status, both the contemporary itinerant migrant and Thrasymachus give place to a democratic politics.

I have discussed in detail how Socrates is, at once, the guest (foreigner) and host (sovereign), and that it is he who extends an almost impossible hospitality to Thrasymachus, the indecidable foreigner (guest/enemy). However, it is also the case that Thrasymachus, the guest, is a host of sorts insofar as it is he, as much as Socrates, who gives place to the dialogue on justice. Thrasymachus, of course, does not extend a welcome into his house, across a threshold, through a border over which he is sovereign, etc. Moreover, Plato's explicit depiction of Thrasymachus suggests that he is an obstacle and danger to the new regime and its efforts to (re)imagine justice. Beyond an obstacle, he seeks to undermine any regime that will limit his economic opportunity, which is dependent upon the silencing of Socrates and philosophy. That said, it is precisely insofar as Thrasymachus is a foreign, itinerant migrant who has no specific allegiance to Athens or the nascent philosophical regime that the reconceptualization of justice in *The Republic* becomes possible.

To strip justice from its traditional, religious, and legal foundations, Plato implicitly suggests that the reconceptualization of justice must originate in the foreign, itinerant migrant who has no need to integrate or assimilate. While it is true that the elaboration and refinement of justice is achieved only when the two native citizens adopt and improve upon Thrasymachus' definition of justice, I do not wish to conjecture on what this might suggest about Plato's understanding of and (de)valuation of natives and foreigners; instead, it reveals that the itinerant migrant, the most unknown, unaccountable, and threatening of the wide variety of foreigners present in Book I, is uniquely able to open up the possibility for the contestation and renegotiation of the political and justice for both citizens and foreigners alike. Although Thrasymachus will not be the sovereign of this new regime, he is similar to Socrates insofar as he is a foreign guest-host, and it is as a foreigner who remains yet refuses to assimilate or integrate that he warrants a prominent place of pride within the new regime. Without swearing allegiance to the regime or its governing norms, Thrasymachus *is* a member of the new regime whose voice is not simply heard but generative of a new politics and justice. In a word, Thrasymachus *qua* foreign itinerant migrant gives place to both citizens and foreigners alike to build a new, more just regime.

In this same way the itinerant migrant, today, is the guest and host who gives place to both citizens and foreigners alike for the possibility of a cosmopolitan, democratic politics and justice. In her demand for political membership, the itinerant migrant—with multiple and uncertain allegiances who need not assimilate or fully integrate—calls into question the legitimacy of democratic hospitality, citizenship, and sovereignty premised upon self-identicality and ipseity. Without the foreigner and foreignness as such, there would be no contestation, no politics, no "place" for democracy, no citizenship, and no justice for the citizen or the foreigner. It would be u-topic in the worst imaginable way, the no-place at all and death that is the infinite repetition of the self-same. The refusal to assimilate or integrate fully and the foreignness of the itinerant migrant that challenges the self-identicality of sovereignty make possible and demand the perpetual contestation and (re)negotiation of the scope and meaning of democratic citizenship.

Democracy *is* risk, and it is precisely on account of the multiple allegiances of the itinerant migrant and the lack of reassurances that she will assimilate or integrate—the risk she poses to sovereign self-identicality—that she exemplifies the figure of the foreign-citizen who merits pride of place within the polity. This cosmopolitan right of political inclusion not only furthers democratic legitimacy by guaranteeing that those subject to the law are also its authors, but it is also the minimal condition of hospitality requisite for disrupting the violent politics of exclusion in the name of sovereign self-identicality. Insofar as the foreign-citizen gives place, foreignness is a cornerstone of democratic legitimacy, cosmopolitan justice, and a vindication (in certain contexts) of the right of the sovereign state to determine its own criteria for citizenship that instantiate universal human rights locally and protect the singularity and incommensurability of all who arrive at its walls.

The cosmopolitan foreign-citizen is im-possible precisely because it undermines the binaristic logic determinative of sovereignty. It will, in other words, never be fully present as such. The foreign-citizen remains to come, and a cosmopolitan future worthy of its name, therefore, must ask several questions: Can we re-imagine democratic citizenship, today, that is no longer determined according to the logic of the nation-state? Can we re-imagine democratic citizenship which would hospitably provide political membership to foreign residents? Can we re-imagine democratic citizenship as a promise—that may never be present as such—which gives place to the singularity of citizen and foreigner alike? The (non)concept of the foreign-citizen suggests that democracy can.

There are, by some estimates, twelve million undocumented (im)migrants in the United States. As Benhabib points out, they may not be effectively silenced, but "not having one's papers in order in our societies is a form of civil death" (2004, 215).[16] The traditional logic of the sovereign nation-state suggests that by welcoming these human beings as members of the community poses a greater risk to democracy than denying them political inclusion. The governing logic of the day suggests that the cosmopolitanism promised by the foreign-citizen is politically naïve and risky. Be that as it may, a future worthy of its name—a cosmopolitan future no longer hindered by the faith in the sovereign immunity of a people—requires that the decision to welcome or exclude be rendered within the indecidable aporia and nearly-impossible distinction between the sovereign and the unconditional. As Derrida writes, "Both of these escape absolutely, like the absolute itself, all relativism. That is their affinity" ([2003] 2005, xiv). They differ, however, insofar as the unconditional demands recognition of and vulnerability to the singularity of the other while the sovereign is itself a form of and attempt at mastery. The unprecedented levels of human migration today across sovereign borders demand that the aporetic, im-possible decision between the unconditional and sovereign must be rendered. If, as I have argued, foreignness is always already constitutive of sovereignty, then the im-possibility of the foreign-citizen provides for a cosmopolitanism attunement to the unconditional singularity and incommensurability of the foreign other. The foreign-citizen is politically naïve, but it is this naïveté that resists good conscience and the violence of sovereign mastery in the name of and for the sake of democracy and its others.

Notes

Introduction

1 In the U.S. alone, there are the torture chambers of Guantánamo, the indefinite detention of U.S. citizens suspected of terrorism, the use of Predator drones to kill U.S. citizens and suspected terrorists abroad, and Arizona's, Alabama's, and Georgia's immigration laws. Further, an entry for each of the approximately (lowest estimate) 100,000 deaths of innocent civilians during the second U.S. invasion of Iraq would provide overwhelming evidence that all of these non-democratic—even anti-democratic—actions, practices, wars, etc. are waged in the name of democracy and democratic ideals and principles.

2 The formation of *demes* in Ancient Greece was designed specifically to replace political organization based on aristocratic familial relations and groups by producing laws and requirements for citizenship in the *deme*. In this way, *ethnos* was political insofar as it was specifically identified as a way to *not* organize the *demes*. Moreover, by the time Athens was at its zenith, the conceptual distinction between *ethnos* and *demos* still remained, but because Athens had no formal naturalization procedures, citizenship was largely reserved to those who fit a particular *ethnos*, i.e., not Athenian *per se* (since not all Athenians were citizens) but predominantly the native-born, Greek-speaking, propertied, adult males, etc. (Walzer 1983, 53). However, the very distinction between these two notions of a people, *ethnos* and *demos*, demonstrates the ancient belief in a non-political and a political community of membership and belonging.

3 The term 'indecidable' is a technical concept to be distinguished from 'undecidable' and is used throughout. Indecidability does not suggest that no decision is or can be made. Sovereign states, of course, make decisions every day regarding how they will respond to the foreigner and foreignness as such. Rather than something that is impossible to decide, indecidability preserves the tension, imbrications, and ambiguity of conceptual oppositions such as guest/enemy, inside/outside, sovereign/foreign, us/them, etc. For more on this distinction, see Hugh J. Silverman's, 1994, *Textualities: Between Hermeneutics and Deconstruction*.

Chapter 1 *Ethnos*, *Demos*, and Foreignness

1 I use the term political ideology intentionally to differentiate between it and various political philosophies. Although modern liberalism is surely influenced by

thinkers like Locke and Rawls while conservative communitarianism brings together thinkers such as Edmund Burke and Michael Walzer, it would be a mistake to assume that the political beliefs and practices denoted by modern liberalism and conservative communitarianism are practical applications of the contributions of these political philosophers whose positions are significantly more subtle than—and, at least in Walzer's case, often opposed to—their ideological counterparts.

2 Restricting my analysis of the political spectrum to modern liberalism and conservative communitarianism fails to bring forth many of the subtleties of democratic political identification and beliefs. For example, both ideologies subscribe to rights discourse of classical liberalism as well as certain tenets of communitarianism. Moreover, the spectrum of Left to Right, even when restricted to democracy, is not fixed in advance. There is no generic political spectrum. Political beliefs are always grounded in the particularity and historicity of a given state. Therefore, while it will be useful for me to speak very generally of modern liberalism and conservative communitarianism in places as divergent as the U.S., France, or Mexico, I do so with the awareness that to home in on the dynamics that shape the identity of the *demos* is a generalization and theorization that requires humility and caution so as not to lose sight of the specificities that make peoples and their political systems unique.

3 There are differences between modern liberalism and conservative communitarianism with respect to the understanding of the relationship among democracy, sovereignty, and foreignness. Yet, what interests me in this work is that both subscribe to a shared idea: Despite the universal scope of democratic principles, sovereign states are obligated to protect its citizens by expunging foreignness from the *demos*. This "purification" and unification of the *demos* may be achieved through greater inclusivity and granting of previously withheld rights or through exclusions and denial of new rights to foreign individuals.

4 The mechanisms and categories of exclusion, marginalization, and oppression are legion. We might note simply here the exclusions are most frequently rooted in language, gender, race, class, and sexuality perpetuated through (legitimate) courts, laws, institutions, and (illegitimate) vigilantes, prejudices, racisms, etc., as well as dominant and accepted socio-cultural norms.

5 This expansion occurs within certain limits, since not everyone can be included in the *demos* (foreigners, non-citizens, and enemies of the state), or if included, they do not have status as full members (children, criminals, guest-workers, etc.).

6 By contrast, in 2011, conservative European leaders such as Angela Merkel of Germany, David Cameron of the United Kingdom, and Nicolas Sarkozy of France all condemned multiculturalism to varying degrees, with Cameron going so far as to claim that it is a failed political experiment that effectively endangers liberal

democracy. See https://www.nytimes.com/2011/02/06/world/europe/06britain.html (accessed February 9, 2013).

7 It is common in the U.S. to hear the claim by proponents of modern liberalism and conservative communitarianism that equality (often ambiguously expressed as either political egalitarianism or equality of opportunity) is not a value specific to a political ideology, but an American value. For example, in a recent speech, President Obama insisted that electing a Republican in 2012 would be dangerous because "the very core of what this country stands for is on the line—the basic promise that no matter what you look like, no matter where you come from, this is a place where you could make it if you try." See http://www.weeklystandard.com/blogs/obama-campaigns-osama-bin-laden-will-never-again-walk-face-earth-s-what-change_616238.html (accessed February 9, 2013).

8 This loss is not theorized as accidental. It is produced through the inclusion of those persons whose experiences, histories, practices, moral and religious values, and languages differ from the original culture and spirit of the *demos*.

9 The supposed unity rests primarily upon a sense of "ethno-genesis," which can be, but is not necessarily, biological; instead, it indicates an idealized set of national and political myths, a "noble lie," that perpetuates faith in a shared (genetic, ethnic, historical) lineage, the coming-to-be, and the perpetuation of the *demos*.

10 Although the 2012 presidential general election campaign in the U.S. has come and gone, we should not forget the Republican primaries, and the candidates' slogans, speeches, and affiliated Super PACs which reflect this point all too clearly. Mitt Romney wanted to "Keep America American" and his Super Pac promised to "Restore Our Future." Rick Santorum was "Fighting to Make America *America* Again," Ron Paul wanted to "Restore America Now," Michelle Bachmann was "Restoring Constitutional Conservative Values." Presumably, whatever America once was has been lost or sullied and is in need of restoration.

11 For example, as Hannah Arendt is right to note, the American Founding Fathers were critical of the idea of public opinion or "the potential unanimity of all" (Arendt 1963, 93). She argues that, "the word 'people' retained for them [the Founding Fathers] the meaning of manyness, of the endless variety of a multitude whose majesty resided in its very plurality" (1963, 93). For our purposes, it is worth remembering that this American idea of productive faction on guard against the tyranny of the majority and unanimity was not necessarily an embrace of diversity for its own sake but an acknowledgement that unanimity must be resisted so long as "the reason of man continues fallible, and he is at liberty to exercise it" (Madison, quoted in Arendt 1963, 94). Moreover, unanimity of public opinion is not the same thing as the unity that results from the shared sense of belonging and identity of a people. In fact, in the U.S. and other countries, the shared sense of unity and belonging is grounded (among other reasons) upon this commitment to open debate and diversity of opinion.

12 Although conservative communitarianism pays homage to family and civil society as a source of political identity, its (and, in many ways, modern liberalism's as well) identity is frequently understood as national identity (e.g., French, British, American) and always, of course, democratic. Only when allegiance is sworn to the nation-state and national identity as well as democracy, should features such as race, class, gender, and sexuality become relevant. These features of identity cannot be primary because they immediately introduce competing experiences, histories, beliefs, and realities that highlight differences over homogeneity, differences that divide rather than unify the *demos*. This does not mean that modern liberalism necessarily embraces identity politics either. There is a sophisticated and ongoing debate among feminists (across the political spectrum but most frequently on the Left) regarding the theoretical (essentialism vs. social-historical vs. discursive constructions of self and identity) and political justifications for promoting or rejecting identity politics. See Mary Daly, bell hooks, Gloria Anzaldúa, Linda Alcoff, Iris Young, Gayatri Spivak, Judith Butler et al. Nevertheless, most conservative critiques of identity politics are less interested in these difficult questions than the insistence that categories of identity that differ from the hegemonic norm are secondary to national identity (which, ironically, is the only acceptable form of identity politics).

13 This respect for the equality of each as an individual, or the equality of each *qua* human being, is an admirable principle, but nevertheless fraught with difficulties insofar as it attempts to conceive of the individuality of each with no reference to those differences of identity that actually mark the individual as individual. A universal equality of all humans leaves unchecked the hegemonic control certain majorities or influential minorities have in states. For example, for more than a century in the U.S., slavery was legal and women were restricted to the private sphere, despite the universal declaration that "all men are created equal." By contrast, in Sierra Leone, the Lebanese ethnic minority has controlled nearly all the economic resources in the country for over a century, although this has begun to change over the past twenty years (Chua 2003: 115–120). The point being that ethnicity cannot always be relegated to a secondary characteristic in favor of a universal conception of the human *qua* individual.

14 Later in *The Politics*, Aristotle insists that the continuity of the identity of a *polis* is not constituted by its "walls" (Aristotle 1981: 1276a24) or the "dimensions of a people [*ethnos*]" (1981, 1276a34) which may change over time or from generation to generation; instead, the continuity of the identity of the state is based upon the constitution, which is nothing more than the form of "association of citizens" (1981, 1276a34). Rather than an *ethnos* circumscribed by walls, the identity of association depends upon what sort of constitution is in place. The identity of a *polis* changes when the constitution changes. This does not mean that *ethnos*

played no role in determining political identity for the Ancient Greeks. However, it does suggest that the continuity of identity of a people and public belonging had as much to do with which constitution was in place as one's ethnicity.

15 Aristotle's identification of language as distinctive of humans has its foundation in his dual methodological approaches of empirical observation and natural hierarchical orderings wherein the most self-sufficient are more valued than the less self-sufficient (Aristotle 1981, 1252b27) and that the whole outranks those parts that compose it (1981, 1253a18). For Aristotle, it is empirically true that language is a unique capacity of humans. This observation is relevant because language allows humans to communicate about the good and the good life. In this way, language is part of a natural hierarchical structuring which not only places humans above plants and animals but also naturally places the husband over wife, master over slave, *polis* over *oikos*, the good life over mere life, Greek over non-Greek (1981, 1252b2), etc.

16 For Aristotle, the distinction between *ethnos* and *demos* is both rigorously delimited and ambiguous. His defense of slavery in Book I of *The Politics* (Aristotle 1981, 1235b1–1256a1) argues for the justness of slavery (admittedly with a certain hesitancy) even when the slave is Greek, is born and lives in Athens, and speaks Greek. Some Greeks, he insists, are and should be slaves and, therefore, excluded from the *demos*. Accordingly, for Aristotle, membership in the *demos* is not and should not be based on *ethnos* alone. Nevertheless, as Michael Walzer points out, Aristotle also believed that the immigrant laborers or *metics* in Athens were not entitled to citizenship (Aristotle 1981, 1278a). Just as slavery exists and was necessary for the functioning of the city, so too was the labor of *metics*. Free and equal citizens tasked with taking turns ruling over each other had limited or no time to attend to the material necessities of life. While slavery was a contentious issue in Ancient Athens, "the ideology that distinguished metics from citizens seems to have been widely accepted by metics and citizens alike. The dominance of birth and blood over political membership was part of the common understanding of the age" (Walzer 1983, 55). Although Aristotle may not have believed that the flourishing and excellence of citizens was hereditary (Walzer 1983, 54) or reserved to a particular *ethnos*, his position on the *metoikia* suggests that the distinction between *ethnos* and membership within the *demos* was, indeed, fixed.

17 This does not mean that there were not others forms of exclusion (gaining citizenship in Athens was notoriously difficult for foreigners and immigrants) or that those who spoke the language were thereby admitted into the *polis*. Nevertheless, the etymology of the term "barbarian" meaning strange, ignorant, uncivilized, savage, wild, beyond the pale, etc. is revealing. Barbarian comes from the Greek *barbarous*, itself derived from the base "*barbar*" which was the Greek

term for the speech of others they could not understand. In other words, the Greeks specifically distinguished between the foreigner (*xenos*) and the barbarian according to the sound and intelligibility of the language.

18 While nationality can and frequently is used to unjustly exclude, it also has the potential to be beneficial insofar as it can bring together individuals and groups to resist oppression or differentiate the experiences and actions of one group versus a different group. Nationalism is often necessary, it seems, to determine past violence and propose future alliances along ethno-national lines. For example, differentiating between Afrikaners, British colonialists and settlers, and the various African populations in South Africa was required for ending Apartheid and establishing the truth and reconciliation commissions.

19 *Ethnos qua* nationality is certainly *real* insofar as it is structured upon material, social, and historical contingencies such as language, memory, religion, culture, custom, and even to whom and where one is born. There are indisputably distinct nationalities, i.e., Mexican, French, German, Chinese, etc. Nevertheless, the fact that *ethnos* marks a *contingent* set of unifying relations is often discarded for the imagined fiction that certain characteristics that exemplify the dominant *ethnos* are immutable, biologically determined, and teleologically destined to rule over other peoples, ethnicities, and nations. Nevertheless, alongside the risk of being manipulated as a guiding force in a politics of fear and prejudiced discrimination, it is precisely because *ethnos* is not a fixed, static, and genetic set of relations that it is also something capable of being re-imaged along new social, historical, and material lines.

20 Balibar recognizes that all forms of association, and especially political association, involve exclusions that produce certain others who are not or cannot be included in the association. Moreover, he recognizes that *ethnos* as an imagined community is required for a shared sense of identity. This is why, in his consideration of a unified Europe, he acknowledges the difficulty or even "impossibility" (Balibar 2004, 9) of the challenge, but nevertheless calls for "inventing a new image of a people" (2004, 9), a European people; however, his point is that when political exclusions result from the construction of borders through subconscious, unintentional, or willful collapsing of the distinctions between a people *qua ethnos* and a people *qua demos*, the legitimacy of those exclusions must be questioned because an untenable dichotomy between citizen and human is made manifest. In this way, all humans have a right to citizenship somewhere, but "here" foreigners can be excluded from the *demos* precisely because they are citizens who have rights elsewhere under another sovereign nation-state. (See Balibar's "Citizenship Without Community," in *We, the People of Europe?*, 2004, especially pp. 58–61.) This exclusionary dichotomy is institutionalized in the Universal Declaration of Human Rights Article XIII where the right to emigrate is protected, but there is no concomitant demand that sovereign nation-states accept émigrés.

21 Certain countries will undertake this process of determining membership in the *demos* in different ways. The two primary mechanisms are *ius soli* and *ius sanguinis*. *Ius soli* grants citizenship and nationality to those who are born within the country's sovereign physical territories. By contrast, *ius sanguinis* does not determine citizenship or nationality by place of birth but by the right of blood, whereby at least one parent must be a citizen of the nation. As Joseph Carens notes, *ius sanguinis* does not necessarily reflect "an understanding of the state as an ethnic community in which citizens are connected to one another by blood, at least in the public imagination" (Carens 2013, 32). In the wake of the French Revolution, for example, France actually adopted *ius sanguinis* as its model in the belief that it served republic citizenship better than *ius soli*, which had traditionally united the anti-republican relation of sovereign and subject. The rest of Continental Europe followed suit with this rule for citizenship. However, "France itself supplemented its *ius sanguinis* rule with a (qualified) *ius soli* rule in the late nineteenth century" (2013, 32). Few other Continental countries, however, followed this lead. (It is worth noting that Germany has recently supplemented its strict *ius sanguinis* rule with a qualified *ius soli* rule precisely in response to the prejudice, discrimination, and disenfranchisement faced by the descendants of immigrants.) While I take Carens' point seriously that *ius sanguinis* is not reducible to an ethnic political identity or *demos*, I would simply emphasize the potential for exploitation of this rule for citizenship, particularly in countries with a history of ethnic-based exclusions. For example, France has just passed a set of new restrictive citizenship requirements in the face of increased Arab immigration and Islamic cultural influence. See http://www.latimes.com/news/nationworld/world/la-fg-france-values-20120103,0,4921057.story (accessed February 9, 2013). These new restrictions include difficult new language tests and oaths of allegiance to French values and France itself. Here, language and its relation to a given group, tribe, and bloodline re-emerges not in the name of republican citizenship but rather as a thinly disguised effort to preserve the *ethnos* through forced assimilation.

22 Some might claim that it is conservative communitarianism that exclusively ties *ethnos* to *demos* or that modern liberalism's commitment to progressive inclusion and expansion of the *demos* undermines this reliance upon *ethnos* to determine the *demos*. However, while the progressive, cosmopolitan left may very well desire a more expansive and inclusive conception of the *ethnos*, the idea a post-national common bond of political identity is still a long way off.

23 Caution is required when using the term sovereignty in these distinct ways. For example, Derrida reminds us that there is not only one form of sovereignty. He writes: "There are different and sometimes antagonistic forms of sovereignty, and it is always in the name of one that one attacks the other" (Derrida 2009, 76). Thus,

in the name of the sovereignty of each person, the universal human rights of each and every person, nation-state sovereignty is attacked. At the same time, the sovereignty of individuals often relies upon nation-state sovereignty as a mode of resistance to the hegemony of more powerful states. Similarly, Judith Butler recognizes that psychologizing a people or state to explain sources of state and non-state uses of violence and perpetuation of injustice is a tenuous move. However, she does insist that when we are speaking about a "subject" and not an individual member of this or that *demos*, then we are speaking about a "model for agency and intelligibility, one that is very often based on sovereign power" (Butler 2006, 45). In this respect, the relationship between subject formation, the citizen, and the state rests on some shared conceptions of sovereignty such as its inviolability and indivisibility. Accordingly, a critique of nation-state sovereignty along the lines of subject formation is helpful not as cheap psychologizing but insofar as it points to "an insurrection at the level of ontology, a critical opening up of the questions, What is real? Whose lives are real? How might reality be remade?" (Butler 2006, 33).

24 In *The Laws*, Plato insists that the best size for a democracy should be precisely and mathematically determined. That size is 5,040 people (Plato 1966, 737e). For Aristotle, an exact number was not necessary, but he did insist upon the appropriateness of having a walled *polis* (Aristotle 1981, 1330b32–40), and that it be large enough so that it is "self-sufficient" and able to provide for the common good of its citizens, but "not so large that it cannot be easily surveyed" (1981, 1326b11–25). Like the ancients, Rousseau also considered the relationship between the size of the state, the extent of its territory, and the type of government instituted ([1762] 1968: 95) as well as the practical concerns of facilitating the assembly of the people in larger states ([1762] 1968: 137–142). However, Rousseau differs from the Ancients insofar as these physical considerations must be measured against the universalizability of democratic principles.

25 Scare quotes are placed around fraternity to make explicit that the consanguinity of fraternity implicitly suggests that despite the universal moral impulse, certain exclusions are necessary, including those who are not democrats, those who are assumed to not be democrats because their differences from "us" as democrats is so stark, those who lack the rational capacity for autonomy (namely women), etc. For his part, Derrida in *The Politics of Friendship* critiques the onto-theological roots of fraternity which excludes the feminine insofar as the community of fraternity appeals to a mystical descent from the father, thereby grounding sovereign legitimacy in the birth and bloodline of God-the-father who creates and gives mankind his being. Derrida is also critical of fraternity insofar as it is dependent upon a measurable equality guaranteed by one's nation and birth, a measuring and

counting that fails to recognize or live up to the unconditional demand that democratic equality is precisely that which is immeasurable and can never be counted (Derrida [1994] 1997, especially pp. 91–99). In *Rogues*, Derrida raises the same issue in his critique of Jean-Luc Nancy and the relationship between mastery and measure (Derrida [2003] 2005, 42–55) noting that fraternity, the brotherhood or political system of equals, requires a measuring that tends toward mastery which Nancy's formulation does not and cannot undo. For Derrida, war, danger, and democratic exclusion are guaranteed "where the fraternity of brothers *dictates the law*, where a *political dictatorship* of fraternocracy comes to be imposed" ([2003] 2005, 50, original emphasis). Peter Gratton notes that Derrida's worry is that Nancy's fraternalism "[is] a thinking of the *dēmos* that repeats a tradition that limits rights and freedoms to men of native birth, to the exclusion of women and immigrants from the rights of the familial circle" (Gratton 2012, 220).

26 At the same time, the emphasis on democratization and democratic nation-building by established democracies also provides the justification for unilateral over-reaching by powerful nations in the name of democracy. For example, Judith Butler points out that the "U.S. extends beyond all geographical limits to include the widest gamut of its 'interests'" (2006, 67).

Chapter 2 Hospitality or War? A Foreigner Approaches

1 The city walls effectively determined the full citizen from the foreigner insofar as Athenian citizenship rested upon a strict conception of *ius sanguinis* and double endogamy in which citizenship was only granted (except in rare cases) to individuals who were born to parents who were both citizens.

2 There is a distinction to be made between pairs of concepts like inside and outside or native and foreigner. These concepts are distinct. However, the fact that these oppositions can be contrasted and distinguished from each other grounds an ontological belief in the purity of each concept where, for example, the foreign is absolutely distinct from the sovereign. The supposed conceptual purity and distinctness of each concept as well as the hierarchical privileging on one pole of the opposition over the other (sovereign over foreign, for example) often functions to justify, as natural, the physical walls that divide up the world in an attempt to physically inscribe this supposed conceptual purity. Against this, I argue that while conceptual distinctions surely allow us to make sense of the world, these binary oppositions are mutually constituting and never instantiated in their purity.

3 For a recent example, think of George W. Bush's infamous statement to the world: "Either you are with us or you are with the terrorists." By eliminating any and all ambiguity between friend and enemy, Bush cleared the way for simplified political

decision-making with respect to war, torture, and unilateralism. See http://georgewbush-whitehouse.archives.gov/news/releases/2001/09/20010920-8.html (accessed February 9, 2014).

4 It is a bit of a running joke in Plato's works (*Symposium*, *Apology*, *Crito*, *Phaedrus*, etc.) that Socrates rarely left Athens. More than a passing reference to Socrates' idiosyncrasies, this unwillingness to leave Athens is also a testament to Socrates' and philosophy's enduring commitment to the city and the *logos* whose proper place is the city, although perhaps not fourth-century Athens (Sallis 1975, 107). Democratic Athens and its laws, as we learn in *Crito* (Plato 1961c, 52a–e), had always been "congenial" to Socrates. Nevertheless, Socrates was also a stranger to Athens. As we learn in the *Apology*, he insists he is a stranger with respect to the courts and its procedures (Plato 1961a, 17d–18a). Moreover, as Allan Bloom suggests, Socrates' philosophizing makes him (and philosophy as such) a stranger and a threat to Athens insofar as he was perceived as being critical of the "city's gods, who are the protectors of its laws" (Bloom 1968, 307). At best he is a bad citizen, at worst he is "no citizen at all" (1968, 307). Moreover, in *The Republic* he builds a city where philosophers challenge the authority of existing rulers (1968, 309). Finally, there is, of course, a deep irony in Socrates reluctance to ever leave the city, namely that it is the city and its men, the "men of Athens" (Plato 1961a, 17a) who are responsible for his death.

5 To examine only a few pages of *The Republic* is incomplete in many ways. However, my intent is not to suggest that Plato has been read in the wrong way for two millennia or that Plato is an overlooked hero for political equality and openness. Instead, I am merely pointing out that in Book I, Plato emphasizes the ambiguity and mixing of concepts, and this conceptual work can be useful for thinking through pressing political issues that foreignness presents for contemporary democracies.

6 The Spartans will destroy this walled road after their victory in the war against Athens (Tschemplik 2005, 8–9). Thus, the protection it is thought to provide and the power it is thought to depict are known by Plato to be ephemeral.

7 However "subversive" (Bloom 1968, 309) the ideas will be, there is not a complete and total rejection of all things Athenian. While many definitions of justice are unsatisfactory and critiqued by Socrates, "from each something is learned which is of the essence of political life and which is reflected in the final definition and the regime that embodies it" (1968, 315).

8 Socrates introduces yet another aspect of force, namely the force of persuasion through reason, a presumably non-violent force, or what Habermas has called, "the unforced force of the better argument" (2008, 157).

9 The symbolic, political, and philosophical significance of this staging by Plato should not be ignored. The renewal of the conceptual resources necessary for

addressing democratic injustices appear to depend upon rethinking the distinctness and purity of the concepts that bind together political space. Plato's staging suggests that novel and more robust formulations of justice require a certain level of displacement, unsettling, and discomfort that accompany any movement away from the safety and security of familiar norms, practices, and customary use of conceptual categories.

10 In a similar recognition by Plato of the importance of tradition and religion with respect to justice, the *Euthyphro* and *The Apology* are important. In *Euthyphro*, Socrates is about to enter the courthouse to learn about his indictment which will lead to his death. Before entering, he encounters the priest, Euthyphro, and an aporetic discussion on piousness ensues. Socrates challenges the respected priest's and the common understanding of piousness, a point not unrelated to Socrates ultimately being convicted for impiousness that is deadly to the city. In *The Apology*, Socrates not only argues that the accusations of impiousness against him are based on doctrines that are not his own (such as Anaxagoras' natural philosophy), but also that his "impiousness" was decreed by the gods themselves insofar as his dangerous philosophical inquiries were begun in response to the renowned, if enigmatic, teachings of the Oracle at Delphi, who claimed that Socrates was the wisest man in Athens.

11 It is worth suggesting why Socrates takes up this point. Socrates has a vested interest in the relationship between seeming and being. He is seen as an enemy, and he is regularly depicted by Plato as a stranger in Athens, critical of its leaders, laws, politics, gods, understanding and practice of justice, etc. In fact, Socrates' philosophical, deontic conception of justice—which counters the popular understanding that the unjust person or the person who appears to be just but is actually unjust is happy—rests on the premise that justice is good in and of itself independent of the benefit to the just person (Plato 1968, 357d). In short, Socrates insists that it is better to be just than to appear to be just, even if one suffers as a result, as Socrates no doubt did when he was executed. The question of seeming and being, therefore, is not merely an epistemological or metaphysical one, but also, importantly, a political one that guides the remaining books of *The Republic*. Moreover, Socrates himself is a visitor to this new community. He has descended to the Piraeus; he is journeying away from his home to this new place. Thus, his status as friend or enemy in Athens as well as this newly formed community is paramount to understanding his conception of justice as well as the relationship between philosophy, politics, and the state, which will be the focus of what occurs after Book I.

12 There is no doubt that Plato is critical of Athenian democracy. His critiques of democracy in Book VIII are extensive and powerful. Nevertheless, Plato also seems to imply that philosophical discourse as such possesses certain democratic

qualities. Plato's ideal city might not be democratic, but at the highest echelons, there is a democratic equality of sorts among aristocratic philosopher kings. Rousseau suggests something similar: "If there were a nation of Gods, it would govern itself democratically. A government so perfect is not suited for men" ([1762] 1968, 114).

13 In his claim that justice is to benefit friends and harm enemies, Polemarchus uses the term personal enemies [*ekthroi*], as opposed to enemy of the state [*polemios*]. However, insofar as Polemarchus' definition of justice emphasizes loyalty according to the insider/outsider distinction, there is some conceptual blurring between the two distinct words even though only *ekthroi* is used. In one sense, Polemarchus is concerned with internal affairs and benefiting friends and harming personal enemies. At the same time, he is also assuming a friendship among insiders that rests upon an enmity with respect to foreigners and outsiders. Socrates' insistence upon differentiating between seeming to be a friend and really being a friend points out that justice is not guaranteed by proximity and consanguinity, thereby suggesting an easy slippage between private and public enemy. Thrasymachus with his aggression and demand for ransom is surely depicted in some sense as the *polemios*. However, as I will now try to show, Plato seems to depict Thrasymachus as both *polemios* and *xenos*, or a guest deserving of hospitality despite (or perhaps even on account of) his hostility.

14 Bloom argues that "Thrasymachus' definition of justice is really the same as the city and he acts as its representative" (Bloom 1968, 326). He supports Athenian laws and practices as the final determination of what is just, including those that lead to Socrates' death. Accordingly, Socrates' execution is just; it is merely an expression of the strength possessed by the *polis* as a whole over and against Socrates' philosophical mission. If Bloom is correct, then Plato's irony is once again emphasized, as the only worthy defense of Athenian democracy is made by a foreigner whose form of engagement is anti-democratic force. Athens—and Thrasymachus—are only just insofar as they are the stronger. If their strength is compromised, their justness is as well. Both, of course, will shortly be defeated.

15 Indeed, Athens was hospitable to foreigners (as expressed by the very meaning of the terms *xenos* and *xenia*), yet this hospitality is of a different order from Socrates' welcoming of Thrasymachus insofar as Thrasymachus is not simply a *xenos*, but also, simultaneously, a *polemios* who would destroy the regime.

16 In Book VIII, Plato argues that democracy undermines an important hierarchy that ranks citizens fist, *metic*s second, and foreigners at the bottom (Plato 1968, 562e). Moreover, the very fact that Cephalus leaves the conversation and

Polemarchus and Thrasymachus are mainly silent after Book I while two Athenian citizens take over the construction of the new city with Socrates makes it fairly clear that Plato is not endeavoring to completely undermine this hierarchical ordering between citizen, *metic*, and foreigner. However, I maintain that Plato's treatment of foreignness in Book I suggests a significantly more complicated conception of political belonging and justice than the simple hierarchy of citizen-*metic*-foreigner entails.

Chapter 3 The Fearful Origins of Sovereignty in the Social Contract Tradition

1 This is not to say that the philosopher-kings are non-violent. Indeed, from infanticide to war to the noble lie, the philosopher-king is both capable of and requires violence. Yet, even this necessity for violence is the product of the dialogic, rational ordering of the regime, which—idealized as it is—is meant to address the empirical fact that not everyone can become a philosopher-king.

2 A revealing analysis of the use of animals as an ethico-political pedagogical tool is developed by Eduardo Mendieta, whose work on political bestiaries examines the distinction within philosophical thought between bestial lawlessness and the well-ordered, lawful regime of humans. His original reading of Homer's famous depiction of Odysseus' request for hospitality and provisions from the Cyclops states: "The Cyclops is your quintessential beast. They are living creatures, and thus, they are a sort of animal. They are above the human and below the gods, although they think themselves more powerful than the gods. They have no religion; no law—no ordinances—and, most importantly, they do not cultivate the land or create political and social alliances. They are lawless and pre-political, even anti-political. They are beastly precisely because they are lawless. They have no law and they are outside the law, and refuse to acknowledge any law" (Mendieta 2010, 3). Odysseus, it is true, is civilized, lawful, a man who fears the gods and lives in social and political relations with others, but in order to survive before or against a lawless violence that has no fear of the gods, "[H]umans themselves have to become lawless. Odysseus has to become no-one, no man, that is, he has to abandon his fear of the gods, the interdictions against killing, by stepping outside the civilized order. To vanquish the Cyclops, Odysseus has to become like the Cyclops" (2010, 4). Moving to Plato's political bestiary, Mendieta argues that for Plato, "The wolf is the metonym for deception, deceit, fierceness, enmity, lawlessness and predatory violence. More specifically still, the wolf is to the sophist as the dog is to the philosopher, and as the tyrant is to the philosopher king. And even if the wolf may become a tyrant, the dog will never become a sovereign. The dog, in the guise of the philosopher, is merely the guardian of the state, qua

philosopher. Once the dog seeks to be more than that, it threatens to become a wolf. The philosopher is a faithful guardian of the state. The philosopher serves the sovereign by discerning between the enemies and friends of the state, something that the sophist could not and would not do" (2010, 6). I think this comparison is revealing and largely accurate, although in Chapter 7, I will argue that the philosopher is a sovereign of sorts, the seemingly contradictory and impossible foreign-sovereign.

3 The central importance of obedience to the law is clearly evidenced by Plato's notions of the noble lie and the program of eugenics, both of which are meant to guarantee that the members of the new regime have no standing or need to challenge the social and legal organization of the regime. More explicitly, in *Crito*, Socrates converses with, and refuses to break, the laws of the city in the face of his unjust execution (Plato 1961b, 50a–54e). In this respect, Plato develops a proto-contractualism in which obedience to the law is paramount to avoid the arbitrariness, dangerousness, and essentially fearful environment of lawless self-interest.

4 For evidence of this fact, it is worth noting that Hobbes took up residence outside of England on multiple occasions to avoid political persecution. This is unsurprising given that his philosophical writings "spanned the reign of Charles I, the Civil Wars, the Commonwealth and Protectorate, and the Stuart Restoration" (Macpherson [1968] 1985, 13).

5 I retain the term "man" here intentionally not only to remain true to the use of the term in Hobbes' text but also to emphasize that the theorizations of sovereignty, the nature of contracts, political rights, etc.—for Hobbes as much as for Locke and Rousseau—are for and about males. For all three theorists, the use of the terms "man," "men," and "mankind" does not refer to the universal category of all humans, which would include women and children.

6 In this regard, the complete title to Hobbes' classic political work is revealing: *Leviathan or The Matter, Forme, and Power of a Commonwealth Ecclesiasticall and Civil*.

7 Hobbes' methodology was inspired by Euclid's geometry (which begins with a small set of self-evident originary principles), materialism (the theory that all objects and phenomena, including human thought, in the external world can be explained by the movements and interactions of matter), and a mechanistic conception of motion (whereby the movements and interactions of objects, including that which moves man's thoughts and compels him to form political society, are explained by physical laws).

8 Hobbes does not use the phrase "state of nature" in *Leviathan*. The term, however, is used by Hobbes nearly a decade earlier in *De Cive* ([1642] 1983).

9 In this way, Hobbes demonstrates his departure from Aristotle: On the one hand, Hobbes rejects Aristotle's theorization of natural slavery by insisting that men are

equal by nature. On the other hand, Hobbes rejects the Aristotelian idea of the naturally social and political man in favor of a conceptualization of man as naturally competitive, violent, and self-interested.

10 Rational man not only leaves behind the state of nature, but he also leaves behind the beasts that lack the reason and speech necessary to assent to the contracts that lead to the formation of political society. Because animals lack reason and speech, it is, therefore, impossible for man to "make covenants with bruit Beasts" (Hobbes [1651] 1985, 197). Similarly, the man who violates the terms of the social contract has given up his right to be protected by the state. He is, therefore, cast back into the state of nature where he can be justly and legitimately hunted and killed like "the beast" that he is. In the same vein, man cannot contract directly with God because his silence fails to indicate whether the terms of the contract and the transference of rights has been accepted ([1651] 1985, 197). Moreover, the sovereign whose qualities are imitative of the divine also need not answer to men. Man makes covenants amongst himself leaving the sovereign unbound by any rules or contracts or norms. The sovereign, like God, is absolute. In this sense, Hobbes' absolute sovereign is above and outside the law. Paradoxically, the silence of Hobbes' absolute sovereign renders him indistinguishable not only from God but also the beast. In *The Beast and the Sovereign Vol. I*, Session 2 (especially pp. 56–57), Derrida (2009) makes much of this distinction insofar as the degrees of being between beasts and God are inadvertently erased in Hobbes' model, as is the strictly human or anthropological artificiality of political sovereignty. The onto-theology Hobbes sought to subvert reasserts itself in the very silence of the sovereign.

11 Just or rightful control over a given territory is a dominant conceptualization of political sovereignty. A representative example of this conceptualization is Carl Schmitt's etymological analysis of the Greek term *nomos*. He writes: "[O]ne should not translate *nomos* as law (in German *Gesetz*), regulation, norm, or any similar expression. *Nomos* comes from *nemein*—a [Greek] word that means both 'to divide' and 'to pasture.' Thus, *nomos*, is the immediate form in which the political and social order of a people becomes spatially visible—the initial measure and division of pasture-land i.e., the land-appropriations as well as the concrete order contained in it and following from it" (Schmitt [1950] 2003, 70). In Wendy Brown's reading, Schmitt's conceptualization of *nomos* expresses "the production of (political) order through spatial orientation" (2010, 45). *Nomos* directs us to the fact that walls serve as enclosures, and it is from this walling off "from the common that sovereignty is born" (2010, 45). On this reading, Locke's "fence of freedom" is a metaphorical substitute for the inviolable and impermeable border between free, equal, distinct, and sovereign individual men. Freedom is the source of the sovereignty of the self, a portion of which must be given up to establish the

sovereign commonwealth so that free men can live together protected against those within and outside of the walls.

12 In Chapter 4, this link between individual and political sovereignty is shown to be rather complicated. Locke is explicitly critical of Filmer (Locke 2003, *First Treatise* §21–43, 18–30), who argues that God's donation of the earth to Adam resulted in his and his male heir's sovereignty over all men. Against Filmer, Locke insists that God gave the gift of the earth and the inferior creatures not to Adam alone but to all of mankind in common. Thus, while property is essential to Locke's account of political power, he adamantly rejects the idea that God gave private dominion over the earth to Adam and his heirs. This point has deep implications for Locke's conception of political power as distinct from paternal power. At this juncture, I make a different argument regarding the rational implications of natural law as put forth by Locke in the *Second Treatise* whereby property (the individual man's body, life, liberty, and labor) is directly "inherited" or derived from God's creation of mankind in general and his giving of the earth in common to all men so that it might be appropriated through labor. In this respect, freedom secures the sovereignty of the self, one's property in his person, and is also that which must be protected by civil government whose ultimate end is the preservation of property.

13 The properties of the beast are not only noxious to what is proper to "mankind," but they are also qualities commonly assigned to the foreigner.

14 Awareness implies a rational capacity that men possess which animals do not; Rousseau, nevertheless, resists identifying reason as the primary distinction between man and beast. Instead of rational capacity, the distinction between men and beast is the awareness of the possibility of disobedience. The political effects of this endorsement of disobedience should be fairly obvious.

15 Ever attentive to the paradoxical features of progress, Rousseau acknowledges that technology and innovation make the life of civilized man easier and safer; yet, what civilized man gains in comfort and safety, he loses in self-sufficiency and the simplicity of living free from civilized man's dependence upon technological innovations.

16 Rousseau famously writes: "The first man who, after enclosing a piece of ground, took it into his head to say, 'This is mine,' and found people simple enough to believe him, was the true founder of civil society" ([1754] 2004, 27).

17 The implication here, of course, being that both the rabble and women do not have highly developed rational capacities.

18 With this point, Rousseau ([1754] 2004, 21) rejects a major theme within the philosophical tradition by claiming that reason cannot be the source of the virtues of kindness, generosity, mercy, friendship, etc. Instead, these virtues arise directly from pity being applied to or fixed upon an individual or the weak, the poor, etc.

19 It is worth noting here that up to this point, we have only considered Rousseau's genealogical description of property, *amour propre*, and fear as the conditions that led to the formation of political society. However, it is not until *The Social Contract* that Rousseau takes up the formation of a people, the event of the origin of political sovereign authority, and its characteristics. Hence, the famous opening "Man is born free, and he is everywhere in chains" ([1762] 1968, 49) presupposes the genealogical account developed in *Discourse on Inequality*.

Chapter 4 The Qualities of Sovereignty in the Social Contract Tradition

1 For example, France's appropriation of Rousseau's notion of the general will provided the justification for a radical democracy of the people necessary to overthrow the deeply entrenched and powerful models of property and politics enshrined by the monarchy. By contrast, the specific historical context of the United States as a settler state controlled from afar by a king through taxation made Locke's replaceable, neutral umpire whose function was precisely to protect individual rights (property) more useful and appealing to the drafters of the Constitution.

2 "Sovereign rights" is a strategic term for Hobbes. Despite the artificiality of the sovereign, it paradoxically comes to resemble something natural insofar as the artificial rights of the sovereign are derived from the natural rights of individual men.

3 While the sovereign possesses the right to punish men as he sees fit, Hobbes maintains that subjects have the liberty to resist the sovereign in order to "defend [his] own body" ([1651] 1985, 268). This right to resistance is retained from the natural right of liberty to pursue one's survival. Nevertheless, because men authorize all acts and judgments of the sovereign, the liberty of the subject does not mean that "the Soveraign Power of life, and death, is either abolished, or limited" ([1651] 1985, 264). Death at the hands of the sovereign in defense of one's body is an expression of one's natural liberty and is qualitatively different from violating the laws of nature by killing oneself or refusing to resist when one's body is endangered.

4 Locke, who rejects this conceptualization of the contract, argues that each individual subject contracts with the sovereign umpire or community as a whole. In this way, Locke envisages a fiduciary conception of the contract that allows men to "fire" the umpire if he fails to equally and fairly execute the promulgated law of civil society.

5 If it be thought that each man enters into a contract with the sovereign for his own protection, then the sovereign possesses no right to punish this subject for disobedience. By contrast, Hobbes insists that the sovereign does have this right to demand obedience and punish transgressors. Accordingly, this right is *authored* by

the individual who has agreed to contract *as a people* not as an individual. Thus, if there is a previous contract that the sovereign sees fit to breach, he does so solely upon the authority of the individual, thereby rendering the earlier contract void.

6 Through this analogy, Hobbes begins the "naturalization" of the artificiality of man's creation by intentionally blurring the lines between nature and artifice so that the artificial sovereign effectively resembles the immutability and eternalness of nature. As such, Hobbes gestures towards the futility of endeavoring to overthrow or challenge the sovereign who is as unyielding and absolute as nature.

7 Absolute power is a necessity not merely for monarchy and aristocracy but also democracy. For example, Hobbes cites the Roman senate and the people of Rome, neither of which "pretended to the whole Power" ([1651] 1985, 365), a failure which led to sedition and eventual collapse.

8 Schmitt was a strict Hobbesian, seeing *Leviathan* as a Catholic writing, a political theology, which Schmitt secularized; however, in *The Leviathan in the State Theory of Thomas Hobbes*, Schmitt claims that Hobbes insists upon the "importance of absorbing the right of private freedom of thought and belief into the political system. This contained the seed of death that destroyed the mighty leviathan from within and brought about the end of the mortal god" (Schmitt [1938] 2008, 57). Drawing on Spinoza's reversal of Hobbes' hierarchical ordering of sovereign right and the private freedom of thought, Schmitt argues that it is exactly at this moment when the sovereign must protect or be killed that an opening for modern liberalism (as opposed to absolutism) is established insofar as one can always claim that the sovereign fails in its duty to protect. One can always resist. Schmitt concludes: "Although Hobbes defended the natural unity of spiritual and secular power, he opened the door for a contrast to emerge because of religious reservation regarding private belief and thus paved the way for new, more dangerous kinds and forms of indirect powers" ([1938] 2008, 83).

9 Locke's disdain of absolutism and his overarching fear that sovereign power is too easily concentrated in the hands of private men and not the public is also a driving force for his division of powers. While Locke's commonwealth is structured upon the public right to make and execute the law toward the end of protecting and preserving property, this power is divided into three branches: the legislative, judicial, and executive. What is lacking in the state of nature is "an established, settled, known law" (Locke 2003, *Second Treatise* §124, 155). In civil society, the function of the legislative branch of sovereign power is to make the laws that bind all men. The state of nature also does not have "a known and indifferent judge" (2003, *Second Treatise* §125, 155) who can fairly decide the law when disputes arise. This is the function of the judicial branch of sovereign power. Finally, men in the state of nature often lack the "power to back and support the sentence when right" (2003, *Second Treatise* §126, 155). This executive function is the third branch of sovereign power.

10 In Chapter V of the *Second Treatise*, Locke explains that because Native Americans did not enclose their land or farm it in the same way as the English landowners, they failed to improve it for the betterment of all. Therefore, this land was not their property. Because Native Americans farmed differently than Englishmen, they effectively remained in the state of nature, and English settlers could appropriate their land without violating the laws of nature. Moreover, Locke's acceptance of the rule of husbands over wives, and his personal profiting from the race-based slave trade suggests that Locke's notion of the public is that it is largely homogeneous.

11 J.S. Mill in "The Subjection of Women" points out that it is common and longstanding practice that in marriage a woman can "acquire no property but for him [her husband]; the instant it becomes hers, even if by inheritance, it becomes *ipso facto* his [her husband's]" (1996, 145).

12 In "John Locke on Women and the Family," Ruth W. Grant does not argue that Locke should be read as a feminist thinker, but she does identify in Locke's liberalism a conceptualization of women aligned with its universal principles. As Grant notes, Locke rejects the ideas that Eve is subjected to Adam's rule because of her natural inequality (2003, 289–290), that marriage is a voluntary contract (2003, 291), and the dominance of husbands over the household is acceptable as a result of man's natural strength, but this does not imply, for Locke, "a general inequality of rights between men and women" (2003, 292). She writes, "Just as Locke clearly condemned cannibalism and infanticide, he would surely condemn practices such as killing women upon the death of their husbands. Some rights are inviolable; Locke would say inalienable—the right to life, the right to own what you earn, the right to be a party to a marriage contract, the right to choose your own religion, the right to remain free from subjection to the arbitrary will of another" (2003, 302). I agree that in many places, Locke's consideration of women represents a vast improvement from his contemporaries. Nevertheless, his depiction of women as equals with respect to the contractual and voluntary assent to marriage and rearing of children confines woman to the de-politicized, subjective, private sphere of the home. I am not suggesting that Locke actively seeks to perpetuate the inequality of women; instead, I argue that he draws upon the extant conceptualizations of women and men as well as the social order of his day in order to envisage the liberal subject. The result is that his supposedly generic and universal depiction of the human being possesses those traits associated with masculinity and rejects those associated with femininity.

13 In many respects, it is the desire for these lost, mythical origins of homogeneity, unity, unanimity, and peaceful wholeness that spur the dreams of progressive and conservative ideologies of the teleological fulfillment of the (re)establishment of the unity of the *demos*.

14 Maurice Cranston notes in the introduction to *The Social Contract* that, beyond rights, earlier theorists such as Locke also believed sovereignty is transferred from individuals to the commonwealth. Rousseau's theorization rejects this by arguing that "no such transfer of sovereignty need or should take place: sovereignty not only originates in the people; it ought to stay there" (Cranston 1968, 30).

15 As noted, natural and social inequalities may exist, but "men become equal by covenant and by right" (Rousseau [1762] 1968, 68).

16 Hobbes also confronts this paradox when he insists that a multitude is united into a people through a majority vote. In principle, there is nothing to stop a multitude from voting, but for a vote among a multitude to be legitimate already presupposes certain norms, procedures, laws, rights, and exclusions. This must be the case otherwise Hobbes could not claim that even those who vote against the contract authorize the contract. In this way, Hobbes' brief mention of a vote and the majority suggests a form of political sovereignty that precedes the formalization of the political as such. Rousseau picks up on this tension by re-enforcing the idea of an originary unanimity when he argues that "the law of majority-voting [whereby a people gives itself willingly to a sovereign] itself rests on a covenant, and implies that there has been on at least one occasion unanimity" ([1762] 1968, 59). For example, the U.S. Declaration of Independence begins with, "We the people . . .". In this case, "We" implies consent. But, consent among who? There is not yet, *a people* empowered to consent, to declare the "we." The paradox of sovereignty, then, is that sovereignty comes into being through the performative act of an already sovereign "we" declaring itself to be sovereign.

17 Rousseau is particularly dismissive of the idea that sovereignty can be divided, comparing theorists who would see it divided to "Japanese mountebanks [who] can cut up a child under the eyes of spectators, throw the different parts into the air, and then make the child come down, alive and all of a piece" ([1762] 1968, 71).

18 I leave out the highly influential theorizations of Schmitt's sovereign decisionism, which, with increasing frequency, is coming to dominate justifications for executive actions on the parts of states. In the U.S. alone, George W. Bush once famously declared himself "the decider" [http://www.cnn.com/2006/POLITICS/04/18/rumsfeld/ (accessed September 27, 2012)]. Nevertheless, sovereign decisionism is not a tool of Republicans alone. President Obama regularly cites executive authority to justify his decision to use unmanned drones to kill both foreigners and U.S. citizens abroad, chosen from Obama's "kill list," who are deemed by the president and his security officials to pose a threat to U.S. security [https://www.nytimes.com/2012/05/29/world/obamas-leadership-in-war-on-al-qaeda.html?pagewanted=all&_r=0 (accessed September 27, 2012)]. These

examples show just how deeply entrenched these historical conceptualizations of sovereignty remain in today's world.

Chapter 5 Foreignness, Sovereignty, and the Social Contract Tradition

1 There is interesting work to be done in providing a genealogical account of the psychosocial and political construction of the threat of foreignness. Plato himself suggests this project in Socrates' conversation with Polemarchus regarding who is a true or real friend. As noted, Allan Bloom's reading of this exchange points to the presumed naturalness of loyalty to family and city grounded in the making and taking as one's own the concrete relations exclusive of outsiders and foreigners. Nevertheless, this genealogical reconstruction is not my aim here. Instead, because of the continued influence of the social contract tradition upon the contemporary understanding of legitimate sovereignty and foreignness, I simply identify the ways in which these extant notions of foreignness are conceptualized as the conceptual antipode of and absolute threat to legitimate sovereignty.

2 Below I examine in what sense internal discord is itself conceived to be a foreign threat.

3 The presumed foreignness of President Obama by many of his critics is a case in point.

4 This observation should not surprise insofar as Hobbes, Locke, and Rousseau all rely upon economic terms such as contracts, property, estate, goods, etc. in their telling of the story of legitimate sovereignty.

5 One might argue that this conception of a bounded or limited economy is an antiquated notion. No doubt, today, economic activity is a trans-national enterprise. Nevertheless, the very fact that the actions of and allegiance to trans-national economic regimes are often at odds with or weaken local political sovereignty demonstrates the presupposition of limits to sovereign economies of currency and power.

6 Sovereign control of territory is often, though not always, coextensive with the borders of the sovereign state. However, by sovereign control of territory, I also include all lands controlled by a given sovereign state. Thus, colonies, protectorates, satellite states, etc. are included in the category of sovereign territory even if the subjects of these "external" lands are denied membership in the body politic.

7 The existence and growing popularity of terms such as "anchor babies" as well as attempts in some corners to change the U.S. model of *ius soli* to exclude children born to so-called "illegal aliens" suggests that while inclusion within the *demos* is founded upon the law, full inclusion is dependent upon the way in which foreignness is understood and deployed by the sovereign state.

8 Even a pluralistic country like the U.S., which grants legal citizenship according to *ius soli*, continues to rely upon the spatiality that gives rise to an *ethnos* to determine *full inclusion* within the *demos* of its citizens. Historically, *ius soli* was instituted after the end of slavery through the 14th amendment to grant citizenship to former slaves. Yet, for another hundred years, Jim Crow laws denied black citizens full inclusion within the *demos* through the segregation of public spaces.

9 The usage of "brothers" here is intentional. This term signals the patriarchal and masculine ordering of sovereignty. The notion of fraternity not only reflects the historical reality of women's exclusion from the public sphere, but also has its basis in the false conviction that women lacked the rational capacity to be full members of the people Also, see Mary O'Brien's, 1981, *The Politics of Reproduction* (especially pp. 67–76) for a feminist critique of the masculinist construction of political society based upon men's alienation from nature and the labor of reproduction. To counter this alienation, men endeavor to replace nature with the creation of the artificial state, a public sphere, which they rule while simultaneously relegating women to the private sphere of necessity and nature where their experiences of childbirth and motherhood are devalued when contrasted with the state.

10 This is why *assimilation* of immigrants is so frequently stressed even by tolerant, pluralistic sovereign states. Anything short of full assimilation leaves open the question of whether the foreignness of the foreigner (i.e. the threat of foreignness to the sovereign) has been expunged.

11 For example, in the U.S., a common justification for excluding Latino/a immigrants who enter the U.S. without documentation is the fact that they have violated the rule of law, an indispensable feature of democracy that unifies its people. Thus, these immigrants are not excluded because they are foreigners, but rather because they are criminals or lawbreakers whose actions threaten the common bonds that establish the stability and unity of the people.

12 Although the term has appeared previously, the various subtleties of "self-identicality" will be fleshed out in this and future chapters with explicit reference to foreignness. By way of an immediate definition, self-identicality is the essence of sovereign identity. Put differently, self-identicality identifies a conceptualization of sovereignty in which both individuals and the people as a whole are what they are only through the *exclusion of differences*. Conceptually, then, foreignness is conceived of and fabricated as that which is threatening and absolutely opposed to sovereignty.

13 This does not mean that the desire for self-preservation is not a central tenet of civilized man living under a sovereign. However, the means for achieving self-preservation change. Instead of natural strength and intelligence, they achieve self-preservation through obedience to the law of the sovereign.

14 This claim regarding the sovereignty of the self is only implicit in Locke. He argues that, "by this grant [God's gift of dominion over the lesser beasts of the earth] God gave him [Adam] not private dominion over inferior creatures, but right in common with all mankind" (Locke 2003, *First Treatise* §24, 20). For Locke, this donation or grant from God is a right in common to all mankind. Adam and his heirs, therefore, are not sovereign over all men. Nevertheless, the very fact that each man has property in his person and freedom is the fence which protects each man from the trespasses of others who would limit another's liberty or destroy another's property does suggest a formula for the sovereignty of the self shared by all of mankind. The gift from God to man over the inferior creatures is a "right in common with all mankind" only if each individual is sovereign over himself and, hence, equal with all other men.

15 Although foreignness is determined by one's physical status as an outsider to the unified political body, Locke recognizes the everyday experience of foreigners visiting or living as resident aliens in a commonwealth. Foreigners are tolerated assuming they follow the laws of the commonwealth during their stay. Yet, as foreigners, once they depart the commonwealth, they are no longer subject to its laws.

16 A contemporary instantiation of this position is the second U.S. war with Iraq, which was justified through appeal to the legitimacy of pre-emptive attacks on any sovereign state that the U.S. deems to be a threat.

17 The inclusion of toleration in this list appears prima facie wrong given Locke's explicit endorsement of its tenets in "A Letter Concerning Toleration." He argues (contra Hobbes) that civil society ought to tolerate private conscience even if it is at odds with the most widely practiced religion of a given state. Private conscience and religious belief concern the "inward and full persuasion of the mind" (Locke 2003, 219) toward the end of eternal salvation. The state is concerned only with "outward things" (Locke 2003, 218), namely the protection of the life, liberty, and estate of its subjects. The state is not responsible for the "care of souls" (Locke 2003, 218). Moreover, the state's power to force obedience through punishment has no place in matters of religious practice and private belief. Coerced belief is not faith and is, therefore, an obstacle to salvation (Locke 2003, 219); it is also an affront to the liberty of each man to care for his soul as he sees fit so long as his actions do not infringe upon the freedom and rights of other men. Therefore, civil society must tolerate distinct religious practices and private conscience. Toleration of religious beliefs, therefore, requires the separation of church and state. Locke insists: "It is not the diversity of opinions, which cannot be avoided; but instead the refusal of toleration to those that are of different opinions, which might have been granted, that has produced all the bustles and wars" (Locke 2003, 249). Locke's famous call for toleration represents a prescient openness to different practices

and beliefs that will become the norm in contemporary liberal democracies. Be that as it may, Locke infamously withholds tolerance from certain religions (e.g., Roman Catholics and Muslims whose very faith and belief place their loyalty and obedience in a foreign power or prince) and atheists (Locke 2003, 245–246). More specifically, toleration for Locke is reserved for certain Christian denominations and, perhaps, Judaism, thereby recommending tolerance not for that which is foreign but rather that which is simply regarded as unfamiliar. I do not wish to underestimate the subtle differences between Christian denominations or the seriousness of thought dedicated to toleration by Locke. Instead, my claim here is that Locke acknowledges the practical fact that foreigners live among citizens and that a basic tolerance by both parties will facilitate the protection of private property and liberty. Nevertheless, Locke's conceptualization of sovereignty as such affords no place for and extends no tolerance to foreignness conceived of as irrationality, particularism, and bestial/uncivilized men in want of a public and universal law. The reason seems clear: tolerance, within limits, can strengthen (or at least not threaten) a liberal civil society, but the sovereign cannot tolerate that foreignness which would threaten the self-identicality and inviolability upon which sovereignty is premised. A foreign-sovereign is no sovereign at all. To tolerate foreignness is to welcome the illegitimacy, particularism, and privation of irrationality, i.e., to crown as legitimate a bestial, intolerant absolute sovereign that preys upon—rather than protects—its subjects. Paradoxically, on the conceptual level of sovereignty, foreignness must not be tolerated so that the sovereign might extend tolerance to the foreigner. Whether and to what extent tolerance is extended to the foreigner is a practical matter of history, geography, national sentiment, public policy, etc.

18 For Rousseau's position on women's rationality, equality, and agency, I refer to his analysis of Sophie in Book V of *Émile*. While he recognizes certain similarities, sexual difference is the source of a fundamental lack of similarity between men and women. As he writes, what men perceive to be women's faults are "faults in you [man], but they are virtues in them" (Rousseau 2003, 262). He continues, "Woman is worth more as a woman, but less as a man; wherever she improves her rights she has the advantage, and whenever she attempts to usurp ours [men's] she remains inferior to us [men]" (2003, 262). With respect to sexual difference, Derrida's conception of ipseity is useful. Ipseity points out that there is a gathering of the same, of those who share a semblance, are assembled into an inviolable whole, etc. Insofar as women are dissimilar and do not share a semblance with men in many respects, they are not a part of the self-identical assembly or whole of political sovereignty; indeed, for Rousseau, women represent a passive force whose proper place is the private sphere and whose proper role is one of submission and subservience to men.

19 In this respect, the psychological impulse behind the European fetishization, sexualization, and exoticization of the non-European foreigner would seem to have some basis in the impossible to fulfill desire to become one, once again, with his natural state.

20 Here, Rousseau is attempting a critique of reason, but he does so by implicitly assuming that reason attaches exclusively to men of a certain class and not to the women of the marketplace or the rabble.

21 Rousseau articulates this problem of legitimate authority in another way when he considers whether the general will can err. Because the general will can never err, since it is always directed toward the common good, the problem of legitimate authority in a democracy is ostensibly solved by giving power to the people, yet Rousseau immediately recognizes that the people are often "misled" (Rousseau [1762] 1968, 72), leading to the partial wills of individuals or the majority unjustly taking the place of or undermining the general will. Thus, to avoid partiality, divisions, illegitimate authority, and the potential for a tyranny of popular sovereignty, Rousseau posits the figure of the lawgiver as a solution to this problem unique to democracy.

22 The fact that Rousseau insists upon this originary unanimity of a people stands in contrast to his positing of the non-self-identicality of man in the earliest stages of the state of nature. Even if individual self-identicality is always already lost, the originary self-identicality of political sovereignty suggests that the exclusion of foreignness is central to his theorization of legitimate political authority.

23 As Bonnie Honig notes, "Democracy is always about living with strangers under a law that is therefore alien (because it is the mongrel product of political action—often gone awry—taken with and among strangers). Even at its very best, or especially so, democracy is about being mobilized into action periodically with and on behalf of people who are surely opaque to us and often unknown to us" (2001, 39).

24 Of course, Rousseau's account of the state of nature is developed to explain the origins of inequality. His work on the social contract is distinct from that earlier work, but since his analysis of the social contract is deeply informed by this earlier work, it is appropriate to examine the claims made in *The Social Contract* through the lens of his account of the state of nature.

25 This is why the originary myth must be repeated and performed in our daily pledges of allegiance to "one nation."

Chapter 6 The Naturalization of Artificial Sovereignty and Foreignness

1 Ironically, the state of nature as conceived of by Hobbes, Locke, and Rousseau is also something posited; it is a story or fable each tells about "natural man" before

his entry into civil society. In this sense, nature is no more natural than the state fashioned by men.

2 Of course, both Locke and Rousseau preserve the people's right to revolution; however, in both instances, this right is an expression of popular sovereignty directed against inept or tyrannical leaders and not sovereignty or political power as such.

3 In the first case, only an artificial sovereign enshrined through the social contract can achieve legitimacy, since God's will is ultimately subject to instrumental, subjective interpretations. In the second case, Hobbes' science of man tells us that men are naturally violent and competitive; therefore, reason dictates that self-preservation can only be secured through a covenant or agreement to give up their natural right to everything in the state of nature by creating a common power to enforce the terms of their covenant.

4 While individual men can never give up the right to self-preservation, the sovereign, nevertheless, has the right over the life and death of its subjects. The sovereign right, therefore, is a right to everything, including men's bodies.

5 Locke critically notes that Filmer fails to convincingly explain how and why the mother has no authority over her children since he fails to consider seriously the entirety of the 5th Commandment to "Honor thy father and mother" (2003, *First Treatise* §61–63, 40–42). He concludes that since procreation requires a joining together of man and woman, both fathers and mothers have a "common right [over their children] belonging equally to them both, that neither can be excluded" (2003, *First Treatise* §61, 41).

6 Interestingly, Locke challenges the legitimacy of the father's rule over his wife, children, and the household as a whole. He suggests that, by nature, men possess greater strength than their wives, and that this fact of nature underpins the customary laws and practices of many nations wherein the husband and father is the absolute power and legitimate ruler of the household; nevertheless, Locke insists that God "gives not, that I see, any authority to Adam over Eve, or to men over their wives, but only foretels what should be the woman's lot" (2003, *First Treatise* §47, 33). In other words, the story of Adam and Eve is not a divine decree or normative claim that men have absolute, royal authority over their wives, children, and households, but simply an explication of the state of women in society and prevalent customs which see men in charge of the household.

7 For example, Rousseau's foreign lawgiver, as discussed, is required to solve the conceptual problem of democracy regarding who, among equals, has the authority and legitimacy to establish the sovereign state.

8 Rousseau suggests that democratic government might not be possible. He writes: "In the strict sense of the term there has never been a true democracy, and there never will be" ([1762] 1968, 112). That said, Rousseau insists—like Plato and

Aristotle before him—that if a democratic government is to exist at all, it must be small in size. In this way, Rousseau emphasizes a political geography or a politics of space, which quite literally naturalizes sovereignty by "grounding" the state in the earth and spatial distribution of land and people within it. As discussed above, a more modern formulation of the politics of space is Carl Schmitt's *Nomos of the Earth* ([1950] 2003), wherein he links the political order as such to the physical space and division of the land.

9 The idea of a "proto-general will" is not far removed from the "proto-unity" in Hobbes outlined above. Both thinkers want to hang the formation of a sovereign people on the assent to the social contract, yet in both, this transformative moment implies that there is already a pseudo-sovereign, pre-political people who share a commitment to, at a minimum, the legitimacy of majority voting. That said, Rousseau's sovereign general will is distinct from Hobbes' sovereign absolutism, and it is, therefore, necessary to differentiate between the "proto-unity" in Hobbes, which accounts for the "real unity" forged from the multitude through the social contract, and Rousseau's "proto-general will," which provides the basis for a self-identical, homogeneous people aware of the divisiveness and dangers of *amour propre* but who have not yet formalized the general will and its institutions through the social contract.

10 This quote might appear to undermine my position. If majority voting rests on a covenant, then even this deliberative procedure is artificial. First, if there is an artificial covenant that enshrines majority voting, then there is another covenant, the social contract, which establishes the sovereign general will. Yet, the problem with this formulation is that it introduces an infinite regress because there must be a covenant which enshrines the covenant of majority voting, which then establishes the social contract and so on. Thus, Rousseau counters this regress of artificiality by insisting that this covenant established, on at least one occasion, unanimity, and as I have argued, there is good reason to understand this originary unanimity as grounded in nature and not simply the supernatural or mythical.

11 In Chapter 7, I raise concerns regarding the democratic basis of Rousseau's "proto-general will" and originary unanimity that authorizes majority voting. Specifically, this unanimity points to the explicitly undemocratic, namely a single voice and a silencing of dissent anathema to democracy and even politics as such (even the tyrant or monarch must make his decrees known). Acknowledging this point, however, does not suggest that the naturalization of sovereignty does not occur. As I argue below, the silence and secretiveness of the sovereign is the animating force of the law.

12 This claim helps to further explain why, for example, international relations in Locke's work are organized according to the precepts of the state of nature. That which is different, apart from, outside the sovereign is foreign and, therefore,

relations between foreign states are governed not by artificial law but the law of nature.

13 An illustrative example of the perpetual threat of "natural" foreignness is the so-called "War on Terror" being waged by the U.S. This war appears to be interminable because it rarely targets states that, once defeated, would signal the end of conflict. Indeed, the "War on Terror" has no obvious end because it is directed against non-state actors, including terror cells, social movements, non-governmental organizations, businesses, foreign individuals, and U.S. citizens. In this sense, the "War on Terror" is an ideological war against foreignness as such, i.e., a war against men and women—independent of their artificial political membership—who are deemed by the U.S. to be engaged in, sympathetic to, and/or material supporters of beliefs and practices opposed to the fundamental tenets of secularized democracy.

14 The U.S. military presence across the globe from the Korean peninsula to Latin America to the Middle East reflects a permanent war footing, a constant vigilance and state of emergency, against real or imagined threats to its sovereign "interests."

15 Against this point, one might argue that I omit the one distinctive feature of sovereignty, namely the law. However, whether viewed in light of Hobbes' absolutism, Rousseau's general will, or even Carl Schmitt's claim that the sovereign is he who decides on the exception, the sovereign, as it is traditionally conceived, is precisely that figure which, in the name of total security, is either above or beyond the law. Thus, even in the U.S. where citizens are regularly reminded that no one is above the law, the occasional and rare public outcry that leads to the imprisonment or deposing of powerful leaders in no way touches upon the sovereign right and power to act outside of the law. Either the law, *ex post facto*, is brought into agreement with formerly illegal actions of the sovereign (e.g. the "Torture Memos") or, more commonly, executive privilege is invoked to eliminate the very possibility of legal review of sovereign actions (e.g. the use of unmanned predator drones to assassinate U.S. citizens without due process of the law). In short, the law may be distinctive of a sovereign people, but the sovereign itself, if only in cases of emergency, is empowered beyond the law. Yet, in a state of perpetual emergency, the sovereign is perpetually empowered to act outside of and beyond the law.

Chapter 7 The Foreign-Sovereign

1 In his analysis of the qualities associated with the general will, Peter Gratton notes Rousseau's theoretical reversal of the conceptualization of sovereignty moving from a political theology to popular sovereignty. For Rousseau, the "people will have all of the qualities associated with traditional monarchical sovereignty:

sacredness, indivisibility, inalienability, nonrepresentability, and even nonrepresentability in language" (Gratton 2012, 48). Most important for the current discussion is the sovereign quality of silence. In Gratton's analysis of the radical and revolutionary underpinning of popular sovereignty, he suggests that, for Rousseau, "sovereignty, at its moment of founding acts with such force that there is and can be no voice" (2012, 48).

2 For Rousseau, the law yesterday or even today does not bind a people tomorrow. Yet, as long as the people remain silent, tacit consent to the law, the state, and the government has been granted. As Peter Gratton suggests, "sovereignty supplements the laws as the active element that gives it force, even if the force is given only by the silence of the present sovereignty" (2012, 57).

3 It might appear that Locke's sovereign is neither silent nor unrepresentable. The neutral umpire who decides and executes the promulgated law appears to hold no secrets. The law and its adjudication are public, and those legislators, executives, and magistrates who fail to serve as neutral umpires of the promulgated laws are legitimately disobeyed. Nevertheless, the sovereign force of the law is not held by this or that representative making this or that decision. Rather, the force of the law is the silent moment of rational neutrality and decision as such.

4 In addition to torture, the "War on Terror" is rife with other sovereign violations of the law: from CIA blackspots to the indefinite detention of U.S. citizens without due process, to evoking state secrets as a justification for withholding evidence, to executive kill lists, to drone strikes in violation of the sovereign rights of other countries, to the NSA's data collection program for spying on U.S. citizens. Indeed, the constitutionality and legality of the U.S. surveillance of its citizens' private communications cannot even be challenged in court. The surveillance of U.S. citizens is shrouded in such secrecy that the state is under no obligation to reveal who has been surveilled; hence, no citizen can prove that she has been surveilled by the state. (Of course, the release of documents by Edward Snowden made public this secret spying regime.). Because she can prove no harm or violation of her rights, she lacks the legal standing to bring any charges against the state. The surveillance of U.S. citizens is absolutely outside of the law. See the Supreme Court's recent ruling in *Clapper v. Amnesty International USA* on the FISA wiretapping laws: https://www.nytimes.com/2013/02/27/us/politics/supreme-court-rejects-challenge-to-fisa-surveillance-law.html?_r=0 (accessed February 9, 2013).

5 By extension of its power to create the natural order, sovereign self-identicality is also conceived of as divine. Recall, for example, Hobbes' claim that the absolute sovereign is a "mortal God." Similarly, Rousseau famously claimed that the "social order is a sacred right" (Rousseau [1762] 1968, 50).

6 Derrida's "Force of Law" provides a useful guide for thinking through the relationship between the performative and voiced force of law and the mystical,

silent law of force. Derrida argues that a law—if it is to be instituted and authorized—must be enforced, and in this respect, "Law is always authorized force" ([1994] 2002, 233). Even if a law is deemed unjust, it is always, where and when it is applied as law, an authorized force. Force, therefore, is not external to law, something added in later; instead, it is "implied in the very concept of *justice as law* of justice as it becomes law" ([1994] 2002, 233, original emphasis). Just as Socrates in *The Republic* endeavored to establish a just city distinct from the religious, traditional, and legal foundations of Athenian justice, Montaigne also differentiates between the law and justice. Yet, he diverges from Socrates by claiming that there is a mystical foundation to the law because laws as such are not just. Their authority and their justness are banked, on credit, simply because they are laws. This is mystical because it is on faith that subjects under the law believe the laws to be authorized and, hence, just. Exploiting this longstanding distinction between law and justice, Derrida argues that the founding and establishment of the law is grounded in a "performative and therefore interpretive violence" ([1994] 2002, 241); however, this violence is itself neither just nor unjust. For Derrida, the law is a "violence without ground" ([1994] 2002, 242), and it is in this respect that he claims discourse in its performative power to make law is the mystical, a "silence walled up in the violent structure of the founding act" ([1994] 2002, 242), since there is no previously existing basis or foundation that can guarantee if the law is just or unjust. We cannot go back and say that the founding of (just) laws is based on this or that historical precedent. Justice is not inscribed on the fabric of existing history, since it is the very moment and decision of establishment and enforcement that shreds that fabric. Justice is an irruption, an event, and an incalculable moment. As such, there is no origin or foundation for law as justice.

7 The pageantry and performance of sovereignty never stray too far from the symbols which remind a people of its natural and divine origins, including appeals to God, self-evident truths, mythical stories of the founding, and invoking national heroes whose violence, disobedience, and dissent must be sterilized so as not to be repeated.

8 As John Jay writes: "Providence has been pleased to give this one connected country to one united people—a people descended from the same ancestors, speaking the same language, professing the same religion, attached to the same principles of government, very similar in their manners and customs, and who, by their joint counsels, arms, and efforts, fighting side by side throughout a long and bloody war, have nobly established general liberty and independence." He continues: "This country and this people seem to have been made for each other, and it appears as if it was the design of Providence, that an inheritance so proper and convenient for a band of brethren, united to each other by the strongest ties, should never be split into a number of unsocial, jealous, and alien sovereignties" (Hamilton et al. [1787] [1961] 1999, 32–33).

9 Examples of this important critique abound. From Carl Schmitt's analyses of the secularization of divine concepts that undergird modern political theology to Michel Foucault's genealogical tracing of the transformation of sovereign power to biopower in which the kingly right to "take life or let live" (Foucault [1976] 1997, 241) is replaced and reversed by the violent disciplining of a people by the nation-state whose power is to "make live and let die" ([1976] 1997, 241). In *The Beast and the Sovereign Vol. I*, Jacques Derrida argues that despite attempts to cover over its artificiality, sovereignty is always posited. Accordingly, the opposition between *physis* and *nomos* in the social contract tradition "is decisively functional" (2009, 42); therefore, "law, sovereignty, and the institution of the state are historical and always provisional, let's say deconstructible, essentially fragile or mortal, even if sovereignty is *posited as immortal*" (2009, 42, original emphasis). Peter Gratton argues that Rousseau's conceptualization of an originary unanimity of a people "is the necessary fiction—theological in provenance, perhaps, but not reducible to it—that takes hold of the logic of the *Social Contract*" (2012, 30).

10 History is rife with examples of holocaust and ethnic cleansing in the name of national unity and identity. By contrast, it might appear that pluralistic sovereign nation-states are living examples of a sovereignty not premised on self-identicality. Yet, as Bonnie Honig convincingly argues in "Difference, Dilemmas, and the Politics of Home", contemporary political theorists have endeavored to "domesticate" (1996, 258) difference through theories of pluralism and multiculturalism. They take identity to be the fixed starting point of groups and political affiliations, which then come into contact with or experience political dilemmas with different groups that are also conceived of as having a fixed identity. On this model of difference, pluralism and multiculturalism function as political solutions for the dilemmas which often arise from the collision of ideas, practices, languages, and cultures which differ from those of the dominant group within a political community. By recognizing the difference *between* distinct groups, pluralist approaches to political dilemmas allow the destabilizing and threatening features of difference to be affirmed and recognized, yet, nevertheless, be "reassuring as it does not threaten to be ungovernable" (1996, 258). By contrast, Honig argues that difference is better understood as that which "resists or exceeds the closure of identity" (1996, 258), since difference is not a description regarding identity but rather a constitutive feature within identity that identity unsuccessfully endeavors to eliminate or stabilize. In this respect, it is precisely the ungovernability of difference that must be taken seriously because it points to and "affirms the inescapability of conflict and the ineradicability of resistance to the political and moral projects of ordering subjects, institutions, and values" (1996, 258).

11 It is worth noting that with this quote Derrida is specifically concerned with Carl Schmitt's work, and the way in which this "indivisible instant" is the ground for the

"decisionist exceptionality" (Derrida [2003] 2005, 101) determinative of Schmitt's sovereign. Nevertheless, this deconstruction of sovereign ipseity is equally compelling when used as a lever of intervention for deconstructing the instrumentalization of foreignness with respect to the implicit and explicit positing of sovereign self-identicality in Hobbes, Locke, and Rousseau. The unrepresentability of Rousseau's general will is a case in point.

12 This claim, of course, rests in tension with Socrates' insistence that imitative poetry (and the poets responsible for this poetry) must be banished from the city in speech for their corrupting influences upon the people (Plato 1968, 595a). But, strictly speaking, what is banned is not simply that which is opposed to philosophy but rather that which perpetuates the authority of a tradition incapable of securing or even providing a consistent account of justice.

Chapter 8 Foreign Unto It-Self, the Democratic Nation-State

1 Recall Thrasymachus' claim that "democracy sets down democratic laws; a tyranny, tyrannic laws; and the others do the same. And they declare that what they have set down—their own advantage—is just for the ruled" (Plato 1968, 338d). The just regime is simply the regime in power, in this case the Athenian democracy. On this model, the trial and execution of Socrates is just. It represents the victory of the stronger, of the *polis*, over philosophy. Like the just regime, the legitimate sovereign compels obedience from its members when it is able to successfully use force, in all of its forms, to its advantage.

2 To be sure, non-democratic nation-states also commit in various ways to protecting human rights. I will say more about why the democratic state is often posited to be uniquely able to protect human rights, but, for now, it is sufficient to note that I focus solely on the democratic nation-state because the tensions between it and universal human rights provide a clear view into the relationship between democracy, sovereignty, foreignness, and rights, which will be the primary consideration going forward.

3 Peter Gratton's reading of the Biblical story of Abraham and Isaac provides important insight into the relationship between the right of force and a patriarchal and fraternal politics that targets women, children, and the vulnerable for exclusion from political and legal rights and recognition. While acknowledging Kierkegaard's analysis, which reads this story as a lesson on morality as such, Gratton suggests that Abraham's silence as he prepares to sacrifice his only son to God can also be read as "a story of man who stands with the strongest of the strong, God, against *les hommes faibles*, against his son, against his wife, in giving death to the other" (2012, 215). With this emphasis, Abraham's story is "about the theology that has long been the mystical foundation of sovereigns (operating in

silence, beyond the laws in order to protect the law), those men who would save the community by breaking its commandments against murder" (2012, 215). God, the father and highest sovereign, is forever silent yet requires Abraham to sacrifice his only son. Likewise, Abraham, the sovereign father and master of his son, is also silent as he takes Isaac from his home and leads him to the sacrificial pyre. Isaac is ultimately spared, but Abraham's faith is rewarded. His offspring will be multiplied, and he will become the patriarch of the Jewish nation and, subsequently, of the three monotheisms. Thus, we receive one instance of the "continuous story of the right of the father passed onto the son by the duty of sacrifice . . . [and] . . . the right of force of the strongest over the weakest; it is a story of the reasoning of the strongest, that coercive power that must remain silent" (2012, 215). To speak would be to introduce morality and the law by demanding a justification for the sovereign decision to violate the law. The silent authority of nature and biological inheritance upon which the patriarchal and fraternal nation rests would be compromised and weakened. Gratton concludes that if we wish to challenge the silent reason and force of the strongest undergirding the legitimacy of both patriarchal and fraternal politics, then "we must first and foremost, in the name of the other, question the silence of Abraham in the face of the weak, in the face also of the feminine, all those that have already been sacrificed to the sacred order" (2012, 215).

4 Democracy's others also refers to non-statist forms of affiliation such as trans-national economic or religious alliances and non-governmental organizations, each of which threaten the primacy of political sovereignty as such and democracy in particular. This formulation is explored further in the analysis of cosmopolitanism.

5 This requirement for unity is particularly important for democracy because the people is sovereign. A people or *demos* that is not unified is divided, and a divided sovereign is not self-identical, i.e., is not sovereign.

6 In Arendt's consideration of the Minority Treaties developed after the First World War in response to the massive number of stateless refugees and the weaknesses of the declarations and agreements signed by the League of Nations, she states: "[O]nly nationals could be citizens, only people of the same national origin could enjoy the full protection of legal institutions, that persons of different nationality needed some law of exception until or unless they were completely assimilated and divorced from their origins" (1968, 275). When the statesmen from countries with no "minority obligation" interpreted the Minority Treaties, they made it clear that "the law of a country could not be responsible for persons insisting on a different nationality. They thereby admitted . . . that the transformation of the state from an instrument of the law into an instrument of the nation had been completed; the nation had conquered the state, national interest had priority over

law long before Hitler could pronounce 'right is what is good for the German people'" (1968, 275).

7 Denationalization should not be misunderstood as a remedy to the dangers of ethno-nationalism. As Arendt explains, the historical lesson from the French Revolution, which inaugurated both national sovereignty and the universally applicable Declaration of the Rights of Man, is that "true freedom, true emancipation, and true popular sovereignty could be attained only with full national emancipation, that people without their own national government were deprived of human rights" (1968, 272). On this measure, denationalization ensures statelessness and the subsequent legitimacy of sovereign nation-states to deny human rights to foreigners and those who have no nation. Arendt explains: "Denationalization became a powerful weapon of totalitarian politics, and the constitutional inability of European nation-states to guarantee human rights to those who had lost nationally guaranteed rights, made it possible for the persecuting governments to impose their standards of values even upon their opponents" (1968, 269).

8 Arendt notes that, "mass denationalizations were something entirely new and unforeseen. They presupposed a state structure which, if it was not yet fully totalitarian, at least would not tolerate any opposition and would rather lose its citizens than harbor people with different views. They revealed, moreover, what had been hidden throughout the history of national sovereignty, that sovereignties of neighboring countries could come into deadly conflict not only in extreme cases of war but in peace. It now became clear that full national sovereignty was possible only as long as the comity of European nations existed" (1968, 278). Yet, I would argue that this belief is also held in a moderated form by many modern democratic nation-states, even if they do not actively pursue denationalization. One might point to the resiliency of structural racism in countries like the U.S., which continues to disenfranchise and marginalize persons of color, but a more telling example is the recurring mantra—most frequently incanted by the white majority—that the U.S. (particularly after the election of President Obama) has proven itself to be a post-racial society. The idea, of course, is that American national identity trumps or ought to trump differences of race, but it is also suggests the desire—even within pluralist societies—for a certain homogeneity which accommodates foreign difference only insofar as it does not oppose itself to the nation. Bonnie Honig notes that pluralism is a political solution for the dilemmas that often arise from the collision of ideas, practices, languages, and cultures that differ from those of the dominant group within a political community. By recognizing the difference *between* distinct groups, pluralist approaches to political dilemmas allow the destabilizing and threatening features of difference to be affirmed and recognized yet, nevertheless, be "reassuring as it

does not threaten to be ungovernable" (Honig 1996, 258). On the one hand, a post-racial society appears to be an explicit rejection of pluralism. On the other hand, as its proponents suggest, a post-racial society epitomizes pluralism insofar as foreign differences are recognized and affirmed without rending the fabric of national identity. By contrast, Honig suggests that it is precisely the ungovernability of difference that must be taken seriously because it points to and "affirms the inescapability of conflict and the ineradicability of resistance to the political and moral projects of ordering subjects, institutions, and values" (1996, 258). I pick up this argument in the final chapter to explore how foreignness and difference can be affirmed in order to go beyond pluralism, i.e., beyond merely managing the various needs of identifiable groups, which all too often results in the "violent and resentful dynamics of identity/difference" (1996, 258).

9 In "Declarations of Independence," Derrida asks: "How is a state made or founded, how does a State make or found itself? And an independence? And the autonomy of one which both gives itself, and signs, its own law? Who signs all these authorizations to sign?" (1986, 13). These questions are germane to the questions undergirding the present discussion, namely: Who is the "We" of a democratic people? Is it proper to itself? Is it sovereign? Where does it come from and what is its source of authority? Does it precede the declaration that names it as in "We the People . . ."? Or, is it forged in the moment of declaration and signature, and if so, by whom? Who grants authority to the "We" that "hold these Truths to be self-evident . . .?" While I will not revisit the entirety of Derrida's responses, his tentative answer to these questions reflects what has been argued here. There is, he suggests, a perpetual substitution that precedes and constitutes the "We." The "We" is at once the people, its representatives, the signatories of the declaration, the future citizens, etc. In short, even the founding moment of constitution of the sovereign *demos*, which would be the expression or announcement of sovereign indivisibility and inviolability, is itself put into question insofar as it is already divided, a pure supplementation and substitution.

10 There is no easy way to unchain the nation and cosmopolitanism, since the spread, growth, and success of the European (and American) nation rooted in the Enlightenment, the Rights of Man, and the intertwining of freedom, equality, and democracy are advances toward a new cosmopolitical order, despite the threat this new universal order might pose to the particular nation. Derrida, in his analysis of a unified European nation following the collapse of the USSR, emphasizes the complex relationship between European (and we might add American) nationalism and cosmopolitanism. He writes, "Nationalism and cosmopolitanism have always gotten along together, as paradoxical as this may seem. Since the time of Fichte numerous examples might attest to this. In the logic of the 'capitalistic' and cosmopolitical discourse, what is proper to a particular nation or idiom would

be to be a heading [the head, the lead, the spirit, etc.] for Europe; and what is proper to Europe would be, analogically, to advance itself as a heading for the universal essence of humanity . . . [] . . . Europe takes itself to be a promontory, an advance—the avant-garde of geography and history. It advances and promotes itself as an advance, and it will have never ceased to make advances on the other to induce, seduce, produce, and conduce, to spread out, to cultivate, to love or to violate, to love to violate, to colonize, and to colonize itself" (Derrida 1992, 48–49).

11 Not even the President of the United States is safe from this attempt to control the trajectory of the (re)imagining of national identity. In 2008, as much of the U.S. celebrated the election of its first African-American president, a potent and durable counter-movement emerged which challenged the legitimacy of Obama's presidency based on the belief that he was not born in America, and, therefore, not legally entitled to be president. Insofar as President Obama's race and heritage was taken—by the aptly named "birther" movement—to be a threat to the dominant (and "natural") *ethnos* of the nation, he was cast as foreign to the people. To dismiss the "birthers" as fringe is to fail to accurately recall that its ranks were and are filled with prominent politicians, business leaders, and members of the media. The seriousness of this attempt to cast Obama as foreign is countenanced by the fact that President Obama, several years into his presidency, released his official birth certificate to reassure the people that he was, in fact, a citizen with the legal and constitutional right to be president.

12 Before women's suffrage, white women were held in higher regard than black women and they received a plethora of benefits through their association with white males, even if they lacked the vote. The point is to show that the exclusion of white women from the *demos* depended in large part by casting them as inferior to men because of their irrationality. In this regard, women were foreign to the dominant *ethnos* of the day, namely white males.

13 In the U.S., conservative politicians and lobbying groups critical of recent immigration reform legislation cite the use of the term "integration" as a justification for opposing the legislation. These critics demand removing "integration" because it suggests a multicultural receptivity to the immigrant. Because these critics view multiculturalism as a threat to the homogeneity of the nation, they plan to structure formal legal recognition of immigrants by the state upon proof of assimilation (English skills, education in civics and patriotism, etc.). See http://www.politico.com/story/2013/06/assimilation-a-flash-point-in-immigration-debate-92469.html (accessed September 25, 2013).

14 The exclusion of "foreign insiders" from the *ethnos* and, by extension, the *demos*, results in the production of an excluded political class whose inequality under the law undermines not only democracy but also the nation-state itself. As Arendt writes: "For the nation-state cannot exist once its principle of equality before the

law has broken down. Without this legal equality, which originally was destined to replace the older laws and orders of feudal society, the nation dissolves into an anarchic mass of over- and underprivileged individuals. Laws that are not equal for all revert to rights and privileges, something contradictory to the very nature of nation-states" (1968, 290).

15 As global regimes of law, trade, and non-statist affiliations make borders ever more porous and weaken traditional notions of territorially bounded sovereignty, sovereign states retain the right to limit immigration and institute rigorous requirements for citizenship in a fevered attempt to control their territories, population, and national identity. As Seyla Benhabib claims: "*territoriality* has become an anachronistic delimitation of material functions and cultural identities; yet, even in the face of the collapse of traditional forms of sovereignty, monopoly over territory is exercised through immigration and citizenship policies" (2004, 5, original emphasis).

16 Michael Naas' explication is useful. He states: "*[F]reedom*, an essential attribute of democracy since Plato and Aristotle, is traditionally grounded upon a notion of sovereignty that is itself grounded in the *autos*, that is, in the self or the selfsame, in the sovereignty of a self-sustaining, self-asserting, and deciding self that has the capacity in and of itself to choose something for itself, to vote one way or another by itself, to affirm or deny out of itself in order to sustain itself and assert its sovereignty as a self" (2008, 125–126, original emphasis).

17 Importantly, Derrida notes that Plato is simply "convey[ing] a commonly held opinion" ([2003] 2005, 22) about democracy. On the one hand, Plato is explicit in his rejection of democracy, which conflates freedom and license. On the other hand, by couching his critique in what is commonly held about democracy, he hesitates by withholding his own judgment, and, perhaps, holding in reserve a hope for democracy, albeit one that is profoundly different from the common conception. In the following chapter, I trace out one possible alternate conception of democracy, Derrida's democracy to come. While the democracy to come is certainly not an application of Plato or Platonism, it is, in some sense, informed by this hesitation within Plato's critique, which leaves open the possibility for rethinking anew the relationship between freedom, license, autonomy, force, and democracy.

18 Each man, Locke argues, ought to respect natural law and the fence of freedom that marks each man's sovereignty and property in his person. When license reigns and men fail to respect natural law, the state of war is introduced, which can only be mitigated through a commonwealth that neutrally judges and punishes these excesses of license that threaten the *liberty* of each signatory to the contract.

19 The relationship between the democratic nation-state and the foreigner has a rich and complex history. In *Guests and Aliens* (1999), Saskia Sassen traces the

nation-state's conceptualization of the foreigner through its response to the political exigencies brought on by the high levels of stateless refugees in Europe, a phenomenon that preceded and was then exacerbated by the First World War. Paraphrasing Arendt, she writes: "The coupling of state sovereignty and nationalism with border control made the 'foreigner' an outsider. The state was correspondingly able to define refugees as not belonging to the national society, as not being entitled to the rights of citizens. Unlike the refugees of an earlier period who had been outsiders in the same way transients or vagabonds were, refugees in the twentieth century were identified as a distinctive category; the state now had the power and the institutional legitimacy to exclude refugees from civil society (Arendt 1958)" (Sassen 1999, 78). This is fascinating in its own right, and speaks importantly to the way in which foreigners and foreignness were and continued to be conceived of by the sovereign nation-state. However, the point here in following Derrida is to trace the ways in which ipseity structures sovereignty even before we speak of the sovereign state or nation. In short, that the exclusion of foreign difference—if not the specific figure of the foreigner *qua* refugee or (im)migrant—is a structural feature of sovereignty as such.

20 In Peter Gratton's formulation, Derrida offers "another freedom, one without autonomy, one without power and force, one that troubles and trembles the thinking of democracy but nevertheless ultimately confronts a long line of the fear and trembling of the politics of sovereignty" (2012, 216).

21 The question of who decides is a questioning of sovereign ipseity. What sources of authority, local laws, or parochial practices will inform the decision? In what language will the decision be announced? What styles of language will be used to debate the outcome (legal, political, dialectical, common, passionate, dispassionate, etc.)? Recall, for example, Socrates' trial: He is tried because of the presumed threat he poses to traditional sources of authority; he has taken license with the liberty guaranteed him by the Athenian democracy. During his defense, he acknowledges his disadvantage arising from his lack of familiarity with the style of language common to the courts. He requests leniency to speak in his customary manner (dialogue, elenchus, aporia, etc.), foreign as this manner of speech is to Athenian legal discourse. He states: "This is my first appearance in a lawcourt: I am therefore simply a stranger to the manner of speaking here. Just as if I were really a stranger, you would certainly excuse me if I spoke in that dialect and manner in which I had been brought up . . ." (Plato 1961a, 17d–18a). His request is granted, but his defense falls on the deaf ears of the majority who would have granted leniency, it is implied, if he had simply addressed himself in the manner to which those who decided his fate were accustomed, namely by humbling himself and begging their forgiveness (Plato 1961, 37b–38b). Similarly, from his prison cell in Birmingham, Martin Luther King, Jr. argued that an unjust law which does not square with the

moral law can be broken (1986, 293). This is a challenge to both rabid segregationists and the apologists of the racist state who decided, in a sovereign fashion, to punish license at the cost of liberty, as if freedom could be so easily parsed. In sum, the question of who decides is a challenge to sovereign force and identity, and in the following chapter we see how who decides is central to the reconceptualization of democracy.

22 See Luce Irigaray's *An Ethics of Sexual Difference* (1984, especially pp. 20–34) for a more detailed reading of the biological metaphors in Plato's *Symposium* and their relationship to the metaphysical basis of the neutral and generic subject (always male and, therefore, neither neutral nor generic) who functions as the locus of moral and political autonomy and consideration.

23 In *Rogues* ([2003] 2005, especially pp. 42–55), Derrida rejects Jean-Luc Nancy's efforts to reconceptualize fraternity as a useful concept for a future politics and a future democracy. The details are outside the scope of this work, but central to Derrida's critique is that one cannot simply deconstruct any concept in order to reconceptualize it and reappropriate it anew for one's purposes. As Peter Gratton concisely summarizes: "This is the place of Derrida's politics: to point out not just the free-play of concepts but also the way that they have sedimented into particular hierarchies throughout the tradition. The continued use and affirmation of certain terms, for example, fraternity, Derrida argues, risks foreclosing the free-play of freedom and the democratic, which is an 'experience of the impossible,' the trembling of difference between fraternity and its other" (2012, 221). While Nancy's attempt to reconceptualize fraternity may be directed against the traditional democratic exclusions premised on this concept (of women, of foreigners, of all those who are not native born men of a certain age and ability, etc.) are laudable, Derrida's concern is that fraternity—even when deconstructed—cannot shed the exclusions generated by the biological and natural aspects of its traditional meanings.

24 The threat of rogue states is real, and the U.S. and its allies often appeal to the dangers they pose in order to justify the global scope of their economic and military interests—often through pre-emptive, even roguish, offensive actions. Indeed, a quick look at recent U.S. global operations makes it clear why Derrida claims that the "most perverse, most violent, most destructive of rogue states would thus be, first and foremost, the United States, and sometimes its allies" ([2003] 2005, 97).

25 Naas elaborates: "While a monarchic, aristocratic, or plutocratic regime *may* change over time, may improve or be destroyed—the monarch may be overthrown or may die, the aristocracy may become corrupted and lead to plutocracy, the members of the wealthy class may shift—such changes are not *intrinsic* possibilities of these regimens" (2008, 136, original emphasis). Rather, it is the "by

turns" of democracy, the coming to rule of one part of the *demos* over the other, that distinguishes democracy as intrinsically and structurally open to its own suspension—temporary or permanent.

26 The claim that democracy takes time is intended to contrast with Derrida's reading of sovereignty, which, he insists, is outside of time and "ahistorical" ([2003] 2005, 101). In its attempt to immunize itself against the other, "sovereignty neither gives nor gives itself the time; it does not take time" ([2003] 2005, 109). While I am actually sketching out the shared autoimmunity of democracy and sovereignty, I mention this tension between democracy and sovereignty—between taking time and not taking time—in order to foreshadow a discussion in the following chapter of the way in which democracy both requires and resists sovereignty.

27 Kant had already made a similar observation in 1795. He claimed that democracy is, properly speaking, a form of despotism because "it [democracy] sets up an executive power in which all citizens make decisions about and, if need be, against one (who therefore does not agree); consequently, all who are not quite all, decide, so that the general will contradicts itself and freedom" ([1795] 1983, 114).

28 In Ancient Athens, this might mean excluding Athenian women and slaves, or foreigners such as *metics*. Today, the exclusion of (im)migrants or citizens deemed to be internal threats to the *demos* is also common. There is no shortage of criminals or traitors who fit this criterion, but the nation-state also excludes those who are foreign to the hierarchical ordering of *ethnoi* upon which the identity of the nation is forged and through which citizenship is determined.

29 Democracy is a unique political constitution because it is free to be other than it is, and there is no telling in advance what effect the free, democratic decision will have on the democracy. Derrida writes that the free decision of democracy suggests "a freedom of play, an opening of indetermination and indecidability in the very concept of democracy" ([2003] 2005, 24). Democracy is free to decide to include or exclude, neither of which can, in advance, guarantee more or less democracy, freedom, equality, etc. Indeed, the very act of free decision generates exclusions from itself. This indetermination and indecidability of the very concept of democracy—the freedom for democracy to be other than it *is* or, alternatively, a democracy that is foreign to itself—is developed in the following section.

30 In particular, I am thinking of the influence Giorgio Agamben's *Homo Sacer* ([1995] 1998) has had upon the recent theorizations of sovereignty and political exclusions.

31 In his "Letter from Birmingham Jail," Martin Luther King, Jr. writes: "One of the basic points in your statement is that acts are untimely. Some have asked: 'Why didn't you give the new administration time to act?' . . . We know through painful experience that freedom is never voluntarily given by the oppressor; it must be demanded by the oppressed. Frankly, I have never yet engaged in a direct action

movement that was 'well timed,' according to the timetable of those who have not suffered unduly from the disease of segregation. For years now I have heard the word 'Wait!' It rings in the ear of every Negro with piercing familiarity. This 'Wait' has almost always meant 'Never' . . . We must come to see, with one of our distinguished jurists, that 'justice too long delayed is justice denied'" (1986, 292).

32 It is not uncommon in the U.S. to hear that someone "bleeds red, white, and blue," a compliment and reference to the colors of the flag, and, hence, a biological and consanguineous proof of one's patriotism and "Americanness."

33 Importantly, the universal freedom and equality of all humans is granted by virtue of one's birth as a human being regardless of the particular state or nation to which one belongs or even if one has no state. Yet, even this requirement retains the biological, genetic, and natural foundations for inclusions within the regime of universal (human) rights. This, it seems, is why Derrida is at pains to emphasize that democracy welcomes the "no matter who" and "the indeterminate 'each one.'" He writes: "[D]oes this measure of the immeasurable, this democratic equality, end at citizenship, and thus at the borders of the nation-state? Or must we extend it to the whole world of singularities, to the whole world of humans assumed to be like me, my compeers [*mes semblables*]—or else, even further, to all nonhuman living beings, or again, even beyond that, to all the nonliving, to their memory spectral or otherwise, to their to-come or to their indifference with regard to what we think we can identify, in an always precipitous, dogmatic, and obscure way, as the life or the living present of living [*la vivance*] in general?" ([2003] 2005, 53).

34 In the wake of the 2013 U.S. Supreme Court decision dismantling major pieces of the 1965 Voting Rights Act implemented to ensure equal access to the polls by prohibiting voting discrimination, many states—notably Texas— immediately enacted restrictive voter identification laws under the auspices of eliminating voter fraud. However, the U.S. Justice Department recently blocked one new law that disproportionately impacted Latino voters. See http://articles.washingtonpost.com/2012-03-12/politics/35450319_1_voter-id-laws-library-card-or-board-combat-voter-fraud (accessed October 27, 2013). More recently still, Texas is being scrutinized for the effects these laws have on making voting more difficult for women. See http://swampland.time.com/2013/10/24/what-voter-id-laws-really-mean-for-women-voters-in-texas/ (accessed October 27, 2013).

35 Take, for example, the recent immigration reform legislation to be offered by Congressman Darrell Issa, a prominent Republican. He describes his legislation as "a 'come-from-the-shadows' effort that would allow the government to do a full accounting of those who are in the U.S. illegally." In this way, undocumented immigrants could be categorized—for example, have or do not have family members who are citizens, interested in guest-worker programs, criminals, etc. The implication being that if one is undocumented or present "illegally," then one

is outside the scope of the law and, as such, not accounted for or accountable to the nation-state. See http://www.politico.com/story/2013/10/darrell-issa-immigration-reform-bill-98764.html (accessed October 30, 2013).

36 This blind application of a universal ethical law would be no different from the blind application of a particular law that refused to welcome any and all that might arrive.

37 Recall Rousseau's famous proclamation: "If there were a nation of Gods, it would govern itself democratically. A government so perfect is not suited to men" ([1762] 1968, 114). Rather than the ideal of democracy, a nation of self-legislating Gods, Derrida is endeavoring to consider democracy otherwise, not as a regime or type of constitution to be perfected in the future, but rather an ethical and political orientation and openness to foreignness that resists the force indissociable from sovereign ipseity.

38 Former U.S. President George W. Bush's memoir is titled *Decision Points*, an appropriate title for the man whose response to the question of whether the then-Secretary of Defense, Donald Rumsfeld, should be fired in light of the torture and abuses of prisoners by American soldiers in Abu Ghraib was: "I listen to all voices, but mine is the final decision ... I hear the voices, and I read the front page, and I know the speculation. But I'm the decider, and I decide what is best. And what's best is for Don Rumsfeld to remain as the secretary of defense." See http://www.cnn.com/2006/POLITICS/04/18/rumsfeld/ (accessed December, 8, 2013).

39 For Derrida, violence is inextricable from the law since any new law or constitution inevitably excludes some for the sake of others. In *Force of Law*, he writes: "law is always an authorized force, a force that justifies itself or is justified in applying itself, even if this justification may be judged from elsewhere to be unjust or unjustifiable" ([1994] 2002, 233). He continues, "The very emergence of justice and law, the instituting, founding, and justifying moment of law implies a performative force ... [T]he operation that amounts to founding, inaugurating, justifying law, *making* law, would consist of a *coup de force*, of a performative and therefore interpretative violence that in itself is neither just nor unjust" ([1994] 2002, 241, original emphasis).

40 While committed to thinking "another experience of freedom," it is the freedom internal to the concept of democracy that appeals to Derrida. It is democracy, not freedom, which Derrida will attempt to reconceptualize and deploy anew in the name of a future justice. As Michael Naas notes, by drawing upon the aporetic and paradoxical aspects internal to democracy as such, including freedom and license and freedom and equality, "it is not the decentered subject that is radically free but, for Derrida, the quasi-concept of democracy ... a democracy that remains to come to the extent that there is a radical freedom or free play in its concept" (2008, 134).

41 Derrida writes, "democracy hesitates always in the alternative between two sorts of alternation (where the power of one party, said to be republican, replaces that of another party, said to be equally republican) and the alternation that risks giving power, *modo democratico*, to the force of a party elected by the people (and so is democratic) and yet is assumed to be nondemocratic" (Derrida [2003] 2005, 30) The example of Algeria discussed above is illustrative.

42 Derrida claims that the democratic right to publicly criticize everything, including the very concept and meaning of democracy, is what makes it unique as a regime. He writes: "It [democracy] is thus the only paradigm that is universalizable" ([2003] 2005, 87). In other words, the fundamental principle of freedom—the freedom of speech and of giving and receiving justifications—is a universalizable process in which the meaning of the democratic is open to perpetual revision with no guarantees in advance how this sharing out of itself will affect the instantiation of democracy in any given polity.

43 Derrida is quick to note that pure sovereignty does not exist. It must speak, and this positing of itself is a violation of itself; hence, sovereignty's autoimmunity that "betrays" the democracy it is supposed to protect.

44 Derrida opposes deconstruction to sovereignty by linking deconstruction to democracy's historicity when he claims that there is "[N]o deconstruction without democracy, no democracy without deconstruction" ([1994] 1997, 105). Insofar as democracy is historical, it is radically open to self-critique and questioning. In a word, it is free to be deconstructed. Thus, deconstruction *qua* free speech is an indispensable normative value and right guaranteed by democracy. At the same time, democracy requires the deconstruction of itself and its fundamental principles if existing democratic states are to remain open to a future resistant to the force and violence of sovereign ipseity.

45 It should be fairly clear that the *double renvoi* of democracy—democracy's structural autoimmunity— shares much in common with the early deconstructive figure of *différance*. Much hinges on these similarities, since Derrida's critics often point to the lack of political engagement or even nihilism of his earliest works of deconstruction while his defenders cite these similarities as proof that deconstruction was political all along. These debates are outside the scope of this work, but in passing it is worth noting that Derrida, without addressing his critics or defenders, does comment explicitly on the similarities and differences between autoimmunity, *différance*, and a vast array of other deconstructive figures developed in Derrida's various work (see *Rogues* [2003] 2005, 35).

46 Derrida would argue that the structure of the promise is "hauntological," a play on words that suggests a certain ontology distinct from the metaphysics of presence (see *Specters of Marx* [1993] 1994, 63).

47 As Michael Naas notes, "Autoimmunity is presented not only as a threat but as a chance for any living organism: a threat insofar as it compromises the immune system that protects organisms from external aggression, but as in the case of immuno-depressants, a chance for an organism to open itself up to and accept something that is not properly its own, the transplanted organ, the graft, in a word, the other, which is but the cutting edge, the living edge, of the self" (2008, 131).

48 In his consideration of the free, responsible, and just decision, Derrida writes that the freedom requisite to make a just or unjust decision "must follow a law [*loi*] or a prescription, a rule. In this sense, in its very autonomy, in its freedom to follow or give itself the law [*loi*], it has to be capable of being of the calculable or programmable order, for example as an act of fairness [*équité*]. But if the act simply consists of applying a rule, of enacting a program or effecting a calculation, one will perhaps say that it is legal, that it conforms to the law, and perhaps, by metaphor, that it is just, but one would be wrong to say that the *decision* was just. Simply because there was, in this case, no decision . . . In short, for a decision to be just and responsible, it must [*il faut*], in its proper moment, if there is one, be both regulated and without regulation, it must preserve the law [*loi*] and also destroy or suspend it enough to have [*pour devoir*] to reinvent it in each case, rejustify it, reinvent it at least in the reaffirmation of the new and free confirmation of its principle. Each case is other, each decision is different and requires an absolutely unique interpretation, which no existing, coded rule can or ought to guarantee absolutely" (Derrida [1994] 2002, 251, original emphasis).

49 Justice, like democracy, remains to-come; it is never fully present as such. The calls for justice by the other are always in want and never adequately represented. While there is no justice without law, justice is not reducible to it. Like equality, democratic law is conditional, it calculates, counts, and measures in order to protect its subjects. There is the risk that it might destroy the singularity and incommensurability of those outside or marginal to the law, but it is also that which gives access to the unconditional by attending to the calls for justice by those outside of the protection of the law.

50 This is yet another way of stating that the question of life or death is no longer proper to the sovereign. It hinges on the reconceptualization of foreignness that both constitutes and enervates sovereignty.

51 The consideration of khōra is explicitly concerned with metaphysical necessity and rational justification of this necessity, but what should not be lost in this complex consideration is the theme of justice. *Timaeus* takes place the day after the analysis of justice in *The Republic*. Socrates briefly summarizes the previous day's highlights before the dialogue is taken over by his interlocutors who, in

hopes of furthering the analysis of justice, embark on a creation story within which the idea of the khōra is developed.

52 Derrida's "hope now" for a future justice rests upon distinguishing between the double meaning of the French term "*salut*" (both salvation and salutation). He writes that, "it [hope] remains, in itself without hope. Not hopeless, in despair, but foreign to the teleology, the hopefulness, and the *salut* of salvation. Not foreign to the *salut* as the greeting or salutation of the other, not foreign to the *adieu* ('come' or 'go' in peace), not foreign to justice, but nonetheless heterogeneous and rebellious, irreducible, to law, to power, and the economy of redemption" (Derrida [2003] 2005, xv). This emphasis upon greeting and welcoming, the available responses by the sovereign to the foreign as well as the responsibility of the sovereign to avail itself to the other, has already been touched upon but will become more central in the consideration of the democracy to come addressed in the final chapter.

53 While caution is required when comparing the vulnerability of the sovereign "we" or *demos* to the corporeal vulnerability of an individual subject, this comparison is revealing insofar as the model of corporeal vulnerability has important political and ethical implications which allow for a reconceptualization of sovereign inviolability on an ontological level. Judith Butler's work is revealing: "I find that my very formation implicates the other in me, that my own foreignness to myself is, paradoxically, the source of my ethical connection with others. I am not fully known to myself, because part of what I am is the enigmatic traces of others. In this sense, I cannot know myself perfectly or know my 'difference' from others in an irreducible way. This unknowingness may seem from a given perspective, a problem for ethics and politics. Don't I need to know myself in order to act responsibly in social relations? Surely, to a certain extent, yes. But is there an ethical valence to my unknowingness? I am wounded, and I find that the wound itself testifies to the fact that I am impressionable, given over to the Other in ways that I cannot fully predict or control. I cannot think the question of responsibility alone, in isolation from the Other; if I do, I have taken myself out of the relational bind that frames the problem of responsibility from the start" (2006, 46). With this model, it is not the vulnerability of the other in need of a sovereign gift of refuge, shelter, or hospitality, for example, which opens the sphere of ethics. Instead, it is one's own constitutive foreignness to oneself, one's imbrication with the radically unknowable other that introduces a fundamental and inescapable precariousness and vulnerability. This vulnerability of and to the foreign is the spacing and opening of the ethico-political. For this reason, Butler concludes rather intriguingly with this: "what was once thought of as a border, that which delimits and bounds, is a highly populated site, if not the very definition of the nation, confounding identity in what may well become a very auspicious direction" (2006, 49).

Chapter 9 The Foreign-Citizen at the Threshold of Democratic Cosmopolitanism

1 Benhabib's concern is reflected in her taking up of Hannah Arendt's famous formulation "the right to have rights" (Arendt 1968, 296). Arendt's work on denationalization and statelessness revealed that those who lost their rights as citizens were effectively stripped of their human rights. For Benhabib, Arendt's analysis points to the key insight that: "The rights of man and the rights of the citizen, which the modern bourgeois revolutions had so clearly delineated, were deeply imbricated. The loss of citizenship rights, therefore, contrary to all human rights declarations, was politically tantamount to the loss of human rights altogether" (Benhabib 2004, 50). In this sense, "the right to have rights" suggests that there is a moral and human right to voice one's opinion, act as a political agent, and "belong to some kind of organized community" (Arendt 1968, 296) that both requires and exceeds the rights of citizenship. Arendt, in this sense, recognizes the paradox that there is a need for sovereign states to enforce and protect human rights and that these states necessarily create exclusions of those who are not members. Nonetheless, her formulation shows that the denial of hospitality—including political membership—provides for an unambiguous judgment that the denial of hospitality to foreigners is a clear violation of human rights. Paradoxically, "the right to have rights" deconstructs the legitimacy of the sovereign state it nevertheless requires insofar as this right suggests that "we" as sovereign citizens cannot know what rights the foreigner will demand from "us." The sovereign state must remain absolutely open and vulnerable to its foreign others even when their inclusion might very well threaten the stability and powers of the sovereign. It is worth noting that, for Benhabib, Arendt's phrase, useful as it is, ultimately fails to found a viable cosmopolitanism. Benhabib argues that Arendt, like Kant, is unable to resolve the paradox between human rights and sovereign self-determination. Arendt, as much as Kant, believed that "exclusionary territorial control is an unchecked sovereign privilege which cannot be limited or trumped by other norms and institutions" (Benhabib 2004, 67). As we will see below, Benhabib's elaboration of democratic iterations and disaggregated citizenship embrace the cosmopolitan right to hospitality and the right to have rights, but she resolves the tension between the state and human rights by articulating the various networks and communities of obligations and allegiances that exist alongside and within the bounded democratic polity which compel the sovereign democratic state to justify its decisions to exclude against the universal scope of its founding principles.

2 Seyla Benhabib provides a useful analysis of the legal status of various categories of foreigners within the sovereign nation-state, including refugees, political minorities, stateless persons, and displaced persons (2004, 55).

3 The International Convention on the Protection of the Rights of All Migrant Workers and Members of Their Families was adopted by the United Nations in 1990 and entered into force in 2003. It requires signatories to the convention to recognize and protect the human rights of migrant laborers as well as guarantee equal working conditions for both nationals and migrants. This is an important document insofar as it recognizes the tenuous relationship between human rights and migration, but it is worth noting that not one receiving nation or host country in North America or Europe is a signatory.

4 For this reason, undocumented (im)migrants who arrive without giving an account of themselves are not hospitably welcomed, even though they might be tolerated.

5 I am in concord with Derrida's claim that the foreigner is not the absolute other, even if the differences between them is "sometimes ungraspable." However, I would suggest that we can conceive of the absolute other along the lines of foreignness as such. Perhaps the most obvious case is when the foreigner becomes a citizen through naturalization. In this moment, she becomes known or knowable to the sovereign, accountable and responsible to the state and its citizens. Her unknowability, her protean and indefinite essence (always oscillating between the artificial, the natural, and the perversion of nature) is eliminated. In a word, she sheds her foreignness, which remains absolutely opposed to sovereignty.

6 Unconditional hospitality is outside and above the law. This articulation is reminiscent of Hobbes' claims regarding the qualities of the sovereign. Derrida does not juxtapose the unconditional and the sovereign without explicit knowledge of the difficulty between distinguishing between them (see, for example, *Rogues* [2003] 2005, xiv). It is in this respect that the emphasis on inflection and accent matters. Is the decision to welcome or exclude rendered according to sovereign self-mastery, or is it rendered according to the structural vulnerability and autoimmunity of the sovereign in the name of and for the sake of the other?

7 In his article, "Derrida's Democracy to Come," Matthias Fritsch provides a nuanced critique of the scope and normative applicability of Derrida's democracy to come and unconditional hospitality. Most generally, he argues that Derrida's emphasis upon a radically open future and the perpetual negotiation, each time, of the sovereign (in)decision requires recourse to the practical norm of the "lesser violence" which can only be decided in each situation. Most plainly, sometimes excluding the foreigner will result in "lesser violence." In this regard, because the determination of "lesser violence" is only possible within a specific context, unconditional hospitality cannot be a universal normative rule. Fritsch concludes that "thinking of ethics and politics in terms of aporia, and insisting on singularity,

may be useful and even necessary, but they disallow universal normative recommendations on their own terms" (2002, 589). Despite his critique, Fritsch also suggests a reading of unconditional hospitality that supports what I have endeavored to develop here. He writes, "The call [for unconditional hospitality] attempts to bring to our awareness this space of aporetic negotiability [the impossibility of sovereign closure], and reactivates the democratic possibilities at the heart of frontiers, politically relevant distinctions, and sedimented structures. If we presuppose that in an economy of originary violence, violence is to be reduced, Derrida can legitimately argue that this democratic space of contestations as well as invention is normatively demanded. The Derridean call for democracy to come calls for the back and forth, the undecidability that often only results if we experience or admit the hyperbolic call to absolute openness and unconditional hospitality to the singular other" (2002, 589).

8 Drawing upon Benhabib might, initially, seem counter-intuitive. While she adopts the Derridean notion of iteration, she explicitly approaches the rights of (foreign) others to political membership "from the standpoint of discourse ethics and a normative theory of deliberative democracy" (Benhabib 2004, 12). There is a longstanding and ongoing debate about whether or not the theoretical tensions between discourse ethics and deconstruction can be reconciled. Derrida himself voices his concern in *The Other Heading* when he claims: "Under the pretext of pleading for transparency . . . for univocity of democratic discussion, for communication in public space, for 'communicative action,' such a discourse tends to impose a model of language that is supposedly favorable to this communication. Claiming to speak in the name of intelligibility, good sense, common sense, or the democratic ethic, this discourse tends, by means of these very things, and as if naturally, to discredit anything that complicates this model. It tends to suspect or repress anything that bends, over determines, or even questions, in theory or practice, this idea of language" ([1991] 1992, 54–55). Derrida balks at what he sees as the implicit power that accompanies the governing norms of rational discourse that may function to silence the voice not only of deconstruction but also of democracy's others, those regimes, ideas, and individuals that merely question or explicitly resist the norms of secular, democratic modernity. It might be argued that there was progress on this front. Nearly a decade later, Derrida and one of the most prominent theorists of discourse ethics, Jürgen Habermas, collaborated—without necessarily achieving a rapprochement—on the relevance and meaning of philosophy in the post 9/11 era of terror (see *Philosophy in a Time of Terror: Dialogues with Jürgen Habermas and Jacques Derrida* [Borradori 2003]). My interest here, however, is not to engage in a tangled debate which would take us far afield but rather to emphasize the shared concern between the two approaches for (re)negotiation of the laws

which all-too-frequently result in untenable political and moral injustices suffered by democracy's others. For more on this debate, see Jürgen Habermas, *The Philosophical Discourse of Modernity* (1987); Seyla Benhabib, *Democracy and Difference: Contesting the Boundaries of the Political* (1996); Matthias Fritsch, "Derrida's Democracy to Come" (2002); Richard Gannis, *The Politics of Care in Habermas and Derrida: Between Measurability and Immeasurability* (2011).

9 Drawing on the normative claims of discourse ethics. Benhabib further argues that, "The human right to membership straddles two broad categories: human rights and civil and political rights. I [Benhabib] am arguing that the *entitlement* to all civil rights—including rights to association, property, and contract—and eventually to political rights, must be considered a human right. This suggests that the sovereign discretion of the democratic community is circumscribed: once admission occurs, the path to membership ought not to be blocked . . . I cannot justify to you why you should remain a permanent stranger upon the land. This would amount to a denial of your communicative freedom and moral personality (2004, 140, original emphasis).

10 As Eduardo Mendieta observes, "*By labelling irregular immigrants 'illegals' and treating them as 'criminals,' we are consigning them to a permanent social disability that will turn them into a permanent untouchable caste.* How we treat immigrants, both regular and irregular, above all in the age of mass migrations in a nation of immigrants, is a hallmark of our commitment to our democratic morality" (2011, 182, original emphasis).

11 Benhabib's discourse ethics also challenges Kant's claim regarding the sovereign gift of political membership, but I emphasize the relationship between the foreign-citizen and unconditional hospitality at this point to foreshadow the ways in which the deconstruction of democratic citizenship provides a normative basis for a cosmopolitanism that both requires and resists the sovereignty of the democratic state.

12 There are well-known examples such as John Walker Lind and José Padilla. Most recently, a white paper titled "Lawfulness of a Lethal Operation Directed Against a US Citizen Who is a Senior Operational Leader of Al-Qa'ida or An Associated Force" crafted by the Department of Justice under President Obama has been revealed. It provides a (secret until now) legal justification for President Obama to target American citizens for assassination without due process of the law. See http://www.theguardian.com/commentisfree/2013/feb/05/obama-kill-list-doj-memo (accessed February 9, 2013).

13 In his discussion of the *double renvoi* of autoimmune democracy, Derrida writes: "One electoral law is thus always at the same time more and less democratic than another" ([2003] 2005, 36).

14 I admit that there is something counterintuitive—even dangerous and vulnerable to exploitation—to claim that voting might weaken or even destroy democratic citizenship. Be that as it may, I stand by the claim that, *within a democracy*, the weakening of the status of citizenship, if it occurs, will ultimately be the result of a democratic vote by its citizens. This is not to suggest, however, that voting should be circumscribed or limited in order to save democratic citizenship. In fact, I am making the opposite claim that, despite the risk to democratic citizenship, voting ought to be extended to non-citizen, foreigners residing with a given polity. The possible perversion, weakening, or destroying of democratic citizenship is also its only chance for (re)invention.

15 Communicative freedom is the right to give, receive, accept, and reject justifications possessed by all humans in virtue of their humanity. This is a cornerstone of discourse ethics that "asks which norms and normative institutional arrangements would be considered valid by all those who would be affected if they were participants in special moral argumentations called discourses" (Benhabib 2004, 131–132).

16 Undocumented immigrants are increasingly vocal in the U.S. From constitutionally protected political rallies by undocumented (im)migrants in the streets of Los Angeles (see Butler and Spivak 2007) to recent actions on university campuses in support of the Dream Act to the continued efforts and activities of the Farmworkers Union, non-citizen status does not automatically entail losing one's political voice, but, as Benhabib notes, it does result in a "civil death" of sorts.

Bibliography

Agamben, Giorgio. [1995] 1998. *Homo Sacer: Sovereign Power and Bare Life*. Translated by Daniel Heller-Roazen. Stanford, CA: Stanford University Press.

Arendt, Hannah. 1963. *On Revolution*. London: Penguin Books.

Arendt, Hannah. 1968. *The Origins of Totalitarianism*. San Diego, CA: Harvest Books.

Aristotle. 1942. *On the Generation of Animals*. Translated by A.L. Peck. Boston, MA: Harvard University Press.

Aristotle. 1981. *Politics*. Translated by Ernest Barker. Oxford: Oxford University Press.

Balibar, Etienne. 2004. *We, the People of Europe? Reflections on Transnational Citizenship*. Translated by James Swenson. Princeton, NJ: Princeton University Press.

Benhabib, Seyla. 1996. *Democracy and Difference: Contesting the Boundaries of the Political*. Princeton, NJ: Princeton University Press.

Benhabib, Seyla. 2004. *The Rights of Others: Aliens, Residents, and Citizens*. Cambridge: Cambridge University Press.

Bloom, Allan. 1968. *The Republic of Plato*, Second Edition. Translated, with notes and an interpretive essay, by Allan Bloom. New York: Basic Books.

Borradori, Giovanna. 2003. *Philosophy in a Time of Terror: Dialogues with Jürgen Habermas and Jacques Derrida*. Chicago, IL: University of Chicago Press.

Brown, Wendy. 2010. *Walled States, Waning Sovereignty*. Cambridge, MA: MIT Press.

Butler, Judith. 2006. *Precarious Life: The Powers of Mourning and Violence*. London: Verso.

Butler, Judith and Gayatri Chakravorty Spivak. 2007. *Who Sings the Nation-State?* Oxford: Seagull Books.

Carens, Joseph H. 2013. *The Ethics of Immigration*. New York: Oxford University Press.

Casey, Edward. S. 2011. "Strangers at the Edge of Hospitality." In *Phenomenologies of the Stranger: Between Hostility and Hospitality*. Edited by Richard Kearney and Kascha Semonovitch. New York: Fordham University Press, pp. 39–49.

Chua, Amy. 2003. *World on Fire: How Exporting Free Market Democracy Breeds Ethnic Hatred and Global Instability*. New York: Anchor Books.

Cranston, Maurice. 1968. "Introduction." In Jean-Jacques Rousseau, *The Social Contract*. Translated, with an introduction, by Maurice Cranston. Harmondsworth, UK: Penguin Books.

Derrida, Jacques. 1986. "Declarations of Independence." *New Political Science*, 7 (1): 7–15.

Derrida, Jacques. 1973. *Speech and Phenomenon and Other Essays on Husserl's Theory of Signs*. Translated, with an introduction, by David B. Allison. Preface by Newton Garver. Evanston, IL: Northwest University Press.

Derrida, Jacques. 1978. "Violence and Metaphysics: An Essay in the Thought of Emmanuel Lévinas." In *Writing and Difference*. Translated, with an introduction and additional notes, by Alan Bass. Chicago, IL: University of Chicago Press.

Derrida, Jacques. 1982. "Différance." In *Margins of Philosophy*. Translated, with additional notes, by Alan Bass. Chicago, IL: University of Chicago Press.

Derrida, Jacques. [1991] 1992. *The Other Heading: Reflections on Today's Europe*. Translated by Pascale-Anne Brault and Michael B. Naas with an introduction by Michael B. Naas. Bloomington: Indiana University Press

Derrida, Jacques. 1992. "Passages—From Traumatism to Promise." In *Points . . . Interviews 1974–1994*. Edited, with an introduction, by Elisabeth Weber. Translated by Peggy Kamuf. Stanford, CA: Stanford University Press.

Derrida, Jacques. [1993] 1994. *Specters of Marx: The State of the Debt, the Work of Mourning, and the New International*. Translated by Peggy Kamuf. New York: Routledge.

Derrida, Jacques. [1994] 1997. *The Politics of Friendship*. Translated by George Collins. London: Verso Books.

Derrida, Jacques. [1994] 2002. "Force of Law: The 'Mystical Foundation of Authority.'" In *Acts of Religion*. Edited, with an introduction, by Gil Anadjar. New York: Routledge.

Derrida, Jacques. [1996] 2002. "Faith and Knowledge: The Two Sources of 'Religion' at the Limits of Reason Alone." In *Acts of Religion*. Edited, with an introduction, by Gil Anadjar. New York: Routledge.

Derrida, Jacques. [1997] 2000. *Of Hospitality: Anne Dufourmantelle Invites Jacques Derrida to Respond*. Translated by Rachel Bowlby. Stanford, CA: Stanford University Press.

Derrida, Jacques. [1997] 2001. *On Cosmopolitanism and Forgiveness*. Translated by Mark Dooley and Michael Hughes with a preface by Simon Critchley and Richard Kearney. New York: Routledge.

Derrida, Jacques. [2003] 2005. *Rogues: Two Essays on Reason*. Translated by Pascal-Anne Brault and Michael Naas. Stanford, CA: Stanford University Press.

Derrida, Jacques. 2009. *The Beast and The Sovereign Vol. I*. Edited by Michel Lisse, Marie-Louise Mallet, and Ginette Michaud. Translated by Geoffrey Bennington. Chicago, IL: University of Chicago Press.

Derrida, Jacques and J.-L. Houdebine. 1973. "Interview/Jacques Derrida: Positions." *Diacritics*, 3 (1): 33–46. Stable URL: http://www.jstor.org/stable/464590 (accessed December 18, 2008).

Derrida, Jacques and Elisabeth Roudinesco. [2001] 2004. *For What Tomorrow . . . A Dialogue*. Translated by Jeff Fort. Stanford, CA: Stanford University Press.

Foucault, Michel. [1976] 1997. "17 March 1976." In *Society Must Be Defended: Lectures at the College de France 1975–1976*. Translated by David Macey. New York: Picador, pp. 239–263.

Fritsch, Matthias. 2002. "Derrida's Democracy to Come." *Constellations: An International Journal of Critical and Democratic Theory*, 9 (4): 574–597.

Gannis, Richard. 2011. *The Politics of Care in Habermas and Derrida: Between Measurability and Immeasurability*. Lanham, MD: Rowman & Littlefield.

Grant, Ruth W. 2003. "John Locke on Women and the Family." In *Two Treatises of Government and A Letter Concerning Toleration*. Edited, with an introduction, by Ian Shapiro with essays by John Dunn, Ruth W. Grant, and Ian Shapiro. New Haven, CT: Yale University Press.

Gratton, Peter. 2012. *The State of Sovereignty: Lessons from the Political Fictions of Modernity*. Albany, NY: SUNY Press.

Habermas, Jürgen. 1987. *The Philosophical Discourse of Modernity*. Cambridge, MA: MIT Press.

Habermas, Jürgen. 2008. *Between Naturalism and Religion: Philosophical Essays*. Translated by Ciaran Cronin. Malden, MA: Polity Press.

Hamilton, Alexander and James Madison and John Jay. [1787] [1961] 1999. *The Federalist Papers*. With an introduction by Charles R. Kesler. Edited by Clinton Rossiter. New York: Penguin Books.

Hobbes, Thomas. [1642] 1983. *De Cive*. Edited by Howard Warrender. Oxford: Oxford University Press.

Hobbes, Thomas. [1651] 1985. *Leviathan*. Edited, with an introduction, by C.B. Macpherson. New York: Penguin Books.

Honig, Bonnie. 1996. "Difference, Dilemmas, and the Politics of Home." In *Democracy and Difference: Contesting the Boundaries of the Political*. Edited by Seyla Benhabib. Princeton, NJ: Princeton University Press.

Honig, Bonnie. 2001. *Democracy and the Foreigner*. Princeton, NJ: Princeton University Press.

Irigaray, Luce. 1984. *An Ethics of Sexual Difference*. Translated by Carolyn Burke and Gillian C. Gill. Ithaca, NY: Cornell University Press.

Janouchová, Petra. 2013. "The Cult of Bendis in Athens and Thrace." *Graeco-Latina Brunensia*, 18 (1): 95–106.

Kamuf, Peggy. 2006. "From Now On." *Epoché*, 10 (2) 203–220.

Kant, Immanuel. [1795] 1983. *Perpetual Peace and Other Essays on Politics, History, and Morals*. Translated, with an introduction, by Ted Humphrey. Indianapolis, IN: Hackett Publishing.

King, Martin Luther, Jr. 1986. "Letter from Birmingham Jail." In *A Testament of Hope: The Essential Writings and Speeches of Martin Luther King, Jr.* Edited by James M. Washington. New York: HarperCollins, pp. 289–302.

Locke, John. 2003. *Two Treatises of Government and A Letter Concerning Toleration*. Edited, with an introduction, by Ian Shapiro with essays by John Dunn, Ruth W. Grant, and Ian Shapiro. New Haven, CT: Yale University Press.

Lysias. [1979] 2005. "Oration XII, Against Eratosthenes." Translated by W.R.M. Lamb, Loeb Classical Library. Included in *The Republic: The Comprehensive Student Edition*. Edited by Andrea Tschemplik. Lanham, MD: Rowman & Littlefield, pp. 387–390.

Macpherson, C.B. [1968] 1985. "Introduction." In *Leviathan* by Thomas Hobbes. New York: Penguin Books.

Mendieta, Eduardo. 2010. "Political Bestiary: On the Uses of Violence." *Insights*, 3 (5): 2–14.

Mendieta, Eduardo. 2011. "The Right to Political Membership: Democratic Morality and the Rights of Irregular Immigrants." *Radical Philosophy Review*, 14 (2): 177–185.

Mill, J.S. 1996. "The Subjection of Women." In *On Liberty and the Subjection of Women*. With an introduction by Jane O'Grady. Ware, UK: Wordsworth Editions Limited.

Naas, Michael. 2002. *Taking on the Tradition: Jacques Derrida and the Legacies of Deconstruction*. Stanford, CA: Stanford University Press.

Naas, Michael. 2008. *Derrida From Now On*. New York: Fordham University Press.

O'Brien, Mary. 1981. *The Politics of Reproduction*. Boston, MA: Routledge & Kegan Paul.

Plato. 1921. "The Sophist." In *Plato in Twelve Volumes, Vol. 12*. Translated by Harold N. Fowler. Cambridge, MA: Harvard University Press.

Plato. 1956. *Plato's Protagoras*. B. Jowett's translation extensively revised by Martin Ostwald. Edited, with an introduction, by Gregory Vlastos. New York: The Liberal Arts Press.

Plato. 1961a. "Apology." In *The Collected Dialogues of Plato Including the Letters*. Edited by Edith Hamilton and Huntington Cairns. Translated by Michael Joyce. Princeton, NJ: Princeton University Press.

Plato. 1961b. "Crito." In *The Collected Dialogues of Plato Including the Letters*. Edited by Edith Hamilton and Huntington Cairns. Translated by Michael Joyce. Princeton, NJ: Princeton University Press.

Plato. 1961c. "Symposium." In *The Collected Dialogues of Plato Including the Letters*. Edited by Edith Hamilton and Huntington Cairns. Translated by Michael Joyce. Princeton, NJ: Princeton University Press.

Plato. 1966. *The Laws*. Translated, with an introduction, by A.E. Taylor. London: Everyman's Library.

Plato. 1968. *The Republic of Plato*, Second Edition. Translated, with notes and an interpretive essay, by Allan Bloom. New York: Basic Books.

Plato. 1987. *Gorgias*. Translated, with an introduction and notes, by Donald J. Zeyl. Indianapolis, IN: Hackett Publishing.

Plato. 2000. *Timaeus*. Translated, with an introduction, by Donald J. Zeyl. Indianapolis, IN: Hackett Publishing.

Rawls, J. 1971. *A Theory of Justice*. Cambridge, MA: Harvard University Press.

Rousseau, Jean-Jacques. [1754] 2004. *Discourse on the Origin of Inequality*. New York: Dover Thrift Editions.

Rousseau, Jean-Jacques. [1762] 1968. *The Social Contract*. Translated, with an introduction, by Maurice Cranston. Harmondsworth, UK: Penguin Books.

Rousseau, Jean-Jacques. 1985. *The Government of Poland*. Translated, with an introduction and notes, by Willmoore Kendall. Preface by Harvey C. Mansfield, Jr. Indianapolis, IN: Hackett Publishing.

Rousseau, Jean-Jacques. 2003. *Émile or Treatise on Education*. Translated by William H. Payne. Amherst, NY: Prometheus Books.

Rousseau, Jean-Jacques. [2004] 2009. *Discourse on the Origin of Inequality.* New York: Classic Books America.

Sallis, John. 1975. *Being and Logos: Reading the Platonic Dialogues*, Third Edition. Bloomington, IN: Indiana University Press.

Sassen, Saskia. 1999. *Guests and Aliens*. New York: New Press.

Schmitt, Carl. [1938] 2008. *The Leviathan in the State Theory of Thomas Hobbes: Meaning and Failure of a Political Symbol.* Translated by George Schwab and Erna Hilfstein with an introduction by George Schwab and a new foreword by Tracy B. Strong. Chicago, IL: University of Chicago Press.

Schmitt, Carl. [1950] 2003. *The Nomos of the Earth in the International Law of the Jus Publicum Europaeum*. Translated and annotated by G.L. Ulmen. New York: Telos Press.

Schmitt, Carl. 1985. *Political Theology: Four Chapters on the Concept of Sovereignty.* Translated by George Schwab. Chicago, IL: University of Chicago Press.

Schmitt, Carl. 2007. *The Concept of the Political*, Expanded Edition. Translated, with an introduction and notes, by George Schwab; with "The Age of Neutralizations and Depoliticizations" (1929) translated by Matthias Konzen and John P. McCormick; Leo Strauss's notes on Schmitt's essay translated by J. Harvey Lomax; with a foreword by Tracy B. Strong. Chicago, IL: University of Chicago Press.

Silverman, Hugh J. 1994. *Textualities: Between Hermeneutics and Deconstruction*. New York: Routledge.

Thucydides. 1996. "Pericles' Funeral Oration." In *The History of the Peloponnesian War.* In *Princeton Readings in Political Thought: Essential Texts Since Plato.* Edited by Mitchell Cohen and Nicole Fermon. Princeton, NJ: Princeton University Press, pp. 13–18.

Tschemplik, Andrea. 2005. "Introduction." In *The Republic: The Comprehensive Student Edition*. Edited by Andrea Tschemplik. Lanham, MD: Rowman & Littlefield, pp. 1–13.

Walzer, Michael. 1983. *Spheres of Justice: A Defense of Pluralism and Equality*. New York: Basic Books.

Wollstonecraft, Mary. [1792] 1996. "A Vindication of the Rights of Women." In *Princeton Readings in Political Thought: Essential Texts Since Plato.* Edited by Mitchell Cohen and Nicole Fermon. Princeton, NJ: Princeton University Press, pp. 362–370.

Index